Paranormal Nation

Why America Needs Ghosts,
UFOs, and Bigfoot

MARC E. FITCH

 PRAEGER

AN IMPRINT OF ABC-CLIO, LLC
Santa Barbara, California • Denver, Colorado • Oxford, England

Library of Congress Cataloging-in-Publication Data

Fitch, Marc E.
    Paranormal nation : why America needs ghosts, UFOs, and bigfoot / Marc E. Fitch.
        p. cm.
    Includes bibliographical references and index.
    ISBN 978–0–313–38206–2 (hardback) — ISBN 978–0–313–38207–9 (ebook)
1. Parapsychology—United States—History. 2. United States—Social life and customs. I. Title.
BF1028.5.U6F58   2013
130.973—dc23   2012040011

ISBN: 978–0–313–38206–2
EISBN: 978–0–313–38207–9

17 16 15 14 13   1 2 3 4 5

This book is also available on the World Wide Web as an eBook.
Visit www.abc-clio.com for details.

Praeger
An Imprint of ABC-CLIO, LLC

ABC-CLIO, LLC
130 Cremona Drive, P.O. Box 1911
Santa Barbara, California 93116-1911

This book is printed on acid-free paper ∞

Manufactured in the United States of America

Dedicated to my wife, Erin. For all your love and support.

For my wonderful
Aunt Liz!

Contents

Acknowledgments

Special thanks to my mother, Paulette, for her time, encouragement, and editorial skills. Thanks to Praeger/ABC-CLIO for giving a new author a chance. Thank you to Tom and Rita McCullough for letting my family live in your home while I finished this manuscript and, of course, thank you to all those who helped and contributed their stories to this work.

(If you don't believe in miracles, I wrote this book while working two jobs and living in a one-bedroom apartment with our two children under 3 years old.)

CHAPTER 1

Introduction

A frightened family and a paranormal research group known as the Spirit Seekers out of Montgomery, Alabama, sit around a wooden table in a dark recess of the Shea family's new home. Ben and Jamie Shea and their three young children, Jackson (3 months), Bridger (5), and Tory (11) have been experiencing a living nightmare since purchasing and moving into the previously empty house. Demonic phantoms appear to them; ghosts of children and the elderly walk up and down their stairs at night; their young son cannot sleep because of the voices that keep sounding in his room and, worst of all, the Shea's oldest child is involved in a near-fatal car accident. After enduring these apparitions, frightening sounds, near misses, and paranoia, the Sheas finally called the Spirit Seekers. Alan Lowe and his wife, Angela, run the Spirit Seekers. Together they investigate paranormal phenomena such as hauntings. Joining them is their daughter Violet, a medium who can converse with the dead, and Karen Shillings, a historical researcher who tries to discover a historical source of the haunting. They have come to help the Sheas rid their home of its unwelcome guests.

The Spirit Seekers set up shop quickly. The focus of the terror appears to be a little boy's room at the end of a hallway. It was in this room that the Sheas found evidence of a satanic ritual when they first bought the abandoned house. Not believing that there was anything to worry about, they purchased the home anyway and turned the bedroom into their son's room. The Spirit Seekers have placed a video camera in the hallway to monitor activity. In fact, they have placed several video cameras throughout the house with viewing monitors, recording devices, and infrared cameras to capture any negative heat signatures left by an entity. The house is rigged, and the investigators are ready to confront whatever evil lies in wait.

Violet, the medium, senses an evil presence in the house—something inhuman. She believes that whoever performed the satanic ritual in the house may have opened a door to an evil world. After some discussion the investigators decide to try to communicate with the spirits through use of a Ouija board. The Spirit Seekers and the Sheas gather around a table in the living room and place all their hands lightly on the planchette. Victoria calls out to the spirit and asks its name. Slowly the planchette begins to move across the board to form the word S-E-T-H. Then Victoria asks when Seth was alive. Again the planchette moves and spells out N-E-V-E-R. The Sheas are now terrified, and the investigators realize that they may be dealing with a demonic entity—something that is not the ghost of a former resident but something straight from hell. They all take their hands away from the planchette and begin to discuss what should be done to rid the house of a possible demon. Suddenly the group watches in horror as the planchette, now without anyone's hand on it, begins to move wildly across the board forming words faster than the investigators can write them down. Alan asks if the presence will reveal itself. The planchette turns, points toward one of the video monitors and stops dead still. The lights in the house suddenly turn off, and on the screen they see a tall, black-robed figure ambling down the upstairs hallway and disappearing into the young boy's bedroom.

The Spirit Seekers attempt to cleanse the house of its demons; however, two months later, the Sheas flee the house in terror as this same black entity descends upon them in the hallway. They leave all their possessions behind.

This was a scene from the Discovery Channel's program *A Haunting*. The premise of the program, which as of this writing is in its fourth season, is to tell the true story of a haunting.[1] Discovery reenacts haunted experiences using actors, scripts, and some fairly spooky special effects based on witnesses' testimonies. The witnesses tell their story through interviews during the program, and the actors act it out with the help of a network studio. *A Haunting* has enjoyed favorable ratings since its release in 2004 and is slotted for another season.

It is just one of many new television shows that have appeared since 2000. Prompted by the success of the British program *Most Haunted*, networks such as Discovery, History, Syfy, A&E, Travel, Biography, and TruTV (formerly CourtTV) have hopped on the bandwagon of paranormal television and have been enjoying the rating benefits ever since. Indeed, some of these programs have even served to put these networks "on the map." Television programs such as *MonsterQuest* and *UFO Files* featured on the History Channel,

Ghost Hunters and *Ghost Hunters International* on Syfy, *Paranormal State* on A&E, and *Ghostly Encounters* on Biography have captured the imagination and rating share of the nation. These shows have garnered considerable ratings for otherwise small cable networks and reinvigorated some channels like Discovery, History, and Travel.

According to the Gallup News Service, approximately "... three in four Americans profess at least one paranormal belief... ,"[2] the most popular being extrasensory perception followed closely by a belief in haunted houses. Interestingly enough, this is nearly identical to the percentage of Americans that believe in God. Obviously, television network executives have tapped into a widespread and profitable consumer base. But what does this say about U.S. culture? Oftentimes we can tell more about the state of the United States through the study of pop culture than we can through polls and demographic studies. Popular culture can be viewed in historical context to reveal anxieties, concerns, and belief systems of a culture, particularly when dealing with the supernatural or paranormal. Is it just coincidence that belief in sightings of UFOs skyrocketed in the late forties and fifties after the development of nuclear arms and the Cold War? Is it coincidence that spiritualism and communication with spirits became a popular social movement in the late 1800s and early 1900s following Darwin's release of *On the Origin of Species?* The United States has undergone many social changes over the past century, which can often be reflected through popular media outlets such as television and movies. Each generation either embraces or rejects the values of the previous one and finds its own way through our ongoing history. So what is it about this time in U.S. history, a time of unprecedented scientific and technological progress, that has made the public so interested in ghosts?

The paranormal is defined as that which cannot be explained by any known scientific explanation and is outside the realm of normal experience. As we begin to comprehend the extent of our knowledge, we may find that it is infinitely smaller than we suppose. The public generally accepts things they cannot see or explain as fact and the basis for their reality. Take, for instance, gravity; the force that keeps our feet on the ground and causes the rotation of the planet in the solar system and the passage of time—day to night, month to month, year to year, and eon to eon. How exactly does gravity function and what causes it? Truth be told, there is much about gravity that we do not understand, particularly in lieu of new advances in quantum physics; and while we have given it definition, we have not yet been able to assign a comprehensive and definitive theory by which the force operates.[3] And even if we did (or "could"), it would still be a "theory," albeit one that is provable every time we get up in the morning and put our feet on the ground. The point is that our knowledge has limits. We accept gravity without understanding it; we assume that someone out there does, and that he or she is really smart and has it all quantified into an absolutely provable science. But, in reality, that is not the case. We live our lives with an assumed understanding of our reality, but there are limits to our understanding.

Like gravity and any number of other functions of physics and science that guide our everyday lives, there are certain experiences that defy our understanding of the known universe. These mysterious, anomalous events are called paranormal because they are outside our normal experience and outside our normal understanding of the universe. In fact, it is this very idea of being "outside" that defines the paranormal. It exists in the periphery of our society, whispered in secret or not at all, only to those who one believes will not ridicule. And these experiences are not isolated to one particular group or society; rather, they have formed the basis of human interaction and progress since the dawn of time. Since the first lightning bolt struck the earth and caused primitive man to fear a god and try to appeal to his mercy, the paranormal— that which is outside our understanding or normal lives—has been with us; it has shaped the progress of science, religion, and social changes. For when the paranormal is no longer paranormal, it becomes science.

But there are limits, and at this point in the progress of science, technology, and humanity, one could argue that society is bumping up against those limits of understanding. Perhaps the most definitive examination of the paranormal came from George P. Hansen's work, *The Trickster and the Paranormal*, in which he defines the paranormal as something that defies boundaries, limits, and institutionalization. "The supernatural is irrational, but it is also real. It holds enormous power. We ignore it at our peril. It operates not only on the individual psyche, but at a collective level, influencing entire cultures. The witchcraft persecutions and the demagoguery of charismatic leaders are only two of many dangers. If we fail to recognize the limits of our 'rational' way of thinking we can become victims of it."[4] It is because of our culture's focus on the rational and scientific that the paranormal is relegated to the outside of the cultural norm. In previous civilizations the inverse may have been the norm; the supernatural was accepted as fact while science was derided as "witchcraft." Hansen warns that we ignore the irrational and paranormal at our own risk, but history has shown that we ignore science and rationality at our own risk as well.

However, today's society is the inverse of the Middle Ages; we have accelerated beyond the Enlightenment, the Industrial Revolution, the Atomic Age, and have now entered the Information Age, fueled by the technology of the Internet. During this age, however, popular culture has become fascinated once again with the paranormal, that which defies science and technology and institutionalization. Humanity has, in fact, never forgotten its ghosts and demons and monsters; the stories and traditions have been passed down from generation to generation and country to country. But there have been "ages" of paranormal fascination and upheaval similar to those times of social upheaval and changes, and, oftentimes, coinciding with them. This begs the cultural question: why now?

Paranormal Nation is a work that will seek to answer the question of why the paranormal has experienced such a revival in the past 12 years and why humanity seeks out and, in fact, needs the paranormal. It will look at the history of the paranormal, its relationship to social changes, and the implications therein and will then look at the current state of the paranormal in the United States and explore our need for the mysterious in our lives. Ultimately, we will ask the question, "What is more frightening: the idea that we do not completely understand the workings of the world or the idea that we do?"

But there are people who make the exploration of the dark and unknown their life's work. People such as ghost hunters, paranormal investigators, cryptozoologists, scientists, ufologists, mediums, and amateur interested sleuths define their worldview and, thus, their lives through the pursuit and exploration of the unknown. And there are those who, while not in pursuit of these paranormal experiences, have experienced them nonetheless and have remained forever changed because of it. But what would drive someone to seek the unknown? What would make someone spend their lives in pursuit of the paranormal, or allow themselves to be shaped and changed by it? Of course, many people live their lives steeped in religion, but church attendance numbers have been dwindling in recent years—43 percent according to ReligiousTolerance.org—while belief in a God or gods has remained fairly steady at approximately 80 percent.[5] This leaves a large discrepancy of people who believe in the spirit world and believe in a God or gods, but who do not regularly attend services. Could this most recent incarnation of paranormal beliefs actually be a result of diminished religious affiliation? How do today's religions view the paranormal? These are some of the questions that will be explored in *Paranormal Nation*.

Even more importantly, we will explore why it appears that the United States *needs* its ghosts, UFOs, and Bigfoot. Do these paranormal phenomena merely symbolize the darkness of human imagination, or do they represent something more essential to humanity?

In the ancient world, stories were developed and passed from generation to generation that told of how the world and everything in it was created. They became the blueprints of how to live one's life in relation to this world.

Almost everyone is familiar with the gods of ancient Greece and Rome, and with the story of the Garden of Eden, which shows how the world was created by God and how the natural world came into being. It is these stories of origins that became the myths that guided the ancient world. Today many of those myths have been discarded in favor of science and a naturalistic view of the universe. However, the abandonment of myth has left a void in society, and it is one that those who seek the paranormal try to fill. To seek out the mysterious is to seek a fundamental change in one's own life. Those who try to bring that change to society as a whole engage in a noble, if not impossible, task. But it is this very task that makes them, in some sense, heroic. If those who seek to verify and prove the paranormal were to ever succeed in their quest, it would fundamentally change our understanding of what it means to be human and what our role is in the universe. Thus, those who seek out the paranormal are seeking to change our society and, in their view, it is for the better.

What does it mean to believe in ghosts, UFOs, and Bigfoot? That is the fundamental underlying question that will be examined in this work. It is obvious through the persistence of paranormal beliefs throughout history that there exists a need to believe, and clearly people do. So what does it mean for both the individual and society as a whole?

There are those people who pursue this primal fear and belief as a noble cause, and they are the individuals who shape and influence paranormal belief in today's society. *Paranormal Nation* examines the paranormal as it exists today in its modern incarnation and also explores the motivations behind those who have been shaped and influenced by their belief in ghosts, UFOs, and Bigfoot. These individuals can be found in nearly every town and city across the country. Their work has sometimes been memorialized and sometimes scorned and discredited, but their motivations stem from a common goal: to seek a new definition for life through exploration of the unknown reaches of both our psyche and our reality. Those interviewed in this work are neither "kooks" nor liars and to call them so is to do a disservice to the spirit of humanity and civility. *Paranormal Nation* seeks to portray the paranormal not as a *supernatural* experience, but rather, a very *human* experience.

Unlike so many books and programs concerning the paranormal, *Paranormal Nation* does not seek to either prove or disprove the paranormal. There can be no assertion of the reality of such experiences without personal experience verified through institutionalization and definition and, as of now, this does not exist. However, the paranormal does exist in the fact that people believe in it and are influenced by and act upon those beliefs. Paranormal beliefs have penetrated our culture to the very core of our understanding of reality, though few realize it. This work will examine the defined impact of those existent beliefs on our society and our individual lives.

Religion is, by definition, paranormal, though many would like to separate the two. Religion is based entirely on the belief of that which cannot be proved and is not part of the normal everyday experience. It is based on faith, not science, and involves belief in ghosts, demons, witches, angels, miracles, and various other phenomena that can only be described as paranormal. With the understanding that religion is paranormal, it is then easy to see how it has influenced our lives and our shared history, but the influence is far deeper than only religion. The paranormal calls into question all that we believe we know about reality. While the average person does not consciously walk around day to day debating the existence of ghosts and how it is tied to the birth of our nation (as will be discussed in Chapter 4), the influence of the paranormal is working on a subconscious level, contributing to influences in our culture including religion, politics, science, entertainment, and economics. But it is also an exploration of what it means to be human, to have faith and belief and to question what we know. It is about the need for mystery, the defining of truth, and the search for identity. We are a nation of believers; believers in a wide variety of different institutions, religions, people, and philosophies. It is that very belief upon which the paranormal feeds and prospers, and it is that very belief that ultimately makes us a Paranormal Nation.

CHAPTER 2

A Brief History of the Paranormal in America

There are countless ghost stories, legends, and tales of mythical and mysterious creatures that comprise the very human experience of the paranormal in the United States. But in the history of the United States there are several influential and persisting paranormal mysteries that have formed the haunted landscape of our shared country and cultural experience and have formed the basis of the themes and motifs examined in this work. From Colonial America to the present day, the paranormal has become part of the ethos of the American experience. Today's fascination with the paranormal has its roots in the ancient history of humanity. Belief in the paranormal is nothing new; ever since man first witnessed a strike of lightning across the sky, belief in gods, witches, ghosts, and monsters have haunted the human psyche and inhabited the social mediums of every age. Ancient Greek plays incorporated ghosts and gods; the Bible tells of Satan and his horde who terrorize humanity for evil purposes and witches who call forth the dead; the Middle Ages and the Renaissance in Europe were preoccupied with the existence of magic and witchcraft; Shakespeare's ghosts were bent on revenge and justice; and the colonialists believed that the Native Americans were ghostly creatures that haunted the very earth and trees, a belief that persists today. The history of the paranormal also involves a history of the mediums through which the world is experienced. Drama, fiction, radio, television, and the Internet have heralded and fueled beliefs in the paranormal. They have been the mediums through which individuals have connected with others and shared experiences. These mediums draw upon the paranormal—the belief in ghosts, gods, demons, witches, and monsters—and present them with their interpretations and representations of reality. This fueled paranormal belief and, as will be examined in later chapters, today's medium, the Internet, has reached many more people in new and powerful ways.

Author and folklorist Bill Ellis uses the term "ostension" to define the physical acting out of a legend or "a dramatic extension into real life."[1] When expanded to include the effects of an entertainment medium, such as oral storytelling, books, television, film, or the Internet, the role of ostension becomes a large and looming social force. Oral or written stories inspire film and television programs which are able to involve a large segment of the population in a dramatic rendering of a legend, ghost story, or any other tale of paranormal manifestation. The medium depicting the story feeds belief among the population and engrains the story into the social consciousness. This inevitably leads to hoaxes, falsities, rumors, and experiences that mimic what has been portrayed through the entertainment medium. It is one of the reasons that the paranormal can be such a difficult area to study: the question of the chicken and the egg can never truly be answered.

For the purposes of this work, we will concentrate on the American paranormal experience and the examination of the legends that have developed over our short history. We must also incorporate books, radio, and film in the history of the paranormal experience because it is these mediums that have passed down the knowledge and legends and, in some cases, fueled and even created them. The American paranormal experience has been an odd mixture of experience and entertainment, fact and fiction, belief and skepticism—each needing the other to survive and continue. It is necessary to recount these iconic American paranormal experiences and legends due to their relation to the rest of this work and their inherent significance in the history of the United States. The paranormal landmarks listed in this chapter continue to this day, still mired in mystery and always drawing new interest from new generations. Their stories, at times, seem almost archetypal to the human experience as a whole and thus justify their continued existence and retelling.

SALEM WITCH TRIALS

The Salem witch trials occurred in Salem, Massachusetts, in 1692. While they were not the first or the last witch trials to be held in the New World, this particular outbreak was appalling in the history of America due to the high number of people accused and the high number of people (mostly women) executed for witchcraft. In 1692, rumors and accusations of witchcraft within the small town of Salem, Massachusetts, culminated with 150 arrests and

19 hangings of innocent people. Much has been speculated about the true origins of this tragedy; some researchers link it to mass hysteria brought on by tainted drinking water, while others argue that the accusations were ways of settling land disputes between neighbors. The accusations were originally lobbed by a group of 10 girls who were displaying "odd postures, foolish, ridiculous speeches, and distemper fits."[2] The girls testified that they were being controlled through forces of witchcraft and began accusing some of the town's resident outcasts. The witch trials represented the dying gasp of the European witch craze that had worked its way across the Atlantic to the New World. By 1692, most of the witch trials that had been plaguing the European subcontinent had come to an end. They were replaced by a new rationalism and revision of judicial laws that required actual evidence to convict someone of witchcraft rather than mere accusations. The Salem witch trials represented a burning ember from the fire of Europe that landed in the New World and began to burn.

And it has continued to burn. Unfortunately, the United States (as well as Europe) has repeatedly reframed and recycled the witch-hunt every few generations to purge the nation of its perceived ills, scapegoating social tensions and changes on whichever "witch" happens to occupy the national conscious at the time. Europe had the Holocaust against the Jews—who have traditionally been associated with witchcraft and magic in European/Christian belief systems—while the United States had the internment of Japanese-Americans during WWII, McCarthyism, and the satanic panic of the 1980s (which will be examined in detail later). Even through the present day, female politicians have to defend themselves against accusations of witchcraft (as in the case of Christine O'Donnell) and the assignation of blame for tragedy as in the case of Sarah Palin following the Tucson shooting spree that nearly killed Representative Gabrielle Giffords. Tellingly, Palin, in her statement to the public, used the term "blood libel," a term used against the Jews in the European Middle Ages who were accused of witchcraft, cannibalism, and blood pacts with the devil.

The Salem witch trials have also remained relevant in their influence on the judicial system. During the trials, Increase Mather penned *Cases of Conscience*, which argued that much of the "evidence" for those convicted of witchcraft was not evidence at all. He condemned the use of specters, or ghosts, as evidence against the accused and also questioned the witnesses' stories. "*Cases of Conscience* called attention to an obvious fact that had become blurred in the quest for empirical proof: central to the validity of any evidence was the trustworthiness of its source and the circumstances under which it was secured."[3] Mather's argument virtually ended the trials.

His philosophy is still a cornerstone of our present-day legal system. Think of the O. J. Simpson trial; detective Mark Fuhrman's trustworthiness was called into question as well as the method that was used to secure the evidence held against O. J. This lack of trustworthiness on behalf of the accusers and the procurement of evidence led to a not guilty verdict.

The trials have also lived on through various entertainment mediums. Nathaniel Hawthorne depicted the environment of social fear and irony in his work *Young Goodman Brown*. Hawthorne was actually a descendent of William Hathorne, a judge who presided over some of the trials and ordered the execution of several women. It is largely believed that Hawthorne changed his name and penned *Young Goodman Brown* as a means of unburdening himself of his ancestral guilt. Arthur Miller penned *The Crucible*, which is largely considered an allegory for the Red Scare and McCarthyism of the 1950s.

The Salem witch trials collapsed under the weight of its accusations, much like the European witch craze, and much like its various reiterations over the course of the United States' history. Eventually too many people are accused; the accusations are too overwhelming and ridiculous. It is no longer the outcast that is being purged from society, but rather the pillars of the community and the accusers themselves. The Salem witch trials, much like many other aspects of the United States' history and culture, was a cauldron bubble that burst, only to have a new one well up from the depths of our social soup.

THE JERSEY DEVIL

The legend of the Jersey Devil begins not long after the conclusion of the Salem witch trials and before the United States had declared itself independent from Great Britain. As legend has it, in 1735, Mrs. Leeds, a woman living in what is now known as the Pine Barrens in southern New Jersey, was pregnant with her thirteenth child. She cursed the unborn child during contractions. While the baby boy was born normal, it quickly mutated into a creature with a horse-like face, bat wings, and hooves for feet. It ran off into the deep pine forest where it has been stalking ever since. Sightings of this strange and sometimes dangerous creature began occurring shortly thereafter and even prompted a local preacher to exorcise the demon from the Pine Barrens; it didn't work. While local authorities hoped the story would run its course and die off, the legend has persisted till today with sightings, research groups, television specials, and even its very own professional hockey team, the Jersey Devils.

One of the premier and most active Jersey Devil research groups are the Devil Hunters, who have been featured in a number of television programs that have become part of today's paranormal experience. Of course, one of the reasons for the persistence of this story is that people keep seeing something in the Pine Barrens that they cannot explain. According to the Devil Hunters,

> The 1900's started off with a major bang for the Jersey Devil legend. In 1909, the largest batch of Jersey Devil sightings ever recorded occurred, in which the Jersey Devil was seen by over 100 people in the time span of a single week. This week, January 16th through January 23rd, has been justly named Phenomenal Week. During this time, a wide range of people throughout the Delaware Valley spotted the winged beast. Some sightings were seen by large groups of people at once; other sightings were made by residents who were awakened in the middle of the night to strange noises in the darkness.[4]

The persistence of the legend of the Jersey Devil, along with the other paranormal experiences we are examining, form part of the cultural identity of the United States; born before the revolution, they represent a period of mystery, uncertainty, legend, and tradition. The Jersey Devil is part of that history and, real or not, it constitutes an important fiber in the fabric of the American tradition; one that blends modernity with tradition, belief with mystery, and always, a feeling of groundless uncertainty for strangers in a strange land.

WASHINGTON IRVING

The American paranormal experience blurs the lines between reality and fantasy. Often one seeps into the other to form the stories and legends that make up the national landscape. Take, for instance, Washington Irving's classic, *The Legend of Sleepy Hollow*. Sleepy Hollow is generally accepted to be Tarrytown, New York, these days, though a section of Tarrytown was officially changed to Sleepy Hollow as a way to honor Irving's influence in the area. Irving's now-classic story illustrates the blurring of the lines between reality and fantasy. The legend of the headless horseman is now taken as an American cultural legend, but there are many scholarly arguments over Irving's sources when he penned this classic. During the 1800s the Hudson Valley was populated with mostly German and Dutch immigrants. Irving draws on the legends and cultural mythology of these settlers and through his writings is able to actually imbue the Hudson Valley with a legendary hauntedness. Irving managed to tap into a legend that had originally been born in Europe and had made its way across the Atlantic and into the Hudson. Owen Davies writes, "The headless or acephalous ghost is one of the classic ghost stereotypes present in folk tradition across Europe."[5] Davies offers several different explanations of the origins of headless ghosts, from the act of beheading the dead to keep them from rising from the grave to people dying from head and neck injuries. England even had its own headless horseman who, "every New Year's eve, haunted a track between Penselwood and Stourton, in Wiltshire . . ."[6] It is interesting to note that Irving wrote the *Legend of Sleepy Hollow* while living in England, away from the Hudson Valley.

The real question is a matter of the chicken and the egg; which came first? The legend of the headless horseman that Irving heard through his travels or his creation of a story that resonated so well with the people and landscape of the area that it was immediately accepted as truth? A second-hand account of an actual witness of the headless horseman was recorded by Edgar Mayhew Bacon in 1897, when an Irish immigrant woman related to him a terrifying night. "It wasn't late, mebby not mower than tin o'clock, an' me waitin' here be the gate for Dinny to com in . . . when upon me sowl, thrue as I'm standing here, I see right out there in the road a big, black shadder like, widout any head, an' him on horseback at that."[7] The legend blended into reality and vice versa, blurring the line between reality and what a culture experiences collectively through shared mediums, in this case, books and oral stories. "Ultimately, though, two things seem true: first that the specific hauntings, as well as the general atmosphere of hauntedness, that made a literary debut in Irving's writing became ingrained and valued ingredients of regional literary and vernacular culture; and second, that the absorption and perpetuation of images from Irving's tales were possible only because the images were adaptable to the diverse social, political, and cultural conditions and needs of individuals and generations."[8]

HALLOWEEN

Halloween is the annual American festival in which we celebrate all the frightening, funny, and unknown aspects of our culture; we dress to mimic that which we find frightening or entertaining. But the roots of Halloween are in an ancient pagan celebration of the dead in pre-Christian Ireland, Britain, France, Wales, and Scotland. According to Lesley Pratt Bannatyne, "The festival of Samhain was the most sacred of all Celtic festivals. Its rituals helped link people with their ancestors and the past. The Celts believed that the dead rose on the eve of Samhain and that ancestral ghosts and demons were set free to roam the earth . . . Samhain marked the start of the season that rightly belonged to spirits—a time when nights were long and dark fell early."[9]

Christianity coopted the pagan holiday by using their traditions but blending it with new, Christ-inspired meaning. Thus, Samhain was molded to become All Saints Eve and All Saints Day. Similar to the adoption of the

Christmas tree to celebrate Christ's birth, Christianity was able to use the pagan symbols like the jack-o'-lantern (originally made from turnips) to reinforce its belief system for peoples newly indoctrinated to Christianity. Halloween's history is as much a blend of religion, culture, and heritage as is the United States' history as a nation. Through its various rebirths, Halloween evolved to incorporate the Roman festival of Pomona, Protestant Guy Fawkes Day, the Mexican Day of the Dead, and Thanksgiving. It incorporated folkloric beliefs in witchcraft, voodoo from the Caribbean, and the dead returning from the Civil War. The holiday experienced different phases during which it was celebrated in different ways. During the Victorian years Halloween was largely about courtship among young people; upper-middle-class households practiced quaint divinations to determine one's future husband or wife. Today's manifestation of Halloween is a different animal but still maintains its roots in the ancient pagan practices. The holiday has become the source of urban legend (apples with razors and poisoned candy) and pop-culture entertainment such as the film franchise *Halloween*. It has become a night of vandalism and, sometimes, criminal activity, but mostly it has become an adult contemporary holiday during which adults dress up and have parties. Small towns and large cities host parades and parties and, naturally, children still dress as ghosts, goblins, and witches and go door to door asking for treats. While the dressing up in ghoulish costumes may be meaningless to the individual, its popular practice remains an incarnation of the ancient beliefs in ghosts, demons, spirits, and witches.

SPIRITUALISM

Spiritualism was the United States' first great contribution to the world's paranormal experience. It began in 1848 in Hydesville, New York, when two adolescent sisters, Margaret and Kate Fox, began to communicate with a spirit in their home by asking the spirit a question and the spirit answering with a knock on the wooden floor or wall. While trying to communicate with the dead was obviously nothing new, the Fox sisters became extremely popular and launched an actual social movement, which gave cohesion to the varied belief systems that involved communication with spirits. The Fox sisters were studied by scientists and skeptics, lauded by the public, and paid well for their services by the wealthy. As Spiritualism grew and changed, the Fox sisters were replaced by mediums who could display even more astounding paranormal phenomena ranging from levitations to actual fully formed ghosts and even the oozing of "ectoplasm" from the medium's body. While Spiritualism was largely a poor and middle-class phenomenon in the United States, in Europe it became a pastime of the wealthy aristocracy. Europe also produced some of the most talented and controversial mediums of the time. A successful medium could expect to be taken very well care of by wealthy persons with an interest in the spirit world, and therefore, the trade was rife with fraud. In fact, much of the phenomena and manifestations produced during the séances of the Spiritualist mediums have now been proven as hoaxes and trickery; at the time, however, scientists engaged in a bitter battle with Spiritualists on the validity of the phenomena.

Some prominent scientists were won over to believing in the mediums and Spiritualism, while others remained incredulous at the reported manifestations and even went on to form an entire group dedicated to investigating claims of the paranormal, the Society for Psychical Research. World War II all but ended the Spiritualist movements, though séances and beliefs do continue to present day. The movement, while on the whole fraudulent, did produce some mediums who defied explanation, and this paranormal movement will be examined in great detail in a later chapter.

The impact of Spiritualism in our culture is not to be underestimated. Spiritualism was the birthplace of séances, the Ouija board, psychics, mediums, and more recently psychic hotlines, psychic fairs, and John Edwards, a famous psychic and host of his own television show *Crossing Over with John Edwards*. Mediums are used extensively in paranormal television shows such as *Most Haunted* and *Paranormal State* to communicate with the spirits haunting a particular location.

Criticism and skepticism abound concerning Spiritualism, with some people going to great lengths to prove that it is all a hoax pulled off through some sleight of hand or trickery and, of course, the public's willingness to believe. Harry Houdini, famous magician and escape artist, wanted very much to believe that man could communicate with the dead. He gave his wife a secret password that only he would know so that when he died, she would know if the medium was truly talking to his spirit. Following his death she tried in vain for the rest of her life to find a medium that could reveal the password to her. No one ever did.

Even in light of such setbacks and exposure of many, many hoaxers, the Spiritualist church does still exist. John Kachuba, in his book *Ghosthunters*, visited a Spiritualist church in Ohio. The service he describes is almost exactly out of an episode of *Crossing Over with John Edwards*. A medium paces in the front of the congregation and calls out names and images until someone in the audience hears something that is familiar. The medium then delivers his or her message to this individual. In his further investigations, John traveled to the Spiritualist Camp in Cassadaga, Florida, and received a reading of his own.

> Vera told me that I had been "living out of suitcase," which was true; I had been traveling a lot as I researched this book. She said I was "tired," which insight did not require a Ph.D. in psychology. She talked about my three children, calling one "optimistic," another "creative, but not yet successful," and the third, "a late bloomer." I didn't find any of these observations to be particularly impressive, either. I also was not impressed by the fact that she answered her cell phone three times during my $50 session to schedule appointments for other clients.[10]

Spiritualism was the first, but not the last, great American contribution to the world of the paranormal. Indeed, the rise of Spiritualism formed the basis for nearly all paranormal belief, criticism, and entertainment in the modern United States and Europe. It invigorated the public to believe in the spirit world and changed the idea of ghosts from something frightening to be avoided to something to seek out and consult with. In essence, it counteracted the effects of the witch trials, as now witches and spiritualists were not being arrested and hung, but were rather making great wealth off the public's need to summon the spirits. The Euro-American cultural history has long oscillated between the fear of ghosts and interest in ghosts, and the late 1800s marked the height of public interest in the paranormal.

WAR OF THE WORLDS

A classic story of the willingness of Americans to believe in the paranormal, and their willingness to act on that belief, comes from Orson Welles's infamous radio broadcast of *War of the Worlds*, a science fiction classic by H. G. Wells. In the story, alien invaders come to earth to destroy the human race and take over. During a theatrical presentation by Orson Welles on the radio, thousands of people from Pennsylvania to New Jersey came to believe that the radio broadcast was real and began to panic. There are differing reports on the number of people who were convinced that the earth was being invaded and also conflicting reports on the action taken by some, but a panic was indeed caused by the broadcast. This is an accurate example of how fictions can become realities through a given medium. According to *The Encyclopedia of Extraordinary Social Behavior*, the panic was the result of deep-seated American anxieties over invasion and the looming war brewing in Europe.

At the time of the broadcast, most Americans were heavily reliant on radio for news and entertainment. Political conditions were tense with Adolf Hitler, having recently annexed Austria, continuing his incursion in Czechoslovakia. With each passing day, Europe was slipping closer to a Second World War that would soon involve the United States. Listeners had grown accustomed to news bulletins interrupting regular programming with live reports from European war correspondents. It was within this context that the Welles drama, interspersed with a series of live field reports, would have appeared highly realistic.[11]

This incident has become a classic tale of Americana, but it illustrates the thin line between fiction and reality, and how that line can be crossed with a new, technologically based medium such as radio. Up until the invention of radio, the public relied on newspaper reports, and these were prone to have tales of "Airships from Space" and alien life forms on other planets. These reports were hoaxes put forth by editors, writers, and other tricksters (including Benjamin Franklin), but they still had an impact on a manipulated public. As radio gave way to television, Britain experienced its own paranormal panic when the television program *Ghostwatch* depicted a "real" haunting. The program resulted in a public panic and one suicide; it was pulled from the air and fined. The public is willing to believe and may even want to believe. The medium through which the world is experienced at any given point in history, whether it be newspaper, radio, television, or the Internet, can exploit this desire for the mysterious and paranormal and can, ultimately, form those beliefs into a reality such as the panic over *War of the Worlds.*

FLYING SAUCERS

"The modern era for UFOs began on June 24, 1947, when private pilot Kenneth Arnold was flying near the Cascade Mountains in Washington State and saw nine unidentified flying objects that he described flying 'like a saucer skipping over water.' The term *flying saucer*, and the public's interest in the phenomenon, was born."[12] This was followed by the supposed UFO crash in Roswell, New Mexico; an event that has become part of the American paranormal landscape and has inspired countless films, studies, and television programs. Today, Roswell is almost synonymous with alien visitors. This phenomenon sparked public and government interest. In 1954 the National Investigations Committee on Aerial Phenomena was formed, and in the late sixties the Condon Committee was given the task of analyzing all UFO evidence to see if there was need for further government investigation. The committee concluded that there was no basis for belief that we were being visited by alien life forms.

Despite this, the forties, fifties, and sixties were a golden age for UFO phe-nomena, with sightings being reported all over the world and believers and skeptics battling once again as they had over ghosts in the 1800s. Naturally, pop culture picked up on the phenomenon, and films and television shows about aliens and UFOs became all the rage. Flying saucers were depicted in comic books, cartoons, film, and media, and it was during the fifties and six-ties, immediately following the onset of the nuclear age, that flying saucers and aliens became culturally popular. In his book, *Projected Fears: Horror Films and American Culture*, Kendall Phillips examines the link between 1950s culture and the success and popularity of the films *The Thing from Another Planet* and *The Day the Earth Stood Still*:

> *The Thing* brought horror out of the Gothic past and placed it squarely into the continuous world of the near future. The monster was not some creature of lore and superstition, but one based, however loosely, on the possibilities afforded by science. By bringing the monster into the more realistic realm of the continuous world, the points of reso-nance between the elements in the film and broader cultural anxieties seem to become more acute. Wrapped up in the fantastic horror of *The Thing* were American fears of invasion, communism, Fordism, sci-ence, authority, expertise, and gender displacement...Throughout the fifties, American filmgoers faced an amazing onslaught of alien invaders.[13]

The emergence and popularity of UFO phenomena during this time in U.S. history is entangled with the cultural shifts taking place and anxieties experi-enced at all levels of society, from government to the blue-collar worker.

One uniquely American aspect of the UFO phenomenon has been UFO abductions of people. This phenomenon came to public attention during the 1960s when Betty and Barney Hill claimed they had been abducted by an alien spacecraft while traveling through New Hampshire. They claimed that they had lost two hours and had no memory of where they had been or what they had done during those two hours. They only remembered a strange light in the sky following their vehicle. It wasn't until they were hypnotized that they revealed aliens had abducted and examined them and then placed them back in their vehicle, leaving them with no recollection of the events. Similar accounts of alien abduction gradually gained more fame and notoriety throughout the 1980s as more and more people claimed abduction by aliens. The experience was captured by Whitley Strieber's book, *Communion*, which claimed to be a nonfiction account of his various alien abduction experiences.

This phenomenon inspired films, documentaries, television programs, and countless hoaxers, imitators, and skeptics. "Just plain old sightings were way too mundane to be very exciting anymore, what with people being abducted so frequently. Several books claimed that humans were being abducted by the tens of thousands and subjected to various invasive medical procedures."[14] Whatever it was that people had been seeing in the night sky, it had now invaded their nightmares, as people claimed to experience a floating sensation while awake in their beds and having visions and memories of creatures swarming around as they lay paralyzed on a bed. This, of course, was immediately picked up by popular culture, which rendered such films as *Close Encounters of the Third Kind* and *Fire in the Sky*, both of which were successful.

Today, the belief in UFOs and alien abductions is still strong, with much television time being devoted to uncovering this mysterious phenomenon. The History Channel regularly airs marathons of its series *UFO Files*, which addresses the study of UFOs and the culture of belief, as does National Geographic's *Is It Real?*, which takes a decidedly more scientific and skeptical approach to the subject. Either way, the idea of flying saucers and alien abductions has become engrained into modern culture. Whether mocked by comedians questioning why it seems that aliens always abduct the most uneducated backwoods bumpkin or officially reported by an air force pilot who thoroughly believes that he saw a UFO in the sky with him, aliens have abducted a part of the American social conscious, and it is resonating across generations.

BIGFOOT

Of course, UFOs weren't the only paranormal phenomena making the papers during the fifties and sixties. During 1958 Ray Wallace, a contractor who was head of a construction site deep in the mountains of Northern California, began finding 16-inch, human-like footprints in the dirt and mud around the construction equipment. The site was so far removed from civilization and the prints so enormous that the finding immediately gained media attention and the creature, "Bigfoot," was born. Bigfoot, or Sasquatch, as it is also known, was not without precedent. For years explorers and tribes in the Himalayas had been reporting giant human footprints in the snow that supposedly belonged to a giant, hairy ape-like creature that walked on two legs like a man, called the Yeti. The discovery of Bigfoot in the wilds of Northern California led many to believe that this was the same type of creature, and it started a wave of footprint findings and rumors of ape-like creatures in the forest as well as rumors of hoaxes. Ray Wallace eventually quit the contracting job and began to make a name for himself (though not in a particularly good way) by making fantastic claims about his interaction with the animal and claiming that it was guarding gold mines hidden deep in the mountains. After his passing, his family made the claim that the entire Bigfoot phenomenon was entirely a hoax dreamed up by Ray Wallace. They even produced a pair of 16-inch wooden "feet" that Wallace supposedly strapped on and used to stomp about the construction site and, apparently, all over the Pacific Northwest. However, under closer scrutiny by scientists and anthropologists interested in the possibility of a North American Sasquatch, Wallace's stories and "feet" seemed to fall apart. Jeff Meldrum, a PhD in anthropology and professor at Idaho State University, writes in his book *Sasquatch: Legend Meets Science*,

> Another fundamental issue remains—how were such crude devices supposedly used to produce hoax footprints convincing to professional trackers and scientists? Could the Wallaces provide a compelling demonstration of how the carved feet were employed to make the tracks that were impressed sometimes an inch or more into firm wet sand? Apparently the media at large felt no obligation to require such a demonstration. The carved feet had simple leather straps attached to their backs and would be worn like primitive snowshoes. However, a snowshoe's ability to reduce pressure on the ground was precisely the effect the enlarged feet would have on the tracks. They would hardly make an impression except in fine dust.[15]

The wooden feet are rather crude, and it is difficult to imagine how one man could be responsible for tracks found all over the Pacific Northwest and into Canada unless other hoaxers caught on to the idea and began producing their own.

The most famous piece of evidence for the existence of Bigfoot is the Patterson-Gimlin film[16] of a giant, hairy creature walking upright through the woods of Northern California in 1964. This has become the quintessential footage of the paranormal and has been disputed back and forth between believers and skeptics since its release. To this day, no one can prove that this film is a hoax, and there are casts of the creature's footprints that accompany the film. Some skeptics say that it is simply a man in a monkey suit; however, the film has been examined countless times, and it seems no one can find the zipper on the ape costume. The footage of this creature was examined and compared with footage of a normal human walking in the same area only to find that this creature was much larger than the average human. The History Channel's *MonsterQuest* tried to replicate the stride and walk of the creature using professional athletes and could not match the ambulation of the creature in the film.

And the footprint casts taken in the dirt indicate that something stepped on this piece of earth that weighed approximately 500 pounds. This footage is regularly used in advertising television shows dealing with the paranormal.

The Bigfoot, or Sasquatch, is actually nothing particularly new to the North American continent. Anthropologists have found references to the "hairy man" who lives in the woods in Native American folklore, and some scientists feel that this may be an evolutionary missing link, a descendent of *Gigantopithicus*, a giant ape that lived in Asia that could potentially have migrated across the Alaskan land bridge. Nevertheless, Bigfoot has become, probably more than any other paranormal phenomena, a part of the American mythology and culture and, really, what better creature to symbolize the United States' quest for the mysterious? A gentle, giant, human-like creature that lives at peace in the natural world, shies away from civilization, and is revered by the native peoples. Bigfoot is the essence of American longing, and its presence links man to some kind of natural brother that still lives alone, stalking the deep, mountainous forests of the Pacific Northwest and Canada. Some hunters have claimed to have had a Sasquatch in the sights of their rifles and found themselves unable to fire the shot that would end the mystery surrounding this creature. Why? Because it looks too human.

Still today, there are various reports of giant, human-like footprints in the dirt and mud across the Northwest and Canada. There have even been sightings elsewhere in the United States. There is the Grassman in Ohio and the Swampman in Louisiana, and every year sightings are reported of some giant, man-like creature covered in hair that lives in the woods devoid of human contact and apparently not wanting any. Bigfoot is the subject of television shows, movies, symposiums, doctoral theses, and even cartoons. *Bigfoot Presents* is a cartoon show hosted by none other than Bigfoot himself and is quickly acquainting children with the idea of a Sasquatch that lives in the forest nearby. Bigfoot even has his own yearly festival during Labor Day weekend in Willow Creek, California, known as Big Foot Daze, which, according to Joshua Blu Buhs, represents part of the ironic commercialization of this mythical creature. "Bigfoot and Big Foot Daze were part of this new economy. They were advertising icons, commercials for local services and the area. Maps proclaimed the region 'Bigfoot Country.' In time, came Bigfoot burgers, Bigfoot Golf & Country Club, Bigfoot Lumber and Hardware, Sasquatch Second Hand, and the Bigfoot Curio Shop."[17] More recently, the Sasquatch Music Festival was a four-day event held in the Gorge Amphitheater in George, Washington, and featured some of the hottest musicians in the industry.

It is interesting to note that while much of the paranormal phenomena of the fifties and sixties was associated with extraterrestrials and space and technology, that suddenly there emerged from the forest of the American conscious Sasquatch, a being that exists as one with nature and is revered by the Native Americans. A creature that has a definite mythological landscape surrounding its existence and that can possibly give man insight into his own origins. You may look to the stars for answers or you may look to the forests. Either way, the mystery keeps the United States looking, searching, and hoping.

THE MOTHMAN

In the town of Point Pleasant, West Virginia, there stands a statue unlike any other in the United States, if not the world. It is a 12-foot tall, stainless steel creature that resembles a man with giant, tattered wings, clawed hands, and a goblin-like face with giant red eyes. This image was culled from the reports of eyewitnesses in and around Point Pleasant during the year of 1966. The "Mothman," as the creature was dubbed, was characterized by witnesses as resembling a tall, muscular man with wings and hypnotic eyes: "Its face couldn't be seen because the eyes simply hypnotized you when you looked into them . . . the eyes consumed your vision and you couldn't see anything but them."[18]

Throughout the following year, more than one hundred people would see this human-like creature with wings and glowing eyes. In addition to the Mothman, a strange mix of other mysterious phenomena have made their way into popular culture, such as the Men in Black, which became a major Hollywood film. The Mothman himself made it to Hollywood stardom in a rather creepy film staring Richard Gere and Laura Linney, entitled *The Mothman Prophecies*. The film was loosely based on the book by the same name authored by John Keel. Keel was in Point Pleasant during the outbreak of sightings. However, Keel's work is not specifically directed at the Mothman; it incorporates a variety of phenomena in the area at the time, including various UFO sightings. The sightings ended rather abruptly, following the collapse of the Silver Bridge, a tragedy in which 46 people died. It was a devastating loss for a small community; since then, many have come to believe that the Mothman was some kind of strange, paranormal warning. Keel writes that some strange energy was converging on the area around Point Pleasant during the time leading up to the disaster; ". . . the strange ones began to arrive in West Virginia. They trooped down from the hill, along the muddy back roads, up from the winding 'hollers,' like an army of leprechauns seeking impoverished shoemakers. It was open season on the human race and so the ancient procession of the damned marched once more."[19]

More important to the history of the paranormal than the Mothman himself, though he has become a part of American legend, are John Keel's belief system and the actual state of West Virginia. It is difficult to define Keel's beliefs as a "system" because they are built more on doubts and insecurities than on any one defined system. Keel does not believe that humans are the first or only intelligence at work on the planet. Rather, he believes that there have been vast intelligences here for eons; tricksters that toy with the inferior human race, ethereal beings that can manifest in a variety of ways and which, he believes, are evidenced in ancient archeology. Keel's work incorporates far more questions than answers and stems from Charles Fort's work regarding the paranormal and unexplained. Keel's influence can also be seen in the works of Erich von Däniken and Graham Hancock, who use archeological evidence to paint a wildly different history of humanity involving highly evolved and sentient beings from other worlds that have guided the course of humanity and have left their fingerprints in the form of baffling ancient architecture such as the Great Pyramids. Keel writes in *The Mothman Prophecies*,

> There are archeological sites in the Mississippi valley which have been dated to 8000 years ago...long before the Indians are supposed to have arrived. Some of the Indian mounds (there are hundreds of them scattered throughout North America) are laid out and constructed with the same kind of mathematical precision found in the pyramids of Egypt. While it is known that the Indians were still adding to some of the mounds in the south when the Europeans first arrived, other mounds seem to be considerably older. Some are built in the form of elephants. What did the builders use for a model? Others are in the shape of sea serpents. These forms can only be seen from the air. To plan and build such mountains of shaped earth required technical skills beyond the simple nomadic woods Indians.[20]

Beyond Keel's theories however, the state of West Virginia, it seems, has an affinity for the unexplained. Besides the Mothman, the Men in Black, and the UFO sightings, West Virginia was also the location of the Flatwoods Monster. In 1952, several boys reported seeing a bright light in the night sky touch down in the hills near Flatwoods, West Virginia. They told their mother, and she with her two boys and a 17-year-old National Guardsman went to investigate the area. When they arrived, a 10-foot glowing creature that emitted a pungent vapor confronted them; it hissed at them and seemed to glide above the ground. They fled and called the police; the police investigated the area but could find only trace evidences. Other people reported seeing the creature during the next week, and witnesses were afflicted with a sickness that included vomiting and convulsions. Skeptics have tried to argue that the people only saw a falling meteor and an owl, but the theory comes off as weak and desperate for an explanation.

There seem to be certain areas of the world that tend to attract unexplained phenomena, and the hills of West Virginia would be one of those places. Both the Mothman and the Flatwoods Monster inspire annual town festivals that celebrate the creatures and the legendary status they bring to the area. Both remain unexplained, and the Mothman is still reported in other areas of the country today.

THE EXORCIST AND THE AMITYVILLE HORROR

However, the United States never forgot its ghosts, witches, and demons and its ability to blend reality with fiction to create a story that reaches over the bounds to become legend. *The Exorcist* was released in 1973 based on a book of the same name by William Peter Blatty. It told the story of a little girl who becomes possessed by an evil spirit and must be exorcised by the clergy. The disturbing nature of the film and the special effects earned it widespread popularity and even Academy Awards; however, that wasn't what made the film so lasting in the American consciousness. What made the film truly horrifying was that it was supposedly based on a true story that occurred in the United States. Satan and evil spirits were suddenly cast into the American spotlight once again. "Not since Psycho had a film provoked the kind of hysteria accompanied by Friedkin's tale of possession. Around the world, the appearance of the film was accompanied by long lines, vomiting, and claims of supernatural events."[21]

The rumors and tales surrounding the truth of *The Exorcist* is what launched the film into a sort of American legend. Blatty claims that his fiction was based on an incident that occurred in the 1950s when a young boy, following the death of his aunt, began to exhibit strange symptoms and seemingly dual personalities. When science and psychologists at the time could not cure the boy, the family eventually turned to the church, much the same as in . . . *The Exorcist*. While the boy did recover and the priests involved (who are still alive and have been interviewed by the History Channel) claim that this was absolutely a case of possession and contend that numerous supernatural events took place during the exorcism, scientists and psychologists now believe that there may have been an incestuous relationship between the aunt and the boy that may have caused a psychotic break in the child's mind that manifested itself through physical ailments and illnesses. Even the priests agree that the physical manifestations shown in *The Exorcist* were extreme—for Hollywood's sake, of course. Nevertheless, the "true" story of

The Exorcist plunged into the fabric of American culture and reinvigorated interest in the occult, spirits, and demons.

Following *The Exorcist* was another "true" story that became a part of American folklore, *The Amityville Horror*. *The Amityville Horror* was, in many ways, a truer story than *The Exorcist*. In November of 1976 Ronald DeFeo murdered his six family members at his home in Amityville, New York, located on Long Island. Soon after the mass murder, George Lutz, his wife, and their children moved into the home unconcerned about the previous events. Over the next month they would experience such haunting phenomena as furniture being inexplicably moved about the house, family members levitating in their sleep, ghostly eyes glaring at them through windows, numerous destructive acts that damaged the home, the sounds of people and music playing late at night when everyone was asleep, and slime dripping from the walls. This demonic presence finally chased the Lutzes from their home a month later; they left all of their possessions behind. Their experience generated much media attention across the island as well as legal troubles concerning the Lutzes' abandonment of a rather expensive home. Their story also generated the book by Jay Anson, aptly named *The Amityville Horror*, which was Anson's rendering of the Lutzes' story as told by the Lutzes themselves.

> On the top step stood a gigantic figure in white. George knew it was the hooded image Kathy had first glimpsed in the fireplace. The being was pointing at him! George whirled and raced back into the bedroom, grabbed up Missy, and shoved her into Danny's arms. 'Take her outside!' he shouted. 'You go with them, Chris!' Then he bent over Kathy and lifted her off the bed. 'Hurry!' George yelled after the boys. Then he too ran from the room, Harry following him down the steps. On the first floor, George saw the front door was open, hanging from its hinges again, torn away by some powerful force. Danny, Chris and Missy were outside. The little girl, just awakening, was squirming in her brother's arms. Not knowing where she was, she started to cry with fright. George ran for the van. He put Kathy on the front seat and then helped the children into the rear. Harry jumped in behind them, and he slammed the door on Kathy's side. George ran around to the other side of the vehicle, jumped in the driver's seat, and prayed.[22]

This was the dramatic final scene in Anson's book as the Lutz family escaped the house and vowed never to return.

The book became a best-seller, the story became legendary, and there was a media frenzy surrounding the house as reporters and onlookers tried to get into this supposedly possessed house. The attention became so much that eventually the name of the street in Amityville had to be changed to keep trespassers away. Meanwhile, paranormal investigators from around the country were clamoring to get inside and investigate the house. The Lutzes contacted both Stephen Kaplan of the Parapsychology Institute of America, and the Warrens, a paranormal investigating couple who had been working in the area for some time. The Lutzes allowed only the Warrens to enter the home and conduct a séance, similar to the Spiritualist séances of the 1800s. The infamy of this house and the success of the subsequent book and film led the Warrens to fame, where they made a name for themselves that would soon be immortalized in paranormal history.

However, there were many people, including the late paranormal investigator Stephen Kaplan, who believed this story to be a hoax perpetrated by George Lutz in an effort to back out of a mortgage that he couldn't afford. Kaplan debated with the Warrens several times on television and radio, denouncing the Amityville Horror as a hoax while the Warrens defended it many times over, claiming that they had indeed experienced the demonic presence in the house. This led to a lifelong bitter rivalry between the two groups. The house was eventually sold again, and the new owners experienced no paranormal events in the home other than people trespassing, trying to get a glimpse of the house and, in some cases, even stealing shingles from the siding. The police had to be called to the house many times to steer away trespassers and tourists, and, as mentioned earlier, eventually the name of the street had to be changed. Still, the next owners were not above having a little fun with the now infamous house, throwing Halloween parties every year with a special invitation to Stephen Kaplan and his wife.

THE SATANIC PANIC

During the 1980s and early 1990s, the United States once again returned to its witch-hunts. Known now as the satanic panic, rumors of satanic cults that engaged in cannibalism, kidnapping, murder, incest, child pornography, group suicide, and ritual child abuse spurred panics in small towns and led to a media frenzy of wild speculation, massive police investigations, court trials, ruined lives and businesses, and the incarceration of innocent people. It was truly a social movement across the board sparked by psychiatrists and therapists—so-called experts—who began to claim that their clients had suffered childhood abuse at the hands of satanic cults. Fears of Satanism had been growing throughout the seventies following the social upheaval of the counter-culture movement, the emergence of New Age religions, and a number of high-profile murders that the perpetrators claimed were part of a satanic ritual. However, it was a small book, *Michelle Remembers*, written by a psychiatrist that really began the panic. In the book a patient by the name of Michelle recalls terrifying abuse at the hands of her mother and an organized group of Satan worshippers. Much of this was recalled under hypnosis, but the book became a bestseller and started a long string of copycat stories that became more and more gruesome as the years went on. Using the same hypnotic, suggestive techniques, psychiatrists and therapists across the country began to find similar stories in the unknown histories of their patients. Naturally, the patients could not remember any of these incidents taking place except under the influence of hypnosis and psychiatric drugs but, at the doctors' insistence, became convinced of their validity. The movement in the psychiatric world corresponded and fit into the notion of multiple personality disorder and repressed memories that were becoming popular both in the psychiatric world and in pop culture. The psychiatrists believed that, as children, these people experienced such horrific atrocities that it caused their minds to either repress the incidents from conscious memory or fracture into different personalities, and this was why no one could remember any of the abuse actually happening.

This panic became national with the McMartin Preschool Trials, in which the staff of a preschool was arrested on the testimony of preschool children, who claimed, among other things, that they had been molested in hot air balloons and underground tunnels and forced to eat feces and drink blood; but there was absolutely no corroborating evidence. Of course, none of the children actually remembered this, either. Rather, child therapists who specialized in satanic ritual abuse (SRA) used leading questions and untested methods by which to extract this information. No bodies were ever found, nor was any physical evidence of sexual abuse. In the end, all those arrested in the McMartin Preschool case were acquitted in what remains the longest and most expensive trial in U.S. history.

The 1980s was awash in this belief that there was a vast conspiracy of Satanists who were murdering up to 50,000 people a year, according to one police officer's estimate. Those who wanted to believe found evidence for satanic cults everywhere. Heavy metal music was blamed for leading teenagers to Satanism and suicide, teachers and family members were accused of molestation and murder, and talk shows were alive with gruesome stories of forced cannibalism and torture at the hands of a vast underground cult, including a Geraldo Rivera special that garnered some of the highest television ratings in history. Particular police officers became known as "cult cops" and went from city to city warning of the dangers of cults and instructing other departments in what to look for; psychiatrists and therapists began to specialize in

SRA and quickly moved to the forefront of their fields as directors of psychi-atric facilities; heavy metal bands were sued following the suicide of teen-agers; major corporations were boycotted because people found evidence of satanic symbolism in their logos; evangelical preachers used the presence of a formidable and dangerous satanic presence to unite their flocks and rally against the downward plight of the nation; and there were even instances of townspeople arming themselves to go look for the cults as they practiced their rites in the dark woods.

However, no bodies were ever found; no corroborating evidence ever uncovered; no vast cult conspiracy that ruled the nation was ever unearthed; and when the accusations became too ridiculous to be believed by even the most ardent of believers, the movement died, just as the European witch craze and the Salem witch trials had. The U.S. justice system had forgotten what Cotton Mather wrote concerning witness testimony. It was later deter-mined that a majority of the accusations against the McMartin teachers came from a mentally ill mother diagnosed with schizophrenia. In fact, there are several documented cases of the police and therapists taking the word of men-tally ill people as testimony and prosecuting based on said testimony. The accusations also involved testimony from highly susceptible children who, up until that time, could not have been used as legitimate witnesses for pros-ecution. There are a variety of political, cultural, economic, and religious aspects of the satanic panic that will be covered in a later chapter, but it does demonstrate the United States' ability to quickly forget lessons of the past and to resort to panic inspired by folklore and ancient beliefs, if given the right social stressors. Despite three hundred years of technological and eco-nomic progress since the Salem witch trials, the United States has progressed very little culturally and spiritually.

TODAY

Today we find ourselves, once again, in the midst of an uprising of belief in the paranormal. It is not a witch-hunt, but resembles the Spiritualism of the late nineteenth century during which men and women sought to find evi-dence of the afterlife and the spirit world. Television is rife with paranormal-based programming and the Internet has allowed for unprecedented access to other belief systems and other believers so that they can come together and try to find evidence of spirits that walk among us.

The United States is the richest and most technologically and scientifically progressive nation in the world, yet the belief in ghosts, UFOs, and Bigfoot is stronger than ever. We are ultimately a nation built on the belief systems of

Europe, but the United States has coalesced and changed and become its own paranormal nation, awash in belief, mystery, fear, and wonder, despite the skeptics and despite the progress.

This presents us with a cultural contradiction, and it is that contradiction which we will be exploring. Whether or not one believes in the paranormal, the belief therein does exist and manifests in all levels of our society. This continued belief in the paranormal begs the question as to whether or not the paranormal is "real." However, we may be asking the wrong question; perhaps we should be asking what our belief in the paranormal reveals about our identity, our culture, and our nation. Despite all efforts, the paranormal has never been proven or disproven; there is only belief and non-belief. Both reveal deep, innate, cultural relics that have been passed down through generations and both reflect insecurities, fears, and contradictions in the way that we live our lives and the way that we perceive our lives. The United States of America was born of religious freedom and yet occupies a Native American graveyard. We have been haunted from the very beginning. We are truly a paranormal nation.

CHAPTER 3

Paranormal Hoaxes

In August of 2008 two hunters in Georgia named Matt Whitton and Rick Dyer reported to the media that they had found a dead Bigfoot while hunting in the forest and that they had the creature on ice awaiting scientific inquiry. The story and the pictures showing what appeared to be the frozen dead body of a Bigfoot captured national attention and was reported by all major news stations. The story was also supported by Tom Biscardi, CEO of Searching for Bigfoot, who claimed to have personally laid hands on the beast and publicly verified that it was real on Fox News. Biscardi's organization paid an unknown amount to have first access to the body. A couple days later, Biscardi had to go on television and admit to being duped by a frozen rubber Halloween costume mixed with a few real animal parts such as tongues and teeth.[1] This was obviously a major disappointment and blow to the entire Bigfoot research community, which does, in fact, claim some reputable scientific figures. The fallout for those involved, including Biscardi, was substantial. Both men involved in the hoax, one a police officer and the other a corrections officer, were threatened with lawsuits by Bigfoot organizations, and Whitton was fired from his job as a police officer. Whitton stated, "All this was a big joke. It got into something way bigger than it was supposed to be."[2] While the two claim that the story merely "got legs" and ran on its own, they certainly didn't shy away from the media attention, and they even helped the process along. They accepted money from Biscardi's organization, held a press conference claiming that the body was real, and then disappeared while the body was thawed and examined.

I remember that August well. I was just forming the idea for this book at the time, and I remember chatting with some friends at a wedding and telling them the news—they had finally found Bigfoot! We were all skeptical, but bolstered by the news reports and Biscardi's insistence that he had laid hands on the creature, and that it was, in fact, real. We were skeptical, but hopeful. We wanted it to be real and were disappointed when the hoax was revealed. The people I talked with at the wedding were not die-hard Bigfoot hunters, nor were they active believers in the paranormal, but they still hoped it was true that there was some last bastion of wilderness and wildness that had remained untouched by civilization for all these years. We wanted to believe that there was still some mystery left in the world. We were let down, but it was certainly not the first time that the hopeful public had been duped. In fact it happens time and time again and, on some level, is probably happening right now as people routinely call psychic hotlines, follow individuals who claim to be gods, or parade around in crop circles hoping to absorb the power of the space beings who formed them.

The hoax raises many questions regarding our beliefs, hopes, fears, and motivations. What would drive two men at the beginning of their law enforcement careers to throw everything away and face public ridicule and anger for a "joke"? How is it that we, the public, are continually misled down well-worn roads of false prophets and tricksters? And why does the hoax persist after so many years and so many failed attempts that resulted in anger, mistrust, and scrutiny? What role does it play in paranormal belief systems?

The hoax plays a crucial role in the realm of the paranormal because the hoax creates doubt and relegates professed experience to the realm of lies and deceit. In essence, the hoax ensures that the paranormal remains relegated to the outskirts of accepted experience and will not garner true scientific inquiry; it ensures that the paranormal will always remain mysterious and entrenched in doubt.

But before we move on, we should establish a working definition of a hoax for our purposes. A hoax is a deception perpetrated by one or more individuals who claim to have evidence or secret knowledge of the supernatural in an effort to gain fame, money, notoriety, or legal benefits or to ridicule the beliefs of others. It involves fraudulent evidence, public manipulation, and, ultimately, to *truly* be considered a hoax, it must be exposed, though we will examine some cases that have never been proven one way or the other. Proof of a hoax can be quite difficult, as all parties have to agree and admit to the hoax or be caught in such a compromising position that they cannot avoid admitting the truth.

A BRIEF HISTORY OF HOAXING

Hoaxing is as old as supernatural belief itself, dating back to the origins of humanity. Ancient shamans used to communicate with the gods and spirits and manipulate them in order to ensure both the survival of their tribe and to ensure their position of power within the tribe. However, the shamans were not always able to summon "powers" at their command, so they resorted to trickery and illusion to maintain their status in the community. "Generally, two explanations are offered for the sham of shamanism. Briefly they are: shamans use deception to enhance healing via placebo effects, and shamans use tricks to demonstrate power and compel obedience."[3] The history of trickery and the demonstration of supernatural powers through trickery have been recorded in some anthropological texts, but are largely unknown, as many of the ancient rites and practices have all but died out, save for a few primitive tribes around the world that still engage in them.

In recorded history, however, one of the earliest known hoaxes dates back to 1661 England and the Ghostly Drummer of Tedworth. According to the Museum of Hoaxing, "The case of the ghostly drummer of Tedworth soon became famous throughout England. Its notoriety prompted Joseph Glanvill, a clergyman and member of the Royal Society, to visit the Mompesson household and investigate the spirit. He collected eyewitness accounts of the spirit's activities, recorded hearing noises himself, and eventually became convinced that the spirit was real."[4]

Unfortunately for the investigating clergy, skeptics began pointing out serious holes in Mompesson's story, like why no one was ever allowed in the cellar, why the drumming always happened at night, and why it seemed to come from outside the house rather than within. The king himself actually sent men to Mompesson's home to investigate, and they determined there was no evidence of paranormal activity. The Drummer was never actually proven as a hoax, and the story eventually passed into legend.

The story of the Drummer of Tedworth is a good base narrative for how hoaxes generally unfold: a claim, a subsequent investigation by someone with mystical knowledge (in this case a clergyman), a subsequent publication of their finding (often for profit), public interest, and then the descent of the skeptics and outside investigators who break open the psycho-structure of the hoax. For our discussion in this chapter, we will refer to this general sequence of events as the Drummer Cycle.

The psycho-structure of a hoax will be discussed later on, but for our purposes, psycho-structure involves the psychological willingness of direct participants or the public to believe what is being claimed, i.e., those who truly believe the hoax and invest a large personal stake in the belief, often putting reputations on the line in defense of it, and thus, greatly resisting having that belief torn open and exposed as a fraud.

A hoax involves manipulation of the medium used to inform and entertain the public, thus, as the medium (newspapers, television, Internet) changed and evolved with technology, so did the nature of the hoax. When widespread printing and distribution of newspapers emerged, along with increased literacy among the public, the newspaper became the realm of the hoax. One of the most famous hoaxers in U.S. history was Benjamin Franklin, a publisher and avid writer, and one of the founding fathers of our country. Franklin authored several hoaxes through the pages of newspapers that he owned and did so largely through pen names. "Like other eighteenth century literary figures such as Jonathan Swift and Daniel Defoe, he used hoaxes for satirical ends, to expose what he perceived as public foolishness and vice to the light of public censure."[5] Some of his more famous pranks did involve the paranormal. "The Witch Trial at Mount Holly" details a fake witch trial at Mount Holly, which captured the attention of the Philadelphia public and was eventually reprinted in the British *Gentleman's Gazette*. According to the Museum of Hoaxes, "The piece is noteworthy for revealing that by 1730 it had become acceptable for the educated class in America to ridicule beliefs such as witchcraft, even though the majority of the population still clung to those beliefs." It should be noted, however, that it was also the educated upper class that sent the Salem "witches" to the gallows.

In 1835, news of life discovered on the moon swept through New York City on the front page of the *New York Sun*. The article detailed a discovery by Sir John Herschel of a race of beings that he had observed living on the moon; this would become one of the more fantastic hoaxes to sweep across the country.

> It described a lunar topography that included vast forests, inland seas, and lilac-hued quartz pyramids. Readers learned that herds of bison wandered across the plains of the moon that blue unicorns perched on its hilltops, and that spherical, amphibious creatures rolled across its beaches. The highpoint of the narrative came when it revealed that Herschel had found evidence of intelligent life on the moon; he had discovered both a primitive tribe of hut-dwelling, fire-wielding biped beavers, and a race of winged humans living in pastoral harmony around a mysterious, golden-roofed temple.[6]

Sound ridiculous? Yale believed it. "Yale College was alive with staunch supporters. The literati—students and professors, doctors in divinity and law—and all the rest of the reading community, looked daily for the arrival of the

New York mail with unexampled avidity and implicit faith."[7] Eventually the hoax was revealed, but not before the *New York Sun* sold many, many papers.

As the mediums through which people experienced the world changed, so did the methods of hoaxing. As print and newspapers began to contain more and more photographs, those photographs were almost instantly used to create images of ghosts. The public, new to the technology and not fully understanding how it operated and how it could be manipulated, initially met many of these ghost photographs with belief and fear. "An American jewelry engraver and amateur photographer named William Mumler is regularly credited as the first person to produce a photograph of a spirit—that of his young female cousin, who had died twelve years before. He published the photograph in 1862 and the media sensation it provoked inspired him to give up engraving and set himself up as a Spirit Photographic Medium."[8] He was eventually charged with fraud. His defense? That spirits of the dead really did appear to the living, and therefore he had no reason to fake his photographs. He was acquitted.

One of the biggest stirs in paranormal photography occurred in England in 1916 in the case of the Cottingly Fairies. Two young girls photographed a group of fairies dancing in the forest. The photographs eventually became famous and even prompted Sir Arthur Conan Doyle, author of the Sherlock Holmes books, to publish a book entitled *The Coming of Fairies* in 1922. The girls' poor father supposedly never knew of the hoax and believed that his young girls had actually photographed real, live fairies—a belief he died with. While the girls never fully admitted to the hoax, they declined to answer when they were asked in an interview in 1971 if they could swear on the Bible that the photographs were real. One of the women, Elsie, laughed and ended the interview. The photos, by today's standards, wouldn't have warranted a second glance, but people were new to the technology and, for the most part, couldn't understand or fathom that these images could have been faked.

Photographs and print gradually gave way to radio and television. Probably everyone has heard of the *War of the Worlds* radio broadcast done by Orson Welles; however, this cannot be classified as a hoax as there were several announcements made regarding the program that clearly indicated it was fiction. Nevertheless, it caused one of the biggest public panics in U.S. history. The advent of television and its popularity led to an eerily similar incident in Great Britain, the 1992 faux-documentary entitled *Ghostwatch*.[9] Presented as actual video footage of a real haunted house, *Ghostwatch* investigators filmed a small family being terrorized by the ghost of a former inhabitant. The video footage showed young girls running from their rooms as furniture was tossed about, and a BBC presenter, Michael Parkinson, being possessed by a spirit called "Pipes." There were mediums channeling the voices of spirits and further incidents of possessions of the family living in the home. Interviews with neighbors revealed a terrifying history of the house. A former resident had claimed to be possessed by the spirit of a woman and consequently hung himself. His twelve cats, however, were left hungry and eventually fed on the body before anyone discovered it.

As the investigators probed the house, they were confronted with voices, objects moving, possessions, the sound of howling cats, and great gusts of wind. The investigators, to their horror, concluded that by engaging in a national live audience they had actually conducted a séance on a massive scale and the ghosts would now be unleashed upon England. According to the Museum of Hoaxes, "The program elicited a huge, national reaction. Many phoned the police and warned them that the forces of darkness had been unleashed upon the nation. Some women reportedly were so scared that they went into labor early, and rumors circulated later that a few teenagers had committed suicide. However, there was nothing real about the show. It had been entirely staged." When it was later revealed that the program was a fake, there was much public and media outcry. The result was that the BBC put a decade-long ban on the program being repeated; the ban was eventually lifted early. Sadly, there was at least one suicide blamed on the program, for which the BBC was held accountable.

One of the most successful and innocently intentioned hoaxes in history was that of crop circles. Two artists, Doug Bower and David Chorley, met regularly at a pub for some pints and to talk about art. It was there they hatched an idea to make people believe that UFOs were landing in cornfields. Bower had previously spent time in New Zealand and had read an article about circles appearing in reeds and grass in Queensland.

> And one day when we were walking out on Cheesefoot Head [two miles east of] Winchester, one summer evening, in the midst of the cornfields, we sat down there, and, trying to get a bit of inspiration for paintings, and I suddenly remembered this article that I read while in Australia. And I told him about it and I said we could have quite a bit of fun, if we could devise some kind of way to make a circular mark in the cornfields here, and sort of arouse a bit of interest. People would think that a UFO had landed in the night, when they discovered it the next morning.[10]

Undoubtedly, this is how many hoaxes originate, over a couple of beers and some fun ideas. However, sometimes they become bigger than could ever have been conceived. At first, no one really noticed the circles, but when the news did break, it became a media sensation almost overnight. When a weatherman stated that a certain weather or wind anomaly could have caused the circles, the boys changed it up and began putting elaborate designs in the crops. Their work, unrecognized as it was, inspired pranksters in other countries, some of whom took the crop circles to entirely new levels. Cult-like groups were traveling to the circles to immerse themselves in the "energy" left behind by the space visitors, and investigators proclaimed that there was no way these designs could be man-made. Chorley and Bower's admission years later reddened the faces of thousands who had believed.

One of the interesting aspects of hoaxing is that often the belief continues even after the fraud has been exposed. People who begin to wrap their entire belief system around something like crop circles will psychologically resist any breakdown of that psycho-structure. Thus, there are still pockets of people who believe that crop circles are the work of alien forces. This is a phenomenon that has been studied and documented in cults; when the leader of the cult is exposed, either through police intervention or, more commonly, when the prophesies fail to be met, the belief structure of the cult is shaken. This results in some people leaving the cult but also in some members entrenching themselves deeper in the belief system. In his book, *Deadly Cults: Crimes of True Believers*, Robert L. Snow writes,

> Although failed prophesies by cult leaders can cause some members to leave, many don't because of a psychological phenomenon called, cognitive dissonance. This phenomenon makes some cult members become even more dedicated to the cult after a prophecy fails ... individuals have a psychological need to maintain order and balance in their lives, in these instances, the only way they can do that is by rationalizing why the predicted event didn't occur, but to do it within the framework of the cult belief.[11]

Likewise, some people have invested much of their time, energy, money, and belief in things like crop circles, which occasionally turn out to be hoaxes or delusions. In an effort to maintain a secure and familiar world outlook, they will find reasons to maintain their original belief system. For instance, some may believe not all the designs could have been made by humans, or they may believe that Doug Bower is actually lying, or so on. Cognitive dissonance, however, works both ways and can affect the skeptic as much as the believer, but this will be discussed later.

Some of the most popular forms of hoaxes and trickery come in the form of psychics, fortunetellers, and mediums. In 1988 James Randi, magician and professional paranormal debunker, teamed with *60 Minutes* in Australia to create a fake medium sensation known as "Carlos." Carlos was a being over two thousand years old who would pour forth his ancient wisdom to those who listened. Randi recruited an unknown actor named Jose Alvarez and concocted a story in which Alvarez, after a nearly fatal motorcycle accident, suddenly began to channel Carlos. *60 Minutes* and Randi created some faked footage of Alvarez going into a trance-like state (using crystals to focus his energy) and then speaking in the voice of Carlos. They then began to advertise for "The Entity Carlos." The sham swept the nation of Australia. Carl Sagan describes Carlos's first public show at the Drama Theater of Sydney.

> An excited crowd, young and old, milled about expectantly. Entrance was free, which reassured those who vaguely wondered if it might be some sort of scam. Alvarez seated himself on a low couch. His pulse was monitored. Suddenly it stopped. Seemingly, he was near death. Low guttural noises emanated from deep within him. The audience gasped in wonder and awe. Suddenly, Alvarez's body took on power. His posture radiated confidence. A broad, humane, spiritual perspective flowed out of Alvarez's mouth. Carlos was here! Interviewed afterwards, many members of the audience described how they had been moved and delighted.[12]

They followed the appearances with marketing of "Atlantis Crystals," "Waters of Carlos," "Tears of Carlos," and a book entitled *The Teachings of Carlos*. All this in an effort to show the gullibility of the masses, and when the hoax was finally revealed, the masses and other media were not pleased. Even the media had been duped by one of their own whose stated purpose, as news media, was to report the truth. The public backlash was immense. However, "Alvarez and Randi proved how little it takes to tamper with our beliefs, how readily we are led, how easy it is to fool the public when people are lonely and starved for something to believe in."[13]

But this kind of hoax happens on a daily basis. Psychics, mediums, and astrologers are seemingly everywhere in today's society. Predictions for astrological signs are printed in newspapers; there are psychic fairs, and mediums like John Edwards, whose work can easily be replicated by magicians and people practiced in the art of cold reading. There are even government-sponsored psychics. In January of 2000, the *New York Times* reported that the welfare department "has been recruiting welfare recipients to work from home as telephone psychics." If you weren't psychic, they actually provided "training" and then put you to work for the Psychic Network. Unfortunately, the Psychic

Network proved to have many complaints filed against it and was investigated by the Federal Trade Commission. "Investigators typically reacted with disbelief to New York City's welfare-to-work psychic venture, but an enforcement official with the Federal Communications Commission, where 40 percent of all complaints concern psychic pay-per-call operations, laughed uncontrollably, then begged for anonymity."[14]

Some psychic hoaxes have involved vast amounts of money and have degenerated into outright threats on personal safety. *ABC News* reported in 2006 about Jackie Haughn, a 36-year-old mother of two who responded to an ad left on the windshield of her car for a psychic reading. "After her first session, Haughn felt as if she could trust Ann Marie [the psychic], and she agreed to come back. During that next reading, Haughn said the psychic told her something dramatic: There was a curse on Haughn and her family. Haughn said Ann Marie convinced her that by performing a number of rituals, the curse could be removed, a curse that was put on Haughn's family many years ago."[15] Haughn eventually paid a total of $220,000 to Ann Marie and then received a letter demanding $63,000 or else Satan would take someone. The police then became involved and Ann Marie, whose real name was Tammi Mitchell, was arrested for extortion. We read about these incidents, we hear about them on the news, and our skeptical side tells us that they are all scams, but there is also something that wants to believe and is looking for answers. Being deceived by one of these hoaxers isn't necessarily a sign of ignorance. Michael Shermer of *Skeptic Magazine* states, "Smart people on some level are even more gullible if you can get them past their initial skepticism. Because most of what we believe, we believe for emotional, psychological reasons, and then we rationalize the belief after the fact, after we already hold it. Smart people are better at rationalizing these beliefs."[16]

It is the rationalizing of beliefs and actions and the effects of cognitive dissonance that comprise the psychological base of both hoaxers and skeptics. However, there is more to hoaxing than merely the psychological; there are the sociological and symbolic aspects of the hoax, the belief, and the defrauders. There are reasons that these hoaxes persist, that the beliefs persist, that we repeatedly find ourselves committing to and being taken in by these tricksters. In the context of the history of hoaxing we will try to examine why people repeatedly feel the need to trick others into certain beliefs, especially when the costs—public, personal, and legal—can be very, very high. But we also need to look at ourselves; why we are willing to believe and what role the hoax ultimately plays in our world experience.

FOOL ME ONCE, SHAME ON YOU

When you buy tickets to a magic show, what are you really buying? You are buying a time during which you are willing to suspend your disbelief in order to view the supernatural. The ticket is a contract of sorts between the audience and the performer; show us something we cannot explain for which we will graciously acknowledge your "supernatural" ability. Of course, no one actually thinks that Criss Angel or David Copperfield is actually supernatural. In the back of our minds, we know that it is ultimately a trick that has a very real and logical, if not scientific, method for fooling the eyewitness. We know this; it's part of the fun—being amazed at first, trying to figure out how it was done, and when we can find no answer, walking away with the knowledge that it was a trick but also with the slight hope that maybe magic is real.

The hoaxer is in a similar position in that he or she is playing a trick with a very real methodology that is designed to confuse and create wonder and belief in the mind of the viewer. The difference is that the viewing audience has not purchased a ticket, has not entered into that contract with the performer, and has not willingly suspended its disbelief. The magic show is performed in a theater in which people allow their beliefs to be molded; the hoax is performed in the everyday, real world, where we do not allow our beliefs to be molded, but rather, we allow our beliefs to mold us. The hoax is the ultimate deception and betrayal because the victims are deceived by the hoaxer and betrayed by their beliefs. The believer allows the hoax to change them, and when it is revealed as a fraud, they are left with a loss of self. The rationale given in a majority of the hoaxes is, "it was all for fun." But the reaction of the fooled public is one of anger and betrayal, and the public will ultimately make the hoaxer pay. The "fun" can be very costly, as shown in the case of Whitton and Dyer's dead Bigfoot.

But why the drive to create these hoaxes in the light of such public, and often legal, recourses? There are three aspects to the motivation of the hoaxer. The first is the fun aspect, the second is monetary gain, and the third is the magical aspect. Let's begin with the fun.

When Whitton and Dyer said that they did it for fun, who was it that was actually having the fun? Certainly not the Bigfoot researchers, the media, or the public; rather, it was for their own amusement. The "fun" is knowledge of the truth in a world of lies. The fun is watching others who are ignorant of the truth talking about, acting out, and believing in a fraud of the hoaxer's design. The hoax is really a malevolent thing, in spite of the "fun" for the hoaxer. Symbolically the hoaxer retains a god-like knowledge of truth and the masses are beneath him, lost in an illusion. "Dyer, asked whether he ever thought that the hoopla had become more than just a joke, implied that everyone should have known it was a hoax. 'Well, we told 10 different stories,' he said. 'Everyone knew we were lying.' "[17] The implication is that anyone with intelligence—any knowledge of truth—should have immediately known that this was a trick and that the two were lying. However, there was a vast and public effort made by the two to confirm their story: press conferences, discussions with research organizations, and the acceptance of money for the body.

In the case of Whitton and Dyer, they were the possessors not only of the truth in a world of lies, but also possessors of the mysterious; namely, Bigfoot. As possessors of the mysterious they were immediately given nearly god-like influence and power. Suddenly camera crews and news organizations were at their feet, researchers and scientists offered them money—the world was focused on them as the possessors of the paranormal. As the possessors of truth, they enjoyed a personal god-like knowledge; as possessors of the mysterious, they enjoyed god-like treatment by the masses.

The hoax is ancient—as ancient as man's desire for power to act as a god over the masses. The hoaxer imbues his or her self with magical ability. This is not the kind of magic that David Copperfield and Criss Angel perform, because that is a magic that functions on the audience's willing suspension of disbelief. This is a more ancient form of magic; it reaches back to the time when magic was real, and the magician was a priest-like figure allied with the gods.

In ancient Egypt, the god Thoth was the possessor of knowledge and magic. Thoth was the originator of both literacy and astronomy but was also credited with religion, magic, and philosophy. Therefore, the magician in ancient Egypt wielded great divine knowledge. In effect, the magician took on a role normally reserved for priests and prophets. "Priests, magicians, and monks all offered concrete supernatural help to other people. Ancient magical spells promised to tell the future, heal illnesses, curse enemies, create pregnancies, instill erotic passion in desired mates, and so on."[18] These are precisely some of the issues that hoaxers claim to address or the public seeks answers for. Psychics and mediums claim to be able to influence these issues through their interaction with the divine. Someone who is having difficulty getting pregnant may not approach Whitton and Dyer, but they may travel to the cornfields of England to bask in the residual "energy" left in the crop circles by visiting alien beings, or perhaps they will purchase expensive, magical crystals. The hoaxer is an ancient magician; one who uses his tricks not for entertainment but for manipulation.

The hoaxer is the possessor of truth in that he or she is the only one who knows what is actually going on in the hoax, and as the sole possessor of the truth, that individual takes on a god-like knowledge. He or she is also looked upon as having a special connection to the divine, and thus, is sought out by the public. Think of the "fun" that Doug Bower and David Chorley, creators of the crop circles, must have had. While they never publicly claimed their connection to the circles until much, much later, imagine them watching the television as the news analysts, scientists, and believers all debated what the crop circles were and what they meant. Imagine them as they watched people from around the world travel to these circles to bask in their energy or seek out healing. It was "fun" because Bower and Chorley were the only two men on earth who definitively knew the truth of the circles—they were a hoax dreamed up by two artists over a couple pints at the local pub. And when science claimed to have an answer in the form of a weather anomaly, they altered their designs to be sure that everyone knew there was something mysterious, otherworldly, and divine occurring in the fields.

Bower and Chorley's work is largely looked upon with a wink and a nod from the public. They are generally viewed as pranksters rather than criminals because they did not take their hoax to the next level—profiting from the falsified beliefs. While there were people who sought to make money off the crop circles by selling New Age materials supposedly connected with the circles, the two originators never made any money because they never came forward publicly to proclaim the circles as otherworldly. In essence, they let the public deceive themselves.

But there are those who use the hoax for monetary gain, sometimes as psychics and mediums as illustrated earlier, but other times posing as legitimate investigators or believers who try to create sensationalism through the media in order to sell the rights to book publishers and movie companies. Much like an episode of *Scooby-Doo*, the true source of the haunting of a place is often the owners themselves who need an excuse to either get out of a mortgage or create revenue through selling their paranormal story. This is where the Drummer Cycle comes into play. I will use an example of a hotly contested and very well-known case of a haunting in order to demonstrate.

The Amityville Horror captured the nation's attention. It sparked massive interest from both skeptics and believers when it was reported in newspapers that a family in Amityville, New York, completely abandoned their home in the middle of the night, leaving behind all their possessions, only a month after purchase because the home was demonically infested. The house had been the site of a mass murder before being purchased by the Lutz family. Following the newspaper stories and subsequent investigation by Ed and Lorraine Warren, who proclaimed the house demonically infested, there was a best-selling book, *The Amityville Horror*, written by Jay Anson and based on the family's testimony, and then a hit movie that spawned several sequels. The Amityville Horror became a part of American legend and is largely thought to be one of those "true stories" of a haunted house.

However, the story was contested from the beginning. The case was contested on television and radio as skeptics and even other paranormal researchers came forward to debate the legitimacy of the "true" haunting. Stephen Kaplan, a New York–based paranormal researcher, authored the book *The Amityville Conspiracy*, in which he asserts that the Amityville Horror was a deliberate hoax perpetrated by the Lutz family and their attorney in an effort to get out of a mortgage they could not afford. Let's look at this story through the Drummer Cycle.

First, there is the report of paranormal activity in the house through a public forum. In this case it was the newspapers that originally broke the sensational story. Secondly, there was confirmation by those connected with the divine and paranormal, in this case, Ed and Lorraine Warren. Thirdly, there was the public fascination; not only was there the book and film which resulted in great profit for the Lutzes, but people traveled from all over the country to trespass on the property. There were reports of vandalism as people stole shingles (pieces connected with the mysterious), and eventually, the name of the street had to be changed because of the number of people trespassing and causing property damage. Then there were the skeptics and others who descended on the story and called it a hoax after conducting their own investigations. There were numerous on-air debates between the Warrens and fellow paranormal investigator Stephen Kaplan, in which the Warrens vehemently defended their conclusions that the house was indeed haunted and also accused Kaplan of being jealous because he was not invited into the house. The arguments got ugly and, as the Warrens' reputation was at stake, they defended it in light of some damning testimony from the Lutz defense attorney, William Weber, and admitted "artistic license" taken by author Jay Anson. This defense by the Warrens was necessary in order to preserve their belief systems and their characters. The Amityville Horror story fits perfectly in the Drummer Cycle of hoaxing, however, this is not to say that the Horror was or is a definitive hoax. The reader can look at the material and decide for himself; this was just a very well-known case that worked within the parameters of the Drummer Cycle.

It is a cycle that has been repeated throughout history in hoaxes and disputed hoaxes. It should be noted that the Drummer Cycle works for nearly every well-known paranormal case also, though all paranormal cases are suspected of being a hoax. If everyone agreed that it was true, then it would no longer be disputable; hence every paranormal claim has its detractors that claim it is a hoax. This simple fact actually keeps many people from coming forward with their story; they don't want to be thought of as a liar or of as being insane.

The debate between the Warrens and Kaplan, which played out on both radio and television during the late seventies, leads us to a strange form of hoax that does not fit into the mold of previous motivations. It is a hoax perpetrated by the believer in an effort to reinforce their existent belief system and convince others to believe as they do. The motivation is not money or fame or even to align oneself with a god, because often the hoax is not perpetrated by the believer on the public, but rather on fellow believers. The Warrens and Kaplan both believe in the spirit world; there was no debate on that issue. However, what was at issue was the Warrens' credibility; their character was on trial and when one's character is on trial, one will generally use all necessary means to defend it. Thus, in spite of certain evidences presented that seemed to contradict the Warrens' story, they still had to maintain and defend their position, because that position was directly tied to their character.

Of course, there is another possibility in the case of the Amityville Horror and the Warrens—the possibility that the Warrens were tricked by the Lutz family, and their willingness to believe forced them into a corner that they were unable to escape from without sacrificing their characters and reputations due to the public nature of the haunting. We will discuss this further in the next section.

FOOL ME TWICE, SHAME ON ME

In 2002, the *Seattle Times* reported on the death of Raymond Wallace and publicly announced "Bigfoot is dead."

Ray Wallace was the first to discover the giant tracks of an unknown beast high in the Pacific Northwest mountains while his crew was working on road construction. Following Wallace's discovery, the name Bigfoot was assigned to the mysterious track-maker by the local media. Wallace then began an odd personal and public journey with his Bigfoot story. At one point he claimed that Bigfoot was actually guarding a secret gold mine, and that he and Bigfoot were well acquainted and that he had hair, recordings, and weapons used by Bigfoot. Immediately following his death in 2002, the family made a statement: " 'Ray L. Wallace was Bigfoot. The reality is, Bigfoot just died,' said Michael Wallace about his father, who died of heart failure Nov. 26 in a Centralia nursing facility."[19] Despite this admission of a hoax that lasted nearly 50 years, the professed guilt by the family, and a pair of wooden feet that were supposedly used in creating the famous tracks, Bigfoot researchers have ignored the confession and have continued to look for the beast. And the public is just as interested in Bigfoot as ever.

Now, there are serious considerations to be taken with the Wallace family's story, many of which are outlined in Jeff Meldrum's book, *Sasquatch: Legend Meets Science*. Much of Wallace's story doesn't add up. However, let's assume that Wallace was finally telling the truth, that it was really just a hoax all these years (the Bigfoot phenomenon does actually fit the Drummer Cycle). Why does the public continue to wonder and believe? There have been countless hoaxes discovered over the years; the public has been burned repeatedly, but we seemingly keep coming back for more. It has been demonstrated that the hoax can take on dimensions far outside the originator. Case in point: the crop circles quickly became replicated by people around the world and became much bigger than the originators. So here we have a man and his family saying that the exact same thing occurred with Bigfoot, but no one in the public, for the most part, believes them. The saying goes "fool me twice, shame on me," so why do we keep allowing ourselves to be duped even in the face of a blatant admission?

The paranormal taps into a belief system that is deep within the human psyche; it is the belief that there is something more than the visible reality in which we live. Therefore, ghosts, UFOs, and Bigfoot provide that mysterious "other world" that lies behind the veil of our accepted reality. This other world is the mysterious, the unknown. The unknown allows for our imaginations to work and extrapolate. Our world is largely governed by logic and accepted realities, social norms and tradition; it does not leave much room for the imagination. The paranormal allows for the imagination to work; the mysterious and unknown lets us think outside of the confines of our everyday reality. Thus, when presented with an opportunity to view the mysterious, when given a great unknown, such as ghosts, UFOs, or Bigfoot, we jump at the chance; we bite at the bait because the mysteries of the world beckon our inner yearnings. As I've asked before, what is more frightening? The idea that we don't know everything about this world or the idea that we do? Absolute knowledge leaves no room for imagination.

When I was very young I believed that Asia was a dark and mysterious land of dense jungle and wild animals. The word itself, Asia, sounded so exotic that I assumed it had to be an exotic land. Imagine my disappointment upon learning that a majority of Asia was made up of cold, barren Russian tundra? I was disappointed; it felt like a big piece of joy and wonder had been taken away.

This is not to say that it is better to be ignorant, but rather to illustrate the disenchantment of the world that is an inherent part of the human experience. The paranormal offers an opportunity to recapture that childhood sense of enchantment and wonder that has been stripped away by the modern, learned, logical world. Malcolm McGrath, author of the book *Demons of the Modern World*, draws a comparison to childlike wonder and belief in magic and primitive cultures: "Nonetheless, there is one similarity in their style of thinking; that is, neither of them has learned to make a clear distinction between the mechanical and the symbolic worlds we live in at the level of secondary theory. Neither of them has learned, for example, that the planets move entirely on the basis of mechanical principles, or that magic and ghosts are not possible."[20] Hence, in my youth I was still thinking in symbolic terms—*Asia* was a word symbol that represented something to me that was not reality. However, as we grow and learn, that symbolism is largely replaced by the mechanical world. "The possibility of magic threatens the integrity of the mechanical theory of the physical universe."[21]

The paranormal allows us to relive childhood wonder, to exist in a world that is outside the mechanics of the accepted physical universe, to operate in a world of symbols. Because symbolism is the first form of knowledge that we learn as infants and children, it can often feel as if it is an innate sense of truth—something basic and deeper than the learned reality in which we function today. So we feel drawn to it, not completely willing to believe the world that has been placed before us by society, science, and education. There is a deep, inner feeling that there is a different truth out there, one that functions largely in a world of magic and symbolism, one that thrives in the mysterious and unknown.

The pervasiveness of religion is a prime example of the draw of symbolism and magic. Religions use symbols that are imbued with unseen power—the cross, communion, statues, altars, and rituals are all symbols of a greater truth. A vast majority of the world is religious and drawn to this world of magic and symbolism. Is it possible that these belief systems tap into a childhood sense of wonder, a world in which symbols and magic operate to explain the unknown?

Just like religion, the paranormal provides the public with magic, symbolism, and a mysterious world that is more basic and thus "truer" than our mechanized world of logic and science. The paranormal, like religion, is a belief system that is based on symbols and magic. Our beliefs form the basis of our sense of self. If, deep in our hearts, we believe that there is something more to the mechanical reality of the world, then we will seek out support for that belief system and try to maintain it despite certain difficulties and refutations of that belief system. To have our beliefs challenged and upended is to have our sense of self challenged and upended. And people will try very, very hard to maintain their belief in both a mysterious world and in themselves, because without it, we feel lost.

It also works the other way around—skepticism is a belief system as much as are religious or paranormal belief systems. The belief of skeptics that there is no proof or validity to the countless paranormal claims allows them to make blanket statements that there are no ghosts (as McGrath illustrates in the quoted text), no UFOs, and no Bigfoot. We are warned as children to "never say never," but that is precisely what skeptics do.

But what would it mean to have your beliefs completely disrupted? What would it mean for science to absolutely prove that there is no Bigfoot, no ghosts, no UFOs, or no God? Fortunately, for believers it is impossible for science to absolutely disprove these beliefs. But for argument's sake, let's suppose they can. What would it mean for science if a Bigfoot was actually found and captured?

It is impossible to study anything in depth and not be somehow changed by it, and I admittedly have been affected by the study of this subject. Perhaps the greatest and most difficult moment came as I was reading *The Day After Roswell* by retired Colonel Philip J. Corso. Corso served extensively in the U.S. government in top-secret operations, served in President Eisenhower's National Security Council, and was the head of the Foreign Technology Department for the U.S. Army. In his autobiographical work, he stated clearly and plainly that there was an alien crash at Roswell in 1947 and that there were alien bodies recovered. He also stated that much of the modern technology we have, such as fiber optics, lasers, integrated circuit chips, and super-tenacity fibers were reverse engineered from the technology of the spacecraft. He claims to have funneled the technology to private companies through the foreign technology desk, and he makes a very convincing story. So convincing, in fact, that he had me convinced. I had entered into this project not really knowing what I believed regarding the paranormal and determined to remain that way. However, here was a colonel in the U.S. military, one who had served directly under a president, stating clearly that there were aliens, and they were visiting us regularly. Somehow, my world seemed to change and I suddenly felt an intense anxiety, as if I somehow couldn't tell what was real anymore. I spent several days walking around in a kind of daze, wondering if everything I had thought I knew was false, if everything I had learned had suddenly been wiped out. I was engaged in an inner battle of belief, but regardless of whether Colonel Corso was telling the truth or not, I eventually was able to settle back down into my comfortable world of disbelief with a small addenda of "it's possible." This period of anxiety and feeling lost is called cognitive dissonance, and I had just gotten a brief glimpse as to its effects.

"Whenever someone comes into contact with beliefs, ideas, or information that is in conflict with a belief that they have a strong emotional investment in, they experience a form of anxiety ... In order to reduce that anxiety, they will search for new beliefs, information, or behaviors that reduce that conflict between their current beliefs and the new information."[22] This can be a powerful motivating factor in human behavior. When Copernicus first proposed that the earth revolved around the sun, he was labeled as a heretic. Why? Because his theory flew in the face of accepted beliefs during that time, and rather than face the anxiety of a reality in which earth was not the center of the universe and the usurpation of God's power in the universe, it was easier to call him a heretic. We seek out that which reinforces our beliefs so that we never have to face that intense anxiety. Imagine the loss that was felt by the true believers when Doug Bower revealed that the crop circles were never formed by UFOs? Many of these people had invested time, money, and personal beliefs in these circles. Imagine what the skeptic would feel if tomorrow a UFO landed on the White House lawn or Bigfoot was captured and put on display. It is a feeling of utter loss, an anxiety because the world is no longer your own, your beliefs are dashed against the rocks of reality, and you are left floating in a turbulent sea. Then you have to learn how to swim all over again.

Most people would try anything to avoid having to rethink their entire world, and that includes believing in things that are quite obviously fake or disbelieving things that are most likely true. Or sometimes, adjusting our beliefs to fit the new mold.

Take this for a global example to illustrate the power of cognitive dissonance. In 2002 George W. Bush was authorized by Congress to use military force against Iraq because Saddam Hussein would not allow inspectors to examine facilities suspected of containing weapons of mass destruction. With the stated purpose of invading Iraq to eliminate a percieved imminent threat posed by Hussein's regime, the U.S. military invaded and conquered Iraq. However, after major operations were concluded and the search for the weapons began, we came up empty. The basis of the invasion was nowhere to be found. It was soon after this that the administration and its supporters began to emphasize that the purpose of the invasion was to establish a peaceful democracy in the Middle East and to liberate a people from a vicious dictator. In essence, in light of the new information that contradicted the beliefs held by the U.S. government that Iraq was hiding these weapons, the stated policy had to be amended and changed in order to accommodate these new facts. But there was a period of collective, national cognitive dissonance, and a good majority of the public was all too ready to accept that Hussein's removal was the goal of the invasion, that the world and Iraq were better off without him. The weapons of mass destruction were relegated to the periphery of our collective memory. The new reality had been accepted and (some of) our beliefs reformed to accommodate.

There is another aspect to our willingness to buy into false claims that support our belief systems; it allows us to fulfill a role in that belief system. Individual believers in the paranormal often feel that they are set aside from the rest of society due to their beliefs. Hence, they and they alone know the truth, and only they have had this experience. That feeling can imbue the believer with a feeling of being "the chosen one." The paranormal belief system becomes something of a role-playing game in which individuals have special powers of discernment, can communicate with the dead or aliens from other lands, or have been selected to spread the word of truth to the masses. The paranormal, in essence, gives their life a new meaning, an importance in being singled out and chosen by the paranormal to be both viewer and witness to the masses. George P. Hansen, in his remarkable book *The Trickster and the Paranormal*, describes an example of an obvious hoax that was believed by famed UFO researcher Budd Hopkins, someone who was not generally prone to gullibility and sensationalism. However, he was duped by a woman named Linda into believing that she had been abducted by aliens in full view of the UN secretary general and that conspiratorial acts by the CIA and other government entities were involved. Eventually, much of the claim was discredited, but not before Hopkins released a book about the abduction entitled *Witnessed: The True Story of the Brooklyn Bridge UFO Abductions*. Hansen, who was derided by Hopkins for his research into the case, states,

> Grandiosity frequently accompanies conspiratorial thinking and paranoiac belief [in our terms the paranoiac would be the 'one' separated from the masses, while the conspiratorial thinking is the masses that don't believe the 'one' and therefore have ostracized him from normative social life]. That occurred in the Linda case, and the hoaxers capitalized splendidly on it. One of Hopkins' abductees was chosen by the aliens for the demonstration of power to earth's political leaders. Hopkins was thereby cast in a central role in the drama, and his colleagues would share in the glory of proving to the world the reality of the ET's. This would be the ultimate accomplishment for any ufologist. Even if there was only a slim chance of the case being proven, the payoff was extraordinary, and it would make their lives' work worth all the effort.[23]

Scott M. Peck was a popular psychiatrist and author until his death in 2005, shortly after he completed his last book, *Glimpses of the Devil: A Psychiatrist's Personal Accounts of Possession, Exorcism and Redemption*. In it he describes two exorcisms, which he performed after setting out to disprove that there was a true devil. However, his stories smack of personal narcissism, and it would appear that Peck had so quickly and fully bought into belief in possession that he began to take on a new role outside the boundaries of his expertise, namely, psychiatry.

> I felt that Bishop Worthington's simple faith was badly needed, but that he was not smart enough to be the exorcist, the captain of the exorcism team. Who then? My own name kept coming to mind. Was I crazy? Baptized for less than a year with no formal theological training? Yet something kept calling me to be the primary exorcist, even though I felt certain that Bishop Worthington was being called as well. As the night progressed I began seriously to consider taking on the role of the exorcist with Bishop Worthington as my assistant. Was this calling from the Holy Spirit or my own arrogance.[24]

Obviously, he believed it to be the Holy Spirit, because he names himself primary exorcist and continues with the exorcism. Throughout his book Peck encompasses many heroic roles—at one point demanding that the demon face him one on one without hiding behind a human façade, much the way Father Karras commands the demon to enter into his body in *The Exorcist*, and he spends much time demonstrating to the demons his intellectual superiority. In fact, his role of exorcist is so important that even Satan himself shows up—on both occasions of exorcism, no less.

Peck writes this book in the twilight of his life and acknowledges that he himself has been diagnosed as having a bit of narcissistic tendency and may have overstepped boundaries in his work with the possessed individuals.

> I do not think that I treated Beccah well. As with a number of my other patients, she deserved a psychiatrist who was not simultaneously on the lecture circuit, always rushed, juggling two careers at once. I also think I was too close to her to be her exorcist, having worked with her for over a year and a half before uncovering her possession. To this day I cannot understand why I did not call up Malachi Martin and ask him to take over. For whatever reason—perhaps my growing fame and the applause of audiences—I think that I was arrogant during that period of time. So if I had to do it all over again I certainly wouldn't do it myself.[25]

Peck's reflection at the end of his life is telling. He was a highly educated and well-known psychiatrist and, when writing about psychiatry, a formidable presence. However, he had entered into a new realm, a new belief system, and within that system he was an ignorant child who was led down paths that nearly led to his destruction and the destruction of others. But Peck leapt into these heroic calls because he had felt himself singled out as The One. Afterwards he went on to tell his story to the masses, to tell them of his gifts and of his being chosen by God. Unfortunately, what is revealed through his work is a bit more insight into his weaknesses and flaws rather than any real glimpse of the devil. If the devil truly was at play in either of these cases, it may have been Peck whom he was seeking to confound and confuse. Peck bought right in—hook, line, and sinker—and regardless of the reality of the possessions or of the devil, he showed himself as susceptible as any other person to the lure of fantasy and role-playing.

THE TRICKSTER

Ancient societies used personified gods as a means to explain a world they could not fully understand. Today many of those gods have been explained away through science. We now know that storms at sea are not the work of Neptune but rather of complex weather patterns and oceanic currents; Hermes no longer plunges nations into war but rather complex geopolitical movements and doctrines lead to wars; and no longer is Zeus hurling lightning bolts at a population that has angered him but instead positive and negative ions exchange in vast quantities between the clouds and the earth.

But there is one ancient god, predating the Greeks, the Romans, and the Bible, which has yet to be explained—the Trickster. "The trickster is the wily survivor, the mischievous underdog who defies convention, subverts the system, breaks down the power structure, and gives birth to new ideas."[26] In essence, the trickster is the anomalous result of a world awash in chaotic systems. He is the ghost in the machine, and he has never been explained because the trickster's essence involves a vast amount of complexity, which can probably never be predicted or accurately understood.

George P. Hansen, author of *The Trickster and the Paranormal*, one of the finest books to be written on the paranormal, uses the idea of the trickster to explain paranormal phenomena and how it presents such a conundrum in our world.

Our way of thinking is governed by Aristotelian logic. It too has a binary aspect; something is either A or not-A. In this system, the 'law of the excluded middle' specifies that there is no middle ground. The betwixt and between is excluded from thought . . . The trickster is not eliminated simply by making sharp distinctions and clear categories. There is still a realm that lies betwixt and between a signifier and a signified, between a word and its referent. Tricksters travel that liminal realm, and ambiguities in communication are their province.[27]

It is exactly this realm in which the paranormal operates. Ghosts are neither living nor dead; rather, they are somewhere in between, which our modern, logical thinking does not allow for. Therefore, the ghost presents a great conundrum to our concept of reality. The UFO occupies the realm between the earth and outer space; Bigfoot between man and animal. The paranormal cannot be explained precisely because it occupies the realm of the trickster and the paranormal is evidence of the trickster's continued existence in our world.

But there is an even more important blurring of lines in the paranormal—the line between fact and fiction, truth and lies. This is where the hoaxer, the player of tricks, plays his or her part.

What if there was never a hoax or trick played? How would our understanding of the paranormal differ from what it is today? There would still be people claiming to see things, hear things, and experience things that would be unexplainable by today's standards, but we wouldn't be able to say it was a trick. We would be more readily willing to accept these stories as true because we would have no knowledge or understanding of or experience with the hoax. Obviously, this is impossible and completely outside the realm of human behavior, but it does illustrate the basic purpose and effect of the hoax on the world of the paranormal. Because the paranormal lies in the interstitial area between realms of truth and lie, fact and fiction, life and death, it will never be explained or found "true" by any scientific method. The belief thereof is then relegated to "the kooks," those who exist on the peripheries of our accepted reality. To admit belief in the paranormal feels tantamount to revealing intimacies of one's sex life—it is hidden from the world. Believers are afraid of ridicule and ostracism—belief in the paranormal is to be kept private. Even as I told friends and coworkers of my work on this book, I experienced a certain feeling of shame and embarrassment even broaching the subject in a mixed social group. Indeed, these worries are often cited by paranormal witnesses as their reasons for not coming forward to tell of their experiences. They do not want to be thought of as crazy or, even worse, gullible and weak-minded. The hoaxer, the trickster, ensures that this remains the case, and it pushes believers to the outskirts of society—outsiders to be laughed at and ridiculed.

"Hoaxes assist the rationalization and disenchantment of the world. They help consign the paranormal to the realm of fraud and gullibility, so that the phenomena receive little serious study. With the taint they induce, hoaxes protect the paranormal from close examination."[28]

Perhaps it is this blurring of the lines between fact and fiction that creates a different sort of truth. Perhaps the paranormal cannot be interpreted by the terms and conditions put forth by science. Rather, it constitutes a different realm of reality and truth.

Caitlin lost her mother to cancer during the summer of 2006. She was 19 years old and attending LeMoyne College in northern New York at the time. The loss of her mother was obviously devastating for her and her family, but she returned to school as scheduled in the fall. The previous semester Caitlin had signed up for a course on death and grieving. Caitlin was one person in a rather large class and did not feel ready to discuss her mother's recent death, so she avoided mentioning it to her professor or classmates. "I didn't write about it in my papers; instead, I focused on other family members who had died in the past. I wasn't ready to talk about her." Over the course of the semester, the professor brought in a psychic medium to speak to the class. "She said that she could read auras and offered to do a reading for anyone who wanted, but no one went forward. I didn't really think much of it. My family had never been believers in that sort of thing." Caitlin's family was 100 percent working-class Irish. The only reason she was able to attend LeMoyne was because her mother had been an employee of a fellow Jesuit school in Connecticut, and therefore, her tuition was free as part of the benefits. Now that her mother was gone, she was left with her father and two brothers, none of whom were much disposed to thinking of things outside the course of daily reality. Caitlin had never been exposed to anything like a medium.

The very last day of the semester, as the group was filing out of the classroom, the medium asked for Caitlin to stay behind. "She said that for the past couple weeks, the six weeks or whatever of the semester, she had noticed that I didn't have an aura surrounding me. She said that typically if you don't see an aura around a person it's either because they're very evil or something tragic has just happened in their life, and they haven't been able to repair, to re-establish themselves yet. I was like, 'God, I hope I'm not evil, I hope nothing's wrong'. She said, 'I don't want to make you uncomfortable or anything, but there has been a woman that has been in the classroom; she seems to be near you, and she has the most beautiful blue eyes that I have ever seen.'" Caitlin's mother had auburn hair and striking bright, blue eyes. Anyone who had ever met her would remember those eyes. "I didn't say anything;

I was kind of just taking it in. Of course, on the inside I was freaking out, but I just didn't say anything. She said, 'I don't know if you know who I'm talking about, but she said you would know her by her birthday being in the very middle of January.' My mother's birthday was January 15th. There was no way that this woman could have known these things, and I started just freaking out. She wanted us to know that me and the boys would be okay, and that she was okay. At that point I started to cry, because how in the world would this woman have known those things?

"I was freaking out because I didn't buy into her whole spiel in the first place, but after a couple weeks of processing it and talking to family members about it, I kind of felt at peace. It was kind of nice to hear. My Dad thought I was a psycho because he doesn't buy into that. He thought it was a weird coincidence and nothing more. I told my brothers, but they didn't really say anything. One of them said that it was good message."

The experience ultimately changed Caitlin into a more spiritually focused individual. It opened an entire world of possibility for her—the possibility of life after death, something that was largely closed, or at least foreign, to her before. Following the death of any family member, the usual platitudes are bestowed upon the grieving, "so and so is better off," or "she's in heaven now," but often those platitudes do nothing more than isolate the grieving even more. They are detached from the possibility of life after death because in this world, in this reality, death always wins out. Death looms as the end-all, be-all reality, especially following an untimely death of such a dramatic figure as a mother. It is often not until much later, when we as earth-bound beings begin to reflect, that we begin to find comfort in the old platitudes. Caitlin was plunged into a spiritual understanding through an experience that she can barely comprehend or explain. "Now I totally believe in all that stuff. Before I was skeptical because I was raised not to believe in that stuff, but now I believe. I like thinking that there is something after you die, whether it's an 'in between,' or you're working your way to heaven or another life—I don't know. But it's comforting. It brought some closure for me."

Caitlin concedes that there is a possibility, a small one, that the medium could have found her mother's obituary online and researched her. However, in a large class of college students, why pick Caitlin? The medium wasn't being paid and didn't try to solicit anything in return for the information. The medium did not make a spectacle of Caitlin, performing this feat in front of the class in order to gain respect and potential clients. Rather, this information was given to Caitlin with compassion and intimacy in a private conversation. However, the truth of what was said changed Caitlin's life forever and brought her peace.

There are two different kinds of truth in the world. There is scientific truth and there is spiritual truth—the kind of truth found through art and personal revelation. What Caitlin experienced was not scientific truth. It, most likely, would not hold up under the scrutiny of the scientific method. But what occurred between Caitlin and the medium was a truth of spiritual and personal revelation; something found in the arts and psychology, rather than in the world of science.

One of our greatest living writers, Tim O'Brien, wrote that,

> You can tell a true war story by the questions you ask. Somebody tells a story, let's say, and afterward you ask, 'Is it true?' and if the answer matters, you've got your answer. For example, we've all heard this one. Four guys go down a trail. A grenade sails out. One guy jumps on it and takes the blast and saves his three buddies. Is it true? The answer matters. You'd feel cheated if it never happened. Without the grounding reality, it's just a trite bit of puffery, pure Hollywood, untrue in the way all such stories are untrue. Yet even if it did happen—and maybe it did, anything's possible—even then you know it can't be true, because a true war story does not depend upon that kind of truth. Absolute occurrence is irrelevant. A thing may happen and be a total lie; another thing may not happen and be truer than the truth. For example: Four guys go down a trail. A grenade sails out. One guy jumps on it and takes the blast, but it's a killer grenade and everybody dies anyway. Before they die, though, one of the dead guys says, 'The fuck you do that for?' and the jumper says, 'Story of my life, man,' and the other guy starts to smile but he's dead. That's a true story that never happened.[29]

According to O'Brien, "Absolute occurrence is irrelevant." Caitlin's experience was a truth that was greater than absolute occurrence. Is it possible that the medium was a sham? Of course. Does it matter? I would say not. The trickster blurs the nature of truth, and because of that, science is probably the least prepared to understand the paranormal and its effects on the individual. Perhaps researching the paranormal would best be left to those who make it their job to unravel the trickster: psychologists, artists, historians, and anthropologists—men and woman who understand the nature of human psyche and its relation to the world, rather than people who understand the physical workings of life and seek to confine them within boundaries. The paranormal, like the trickster, will always blur those boundaries and is therefore not subject to scientific investigation.

This may come as a shock to both paranormal researchers and traditional scientists; however, to date neither has been able to grasp a foothold on the nature of the paranormal. Each of them tries to confine the paranormal within boundaries and each repeatedly fails. Both sides seek to establish a "reality"; one reality is that the paranormal does not exist—the other reality is that it does exist. Neither can be proven, thanks to the trickster and the hoaxers and pranksters that he enlists to aid in the blurring of lines between fantasy and reality, lies and truth, fact and fiction. The hoaxer may play the most important role in the realm of the paranormal—an agent whose mission is to defy boundaries and maintain its constant mystery.

CHAPTER 4

The Native Paranormal

Y i-Fu Tuan wrote, "The United States of America would seem to be the country in the world least hospitable to ghosts. It does not believe in the sanctity of the past... A new nation, America lacks the favored haunts of ghosts: old houses that belong to families with blood-stained histories, old inns, and abandoned monasteries. The nation has its face to the future, and it projects a public image of bustling cities, lush cornfields, and superhighways."[1]

While many of the paranormal beliefs and traditions in the United States have stemmed from its colonial ties to Europe, the nation was haunted long before the first white European settlers came to its shores. There exists in the United States a different kind of haunting—a paranormal world that stems from the beliefs of the indigenous peoples that were displaced from their lands and, at times, massacred during the settlement of America. There exists in the national consciousness a foreboding belief in the sanctity of native lands, particularly around burial grounds and ancient sacred lands of the Native Americans. To this day hauntings are regularly blamed on the spirits of Native Americans and the disruption of their grounds, and Indian traditions are used to cleanse haunted houses through the use of sage, salt, and incense. People have reported seeing native spirits in full dress; they have reported poltergeist activity tied to desecrations of sacred lands. Even the infamous Amityville Horror was blamed in part on the influence of a Native American site. "It seems the Shinnecock Indians used land on the Amityville River as an enclosure for the sick, mad, and dying. These unfortunates were penned up until they died of exposure. However, the record noted that the Shinnecocks did not use this tract as a consecrated burial mound because they believed it to be infested with demons."[2] The idea of Native American burial grounds being places of dread is also featured in films such as *Pet Semetary*, in which a child buried in the Native American burial ground returns to life possessed of evil, and in the film *Jeremiah Johnson*, in which the ground is imbued with a sense of dread. It has even worked its way into pop culture, having been featured as the source of paranormal power in television shows such as *South Park*. But the tradition of associating Native Americans with ghosts and spirits dates back to the late 1700s and 1800s following the drafting of the Constitution. During this time, the newly formed United States was embroiled in a continuing battle against the Native Americans in an effort to exterminate their numbers and form the boundaries of the United States of America. It was during this time that the American gothic novel appeared in literature. Renée L. Bergland, in her stunning work *The National Uncanny: Indian Ghosts and American Subjects*, critiques the emergence of this new form of a traditionally European literature. According to Bergland, this new American gothic literature featured Indians instead of ghosts and the American wilderness in place of the traditional Gothic castle. U.S. literature "re-imagines the Gothic protagonist as one who struggles to establish order in the chaotic and savage world of his own soul."[3] Thus, the belief in the ghostliness of Native Americans and their lands has been passed down through the centuries through an ostensible tradition of literature, film, and television as well as oral histories and modern-day legends.

The desecration of sacred Indian grounds was not actually made illegal until 1990 with the passage of the Native American Graves Protection and Repatriation Act. So the fear and superstition associated with these sacred grounds did not translate into any real action or protection until the last 20 years. This seems to be one of many contradictions in the United States' spiritual relationship with its native people, and it is within these contradictions that we may find the Native Americans' paranormal power over the collective imagination of the United States. While the burial grounds were regarded, in a sense, as sacred (or at least worthy of fear and superstition) by the European settlers and their descendents, no action was taken to preserve the grounds until 1990. Another puzzling contradiction is the convergence of European Christian belief systems and those of the Native Americans. While the Europeans, at the time, were believers in witches and devils and magic, they feared the spiritual rites and traditions of the "savages" in the New World. The settlers immediately took possession of the native belief systems and coopted them to become part of the Christian tradition. Viewed through the lens of Christianity, the Native American beliefs were thus labeled demonic. But it seems odd that the Christian-centric Europeans would have reason to fear the beliefs of the Native Americans; in actuality, the two belief systems—the totemism of the native people and European Christianity—were not that different. Thus, the Native American belief systems were easily assimilated into the colonialist beliefs. Lastly, Bergland points out the glaring contradiction that defines the United States: the United States defined itself through the rejection of colonialist rule, but formed itself through that very same colonization. "What I mean is that everyone, Czech to Chickasaw, who tried to imagine him or herself as an American subject, must internalize both the colonization of Native Americans and the American stance against colonialism. He or she must simultaneously acknowledge the American horror and celebrate the American triumph."[4] Thus, the continued haunting of the United States by its Native American ghosts can be defined in terms of national guilt, the convergence of Christianity and totemism, and some of the basest human fears regarding the unknown that began when Europeans first set foot on this land—something that continues today, despite our scientific and modern age.

These contradictions in the American consciousness form an unusual ether—a spiritual limbo—in which the spirits and ghosts of the Native American people exist. George P. Hansen referred to this as the liminal area at the outskirts of rationality where truth and fiction blend; Bergland refers to it as the frontier where two cultures meet and interact. They are both the same in that it is a place for ghosts and spirits; a place of the paranormal where contradictions of fantasy and reality, truth and fiction all blend into a strange soup of belief, tradition, and fear. This is where the Native Americans have been relegated to—the liminal outskirts of the American consciousness, the frontier between man and ghosts. "Europeans take possession of Native America, to be sure, but at the same time, Native Americans take supernatural possession of their dispossessors. It is hard to know who is the victor in such a contest."[5] Because these contradictions concerning the origins of the United States cannot be resolved or buried, they linger as ghosts in the national consciousness. The native haunted-ness of the United States extends further than literature and pop culture and even further than social guilt; it travels to the heart of what it means to be human.

Despite Tuan's assertion that the United States should not be a place of ghosts, perhaps our faces turned forward have allowed the past to sneak up on us. Also, early colonists did not stumble upon a fully formed, forward-facing nation; rather they entered into a dark wilderness inhabited by a strange people who were possessed of beliefs in spirits that roamed the land. The early settlers arrived to a land that was virtually uninhabited when compared to the cities and towns from which they had come. They had left the technology and comforts of their homeland and endured several months' journey across the Atlantic to arrive to a dark, coniferous land, utterly foreign and uncharted to the early Europeans. Even when they had established their colonies, they were still surrounded by the unknown. Early European belief systems incorporated the belief in ghosts, witches, and demons; those beliefs, combined with their surroundings, would naturally lead to myths and stories about ghosts and spirits. Furthermore, the presence of the Native Americans, with their foreign beliefs and practices, contributed to the settlers' fears and beliefs in the supernatural wandering the forests and occasionally impeding upon the colonies. Malcolm McGrath, in his work *Demons of the Modern World*, focuses on early European and primitive thought and postulates that it is similar to that of children; there was no disconnect between the mechanical and symbolic worlds. Therefore, a landscape such as the completely undeveloped Americas would naturally inspire fear of ghosts and magical beliefs. While European thought had progressed somewhat from the Middle Ages, it was firmly believed that the mechanical world could be directly influenced through symbolic action and vice versa. "Modern children cannot make this distinction because they are not born with it and must learn it in school, and non-modern cultures cannot make it because the theories that support this distinction are only a relatively recent invention. Thus, both children and so-called primitive cultures see themselves as living in a world where both magic and nonhuman personalities are a real possibility."[6] Hence, even if early European settlers had come from a progressive and scientifically superior culture, the three-month journey across the Atlantic and into the dark, unknown wilderness of the primitive Americas would have symbolically been a regression from modernism backward into a primitive world where the boundaries between reality and magic were broken down and each flowed into the other. The Europeans entered an uncharted world; any notion of the modern world from which they had come was lost in the unknown landscape and the new world inhabited by a strange people with unknown spiritual beliefs. Tuan's own work, *Landscapes of Fear*, illustrates how the American landscape itself would have produced a haunting dread and fear in the early settlers, based on early childhood fears and the European mythological tradition. "The forest figures prominently in fairy tales . . . It spells danger to the child, frightening by its strangeness—its polar contrast to the cozy world of the cottage. The forest also frightens by its vastness, its breadth and the size of its towering trees being beyond the scale of a child's experience . . . It is a place of abandonment—the dark, chaotic non-world in which one feels utterly lost."[7] Primitive America was truly vast—a larger country than any experienced by the early settlers—and its wild nature broke down the symbolic barriers between civilization and the chaos.

The mythologist Joseph Campbell believed that the basis for much of human mythology comes from an innate fear, something reserved in the collective consciousness of the species, which somehow knows to respond with fear to particular stimuli.

> Chicks with their eggshells still adhering to their tails dart for cover when a hawk flies overhead, but not when the bird is a gull or duck, heron or pigeon . . . The image of the inherited enemy is always asleep in the nervous system, and along with it the well proven reaction. Furthermore, even if all the hawks in the world were to vanish, their image would still sleep in the soul of the chick—never to be roused, however, unless by some accident of art . . .[8]

Thus, according to Campbell, there exists an innate fear in humanity of the lurking unknown—chaos on the outskirts of order. Sigmund Freud also wrote on this subject, which he coined as "the uncanny." While the early settlers had most certainly seen deep, dark forests in the past, and even though ghosts and other such folklore were a regular part of their European lives, the American landscape presented a world that was both new and familiar; something they recognized, and that recognition aroused fear. Freud uses the example of a haunted house. A haunted house is at once familiar, because we have all seen houses, but simultaneously new and frightening, because it contains an element which renders the familiar unfamiliar and the homey (the literal translation of Freud's *heimlichen*) un-homey (*unheimlichen*). "It would seem that each one of us has been through a stage of individual development corresponding to that animistic stage in primitive men, that none of us has traversed it without preserving certain traces of it that can be re-activated, and that everything that strikes us as 'uncanny' fulfills the condition of stirring those vestiges of animistic mental activity within us and bringing them to expression."[9] And Bergland plays on the meaning of "un-homey" by replacing it with a more elegant and appropriate English word, "unsettling." "The sense of unsettledness in the word unheimlich [sic] is important, because it evokes the colonialist paradigm that opposes civilization to the dark and mysterious world of the irrational and savage. Quite literally, the uncanny is the unsettled, the not-yet colonized, the unsuccessfully colonized, or the decolonized."[10] Stephen King defines terror as the sense that "things are in the unmaking";[11] in essence, the world is shedding its veneer of civilization, all the comforts and familiarities that we have come to know, and returning to its primitive and savage state.

Therein lies the basis for the belief in Native American haunting; it was not something that necessarily arose out of direct experience with the native people, the genocide or the proceeding national guilt (though that is certainly part of it today), but rather it began with the mere setting of foot on this new land. The Europeans had certainly left off the vestiges of their familiar and modern society, and during the dangerous three-month voyage across the Atlantic, realized that they were venturing into new territory, something completely unsettled and unsettling. This journey away from civilization called forth the primitive fears in the modern man; primitive fears that man is born with and relates to on a magical level throughout childhood. America was an unsettled, dark and mysterious place after a three-month voyage from civilization into the unknown, and the native inhabitants of this land were imbued with the same mystery and fear. The natives haunted this landscape; they were of the land, and the land was unsettled and filled with potential danger. Thus, the Native American was already a source of fear, foreboding, and superstition without the Christian and racial guilt that would later become part of the modern United States.

The subsequent genocide of the Native Americans did nothing more than contribute to the ghostliness of these people. Freud cites dead bodies as producing an uncanny feeling: "Many people experience the feeling in the highest degree in relation to death and dead bodies, to the return of the dead, and to spirits and ghosts."[12] During the colonization of the Americas, "Citizen soldiers laid their own bodies on the line, and they grew intimately familiar with the corpses of conquered Native Americans... only Indian corpses had concrete reality; before they were dead, Native Americans were representative of the great unknown."[13] What occurred during the colonization of America and the Indian Wars was a strange inversion of reality; dead Indians became real, and living Indians became ghosts. The dead were known, and the living unknown; and thus, Native Americans were relegated to ghosts, and rumors of their ghostliness grew in the American consciousness.

Another factor that contributed to the Native American haunting mythology is the convergence in the United States between European Christianity and Native American belief systems, which can be rather loosely labeled under the term *totemism*. Claude Lévi-Strauss writes, "... totemism assimilates men to animals, and the alleged ignorance of the role of the father in the replacement of the human genitor by spirits closer still to natural forces," and, "Totemism is firstly the projection outside our own universe, as though by a kind of exorcism, of mental attitudes incompatible with the exigency of a discontinuity between man and nature which Christian thought has held to be essential."[14] Thus, the Native American saw himself as part of the spirit of nature, born from it and allied intimately with plants and animals, which were spiritual guides, guardians, provocateurs, and parents. The Indian was

an extension of nature rather than lord over nature as appointed by a patri-
archal God. Primitive peoples expressed this kinship with nature through
the building of totems (like totem poles in North America) that simultaneously captured the spirit of particular plants and animals and also transcended
those spirits and transformed them into something solid and concrete—a
symbol. The Native Americans, by their belief system, were tied to the haunting land, which the settlers had begun to colonize. These beliefs fused both
living and dead Indians to the very land that was being colonized and further
blurred the boundary between tangible native and ephemeral ghost. Lance
M. Foster is a part-time professor of anthropology at the University of
Montana, Helena, and a member of the Ioway Tribe. He also runs a blog
called Native American Paranormal, which traces some of the ideas and influences of Native American haunting, particularly concerning sacred burial
grounds.

> Indigenous peoples, people before Christian times, have a tradition of
> merging with the land, physically and spiritually, after death and of rest-
> less spirits when they have been wronged. So in a way, the spirits of
> Native Americans are more present and powerful in their burial and
> sacred places, because they have merged their essence with the land
> itself and the land spirits there. And when the land is damaged, dis-
> turbed, built on . . . the spirits, the land itself, is unhappy. The average
> American feels that when they die, they go to heaven or hell, or some-
> where else. The traditional Native American may have an idea of a dis-
> tant "happy hunting ground" but also that some part of their spirit is
> fused within the land, especially where they are buried.[15]

The apparent disparity between Christian beliefs in the separation between
man and animal and the totemic beliefs that tied them together was obvious
fodder for European settlers to associate the Native American with witchcraft,
demons, and diabolical magic. Similar to the prosecution of witches in
Europe during this time, the European settlers tried to either convert the
natives or destroy them, thereby completing "God's work" in the new land.
"Christian settlers were soldiers in the war against Satan, who was in turn
determined to unsettle what God had settled. The doubleness of the language is clear: unsettlement is both the undoing of the colonial project of settlement and the uncanny 'feeling of dread and creeping horror' (as Freud
might describe it) that arises when Satan's devices—Indians, diseases, lightning bolts, witches—threaten the settlement."[16]

However, the Native American belief systems were not destroyed along
with the people. The colonists' effort to do "God's work" succeeded in

eliminating the indigenous people, but it failed to destroy their belief system. In actuality, Christianity fused with the totemic belief systems and incorporated the Native American beliefs into its larger and more dogmatic framework. The fear of Indian ghosts, which was prevalent in the seventeenth century through the twentieth century, actually demonstrates that the Native American belief that the soul merged with the land had come to be readily accepted and feared by the U.S. population. The Ghost Dance Massacre at Wounded Knee, which will be discussed later, is ample evidence that the people and the government took the beliefs of the Native Americans seriously and had come to incorporate their totemic paradigm into their own Christian belief structure.

In his work *Psychoanalysis and Religion*, Erich Fromm postulates that Christianity and the U.S. politic are nothing more than primitive totemic beliefs with the veneer of religion, organization, and politics.

> A person whose exclusive devotion is to the state or his political party, whose only criterion of value and truth is the interest of state or party, for whom the flag as a symbol of his group is a holy object, has a religion of clan and totem worship, even though in his own eyes it is a perfectly rational system (which, of course, all devotees to any kind of primitive religion believe). If we want to understand how systems like fascism or Stalinism can possess millions of people, ready to sacrifice their integrity and reason to the principle, "my country, right or wrong," we are forced to consider the totemistic, the religious quality of their orientation.[17]

Although Fromm was writing in the twentieth century and concerned himself mostly with the horror witnessed during World War II, his message speaks also to the Christian settlers during the earliest days of our nation when, in the name of "God," an entire civilization was wiped out, and U.S. nationalism and government justified the near erasure of an entire people. Their belief was in the country as an entity rather than in the individual; and the belief of the Christians was equally in their symbolism of crosses and churches rather than in the actual teachings of Christ. In essence, their belief, their view of reality, and their very lives were extensions of the symbols of the state and church, and in those symbols was the strict adherence to blind faith despite all the contradictions that may arise. These symbols allow faith to become fact. Faith can be difficult because it requires belief in something that cannot be proved and cannot be seen; however, when replaced with a symbol, such as a cross or a flag, suddenly the belief goes from incorporeal faith to tangible gods. Thus, Fromm asserts that to this very day we continue to put faith and blind obedience into symbols and ideas rather than in spirit and reality.

"Like nation, race, class, and gender can all be understood as ghostly entities. They may be imaginary, but they structure our lives nonetheless . . . If hegemonic powers are, in fact, ghostly powers, then all of us must believe in ghosts, just as we believe in stories, histories, or in memories."[18] And as Strauss writes, "In order that social order shall be maintained . . . it is necessary to assure the permanence and solidarity of the clans which compose the society. This permanence and solidarity can be based only on individual sentiments, and these, in order to be expressed efficaciously, demand a collective expression, which has to be fixed on concrete objects . . . This explains the place assigned to symbols such as flags, kings, presidents, etc., in contemporary societies."[19]

Thus, Christianity and U.S. nationalism were able to incorporate the totemic beliefs of the Native Americans into their respective frameworks, which resulted in the spirits of the Native Americans haunting the nation's past and present. Our society and our religions are perfect for Indian ghosts. It has become part of our collective consciousness. Despite Tuan's assertion that the United States should not be hospitable to ghosts, it is, in fact, part of our very soul.

The greatest evidence for the assimilation of Native American beliefs by the new Americans came in the battle of Wounded Knee, also known as the Ghost Dance Massacre.

The Ghost Dance Movement began in 1889 when Jack (Wovoka) Wilson, a member of the Nevada Paiute, had a vision in which he saw God and all of his ancestors in paradise, and God instructed him to tell his people to live in peace and love and harmony; only then would peace come to their people. Wilson advocated a peaceful end to the white expansionism. He believed that the ancestral ghosts whom he had seen in his vision would aid the Native Americans in reclaiming their heritage, their lives and their lands. Wilson's message resonated with other tribes, who sent members to Wilson to learn of his teachings. The practice of the Ghost Dance began to spread rapidly across the Midwest United States. The ritual called for a five-day dance that would cleanse the earth of evil. However, many in the U.S. government believed that the call to cleanse the earth of evil meant the eradication of the white race from American soil. During the reorganization of a Lakota treaty, government officials were sent to observe and monitor the Sioux in their transition and to train them in farming techniques. However, when food rations to the Sioux were cut in half, the tribes began practicing the Ghost Dance ritual with increased fervor, which caused great anxiety and fear in the government watchdog group. Troops were deployed to the area, and on December 15, 1890, Sitting Bull was arrested for not stopping the Ghost Dance ritual. The following day, as troops moved to disarm the Sioux, a struggle ensued and a gunfight broke out. The troops opened fire on the Native Americans and killed 153 within minutes, resulting in the "Battle at Wounded Knee," also known as the Ghost Dance Massacre.

Within this story, there lies an apparent contradiction in the U.S., Christian attitudes toward the native beliefs. Why would the Ghost Dance cause such a reaction? "Wavoka (Jack Wilson), the Ghost Dance prophet, developed the positive implications of Native American ancestral ghosts into one of the central elements of his vision. From the white American viewpoint, the same figure caused abject terror. The massacre at Wounded Knee brutally illustrates the United States' refusal to allow the invocation of Native American ghosts."[20] The only explanation is that the "invocation of Native American ghosts," caused such a stir because the Native American belief system had been adopted into the Christian American belief system. The totemism of the native people, who formed their symbols out of plants and animals, was recognized and incorporated by the Christian religion and U.S. nationalism that were themselves inherently totemic. The Ghost Dance caused fear precisely because the public and the government had come to recognize the Native American beliefs to be as indelible as their own. The white European Christian had come to occupy Native American land; however, the Native Americans had come to occupy the European belief systems. The Ghost Dance was feared because the people believed it would call upon all the evil ghosts of Native American ancestors to invade the waking, civilized world of the post–Civil War United States. It would be an invasion of the colonized, organized world of the new United States by a chaotic force of ghostly power. The Ghost Dance represented a threat to the spiritual boundaries of the new United States and was thus wiped out. However, those very ancestral spirits lived on in the ghost stories and testimonies of haunted people in future generations.

Today, the Native Americans occupy territory outside the federal government's jurisdiction but within the boundaries of the United States. They are truly a liminal people that exist at the boundaries of society and are, at once, part of that society and also separated from it. Their reservations are largely poverty-stricken and rife with alcoholism, and many of the ancient beliefs are feared to be fading from cultural memory. But it's this existence at the periphery of the United States that makes the Native American such a powerful and enduring specter in the paranormal history of the United States and may help explain why, to this day, people still claim to see the ghosts of Native Americans. While the Native Americans have been pushed to the outskirts of our society, they still exist and still serve as reminders to the very atrocities that created this nation.

To be haunted, by its very definition, is to be possessed of the past, and while this nation's face may be to the future, our troubled and contradictory past remains with us. The incorporation of Native American ghosts into the haunted American landscape is a way of addressing the past without facing it. Foster writes,

> When the Irish arrived in Ireland, they defeated and dispossessed the preceding peoples of those lands, the Tuatha de Danaan. After the Tuatha were defeated, through guilt and admiration, they were romanticized as a race of spiritual beings who live in the lands beneath the hills ... the Good People, the Faerie. This also happened in other lands, an older people giving way before a migration of people from another land. And it happened in America as well. We see the same romanticization of Native Americans as the original, spiritual people of a place.[21]

Hence, the Native Americans merged with their sacred lands and became the ghosts that now haunt the American landscape. These ghosts can be seen as symbolic representations of national guilt for the displacement and genocide of the indigenous people. Their ghosts are a way of trying to reconcile the past with the present. While the dispossession of the native peoples was necessary to create the United States as we know it today, it does not relieve the guilt for moral wrongdoing. The United States defined itself through its rejection of colonialism but formed itself through the very same kind of colonialism, thereby leaving a contradiction in the heart of the nation that remains unresolved to this day. Indeed, it is probably not able to be resolved. Thus, the ghosts of the displaced people have returned to remind us of this wrong, similar to the works of Shakespeare, when the ghosts of the murdered return to right the wrongs that were done to them on earth.

The Native Americans exist at the peripheries of our society. Their ancient beliefs were incorporated by the European Americans who became subject to their ghosts, and these were thus passed down through the generations to haunt today's society. Our very own totemic culture absorbed the beliefs of the indigenous people, and their ghosts became a part of our cultural legacy. The pervading national guilt, recognized or not, has left an indelible mark on the national subconscious. The contradictions that formed our society remain in limbo— unable to be laid to rest in our past and thereby haunting our present.

> The American landscape has a time dimension. Drive off the hardtop road in Tennessee, Kentucky, or in the Ozark Hills, and in a matter of minutes you enter another world of closely knit communities that retain

many of the superstitions and customs of Old Europe. In the isolated hollows, ghosts and witches are as much a part of living tradition as dying in one's own home and maintaining the family graveyard. A country lane or covered bridge, so picturesque to the passing tourist on a sunny day, can seem ominous to the old-timer trudging home before the shadow deepens.[22]

CHAPTER 5

The JFK Assassination and the Paranormal

T he assassination of John F. Kennedy as he rode through Dealey Plaza in Dallas, Texas, on November 6, 1963, is often referred to as the moment when the United States' innocence was totally lost. A young, handsome, charismatic president was shot and killed in front of thousands of people at a time in U.S. history when nuclear Cold War tensions were beginning to boil. Nearly everyone alive at that time remembers where they were and what they were doing when they heard the news; likewise, nearly everyone living today remembers where they were and what they were doing when news of the jetliner crashing into the World Trade Center first reached them on September 11, 2001. These were days in U.S. history that marked dramatic turning points. But the assassination of JFK marked a more ominous and paranoid moment in U.S. culture, one that would transcend the decades and haunt the aftermath of 9/11. It would also breed an entirely new wave of paranoia and distrust of the U.S. government; a distrust which formed massive conspiracy theories and quickly found its way into paranormal belief systems, where it has thrived ever since.

At the time of Kennedy's assassination, conspiracy theories were nothing new, though very few remembered the "Ring of Gold" conspiracy of WWI or the Pearl Harbor Conspiracy trumpeted at the outset of U.S. involvement in WWII, which posited that Roosevelt had prior knowledge of the coming Japanese attack but allowed it to occur in order to justify entry into war with Germany. These were times of extreme duress and political outrage that would make today's partisan bickering seem tame. Both the politicians and the public actively feared that the U.S. government was being subverted by outside influences such as Communists, Jews, and bankers. However, that day in Dealey Plaza marked a fundamental change in the U.S. psyche and in the way the government is perceived. Kathryn S. Olmsted, in her work *Real Enemies: Conspiracy Theories and American Democracy, World War I to 9/11*, writes, "No longer were conspiracy theorists chiefly concerned that alien forces were plotting to capture the federal government; instead, they proposed that the federal government itself was the conspirator."[1] The federal government had grown and expanded into something that was big and anonymous, and to many, it had become secretive, threatening, and violent.

In many ways, the idea of conspiracy had been a long-held belief and rallying cry in the past as a means of persecution. During the European witch craze, public officials and clergy preached of a conspiracy of witches that consorted with the devil by moonlight. "Witches were to be found in Europe, in every neighborhood, all linked together in one great conspiracy under generalship of Satan against the Christian Community."[2] The conspiracy of witchcraft is something that would continually reinvent itself in the American consciousness through the McCarthyism of the 1950s, during which Senator Joseph McCarthy questioned whether this time was a "show-down between the democratic Christian world and the Communist atheistic world,"[3] and into the 1980s and '90s with the satanic panic, which will be covered in a later chapter. The witch-hunt and the conspiracy theory have become endemic to U.S. culture.

However, the European witch-hunt and conspiracy was alleged by the elite and powerful government figures, as was nearly every conspiracy theory up until the JFK assassination. But November 6 essentially turned the tables on the elite and powerful; suddenly they were the "witches" being hunted by the townspeople. "The researchers set out to prove that ordinary American citizens had as much authority to investigate the killing of the president as the government did—indeed, that their status as amateurs gave them more claim to authenticity and truth."[4] Furthermore, in an ironic twist on the witch-hunts, for the first time in history the primary investigators and conspiracy hunters were women, something that would continue throughout the rest of the century.

Olmsted notes that, while conspiracy theories tend to eventually spin out of control, they usually begin from a point of truth. In the case of JFK, Lyndon Johnson and the Kennedy family purposefully concealed aspects of the assassination and aspects of Kennedy's life in order to preserve peace and the image of John F. Kennedy. JFK, it turns out, had several skeletons in his closet, both in regards to his Cuban policy and in his personal life, which both the government and his family wanted to keep secret. However, this secrecy concerning the possible causes of the assassination and other aspects involving JFK's anti-communism policies created more distrust in the government and spurred further investigation and accusations of conspiracy by the public. When the Warren Commission was created to investigate the assassination, it was given a script by Johnson as to what the "official story" would be; it was the commission's job to reinforce the official story. "The commission's reconstruction of the assassination, in short, was shaped from the beginning by the members' determination to reach a predetermined conclusion. It was unpersuasive even to the men who came up with it. This does not mean that it was wrong. It does mean, however, that the commission was primarily a public relations exercise, as Robert Kennedy later told an aide, meant to placate the American public. It was not meant to discover the truth."[5] This public relations commission—designed not to find the truth but rather to placate the public—is something that would haunt the American psyche from that point on and would essentially poison the well of public and government relations. The public could not trust the government to investigate itself, and therefore, everything and everyone in the commission was suspect, including the scientists and experts that the panel used as sources. They all became part of the conspiracy. "Besides their obvious distrust of government, the assassination conspiracy theories also reflect a loss of faith in all experts—in government and science—and the whole idea of 'expertise.'"[6]

Following a yearlong rash of UFO sightings in 1947 (including the supposed crash in Roswell, New Mexico), the air force began to investigate UFO sightings. First dubbed Project Sign, then Project Grudge, the compilation and investigation finally settled on Project Blue Book as a name and it lasted through the completion of the investigation in 1969. In 1969 the air force contracted with the University of Colorado to form a panel, headed by Dr. Edward Condon, to review the cases and conduct a study to determine if there was any need for further investigation. Known as "The Condon Report," the panel determined that there was no cause for further investigation and that UFOs were not worthy of further study. While the report included many UFO incidents that the panel could not explain, the official word was that UFOs were weather anomalies, stars, figments of imagination, and so on.

However, this investigation and panel, much like the Warren Commission, left more questions than answers for believers, and suddenly the amateurs took the reigns of the investigation and castigated the "experts." But the believers did have a few experts on their side, one of whom was Dr. J. Allen Hynek, who had been a consultant on Project Blue Book. Dr. Hynek criticized the Condon Report and went on to write his own book, which detailed a number of cases that were deemed unexplainable. More vocal and persistent, however, was a young physicist and rocket-propulsion engineer named Stanton Friedman. Friedman was the kind of person who exhibited a drive and tenacity that bordered on religious fanaticism; but unlike the religious zealot, he had the credentials and arguments to back up his assertions. He was also a skilled researcher. He and several other organizations and believers went through Condon's report piecemeal. "It comes as a great surprise to many that, according to a UFO subcommittee of the world's largest group of space scientists—the American Institute of Aeronautics and Astronautics—one could come to the opposite conclusions as Dr. Condon based on the data in the report. Any phenomena with 30 percent unidentified classifications is certainly worth further investigation, as the AIAA noted."[7] Friedman also pointed to a 1966 memo from the assistant dean at the University of Colorado, which states,

> The trick would be, I think, to describe the project so that to the public, it would appear a totally objective study, but to the scientific community would present the image of a group of nonbelievers trying their best to be objective, but having an almost zero expectation of finding a saucer. One way to do this would be to stress investigation, not of the physical phenomena, but rather of the people who do the observing—the psychology and sociology of persons and groups who report seeing UFOs. If the emphasis were put here, rather than on examination of the old question of the physical reality of the saucer, I think the scientific community would quickly get the message ... I'm inclined to feel at this early stage that, if we set up the thing right and take pains to get the proper people involved and have success in presenting the image we want to present to the scientific community, we could carry the job off to our benefit ...[8]

Once again, it would appear to the believers that the commission had been rigged from the beginning, and that furthermore, its goal was to paint believers as kooks and as people who were experiencing some form of psychosis or sociological phenomenon.

This, of course, was not the first or the last time that critics and conspiracy theorists would be labeled as lunatics. Even during the 9/11 Commission the New Jersey widows were labeled as "harpies" by one political commentator (note the element of witchcraft). And during the JFK investigations, the media and politicians also labeled the women who began their independent study. "The Warren Commission's defenders quickly mobilized to attack these amateurs. With few exceptions, most mainstream media outlets rushed to defend the Warren Report and to blast critics as cranks and obsessives."[9] However, the critics were merely responding to what they knew were glaring omissions of fact and logic from both commissions' reports. The people had begun to recognize the more sinister side of the government and were no longer willing to be spoon-fed the public mandate from on high. The JFK assassination sparked a democratization of investigatory journalism and "expertise." Suddenly, regular citizens were becoming some of the most educated and informed people on the planet about the assassination, and they had some theories that differed from the government's narrative. Obviously, they did not have all the facts because the government was withholding evidence that it deemed necessary for national security. However, the public quickly recognized this and pounced on it as evidence of a greater, more evil conspiracy. The people felt the government was deceiving them, and, for the most part, they were right.

This democratization of expertise and investigatory journalism extended quite naturally into the realm of the paranormal, particularly surrounding the UFO phenomenon, which had experienced the height of public fascination in the late forties and the fifties. People were seeing something in the skies and reporting it to the media and the government. The U.S. cultural landscape was inundated with flying saucer films and books, most of which reflected Cold War fears of nuclear annihilation. The public was responding, and the government launched its investigations with Project Blue Book and eventually the Condon Report. It could be speculated that had the Condon Report come before the Warren Commission debacle and subsequent public rejection, it may have been well received. As it was, the Condon Report was viewed as another government attempt to placate the public with spoon-fed government script.

It was shortly after the Condon Report that Stanton Friedman began investigating what was at that time a little known story out of Roswell, New Mexico. In July of 1947 the local newspaper reported that the air force had recovered a crashed flying saucer in the New Mexican desert. However, the very next day, the air force retracted its statement and said that it was merely a weather balloon. Friedman, doubting the government's honesty and good intentions, sought out the people involved in the Roswell incident, including the air force personnel who inspected the crash. Friedman teamed with some other investigators and authored the first book on the subject, entitled *The Roswell Incident*, which was published in 1980. He then went on to coauthor *Crash at Corona: A Definitive Study of the Roswell Incident* in 1992. These books detail the alleged truth of the Roswell incident in which the air force discovered an actual flying saucer and alien bodies in the New Mexican desert. The bodies and debris were then moved to Area 51, a top-secret government facility in the Nevadan desert, where they were held and used to create new technologies.

This may sound like fantasy, but in 1997 retired Colonel Philip J. Corso authored a book, entitled *The Day After Roswell*, which detailed a similar scenario, and Col. Corso was in a perfect position to know the facts of the case. He had worked in military intelligence during WWII and quickly rose among the ranks, working directly under President Truman and President Eisenhower where he served on the National Security Council and was head of the Foreign Technology Desk for the army's research and development department. Corso claims that this position enabled him to covertly funnel new technology that had been reverse engineered from the downed saucer to companies around the United States, thereby concealing the source of the scientific breakthroughs.

> In 1961, regardless of the differences in the Roswell story from the many different sources who had described it, the top-secret file of Roswell information came into my possession when I took over the Foreign Technology desk at R&D. My boss, General Trudeau, asked me to use the army's ongoing weapons development and research program as a way to filter the Roswell technology into the mainstream of industrial development through the military defense contracting program. Today, items such as lasers, integrated circuitry, fiber-optics networks, accelerated particle-beam devices, and even the Kevlar material in bulletproof vests are all commonplace. Yet the seeds for the development of all of them were found in the crash of the alien craft at Roswell and turned up in my file fourteen years later.[10]

Even as late as 2010, former air force officers were coming forward with incredible stories of UFO encounters at air force bases. One of them, Captain Robert Salas, stated at a press conference on September 23, 2010, "The U.S. Air Force is lying about the national security implications of unidentified aerial objects at nuclear bases, and we can prove it."[11] Salas and six others claimed that UFOs were regularly interfering with U.S. nuclear missile sites. "The group plans to distribute declassified U.S. government documents at the event (press conference) that they claim will substantiate the reality of UFO activity at nuclear weapons sites extending back to 1948. The press conference will also address present-day concerns about the abuse of government secrecy as well as the ongoing threat of nuclear weapons."[12]

Following the tremendous Watergate scandal of the Nixon administration, the Ford administration tried to rebuild public trust in the presidency by exposing previous administrations' secrets and purging the presidency of its secrets. Unfortunately, this only exposed the public to more than it had ever asked for, and trust of the government reached the lowest levels ever. Combined with the Freedom of Information Act, the documents of exposed government activities throughout history inundated the public with the idea of a secret, rogue government that was not working for the people's best interests. Exposure of J. Edgar Hoover's massive wiretapping programs, Kennedy's use of mafia hit men to make assassination attempts against Castro, and the CIA's random drugging of civilians to test the efficacy of LSD and other hallucinogens fueled the fire of distrust and discontent.

Then, in typical conspiracy form, mysterious documents were suddenly making the rounds in UFO groups. Known as Majestic 12, they were first discovered in 1984 and became public in 1987. The UFO conspiracy raged on simultaneously and, in many ways, in confluence with the exposure of political/military conspiracies.

> In May of 1987, as dramatic testimony before the Iran-Contra investi-
> gating committee dominated headlines, three authors announced an
> informant had provided them with proof of the Roswell conspiracy . . .
> Stamped 'Top Secret: Majic Eyes Only,' the memo allegedly briefed
> the president on a complex plot involving a flying saucer crash at
> Roswell, the military's recovery of four decomposed alien bodies, the
> weather balloon cover story, and a massive governmental cover up,
> code named Operation Majestic 12, or MJ-12.[13]

And as reported in the *New York Times*, "Enthusiasts are now even charging that for 40 years the Federal Government has harbored evidence of an encounter with extraterrestrial creatures, including their lifeless bodies and damaged spacecraft. That startling report, dismissed by skeptics and Government officials as laughable, is contained in what purport to be top-secret Government papers from the Eisenhower era."[14]

As the government's lies and indiscretions over the past decades became exposed, the UFO conspiracy theory became even more entrenched. Likewise, popular culture's focus on these conspiracies and their exposure fueled films such as *All the President's Men*. The UFO conspiracy theorists had their own "Deep Throat," someone who was passing top-secret documents to them, and former air force officials who were telling them, point blank, that the government was conspiring to cover up the wreckage of a flying saucer.

Belief systems can often be about role-playing. Indeed we all role-play to some extent in our lives, but belief systems involving conspiracies or the paranormal can often spin wildly out of control or become an all-encompassing role in which the individual sees him- or herself as the sole possessor of knowledge that will somehow change the course of human history. Certainly the knowledge of extraterrestrials is something that would alter our understanding of the world in which we live. However, playing the role of savior of humanity can often lead the individual down paths of logic to illogical outcomes. Their need to expose the "truth" can oftentimes lead them to purport such "truths" that are impossible to verify and thus actually obscure the process of revelation. But the exposure of actual political conspiracies by the government, journalists, and the public has had its effects in the paranormal world. The assassination of JFK and the democratization of expertise and investigation, combined with the Freedom of Information Act, opened the door for believers in UFOs to investigate and document for themselves the inconsistencies of government public policy and to debate the conclusions reached by their investigatory panels. The UFO community is awash in conspiracy—secret documents, hoaxes, government denial, cover stories, whistle-blowers, men in black, government espionage, and inexplicable witness testimony. The UFO believers find themselves in possession of a truth with various forms of evidence, but they are up against a massive entity that has quite successfully labeled them as kooks and laughed off their accusations as paranoid delusions. However, they're not all paranoid . . .

One of the elements to any conspiracy or suspicion of conspiracy is the government involving itself to a greater or lesser extent. Often, that government involvement is disruptive, deceptive, resistive, and anonymous. Some of J. Edgar Hoover's exposed activities involved disinformation and government involvement in several social movements, which Hoover considered communist or detrimental to the United States. Similarly, the CIA was exposed as being involved in the deceptive manipulation of different groups both in and outside of the United States. Subsequently, UFO believers were apt to believe that the government was also engaged in manipulation of their cause. And they have not been altogether mistaken.

"Any legitimate analysis that tries to explain beliefs about UFOs must recognize that the UFO subculture is awash in disinformation spread by government personnel, and that has played an enormous role in shaping the subculture . . . Virtually all UFO investigators who make regular public presentations are from time to time approached by people who claim to have seen materials or documents while in military service that confirmed that the government has UFO projects."[15]

Lawrence Fawcett and Barry J. Greenwood authored a 1984 account of government involvement in UFO research entitled *Clear Intent: The Government Coverup of the UFO Experience*. The account, however, is not a compendium of UFO kookery, but rather an exhaustively researched work that uses the Freedom of Information Act to bolster its assertions and show that the government really does know more than it is revealing, just as it did in the JFK assassination, in Watergate, and in any number of other conspiracy-riddled government flashpoints. Working in conjunction with Citizens Against UFO Secrecy (CAUS), the Mutual UFO Network (MUFON), and Ground Saucer Watch (GSW), Fawcett and Greenwood lobbied the Air Force, the CIA, and the NSA for all of their records concerning UFO activity. Naturally, these organizations resisted; however, CAUS took its case to court and was almost heard by the Supreme Court of the United States. The organizations finally remitted some of their documentation, which revealed numerous studies, incidents, and interactions between the U.S. government and Unidentified Flying Objects, including many intrusions into protected U.S. airspace and restricted airspace over nuclear weapons facilities. There were also many instances of air force fighters being scrambled to intercept the UFO but coming up with nothing. For instance, the following is part of a message from the commander in charge of NORAD, dated November 11, 1975:

Missile Site Personnel, Security Alert Teams, and Air Defense Personnel at Malmstrom, Montana report an object between 9500 ft. and 1500 ft. which sounded like a jet aircraft. FAA advised there were no jet aircraft in the vicinity. Malmstrom search and height radars carried the object from 0807532 thru 09002 Nov. 75. F-106s scrambled from Malmstrom could not make contact due to darkness and low altitude. Site personnel reported the object as low as 200 ft and said that as the interceptors approached, the lights went out. After the interceptors had passed, the lights came on again, one hour after they returned to base. Missile site personnel reported the object increased to a high speed, raised in altitude and could not be discerned from the stars.[16]

This is only one of many incidents that would never have been revealed or known, had CAUS not fought for the right to view the information. So obviously, yes, the government knew more than it told the public, and its repeated assertions that it was not interested in the UFO phenomenon were rendered inaccurate by the records. Certainly, one would hope the government would be interested in anything that could so easily thwart its defenses.

Perhaps even more fascinating was the National Security Agency's assessment of the UFO phenomenon. It offered five possible explanations, none of which is very comforting. First, it postulates that all UFOs are hoaxes, but then determines this cannot be the case because the phenomena have been witnessed all over the world from ancient times. Moreover, if they were all hoaxes then it would signify a "mental aberration of alarming proportions." Second, it postulates that UFOs are hallucinations; however, this assertion would also have serious repercussions for humanity if it were true: "The negative effect on man's ability to survive in an increasingly complex world would be considerable..." Third, it offers the possibility that UFOs are natural phenomena; however, if this is the case, "the capability of air warning systems to correctly diagnose an attack situation is open to serious question" because of UFOs being recorded on radar and missile tracking systems. The fourth option is that UFOs are secret terrestrial projects, which would obviously not be good for the U.S. military dominance. Lastly, the NSA postulates that UFOs are extraterrestrial in origin. This is the most disconcerting of the NSA's assessments because "History has shown us time and time again the tragic results of a confrontation between a technologically superior civilization and a technologically inferior people. The inferior is usually subject to conquest."[17] Presented with these options, the government would have no choice but to take seriously the reports of UFO activity around the world.

However, as intriguing and revealing as these documents were, "conspiracy-think" took over the judgment within the UFO communities. Similar to past instances of government revelation, the groups began to suspect that what the government had chosen to show them was merely the tip of the iceberg. It is certainly true that some top-secret documents were not allowed to be revealed, and many others had been blacked out so extensively that the document amounted to nothing more than a date and a signature. Naturally, the government must have its secrets, but this has caused many in the UFO circles to ask the question, "What haven't they told us?" The logical determination is that the government must have truly earth-shaking information, which it will not reveal for security purposes. Hence, the Roswell conspiracy fits quite well into the history of UFO research and their use of the Freedom of Information Act.

Also, the belief that the government is not revealing the truth creates belief in a "secret government" which is ultimately pulling the strings on world events, all with the backdrop of secret UFO knowledge. Considering the time during which Fawcett and Greenwood published their work and the discovery of the Majestic-12 documents, however, the idea of a secret government had a factual basis. As indicated previously, this was during the Reagan administration and the Oliver North/Iran-Contra hearings in which it was revealed that a subset of the U.S. government had acted on its own and traded with Iranian militants and armed Nicaraguan Contras. The CIA had used money from the sale of Nicaraguan drugs (which probably flowed across the border into the United States, further fueling the drug epidemic) to purchase weapons from the Iranians to give to the Contras. With all this being revealed on Capitol Hill, the idea of a secret CIA/NSA-dominated government cabal did not seem all that impossible. The idea of a rogue, secret government stirred a sense of paranoia. Take, for instance, a man who reported the following about his friend, an air force radar intercept officer who had told him about the disappearance of two F-4 Phantoms as they pursued a UFO. "The last thing I had heard was that he had been killed in action someplace near Da Nang . . . He was part of a special unit in 1969. I'm trying to remember what it was. He had been trained by the NSA, but the group he was working with specifically had their own special radar set up. It was probably sponsored by the NSA . . ."[18] The implication is, of course, that the officer's revelation of the UFO incident led to the NSA moving him to Vietnam and orchestrating his death. A rogue government does not adhere to common laws, and acts with extreme prejudice in its own interests.

In 1980, Linda Moulton Howe won an Emmy Award for her hour-long documentary entitled *A Strange Harvest*,[19] which gave a detailed look at the cattle mutilations that had been occurring in the United States and in other parts of the world since the late sixties. Along with many of these reports of cattle mutilations were coinciding reports of UFO activity and sightings of black, military-type helicopters. UFO groups, who had been tracking the reports for quite some time, quickly pounced upon the film. The cattle were usually found with their blood drained, sexual organs removed, and colon removed with supposedly surgical-like precision. No tracks were found around the bodies, including the tracks of the cattle themselves. Furthermore, reports of mysterious, unmarked black helicopters with armed men dressed in black arriving at the scenes of UFO sightings and cattle mutilations abound in UFO literature. The black helicopters, manned by military-type personnel, appeared to be both in pursuit of UFOs and engaged in an effort to silence witnesses and remove all evidence before it could be made public. All the conclusions reached by the UFO groups appear to point toward a rogue, secret government actively trying to keep the most important discovery in the history of mankind under tight wraps. The idea of a secret rogue government was born out of the Kennedy assassination where, for the first time, the public fear was not that the U.S. government was being subverted by outside forces, but rather that the government itself was acting independently of checks and balances—working in secrecy, committing acts of murder, kidnapping, and worse, all to keep the American public in the dark. This belief was reinforced by Lyndon Johnson's efforts to quickly close the JFK investigation, and by the Watergate and Iran-Contra scandals. Furthermore, it was Johnson's effort to make the government more transparent in order to preserve democracy that enabled these groups to confirm some of their suspicions and to speculate even more fantastically as to the extent of government subversion of the American people. The UFO conspiracy was born out of actual conspiracies, in combination with the mystery of things seen in the sky by ordinary people and a government that continued to deny the reality of those sightings, while privately investigating and cataloguing them.

An obvious example of the influence of government conspiracies on the culture of ufology is the terminology employed by the various groups and individuals: "... one of the four major conclusions to which I have arrived, after 50 years of study and investigation, is that the subject of flying saucers represents a kind of Cosmic Watergate."[20] Stanton Friedman concludes that there are people within the government who know that some UFOs are controlled by intelligent beings, but not everyone in government is aware of this. Thus, it amounts to a conspiracy, modeled after the Watergate scandal.

One of the arguments lobbied against conspiracy theorists is that the very same government officials and agencies thought to be so efficient and secretive as to have kept this information secret and simultaneously discredited investigators through a vigorous disinformation campaign are the same goof-ups that somehow allow information such as the Majestic-12 documents to be leaked. While the argument is true in principle, it does not account for some of the secrets the government has successfully kept throughout the years. The atom bomb, despite its blinding blast, was successfully hidden from the public along with the health effects on local residences; and the stealth bomber was kept under wraps until its unveiling during the first Gulf War. In fact there are many cover-ups and conspiracies that have only come to light when the government determined that it was acceptable. As the CIA often says, "people only hear about our screw-ups, they will never know of our successes." It is conceivable that certain factions of the government could be holding information now that is deemed too important to be divulged at this time. There have been government leaks in the past: take, for instance, the aforementioned press release concerning former military officials stating that UFOs were regularly causing disturbances to nuclear missile sites, something that is documented in Fawcett and Greenwood's work. Or take Lt. Col. Philip Corso's assertion that he was given the task of feeding alien technology into the private sector for development. Government officials have come forward in the past, and some may come forward in the future. If these men were whistle-blowers of a giant corporation asserting that the corporation had engaged in a massive cover-up, such as the Enron case, the press would immediately be investigating, as would the government. Or if there were mysterious insiders detailing how the president was engaged in a massive spying and subversion ring in order to discredit his opponents, there would be front-page coverage and films starring Robert Redford. However, in the case of UFOs, the pleas and testimonies fall on deaf ears of a public and media that either don't want to hear it or believe that these are merely lies and hoaxes perpetrated by publicity hounds and tricksters.

Indeed, the UFO community can become a bit overzealous in the expounding of their theories. UFO proponents have put everything conceivable forth, from aliens orchestrating the JFK assassination to the mysterious black helicopters actually being flying saucers in disguise. The UFO community and the paranormal community in general are defined more by the lunatic fringe than by the moderate, logical, and researched middle. Also, those within the community tend to be at odds with each other, oftentimes perpetrating hoaxes and frauds against each other as a means to prove or disprove their theories. For instance, famed UFO researcher William L. Moore claimed that he was, in fact, a government spy meant to subvert the work of the UFO community. This occurred after Moore was accused of falsifying documents (MJ-12) and impersonating a federal officer. However, Moore's claim that he was an operative actually secured his place in the UFO community and reinforced their beliefs. As in other instances in the realm of the paranormal, exposure of fraud often reinforces belief rather than dissuading the believers.

A final, disturbing instance comes from the memoirs of Travis Walton, one of the most famous cases of UFO abduction in history. Many years after his supposed abduction, when his story was being made into a Hollywood film entitled *Fire in the Sky*, he was contacted by a man claiming that he was military personnel and that he had witnessed the UFO that had taken Travis that fateful night 25 years earlier. However, when the movie studio gave the man a polygraph, he failed. "The results were very strange—with some truly sinister implications. Not only had the man done very badly, things came to light which gave indications of deceit and suggested possible intrigue from high levels in our government!"[21] Walton believes this person was an operative sent by the UFO skeptic and debunker, Philip J. Klass, who has a reputation for using unscrupulous and fraudulent means to attack UFO investigators. Klass and other skeptics' methods create an even greater sense of paranoia in the UFO communities as they worry about government disinformation, fraudulent insiders, and dishonest skeptics. Their world is awash in half-truths, deception, and conspiracies due, in part, to their own actions, but also due to interference by both government and skeptics who pursue the UFO believers as if on some kind of crusade.

However, this is exactly the kind of treatment that fuels belief, because it begs the question, why? Why would the government subvert the work of a group of amateur, independent UFO investigators if there was nothing to their claims? Why would skeptics employ such unscrupulous tactics while claiming to represent science? Their interest and blind dedication raises more questions than answers.

As indicated before, the paranormal is defined more by the lunatic fringe than by the people who actually put forth the most intriguing questions and theories and work to support those theories. Unfortunately, hoaxes, fraud, disinformation, and facts all create a dilution of truth in these paranormal communities and thus drive their belief systems further and further toward the fringes of logic—the edge of reason, where truth and fiction become indistinguishable, and people start to become characters in their own spy novels. Examples have abounded in government conspiracy theories, extending primarily from the JFK assassination. However, the patterns of conspiracy theories and the effects on the investigators and the public have come to define some of the paranormal research groups. The paranormal exists in a realm where truth and fiction, fact and fraud are blended into one, indiscernible mess. Likewise, the conspiracy theories that have plagued the U.S. government through the decades result in a separate world of intrigue, fraud, manipulation, lies, and disinformation. Some of it true, much of it not. When gaps are left in the story, people begin to fill in the blanks using imagination and some semblance of logic.

The difficulty inherent in examining an entity as large and fractured as the U.S. government is that there are various agencies with different goals—all separate, yet connected—with various people acting in their own interest and in the interest of the agency, doing what they think is right or will benefit them the most. Conspiracies often label this massive entity as merely "the government." Theorists try to fill in the gaps in government agencies and personnel through inserting a logic that supports their belief systems. Somehow, a government cover-up of alien life just seems to make sense when looking at a massive bureaucracy that is difficult, if not impossible, to cleanly navigate. The best paranormal researchers understand this and limit the extent of their conspiracy think, while others let it spin wildly out of control. To them, a massive, world-changing secret is the only thing that can account for what the U.S. government has become, and this secret fills in the blanks for that which we cannot or will not answer or just don't understand. It is the pursuit of a truth that may not exist, with the belief that this truth will somehow right the world and that the investigators will become key players in the salvation of mankind through the liberation of this truth. Unfortunately, the need to fulfill that role can sometimes override reason and actually obscure truth more than reveal it.

Their efforts are actually an attempt to give meaning to a world that appears to have gone haywire. The JFK assassination marked a new era in U.S. history—one of chaos. The Cold War, social disruption, the expanding government and media, the exposure of real conspiracies by the government in the form of Watergate and Iran-Contra, the CIA testing LSD on average citizens, and knowledge of the government working with mafia thugs created a sense that the world had been turned upside down. And during this time, unidentified flying objects were appearing in the sky—things unexplainable by the witnesses and undisclosed by the government. Our minds try to make sense of it all, to form cohesion in chaotic environments; and for some, the only thing that forms this cohesion is the belief that an alien presence is visiting earth, and the world governments are keeping this truth from the people in an effort to maintain their hold on civilization.

CHAPTER 6

Social Change and the Paranormal

The history of the paranormal has been one of feast or famine; periods of great renewed, fervent, and sometimes dangerous interest, followed by times of ridicule, skepticism, disbelief, or just plain old disinterest. These pendulous swings of paranormal belief and interest have shaped our modern world in immense ways, though often unbeknownst to the general public. But what brings these swings about? What causes the feast and the famine? Renewed public interest in the paranormal at particular junctures of human history is a signifier of massive social change sweeping across the culture and country. These times in history—the European witch craze, the rise of Spiritualism, the flying saucer invasion, and the satanic panic of the 1980s—all coincided with sweeping social changes, particularly in the realm of the sciences. The divergence of science and paranormal beliefs dates back to the European witch craze of the 1500s and the reformation of the Catholic Church; thus, we will begin our demonstration at this juncture in history.

The coincidence of major scientific developments and fervent public interest in the paranormal is not necessarily directly related, but rather indirectly. What the trend of coincidence demonstrates is an indirect relationship between the two, spurred by a public reaction to the subsequent change in culture. As with anything in life, major changes encounter difficulty and resistance on many levels. The social changes that coincide with the uprising of paranormal belief systems stir public reaction and resistance. Any challenge to widely held personal belief systems such as religion will encounter great resistance, and this resistance to the incursion of science into cultural belief systems will meet with renewed interest in the paranormal. As with any uprising, the interest slowly dies out, or in some cases, the pendulum of culture swings far in the opposite direction toward complete disavowal of the old belief systems and incorporation of the new. Hence, the surges of paranormal belief and interest are public reactions to the sweeping social, ethical, and cultural changes brought on by major developments in science. Following this line of thinking, we will examine some of the major paranormal ages in history and examine the coincidence of cultural and scientific changes. The times to be examined are listed above each section; however, the Bigfoot craze of the 1950s and '60s will not be examined because it has already been examined in great detail in Joshua Blu Buhs's fantastic work, *Bigfoot: The Life and Times of a Legend*, and is, therefore, not worth repeating in this work. Also, please note that the dates listed for each of these uprisings are only approximations to give a point of reference and to outline the times when public interest was at its peak; nearly all the paranormal beliefs listed still occur today in varying degrees.

THE EUROPEAN WITCH CRAZE

Jeffrey Burton Russell writes in his work, *Lucifer: The Devil in the Middle Ages*, "The great witch craze, which built upon this wide popular belief [the devil], was a phenomenon of the Renaissance, and the witch craze was at its height in England at precisely the time that Shakespeare was at his."[1] The European witch craze was responsible for one of the deadliest and darkest times in the history of the paranormal, resulting in the deaths of over one hundred thousand people, mostly women. These days the witch-hunts are looked upon with incredulous disdain and ridiculed as ancient beliefs and medieval practices born in the dark ages of ignorance and religious fervor. However, the witch craze actually occurred during one of the greatest and most earth-changing times of scientific development and enlightenment— the Renaissance. This was the time of the Copernican revolution, the first printing press, the explosion in literacy and scholarship; it was the time of Chaucer and Shakespeare; it was the time when the scientific method was developed, and some of the greatest thinkers focused their attention on the empirical world—men such as Leonardo da Vinci, Isaac Newton, and René Descartes, just to name a few. It was a time when the leading theology had all but abandoned the notion of the devil and his work in the world. "None of the main intellectual currents of the period was conducive to diabology. Scholastic realism had already played the Devil down, and now nominalism, mysticism, and humanism were even more inclined to ignore him. Yet at the same time the great witch craze began ..."[2]

But amidst these scientific, artistic, and philosophical revolutions, thousands were being burned at the stake across Europe for witchcraft. Trials were held with "evidence" based on nothing more than an accusation, and "scientific" tests to determine if someone was a witch included torturous acts designed to confirm the accusation. The public, fueled by sermons from priests and preachers, judges and the aristocratic elite, believed that on any given night, otherwise normal people were riding brooms or flying through the night air as unworldly creatures, to attend sabbats and Black Masses, which included orgiastic sex, ritual child murder, cannibalism, and pacts with Satan himself. These beliefs fueled one of the worst cases of mass panic and murder the world has ever known. But this panic was not fueled by the peasantry and the poor, though they were at the center of the panic; rather, it was fueled by the educated and elite intellectual class. It is often easier for us to accept the idea of ignorant townsfolk, pitchforks and torches in hand, surrounding innocent outsiders and killing them in a frenzy, similar to the famous scene from Frankenstein; but these were not mob killings, they were death sentences vetted by courts and magistrates, and presided over by the educated, wealthy, and pious.

Belief in witchcraft was nothing new. The world up until this point was one of magical religious practice and understanding. The very nature of the cosmos could not be understood without the magical, miraculous intervention of God himself. However, accusations of witchcraft were rare, and the punishment not nearly as severe in the days leading up to the Renaissance. So what made this time of human history different? What spurred the murder of one hundred thousand people? Anne Llewellyn Barstow authored *Witchcraze: A New History of the European Witch Hunts*, which examined the feminist aspect of the European witch-hunts, something that, until her writing, had been largely unexamined. "The gender of the victims no more explains the entire witch craze phenomenon than the legal, religious, political, or societal-functional arguments. All these factors and the generally neglected economic changes as well, are part of a valid explanation."[3] No coherent explanation of any time in history is valid without the consideration of many, many factors, each of which could probably comprise a book in and of itself. This being said, however, in the context of examining the paranormal uprisings from the time of the witch-hunts through the current day, we should examine the common factors; in our case, the strong coincidence of scientific and technological development and renewed interest in the paranormal. While the religious, economic, social, and gender factors are all parts of the complete picture, it was the development of the sciences during this time that laid the groundwork for this paranormal fervor. The fast pace by which God, and the belief in God, was challenged stirred a reaction from the elite and educated down through the masses. These massive changes in the way the magical-religious world was viewed bred fear, panic, a loss of self among the mobs, and, most of all, a power vacuum, which the elite sought to fill. This time was ultimately about control: control of the cosmos, the people, the money, and the pulpit. But it began with the usurpation of God's control over the cosmos.

The *Malleus Maleficarum*, or *The Hammer of Witches*, was published in 1486; however, it had very little impact until the witch craze had already begun and witch- hunters were carrying out their searches and persecution. It is possible that this was due to low literacy rates among the populace (though that was increasing rapidly); however, the witch craze, as indicated before, was largely perpetrated and prosecuted by the educated elite, but it still took nearly 80 years for the *Malleus* to truly be used as a hammer of witches.

Some authors have focused on the *Malleus* more than others. In their *Outbreak!: The Encyclopedia of Extraordinary Social Behavior*, Hilary Evans and Robert Bartholomew write, "By presenting witchcraft as a new heresy and dissociating it from the old peasant sorcery, they were able to add urgency to their mission, to spread the fear that humankind was threatened by a new menace. This was readily taken up by many secular authorities."[4] The *Malleus*, following in the traditions of the Inquisition, made any form of magic heretical, and therefore it could be prosecuted under the laws of the Inquisition and punished by torture, imprisonment, and death. It also established belief in witchcraft as essential to Catholicism and rendered any denial of witchcraft also heretical. But the argument that this was readily taken up by scholars seems a bit extreme. Most scholars at the time were having difficulty trying to reconcile a good and just God with the existence of a powerful, personal devil; and many had already begun to write the devil out of their theology, maintaining that evil was merely a lack of the presence of God, or "privation of God," as Russell puts it. Being that the belief in organized witchcraft is tied to belief in the devil, it seems that the *Malleus* might not have had the influence at first that it had in the later sixteenth and seventeenth centuries. The *Malleus* did indeed become the handbook for witch-hunting (along with several other treatises and quite a bit of ad-libbing), but not until many decades later. This is not to say that there were not trials and convictions of witchcraft when the *Malleus* was written, but they did not reach fever pitch until subsequent centuries.

Shortly before the witch craze began in Europe, Nicolaus Copernicus published *De Revolutionibus*, which showed the sun to be the center of the universe, rather than the earth. Published in 1543, *De Revolutionibus* essentially placed the earth and all her inhabitants on the outskirts of the cosmos; we were no longer the center of the universe. Not only were we no longer the governing body of the universe, Copernicus also developed the theories of guided celestial orbits. He laid the groundwork for nature to be known through empirical observation rather than by divine inspiration and literature. The work of Copernicus set into motion the work of Galileo, Kepler, and Newton, as well as the philosophies of René Descartes and Immanuel Kant. It was truly a revolution of thought and belief systems, and the world was forever changed.

Naturally, this did not happen overnight, and please do not draw the conclusion that the work of Copernicus, Galileo, Kepler, and Newton caused the witch craze. In fact, had their ideas taken root earlier or more quickly, perhaps the witch craze would never have occurred. It was not their theories that influenced the craze, but rather a form of cultural cognitive dissonance and loss that resulted from these discoveries that spurred the craze.

We must remember that the world was a very different place at that time. For centuries mankind had easily accepted that the earth and cosmos were governed directly by God. While there had always been debate among scholars regarding predestination as opposed to free will, it was generally accepted that God controlled the happenings of the universe. The idea that somehow there was an invisible force controlling the heavens, and that we did not sit at the center of God's creation, shook the foundation of hundreds if not thousands of years of belief. The psychological impact of these theories was immense, tantamount to aliens landing on the White House lawn and telling the world that we humans were only part of a lab experiment that they somehow botched. The previously held ideas and beliefs, which centered on God as the creator and primary mover of the cosmos, were suddenly and very soundly refuted using empirical observation and evidence. Copernicus and subsequent scientific revolution removed control of the cosmos and nature from God.

As discussed in the chapter entitled "Paranormal Hoaxes," cognitive dissonance can have disastrous and extreme effects on both an individual and a community. The upheaval of a worldview can result in an extreme effort to preserve and somehow justify the traditional beliefs. Could the witch craze have been a case of mass hysteria spurred by the effects of cognitive dissonance? People will often take illogical, seemingly insane stances in an effort to avoid their worldview being proven inaccurate and will react violently in an effort to preserve their belief systems, something often seen in the study of cults. Jim Jones orchestrated the largest mass suicide in history in an effort to preserve the illusion of his religion. Considering the level of control, enforced by violence, which the church exerted over the entire population, life in Europe leading up to the sixteenth century was not much different from a cult. It supplanted science and reason with blind faith and enforcement through the Inquisition.

As in the case of Jim Jones, the witch craze revolved around control. It wasn't necessarily about science itself, but rather the control of the cosmos that science was quickly changing. The elite, whose power was largely due to their religious and economic stature, spurred the witch craze. Scholarship, government, society, and law revolved almost completely around God's law and theology. The usurpation of God was the usurpation of the basis for their control. Essentially, God's control had been removed from the cosmos, leaving an entire people without direction, understanding, or a solid grasp of the world. Subsequently, the world reacted . . . violently.

As indicated before, no one explanation can completely analyze what happened in Europe in the sixteenth and seventeenth centuries, but the issue of control underlies nearly every facet of the major changes that occurred during these centuries and in the fears expressed by the witch-hunters at the height of the craze.

First, we shall look at the loss of religious control. Religious scholars did not miss the implications of the Copernican revolution; they had been debating the meaning of theological texts for centuries and were very adept at making logical arguments concerning God's role in the world. Subsequently, it did not take a great leap of rational thought to tie Copernicus's theories to the dismissal of God's control over the heavens and the earth. Indeed, it was the church that had first access to Copernicus's theories and to his writings, and it was the church that actually encouraged him to have the work published. "As Copernicus continued work on *De Revolutionibus* throughout the 1530s, interest in his work grew. In 1533, Pope Clement VII was told about Copernicus's theory of the motion of Earth. Cardinal Nicholas Schonberg in Rome wrote to Copernicus in 1536 saying he admired his work, asking for a copy of his manuscript, and offering to pay all expenses. His friend, Bishop Tideman Giese, urged him to publish."[5] However, when Galileo expressed his support in 1610, he was warned by the church to stay quiet; and in 1632, when Galileo published his defense of Copernican theory, *Dialogue Concerning the Two Chief World Systems*, he was convicted of heresy and placed under house arrest for the remainder of his life. Why the sudden change of heart by the church?

The focus on the devil in the witch-hunts also merits inquiry because, as indicated before, many scholars and theologians had begun to dismiss the idea of a separate entity responsible for evil. However, the devil was the main focus of the witch-hunts as it was he who corrupted susceptible women and forced them to copulate with him at sabbats. The professed empowerment of the devil during these times may have been a means of protecting the weakest link in Christian theology. The existence of evil is one of the most difficult aspects of a religion that proposes an omnipotent, omniscient God who is both good and loving. Several different logical theories trying to justify the existence of evil or a devil have been debated for centuries with very little progress. While many scholars were beginning to shy away from the problem of the devil, denial of a personal, knowable evil entity was and is contrary to the base beliefs of Christianity. "The difficulty is that any unbiased, educated agnostic observing the phenomenon of Christianity will perceive that belief in the Devil has always been part and parcel of Christianity, firmly rooted in the New Testament, in tradition, and in virtually all Christian thinkers up into very modern times."[6] The devil, and evil itself, presented one of the more difficult theological problems. The implications of the Copernican revolution could (and eventually did) expose this weakest link in theology. Therefore, the exponential growth of the devil's power and influence in the sermons of the sixteenth and seventeenth centuries could have been a protective, defensive mechanism as the elite ruling party tried to maintain their control through a mythology based on fear. The greater the belief in the devil, the more difficulty the new empirical, scientific thinking would have in discrediting such beliefs ... especially if the existence of the devil and witchcraft could be "proved" through trials and forced confessions of the accused witches. Belief in the devil gave the church and the ruling parties control over the masses and a powerful belief system against the empirical and scientific method.

The great reformation of the church also had its roots in power; firstly, by the Catholic Church trying to maintain their belief and power systems, and secondly, in the usurpation of control by the people themselves. The Protestant Reformation sought to connect the individual directly to God without having to use the church as a medium. As literacy increased and the Bible became more and more available to the people, the centuries of dogma built by the Catholic Church was called into question. Thus, the Reformation largely consisted of the control of peoples' souls, and salvation being transferred from the Catholic Church to the individual. The Protestant Reformation, however, faced some difficulty with belief in the devil and the persecution of witchcraft as well. "The fierce religious differences revealed by the Reformation added another point of instability in this tumultuous century. Lutheran theologians and pastors stressed a demonology different from that of the Catholics. Regarding the devil's power, they taught that misfortune was caused not by the devil but by God's providence, and that the devil, and certainly his servants, did not have the enormous power with which popular belief, and especially Catholic belief, credited them."[7] However, the Protestants continued with witch-hunts, though less fervently than the Catholics. The Protestants, with their focus on scripture and scripture alone actually reacted more vehemently against the Copernican theories. " 'Mention has been made of some new astrologer, who wanted to prove that Earth moves and goes around, and not the firmament or heavens, the sun and the moon,' commented an angry Martin Luther in 1539. 'This fool wants to turn the entire art of astronomy upside down! But as the Holy Scriptures show, Joshua ordered the sun, and not Earth, to halt!' Protestants proved initially more hostile to Copernicus."[8] Also, "Luther, who despised hermetic magic as a vain and prideful attempt to grasp divine knowledge through intellect, hastened to link all magic with witchcraft."[9] Hermetic magic was the search for an underlying connection throughout the natural world, probably more akin to physics than witchcraft. To Protestantism, the Copernican theories were more threatening and dangerous than any form of witchcraft. Witchcraft was ultimately the providence of God, but the budding scientific revolution was a direct threat to the belief in God. Thus, it was essential to the church that fervor, fear, and hunts were maintained, the devil continued to roam the European countryside, and witches continued to have their trials. Control of world perception had to be maintained in order to preserve the current balance of power, whether that power rested with the Catholic Church or the Reformation; both needed the existent, theological worldview in order to maintain their tenuous grasp of the cosmos and the people.

The witch craze also revolved around the establishment of centralized government and the assertion of control over the people. The elite, educated, and pious were taking their place at the head of government and extending their reach to small, country townships. "The ducal and Royal governments of Europe were becoming more efficient, centralized, and powerful; in other words, more capable of controlling many aspects of peoples lives."[10] Also, the trials were presided over by judges who acted on behalf of the state. "The judge became the initiator of charges, compiling evidence against suspects, interrogating the accused in secret, using torture when necessary to ascertain the truth, acting always in the name of the state."[11] The extended government control, along with new taxes and enforcement, tightened the noose around all of society and created new economic hardships for the peasantry. The witch-hunters and judges, on behalf of the state, also showed an expressed fear of a conspiracy of witches. Their torturous methods forced the witches to reveal other witches in the community. Under extreme duress, many of the women would openly confess to their deeds and begin to name other women who attended these blasphemous sabbats. This created in the townsfolk a dependency on the state and church based on fear of a vast satanic conspiracy of witches who kidnapped and devoured people's children, cavorted with the devil, and cast spells which brought disease, famine, and death. The promotion of the belief in witchcraft allowed the townsfolk to blame all their difficulties on a common enemy, one which was being hunted down by the government and the church in the name of preserving life, safety, and souls. It also allowed the townspeople to feel a sense of control in the world. With an enemy responsible for the world's evils, named and known and being hunted, it actually established a sense of purpose, reason, and control in the minds of the townsfolk; it felt as if order was being enacted in the world—God's order.

Such order was not possible in the Copernican universe that was governed, not by God, but by strange, unseen forces. No longer was God the hand that ordered the universe. The witch-hunts, through their use of tortured confessions by the witches, proved the existence of the devil and the need for God's hand in the natural world. The irony being, of course, that the chaos of this mass hysteria was anything but orderly, and certainly not godly.

And was it, perhaps, these strange forces of nature, such as physics, that everyone was so concerned about? Magic is essentially the manipulation of nature through unseen forces. In the case of witchcraft, it was manipulation of nature through the aid of evil spirits, even the devil himself. Suddenly, Renaissance scientists were proposing unseen forces that controlled the cosmos, similar to the way witches controlled the fates of people's health, livestock, and lives. Anne Llewellyn Barstow, in her feminist examination of the witch trials, makes the important point that the victims, more than the perpetrators, should be examined closely when trying to find a cause of the witch craze. The majority of accused witches were poor, single or widowed women who lived on the outskirts of communities, often beggars who were largely involved in the healing arts and midwifery. With science barely existent in the times leading up to the witch craze, many of the healing arts dabbled in sorcery and mysticism, using herbs and medicinal practices that were not understood by either patient or healer; but nonetheless, these folk remedies worked and were readily accepted by the people. However, following the *Malleus*'s decree that all magic and sorcery was heretical, and the imposition from the elite that witchcraft had to be pursued and prosecuted, these women went from healers to witches. Again, it became an issue of control; through the elimination of those who were thought to have the ability to control these forces of nature and healing, control was returned to God, rather than leaving it in the hands of magicians who manipulated unseen forces.

But the real test as to what the elite truly feared and what actually drove the witch craze may lie in what was ultimately its undoing. The new understanding of the world through science was a contributing factor to both the birth of the witch craze and its death. In essence, the old belief system, which so ferociously reared its head during the sixteenth and seventeenth centuries, was now being defeated quickly and quietly by the age of science, reason, and empiricism. "From this combination of decreasing anxiety about the structure of the inhabited world and increasing assurance of people's ability to understand that world in earthly terms, witchcraft, as a Western belief, was ultimately to founder."[12] And Russell writes, "Witchcraft took a steep downturn in the mid-seventeenth century, as people wearied of being terrified—terrified of the threatening presence of hostile spirits, and terrified of prosecution."[13] The confusion, anxiety, and fear that had spurred the witch craze had subsided and been replaced by a new era of thinking that did not allow for such beliefs. The foundations of the world in the sixteenth century had been rocked by several advancements in the sciences beginning with Copernicus's theory of a heliocentric universe—a universe in which basic laws of unseen natural forces guided the planets around the sun, rather than God's divine hand guiding the planets around the earth. The negation of God from the natural realm spurred a reaction beginning with the church and with the scholars who had direct access to Copernicus's work. While he was at first encouraged by the church, within half a century Copernicus's views were regarded as heretical, and Galileo paid a steep price for defending them. This sudden and dramatic change is indicative of the fear that Copernicus and Galileo wrought in those who adhered to the old traditions. Suddenly, the world as they knew it was being pulled out from under them. The witch craze was a violent reaction to this sudden and dramatic change.

However, I am not suggesting that the Catholic Church and the scholars got together and decided to systematically combat these new ideas by promoting witchcraft and the persecution thereof. Rather, I am offering yet another possible road into the cause of this dark time in human history. The Renaissance forever changed the course of human history, but a change so dramatic is going to have psychological effects. The world of spirit was quickly being replaced by a world of natural law and science, but the dramatic change would not come without some form of resistance. As the framework of the known godly universe began to crack and tumble, the people clung to their traditional beliefs in a violent and illogical way. One needs only look at the extent of absurdity to which these beliefs were carried to understand that this was much more than just an aberrance of human behavior. People were desperately trying to prove the spiritual universe. They needed some form of proof that the devil was out there and that his magic was being worked on the population; they found that proof, or rather coerced confession, in witches.

The accounts of orgies, cannibalism, and infanticide during the witches' sabbats were nothing new to traditional beliefs. These were all offenses that had been laid at the feet of Jews, heretics, and even Christians in Rome during the early years of belief. Clinging to this great idea of evil "others" who had consorted with the devil fit perfectly into the spiritual understanding of the universe, and the townspeople were able to accept these accusations with ease. The establishment of folk magic and hermetic magic as heretical by the *Malleus Maleficarum*, as well as its decree that belief in witchcraft was essential to Christianity, set in place a thought pattern that would come to reject Copernicus's theories as heretical and exposed many women who practiced the healing arts as witches. A battle of ideas was fought between the old traditions and the new science, and science ultimately and resoundingly won, but there were casualties. No universal worldview can be shifted without tremendous effect on the population, and that is essentially what science did in the sixteenth and seventeenth centuries, beginning with Copernicus. "In opposition to scholastic modes of thought, the seventeenth century witnessed the rise of philosophies in which there was no place for spiritual or supernatural causes of the events of the natural world. Arising from Descartes's categorical separation of the realms of matter and spirit, from experimental and empirical naturalism, mechanistic modes of explanation increasingly replaced accounts of spirit acting upon matter as satisfactory accounts of events in men's minds."[14] If you want to see who fought a war, look at the dead and then look at the living. In this case, the old traditions were gone, and the modern age of science and reason had arrived.

EARLY AMERICAN SPIRITUALISM

In 1848, in a small farmhouse in Hydeville, New York, the Fox family began to hear strange knocks and rattles in their home. The family quickly came to believe that their house was infested with evil spirits. Two young adolescent sisters, Margaret and Katherine, discovered that they could ask the spirits questions and receive answers back in the form of knocks. Word got out in the surrounding towns, an area of New York known as the "burned-over district" because of the number of religious revivals that had run rampant throughout the countryside, and suddenly people were flocking to Hydeville from all over New York to see the Fox sisters communicate with these spirits. Thus began a movement known as Spiritualism that would capture the imagination of the public and the scrutiny of science for the next 80 years, eventually reaching its peak in the days just before the First World War.

However, before the Fox sisters were even born, a scientist was embarking on a round-the-world trip aboard the HMS *Beagle*. In 1831, Charles Darwin boarded the *Beagle* and began a five-year journey that would take him to the Galápagos Islands and many other lands where he would study nature, flora and fauna, and eventually develop his theory of evolution through natural selection. While the Fox sisters were communicating with spirits, Darwin was communicating with fellow biologists, passing along his ideas and essays. Ten years after the Fox sisters began to hear raps in the attic, Darwin released his work, *On the Origin of Species*, and forever changed the way that science, nature, religion, and the origins of life were viewed. It marks one of the most dramatic scientific and cultural changes in modern history and sparked debates that still rage to this day. Amid this scientific revolution, the public became fascinated with Spiritualism and its practices, which included accounts of communication with dead relatives, levitation, manifestation, spirit hands, approbation, extrasensory perception, and spirit manifestos that focused on the nature of reality and the afterlife. Darwin, despite being a religious man himself, essentially removed God and the soul from the origins of life. His theories had almost immediate acceptance in scientific circles, but also social repercussions. The public reacted by turning toward the very thing that Darwin removed from the equation: the idea of the eternal human soul—that we were not merely animals but divinely created beings that lived on after death. Georgess McHargue states in her work, *Facts, Frauds, and Phantasms*, "Probably the most exact way to describe Spiritualism is to say it is the belief that the individual personality survives after death and can communicate with the living."[15]

It should be noted, however, that Darwin's *On the Origin of Species* and the rise of Spiritualism are not directly related. *Origin* was not released until 10 years after the Fox sisters began to communicate with spirits of the dead. Within that 10-year span, Spiritualism swept across the United States and crossed the pond to Europe where it became a fascination of the Victorian wealthy. Evolutionary theories, however, had been circulating for some time before Darwin. The nature of cultural shifts, reactions, and progress can never be confined to direct causal relationships; instead, it is a complex assortment of different factors. Much like the European witch-hunt that cannot be directly attributed to the *Malleus Maleficarum* or the revolution, neither can Spiritualism be directly related to *On the Origin of Species*. While Darwin's theories were circulating among a select group of scientists, the public was becoming more and more aware of and fascinated with the mysteries of life. The very exploration of these mysteries called into question some of the orthodox religious assertions about the divine origins of the universe.

> Amid all this turmoil were the general hope and uneasiness that coa-
> lesced around the great passion of the age: science. The telegraph,
> which had been invented only four years before the Foxes first sum-
> moned the spirits, revolutionizing communications as surely as the tele-
> phone, television, and the computer would in their time. Railroads were
> just beginning to crisscross America. Most of all, electricity held an
> abiding fascination, fraught with promise and mystery. Everyone knew
> it existed and was immensely powerful, but no one was quite sure what
> it was or how it could be safely or effectively harnessed.[16]

Thus, the public reaction in the form of Spiritualism was not necessarily against Darwin's theories, but against the massive inroads that science was making into the inner workings of life.

However, it was Darwin's theories that would generate the biggest reaction and greatest public outcry as it, ultimately, uncovered the origins of man, plants, and animals, and called into question man's very soul. "Orthodox religion was also fending off attack from discoveries in such diverse fields as biblical criticism and geology. Textual studies of the Bible called into question its divine authorship, and new evidence about the earth's age and development threatened to undermine scriptural cosmogony."[17]

While the overriding concept of the European witch craze centered around the issue of control of the cosmos, and whether that control existed with God, witches, or the government, the concept surrounding the rise of Spiritualism seems to be that of nature, and whether or not man is more than animal. The primary belief of Spiritualism is that the soul of man survives death, thereby separating man from animal and maintaining the belief that mankind is divinely created. While the Fox sisters clearly knew nothing about Darwin's coming revolution, the gate of nature had begun to be opened by current science. The Fox sisters, when they began communicating with departed spirits, were not doing anything essentially new, as these practices had been in existence since ancient times. However, the public reaction to and fascination with the Fox sisters and their subsequent imitators and inno-vators represents a deep-seated yearning to bolster old beliefs in the face of emerging science. Spiritualism was closely linked to Christianity, but it also allowed believers to sidestep some of the more difficult theological questions brought about by science. Spiritualism was hardly ever a set or organized religion; Spiritualists' beliefs ranged from Orthodox Christian beliefs to belief in alien planets inhabited by the souls of the long-departed. This allowed Spiritualism to change and mold itself as science changed and molded society. However, it could not escape the inevitable conflict between the idea of man as an animal that had been produced through natural selection and man as a spiritual, divine being. Ultimately, that is what played out upon the public stage. It was a reaction against the scientific theories that portrayed man as an advanced animal rather than a demigod. The two great passions of the age—science and Spiritualism—clashed, and would continue to clash throughout the next 80 years.

Nowhere is the clash between science, Spiritualism, and the public more manifest than in the exhausting studies conducted on some of the greatest spiritual mediums of the time, and the uproar that these experiments created. The studies would sometimes be conducted over a period of years and showed a scientific methodology at odds with something completely unscientific—the spirit world. And while there were many frauds discovered (probably the majority of so-called mediums were frauds), there were the occasional mediums that seemed to defy the sciences for explanation. Ironically, it was these extensive and often successful attempts to demonstrate a medium's fraud that led to greater belief in Spiritualism. Dr. Charles Alfred Lee toured New York showing how the Fox sisters were able to create the spirit knocks and raps by cracking the joints of their fingers and toes. He demonstrated this by exhibiting a man who was able to mimic the sisters' work through the use of this strange ability. "The results of the tour were unexpected. Instead of being warned away from the tricks of false mediums, many of those in Dr. Lee's audiences became converted to spiritualism by his earnest attempts to discredit it."[18]

Similarly, during a séance with famed medium Florence Cook, in which she manifested a ghost by the name of Katie who would walk around the room and converse with the sitters, a patron by the name of William Volckman grabbed the entity by the arm and refused to let go. The other sitters came to the rescue of Katie and released his hold. The entity then retreated back into the very same closet that held Florence Cook, who was supposedly tied up at the time. When Cook emerged from the closet she was visibly shaken. For a long time there had been comments made by skeptics and believers alike that "Katie" closely resembled Florence Cook, even though Cook, of course, vehemently denied it. However, this clear unveiling of a fraud was met with outrage. "Reaction to this incident among spiritualists was immediate and violent. Mr. Volckman, though an active spiritualist of several years' standing, was angrily condemned . . . At least half of the outrage occasioned by Mr. Volckman's escapade was directed at his supposed breach of good manners (in taking hold of a lady and impugning the reliability of his hosts) rather than at the actual truth or falsity of his charges."[19] Mediums would never allow someone to touch an entity that they had manifested because it would supposedly drain the energy of the medium and possibly cause serious illness or even death. This, of course, gave the medium some confidence that his or her fraud would go undetected by a genteel public, and it also allowed the spiritualists to enact righteous indignation when the fraud was exposed, thus turning attentions to the breach in etiquette and the endangering of a young woman, rather than the truth of the matter.

Florence Cook would have a rather long and illustrious career working with famed scientist Sir William Crookes, who had set out to discover the truth of Spiritualism. But Cook managed to seduce the poor old fellow, and he became one of her greatest advocates, attesting to her abilities as genuine supernatural feats. Crookes, despite his impressive scientific career, was unfortunately swallowed whole by the Spiritualist movement—a testament to man's powerful desire for immortality. Crookes had originally tested D. D. Home, one of the few mediums whose abilities actually did baffle scientists and call into question the nature of mankind. Crookes reported that he felt D. D. Home was genuine and had unexplainable abilities. However, when he turned his attentions to the young and pretty Florence Cook, nearly all the mediocre checks and methodology he had used on Home went right out the proverbial window. While his assertions of Cook's abilities certainly made waves in the scientific and Spiritualist communities, his poor methods and obvious corrupted nature virtually ended his credibility in the science community. But he was certainly not the last of the great scientists to test the Spiritualist waters.

It was during this time in history involving the research of spiritualism that the Society for Psychical Research or SPR began. SPR was an organization of respected scientists who devoted themselves to the study of psychic phenomena and often debunked the mediums as frauds. However, they were open-minded enough to allow that some of the people studied did display abilities that defied explanation, though these incidents were rare exceptions. The research into the possibility of a spirit world captured the attention of many of the world's great scientists, including Harry Sidgwick, professor of moral philosophy at Cambridge and the SPR's first president.

What is truly fascinating about this confluence of science and spiritualism is the dedication with which each side upheld their own belief systems; die-hard spiritualists could not be convinced of fraud even when exposed before their very eyes, while the scientists would routinely deny the reality of the phenomena that could not be explained. Their controls during experiments included holding the mediums' arms and legs while they sat bound to a chair in a room of the scientists' design. However, were the medium to loose a foot or hand for a moment, the scientists would discount the entire experience as somehow being controlled by a trick. Nowhere was this more evident than in the case of Eusapia Palladino, one of the most ambiguous and frustrating mediums that the SPR ever had to deal with. Eusapia was born very poor; she rejected education throughout her life, along with several other niceties such as bathing or social etiquette. Also, her séances were orgiastic in nature and were largely thought of as uncomfortably sexual. Eusapia would often flail her body and arms, which allowed plenty of opportunity for tricks and hoaxes to be played, and it was well known that, at times, Eusapia did fake some of the phenomena. However, her appeal was that a large number of her feats were completely unexplainable, and, in fact, so unbelievable that many, including scientists, did not believe they could be faked. Unlike many of the mediums during the Victorian times, Eusapia was not accepted or admired by the wealthy upper class. They regarded her as rude and crude and uncomfortable to be with. Subsequently, Eusapia spent much of her career as a medium being studied by scientists. Her phenomena were witnessed by Harry Sidgwick and his wife, and included such feats as a wicker chair and a melon levitating and moving to the center of the table, strange lights and ghost faces appearing in the darkness, musical instruments playing themselves, and extra limbs of ectoplasm that could move and push things across the table.

Eusapia's tests were famous but also ambiguous. When she didn't feel like manifesting anything, she would obviously cheat, which led some of those in the SPR to conclude that she was a fraud. Moving her arms and legs was a large part of her conjuring, so the men would hold onto her limbs to be sure that she couldn't cheat. Even her occasional freeing of an arm or leg could not account for the phenomena that she produced in a room that was set up by the scientists to control the experiments. During a performance for Marie and Pierre Curie, who monitored her with electronics, she caused one of their scientific devices to rise in the air and sail past Marie and Pierre. The SPR subsequently sent a second envoy to investigate her in 1908, during which she wowed them with her abilities. Even so, some could not get past her occasional cheating, "But was the SPR so blind to assume that a free hand or foot could account for all the things she did? Did they not see that the very clumsiness of her cheating belied her being an accomplished fraud?"[20] What was probably a more startling feat was that an uneducated woman from the streets could outsmart the world's most prominent scientists and fraud hunters with tricks. Unfortunately, she grew tired of the skepticism and experiments and was caught regularly using her tricks and no longer putting any energy into her conjuring. Following an unimpressive trip to the United States, she retired.

Eusapia's career presents a microcosm of the difficulties that surround scientific investigation of the paranormal. She was ambiguous—an anathema to scientific study, combining trickery with sexuality and spirituality and the unexplainable. In this sense she was similar to the ancient shamans that formed the very first religious experiences in ancient tribes. She would perform a miracle followed by a fraud. She did not fit into any category; rather, she crossed the boundaries that form the basis of science and our understanding of the world. She encompassed the trickster aspect of the paranormal, blending truth and fiction, reality with fantasy, the supernatural with trickery; and for this reason, she was probably the most genuine medium in history, fully embracing the liminal aspects of the paranormal and spiritual. She could not be categorized because she transcended the normal boundaries of human knowledge and experience. Thus, she presented the greatest challenge to science, whose understanding is limited to method and boundary. The scientists defended their beliefs that Spiritualism was a fraud as fervently as the spiritualists defended its credibility—to a fault. For both sides, it became a matter of faith; faith in the spiritual world versus faith in the not yet fully understood natural world.

One of the more telling aspects of the relationship between the Spiritualist movement and the emerging natural sciences were the spirits with whom the mediums communicated, and the secrets of life that said spirits revealed. The Spiritualist regularly claimed to communicate with great scientists of the past—personalities who had moved on to explore the infinite reality of life in the spirit world and had returned to share their experience with humanity. However, "Several critics of the movement had pointed out that humanity had never received a single piece of useful information from the spirit world in spite of all the mediums who claimed to have communed with the great scientists and thinkers of the past."[21] Rather, Spiritualist messages from beyond appeared to be New Age platitudes—spiritual propaganda that may have passed for the teachings of a cult rather than any substantive philosophy or communication. As Spiritualist organizations formed, they began to form solidarity in a message that preached of the unity of all life, but with a decidedly Christian spin. One of the principles of the White Eagle Lodge was "That Christ, the Son of the Father-Mother God, is the Light that shines through Wisdom and Love in the human heart; and that by reason of this Divine Sonship all are brothers and sisters regardless of race, class, or creed; and that this brotherhood and sisterhood embraces life, visible and invisible."[22]

This idea of a world spiritually interconnected is not vastly different from Darwin's theory of evolution—a theory that postulates that we are all related; plants, animals, and man have all descended from the same place, are all made of the same primordial stuff, and therefore, are all brothers and sisters. The White Eagle Lodge was created in 1936 and could possibly be a reconciliation of Spiritualism and Darwinism. Rather than emphasizing the physical relationship of man with the earth, the White Eagle Lodge emphasized the spiritual connection.

However, even before Darwin sought to explain life on earth through natural selection and before the Fox sisters began to communicate with spirits, Andrew Jackson Davis was already exploring the beginnings of the universe through spiritual revelation. While in a spiritual trance, he dictated his work *Principles, Revelations, and Voice*, which was an inspired history of the universe, detailing the divine nature of man and spirit. McHargue states that the book follows an "evolutionary view of life on this planet," but it devolves largely into scientific/spiritual nonsense, highly reminiscent of today's New Age belief systems—that of a spiritual unity of the universe. Little did Davis know that his beliefs were being echoed by science, only instead of a spiritual unity, it was unity based on basic elements, the struggle to survive, and the continuation of life after death through reproduction. Davis's work was extensive and very popular—a blend of infant spiritualism and dawning science. His descriptions of the birds, which inhabit his celestial spirit dwelling known as the Summer Land, invoke the same kind of wonder and exotic beauty Darwin beheld on his trips to the Galápagos and other such locales.

However, perhaps the best example of the collision between Spiritualism and Darwinian evolution was the story of Alfred Russel Wallace. "Independently of Charles Darwin, Wallace had worked out a theory of evolution based on natural selection. But he was disturbed by his own findings. Although convinced that the theory was generally correct, he felt that the human mind was exempt from it. The mind, the human spirit, was a unique act of creation. So believing, Wallace found comfort in spiritualism, which seemed to confirm humanity's spiritual singularity."[23]

Wallace's conflict is a microcosm for the conflict that spurred the Spiritualist movement; the conflict between belief in man as a divine and spiritual being and man as a highly evolved animal. Both science and Spiritualism were trying to answer some of the basic fundamental questions of life; namely, how did we get here and what happens after we die? They both sought to understand the essence of humanity. Wallace's findings were so at odds with what he believed about humanity that he rejected his own work and turned instead to Spiritualism. Likewise, many on both the American continent and in Europe did the same. In the face of emerging sciences that harnessed an unseen force such as electricity and postulated that man was nothing more than a highly evolved ape, the masses turned to Spiritualism to provide proof to the contrary. And the Fox sisters gave them that proof. Even science was scrambling to understand the phenomena surrounding the séances and the mediums—truly looking for the assurance of life after death, of the human soul, and perhaps most of all, God. The scientists wanted to believe, but, save for a few exceptions, they were not willing to believe for belief's sake alone. Rather, they required proof. They hoped, once and for all, to be able to stand on fact rather than faith, that man was more than just a creature who developed down a different evolutionary path. Mankind's belief in its own spiritual immortality had been rocked again and again throughout the past generations, and people were desperately hoping to find something that could not be shaken, that could not be explained away with mathematical equations and fossil records. What they got was Spiritualism, which proved to them that the spirit survives death. Taps on the wall, levitation, spirit hands that touched the hem of a dress, tales of Summer Lands inhabited by benevolent civilizations, a spiritual reality far removed from our own, were the proofs that the public sought and gained from Spiritualism.

Sadly, however, it was largely fraudulent, perpetrated by ingenious social climbers who used their tricks for money, fame, and life with the aristocracy. Many were exposed, but it did not deter the public; in fact, it seemed to encourage the public. Perhaps their need to believe outweighed their capacity for critical thinking. In fact, it would appear that it took World War I to finally put Spiritualism to rest. While the belief and practices continued—and still do—the destructiveness of the Great War was so great that it literally caused a spiritual crisis in Europe, which had been the focal point for much of Spiritualism. The United States, however, remained largely unaffected by the devastation of the war and held its spiritual beliefs more intact. But science was successfully working to discredit the movement as a whole.

However, there were the anomalies. There were the mediums that science could not explain and that common sense could not brush off; D. D. Home and Eusapia Palladino were two such examples. Palladino, in particular, was studied at such length that to deny all her miraculous workings would be to deny the work of a large group of people and scientists. While she could never be a study in scientific method, she did show that some mysteries still existed in the world. "Thus, in the perverse manner so common in psychical research, the experiment ended neither in success nor in failure but only in presenting another problem."[24]

The need to believe that man is a spiritual being conflicted with the scientific developments of the late nineteenth century, particularly Darwinism. This need caused an accelerated belief in something that offered proof that a human spirit existed. In the end, however, the Great War decimated the human spirit and lay before the eyes of the world mangled corpses that revealed man as nothing more than bone, flesh, and blood. Darwin's frightening world had become manifest, and a new era had been ushered in: survival of the fittest, the ascension of technology, the rise of evolution. And Spiritualism, with all its hope, trickery, and mystery, was left in the trenches with the dead.

THE FLYING SAUCER INVASION

On August 6, 1945, the United States dropped the first atomic weapon ever used in war on Hiroshima, Japan. Three days later, it dropped the second on Nagasaki, thus ending the war with Japan. This new weapon unleashed more destruction in one blast than had been seen in the entire history of war. Science had unleashed a new and powerful energy, one that was capable of destroying an entire city and killing hundreds of thousands of people in less than a second. Four years later, the United Soviet Socialist Republic successfully tested an atom bomb. Not only was this new force born of science capable of destroying an entire city, it was a force that was capable of destroying all of humanity. A new era had been born in a flash as bright as the sun— the atomic era. It was a time of fear and anxiety, of scientific revolution and the start of the Cold War with Russia. All eyes were to the sky. It was a time of jet propulsion. It was a time of fast new aircraft capable of great destruction and speed never before attained. The scientific world was jumping forward at incredible rates. Bomb drills were held in classrooms, where children were instructed to hide under their desks to protect themselves from nuclear fallout. It was the Cuban Missile Crisis, the Red Scare, the assassination of John F. Kennedy, Sputnik, and, a mere 20 years later, man's successful landing on the moon. It was also the time of the flying saucer invasion.

And just two years after the bombing of Hiroshima and Nagasaki, newspapers were running stories about flying saucers in the sky—unknown objects that appeared to be of extraterrestrial origin. Pilot Kenneth Arnold was the first to dub them "flying saucers" when he spotted approximately nine of them flying in formation near Mt. Rainier, Washington. Following his report, citizens everywhere began to see these flying saucers, or as they were later named, Unidentified Flying Objects. The next 30 years, from 1947 to 1977, included some of the most famous and infamous moments of UFO lore and also marked the highest point of public interest. It was during these 30 years that all the great stories, moments, and personalities in the UFO subculture would emerge.

The year 1947 marked the flying saucer crash at Roswell, New Mexico; however, this event garnered very little attention until decades later it was rediscovered by Stanton Friedman and others. The late forties and fifties were marked with repeated sightings in both civilian and military circles, and in the sixties the abduction craze began with the first major reported abduction of Betty and Barney Hill.

There was something else that made this time in history unique; the medium through which the public experienced the world and shared information was changing from newspapers to film and television. And it was through these mediums that the fascination and fear of the newfound atomic science revealed itself in the form of flying saucers. Hollywood immediately seized on the idea of flying saucers, which came to represent everything from violent invaders to peaceniks with messages of hope and change. The visions of things seen in the sky were translated to visions of things seen in film, and they came to represent the fears of a society that was now in possession of a destructive power capable of ending civilization. As the reports of flying saucers grew, the military was creating and testing a new nuclear weapon (the hydrogen bomb), putting the first man in space, and reaching for the moon. The rapid advancement of the sciences in rocket technology and atomic energy made the idea of space travel possible, but it also made possible doomsday, as indicated by the oh-so-subtle Doomsday Clock that was set in motion by a group of concerned scientists.

In his nonfiction work *Danse Macabre*, Stephen King recalls the summer of 1957 when he sat in a theater in Stratford, Connecticut, watching, ironically, *Earth vs. The Flying Saucers*, when the manager of the theater stopped the film to announce to the audience that the Russians had just successfully launched Sputnik into orbit. "The Russians had beaten us into space . . . The manager stood there for a moment longer, looking out at us as if he wished he had something else to say but could not think what it might be. Then he walked off and pretty soon the movie started up again."[25] This moment beautifully illustrates the convergence of the flying saucer mania and the social effects of a Cold War spurred by new technology and science seemingly run amok. "Terror—what Hunter Thompson calls 'fear and loathing'—often arises from a pervasive sense of disestablishment; that things are in the unmaking."[26] It wasn't just the Russians making it into space before the good ole United States of America, it was something more; it was the sense of disestablishment that caused the sudden and alarming spike in sightings of and belief in flying saucers. Flying saucers were society's answer to the scientific boom; they were simultaneously cautionary and hopeful, somber and fantastic. New worlds were opening up as our old world balanced on the verge of destruction.

In 1951 the science fiction classic *The Day the Earth Stood Still* was released.[27] It is a story about a flying saucer that lands in Washington, D.C. The alien aboard, Klaatu (who looks very human), comes to earth offering a gift and a message of peace. He is promptly shot, which probably explains why real aliens do not choose to land on the White House lawn. Klaatu lives, and he wants to deliver a message to all the nations of earth, a message of peace and a warning that if we continue upon our current course of destruction, the alien powers will destroy us. He is promptly shot again.

However, the message of this film encapsulated many of the hopes, fears, and fantasies that thrived in the aftermath of the atomic bombs and were incorporated into the belief in flying saucers. Once again, world-changing scientific development coincided with a spike in public belief, interest in, and sightings of the paranormal. In this case, scientific development grew much, much faster than humanity matured, and thus, the United States was left in the grip of the Cold War fear. It was these scientific developments that forever changed the course of human history and preceded the public fascination with flying saucers. This is not to say that flying saucers were not seen before 1947; in fact, there are reports going back to ancient man. However, there had never been such a surge of interest and belief as occurred in the late forties and early fifties. Advances in flight, radar, rocket power, space travel, and atomic energy suddenly had man looking to the sky and beyond, and what he saw defied explanation. The flying saucers offered mankind a hope; a glimpse at something perhaps more stable and peaceful—a civilization that had somehow survived its own technology and sciences. The world had suddenly grown complex on a global scale, and following the assassination of JFK, it seemed that the world was unraveling. This is the environment in which the paranormal thrives.

People who claimed to have been contacted by the space visitors also reflected this message of peace from beyond in many of the UFO cults that arose during these times. Dr. J. Allen Hynek remarked in his book, *The UFO Experience: A Scientific Inquiry*, "The contactee cases are characterized by a 'favored' human intermediary, an almost always solitary 'contact man' who somehow has the special attribute of being able to see UFOs and to communicate with their crew almost at will (often by mental telepathy)... The messages are usually addressed to all of humanity to 'be good, stop fighting, live in brotherhood, ban the bomb, stop polluting the atmosphere,' and other worthy platitudes."[28] Hynek would know, as he had served as an advisor to the Condon Committee, which had been charged with investigating reports of UFOs. Therefore, he had the unenviable job of sifting through the crazies to find the people who may actually have had an unexplainable experience. Hynek laments the fact that the crazy, pseudo-religious fanatic is often what people think of when they think of someone who claims to have seen a UFO, and it's this image that often dissuades otherwise normal people from making a formal report. The congruity between the technological revolution of nuclear technology and the flying saucer invasion is noticeable in some of the flying saucer cults that popped up during the early 1950s. Most notable is George Adamski's claim that aliens from the planet Venus were contacting him. He quickly authored a book entitled *Flying Saucers Have Landed* and set about spreading the message of our "Space Brothers." The Space Brothers, it seems, were very concerned with the plight of humanity during this tumultuous time and urged peace and brotherhood throughout the world. Many similar "contactees" began to come forward with messages from aliens. Supposedly, after meeting with the contactee, the aliens would continue sending messages to their chosen one via mental telepathy, which the contactee would relate to the rest of the group or the world. Invariably, these messages centered around world peace and the inevitable doom that awaited humanity if it continued on its present path. Many contactees would instruct their followers to wait at a specific time and place to be received by an alien spaceship and taken to a new and wonderful world or dimension (depending on the narrative). Jerome Clark authored a brief biography of Dorothy Martin, a contactee who eventually dubbed herself "Sister Thedra" and who acquired a small band of followers. She claimed that the "Guardians" from the planet Clarion were contacting her telepathically to have her warn of coming disaster and to rescue anyone who was willing to listen. However, when Martin told the group that a spaceship was coming to rescue them at a particular time and place, things took an unfortunate turn. "Late that evening Martin received a psychic message that a spaceship was on its way; anyone who was not ready when it arrived would be left behind. For more than three hours, until about 3:20 in the morning, the small band shivered outside in the frigid air. Finally, a message arrived from the space people praising the believers' patience and commitment and releasing them from the vigil."[29]

Basically, the flying saucer cults and contactees were Spiritualism reconstituted to incorporate a narrative of aliens instead of spirits, and superior technology rather than paranormal manifestations. The contactee acted as the medium and delivered messages. While there were no formal séances held in the dark, the messages from the aliens were remarkably similar to the messages from the spirit world. Thus, as Spiritualism was a reaction to major scientific breakthroughs of the earlier century, the UFO cults acted as a cultural reaction to the newest, dominant technological breakthrough— that of the nuclear bomb. Bryan Sentes and Susan Palmer propose a similar theory in their essay, "Presumed Immanent."

> The appearance of UFOs on our historical horizon as objects inspiring religious behavior "stands in compensatory antithesis [Jung]" to the scientific worldview as such and its practical, social, and spiritual effects since the Scientific and Industrial Revolutions, and that this standing "in compensatory antithesis" is ambivalent, being simultaneously an affirmation, critique and transcendence of science and technology and the mortal threats they are seen as presenting (e.g., the environmental crisis and the danger of nuclear war). New religions arising within the context of the contemporary developed world whose sources of revelations are extraterrestrial spontaneously take their space-age deities to be merely natural or immanent rather than supernatural or transcendent, precisely because they exist within the horizon of our postmodern condition (i.e., within the horizon of the death of God).[30]

The contactee cults became religious in nature. Many of the contactees claimed to speak with Jesus and various other religious figures or claimed that Jesus was, in fact, an alien. The idea of aliens replacing God coalesced in Erich von Däniken's best-seller *Chariots of the Gods*, which theorizes that ancient visions of God (or gods) are actually accounts of ancient people's encounters with extraterrestrial life and superior technology. Thus, the entire history of the world was being rewritten in terms of technology and science, and people were attempting to adapt to the new era. Man had split the atom, the basic building block of all matter in the universe, and had unleashed hell with it. Great "signs and wonders" appeared in the skies, and newly born prophets warned the world of the dangers of this new technology.

However, Sentes and Palmer clearly point out that while it was technology and science that spurred these fears, it was also science and technology that offered an answer to the threats that faced humanity. "Alongside or bound up with this assumption of science as a naturally evolving universal tendency of life is the belief that the way out of the profound problems industrialization has presented is technological ingenuity itself."[31] Hence, while it was technology and science that had gotten the world into trouble, the space beings would be able to save us because of the superior technology and wisdom they had gained. This is similar to Spiritualist mediums who had claimed to speak with great thinkers and scientists who had obtained new levels of understanding and were bequeathing their wisdom to the medium in order to make the world a happier place. Instead of the long-dead scientist, however, we are greeted by messages from Orthon, the Venusian who contacted George Adamski in the desert.

> He made me understand—by gesturing with his hands to indicate cloud formations from explosions—that after too many such explosions. Yes! His affirmative nod of the head was very positive and he even spoke the word "Yes" in this instance. The cloud formations were easy to imply with the movement of his hands and arms, but to express the explosions he said, "Boom! Boom!" Then, further to explain himself, he touched me, then to a little weed growing close by, and next pointed to the Earth itself, and with a wide sweep of his hands and other gestures that too many "Booms!" would destroy all of this.[32]

There was a darker, more threatening side to the flying saucer craze as well. Reflected keenly in *Earth vs. the Flying Saucers*, the film was released in 1957 and was a fine example of Cold War technological paranoia reflected in the flying saucer fascination.[33] This film is rife with air sirens, anti-aircraft artillery fire, scientists, and underground bunkers. It even has stock footage from WWII of rockets taking off. In this film the aliens seek to take over the world, starting in Washington, D.C. While they would prefer to make the takeover peaceful, the United States' efforts to thwart them result in major destruction and havoc being wreaked across the globe. The film reflects some of the Cold War fears of the time—that of Communist technology that exceeded our own. The Soviets were much quicker in building a bomb than the U.S. government thought they would be, and the launch of Sputnik sent shivers down the American subconscious. In the film, U.S. scientists are brought face-to-face with aliens whose technology is far superior to our own, and this technological superiority means certain death or enslavement by the aliens. Our weapons are useless against them.

However, in the film, the scientists work together to invent a weapon that causes the flying saucers to lose control and crash. During the alien invasion, this ray gun is used to great effect, causing flying saucers to drop left and right. Unfortunately, the saucers crash into nearly every major political landmark in Washington, D.C.—the Washington Monument, the Capitol

Building, and the White House are all destroyed when the saucers are downed by our newest weapon. The symbolism is slathered on rather thickly, but the message reflects the cultural fears of the time—invasion from above, technology run amok, and enslavement to an alien race (Communists). As the public looked to the skies, as the nuclear fears solidified in the American consciousness, as the air raid sirens sounded across small-town USA, the flying saucers were watching and inspecting. Stephen King's experience in the movie theater that day is the height of irony and is probably why he remembers the incident so vividly. As he watched a film that feared a superior alien technology that would be used to take over the United States, the Soviets launched Sputnik, and suddenly the United States was not the technological supremacy in the world, let alone the universe.

Hynek points out the fear that results from the contemplation of beings from another planet when he discusses close encounters of the third kind, UFO experiences in which the witnesses actually see occupants aboard the craft or outside of the craft. "Perhaps as long as it is our own intelligence that contemplates the report of a machine, albeit strange, we still somehow feel superior in contemplation. Encounters with animate beings, possibly with an intelligence of different order from ours, gives a new dimension to our atavistic fear of the unknown. It brings with it the specter of competition for territory, loss of planetary hegemony—fears that have deep roots."[34] The fears generated by flying saucers and the possibility of alien life were oddly similar to some of the fears experienced as a direct result of new technology, the bomb, and the Cold War. A loss of dominance, a threat to American hubris, and subjugation by an alien force were all fears that bubbled to the surface during these tumultuous times.

The fear of invasion from extraterrestrial forces was not completely without cause. During the night of February 24, 1942, a large UFO was spotted over Los Angeles, California.[35] Feared to be Japanese bombers, the 37th Coast Artillery Brigade began to fire anti-aircraft rounds into the sky at the object(s). As the object(s) moved from Santa Monica to Long Beach, the artillery fire continued, but to no effect. Artillery shells returning to earth struck homes, and many people were injured. The object(s) was clearly seen by hundreds of people and military spotlights were trained on it as tracer fire lit up the night skies. The official air force explanation was that the brigade had actually been firing at a weather balloon or had succumbed to panic and was actually firing at nothing at all. These two explanations did not set the public at ease for two simple reasons: by offering two explanations, the air force implied that it did not have a firm explanation for what had been seen, and secondly, it also implied that either U.S. defenses were incapable of shooting down a balloon or were so ill-prepared that an entire brigade had panicked and suffered from some paranoid mass delusion. Either way, the incident did not speak well of our defense capabilities.

A large percentage of UFO reports involved military installations, nuclear warhead sites, and top-secret military bases such as Area 51. This apparent interest in military sites could be viewed as a threatening gesture, as if the aliens were monitoring our military in preparation for an invasion. The National Security Agency, in its assessment of the UFO phenomenon, warned that history has shown that when an advanced civilization meets a primitive civilization, the result is almost invariably annihilation or subjugation of that primitive society. Naturally, we would be the primitive society.

David Seed discussed the American "narrative of invasion" in his article "Constructing America's Enemies: The Invasions of the USA." In it he discusses American cultural fears of invasion, which were being reflected in literature and film.

In the 1953 George Pal film adaptation, *The War of the Worlds*, one of the men who discovers the mysterious "comet" comments that it must be a "sneak attack" by the Soviets. Similarly, in Norman Edwards's *Invasion from 2500* (1964), the sudden appearance of huge black planes that discharge tanks and ground forces after they have gas-bombed the USA is identified by one observer as "probably them Russians." A series of novels and films thus articulates America's fear of its main Cold War enemy by describing the invasion and the subjugation of the USA by communist—which in practice usually means Russian—forces. What became routine comparisons with the communists were deployed to naturalize the reader's sense of emergency. If the Soviets might come, why not even more alien forces?[36]

Seed also draws an indirect comparison between the Salem witch trials and the Cold War fears of invasion by alien forces.

The godly terrain of the emerging nation is described as under siege from demonic, invisible forces that have forced an entry even into the citadel of the home. Mather initiates a long tradition in American writing in which the underside of manifest destiny is explored—the fear of failure, defeat, and subversion. Since Mather's day, invasion has become such a routine term in American culture that it is now variously applied to biological species, terrorism, Chinese agents, businessmen (Japanese and European), and drug trafficking. The proliferation of American invasion narratives in the late nineteenth century coincides historically with the emergence of the USA as an imperial world power.[37]

The fear of failure, defeat, and subversion were bound with the fear of Soviet superior technology. It was a fear that was compounded by the Soviet's rapid development of nuclear technology and their launch of Sputnik.

The post-modern age was thrust upon the world with the thunderous sound and blinding light of the Hiroshima bomb. What followed was a breakdown of the understanding of science, truth, religion, and culture, and suddenly, the world was seeing strange machines in the sky. This is perhaps the most important period of time in the paranormal history of the United States precisely because the commingling of science, the paranormal, and religion began to blur the boundaries of each area. UFO believers augmented science and technology to study the phenomenon, which simultaneously took on religious connotations. Contactees would regularly claim contact with Jesus, Mohammed, and Moses. But even more so, the belief in alien life forced UFO researchers to examine and question the ancient texts upon which most, if not all, of the world's cultures have been built. Examination of the Bible, the Hindu Vedas, and ancient Sumerian texts, as well as cave drawings, Egyptian hieroglyphs, and ancient architecture suddenly became proof of alien intervention rather than social evolution and supernatural gods. The ancient-alien theorists posited that everything we currently believe about the history of humanity is predicated on ancient peoples who believed that alien visitors were gods and worshipped them as such. They also believe that much of the evidence has been systematically removed or ignored by the scientific community because it does not fit with the current worldview of history and humanity.

Thus, this paranormal phenomenon began to blur the lines between science, religion, and the unexplained. In essence, the accusations of UFO proponents against the scientific community and their questioning of science had turned science into a religion all its own. Because the scientific community was unable to remain transparent during their initial inquiries into the phenomenon, and because they twisted information, as demonstrated by Hynek and several others, science began to employ the same techniques as religion. The Condon Committee was told what conclusion to reach before even beginning the investigative process, and science, in its purest form, was replaced by pre-determined conclusions. Religion relies on faith in that which cannot be known. Religious people have faith that there is something greater than themselves. However, science demonstrates similar faith in the idea that the universe could not operate beyond the current scientific paradigm expressed in the physics of Newton, Einstein, and Bohr. When science subverts itself for the purpose of maintaining a worldview, it becomes a religion based on faith in the current understanding of reality, something referred to as "scientism." The dismissal of the UFO phenomenon by many prominent scientists without direct investigation is a statement based on faith. Two scientists examining the same UFO phenomenon can reach two entirely different conclusions—one based on a belief in extraterrestrials, and one based on the belief that extraterrestrial visitations are beyond the scope of reality. Either way, this discord causes the public to lose faith in the scientific community and to doubt their conclusions. As scientists begin to publish their findings and opinions and base their careers upon their assertions, they begin to have an ulterior motive for maintaining their beliefs even in the face of new evidence. Once someone commits to a worldview he or she believes is truth, it becomes very difficult for that individual to change his or her belief systems or even adjust them to accept new data that may threaten that truth. To be fair, this same psychology is overwhelmingly true for proponents of UFO research and belief. Historically, religion has been trying to compensate for scientific findings through molding science to fit their worldview—but often at great cost to religion and the theology thereof. Hence, religions will offer outlandish, ridiculous, or flawed explanations to maintain their worldview in light of some new discovery, evidence, or so on. Similarly, science has offered outlandish and ridiculous explanations for many UFO sightings, often asserting that the witness is somehow mistaking a flying saucer for the planet Venus or a helicopter or any number of common, everyday objects that most people would easily recognize. This simplistic explanation asserts that the sighting cannot be anything that is unknown. Rather, it is just a mistaken witness or a confluence of coincidental events that have created some kind of visual anomaly. Offering explanations that do not begin to account for new information that threatens a set worldview is more a matter of faith preservation. The public recognized this through the efforts of many UFO investigators and through their own experiences with the phenomenon, thus adding to the distrust of scientists and science. This is unfortunate for a variety of reasons, but perhaps the most damaging of all is the loss of a set sense of truth and reality by the populace. For his part, Hynek never truly asserts that there are extraterrestrials visiting the earth, but he does assert that the Condon Committee did not actually investigate the phenomenon, and that their public proclamation that there was no need to further investigate was based on faulty science and predetermined conclusions.

The questioning of science during this tumultuous time in U.S. history coincides with the questioning of nearly everything else in the wake of the nuclear age. Questions of government transparency (as discussed in the JFK chapter), questions of life and death and morality all began in the time immediately following the explosion of the nuclear bombs and the beginning of the Cold War. In this post-modern world, the truth was no longer known or fixed; it had been replaced with belief and blind faith. Institutions such as government and science were no longer trusted, as it was these two, combined, that had developed a weapon capable of destroying the earth, and they had done it in complete secrecy. And all the while, there were discs appearing in the sky, and people telling stories of alien life forms visiting them and warning of humanity's impending doom. While the Condon Committee publicly stated that there was nothing evidential of alien life in the UFO reports, scientists began to come forward with a different story and different conclusions. There were conspiracies everywhere, and the public could do nothing but guess as to the truth—the official scientific inquiry made by the government, or the defectors who claimed different results from their inquiry.

This blurred line of truth continues today and has been exasperated by the new 24-hour media cycle and the Internet, both of which will be addressed in a later chapter; but the chaos of today had its beginnings in the post–World War II culture. Pia Andersson writes in her essay, "Ancient Alien Brother, Ancient Terrestrial Remains," "An intricate spectrum of relationship, both implicit and explicit, seems to exist between today's two dominant constructors of reality: the advocates of science and the advocates of religion. Therefore, following the current trend, regardless of which methodology ultimately proves its position regarding prehistory, populist theories about our beginning and our evolution still may turn out to be determined by rhetoric, marketing skills, and media exposure rather than by solid scientific research that rigorous academics advocate."[38] It is this "intricate spectrum" that the paranormal tramples through like a stampede of wild Sasquatch. The influence of the paranormal comes from the questioning of truth— something that has defined the post-modern era. The flying saucer invasion during this time in U.S. history called into question the truth of science, religion, and government. The reason the public responded so quickly to the reports of flying saucers was because these things in the sky summed up their fears and their questions; they provided proof of something hidden and unknown and denied by all the institutions that were being openly questioned by the public. The United States was no longer safe in the shadow of the Cold War, and the flying saucers encapsulated that fear, whether they offered hope of a better tomorrow or fear of alien invasion.

THE SATANIC PANIC

The 1980s, for all intents and purposes, were a mess; and it wasn't just the big hair, faded jeans, bad music, and cocaine, it was also a paranormal mess. This time period marked a socially amazing reenactment of the Salem witch trials on a national scale known as the satanic panic. Unfortunately, this time period had no scientific or technological breakthrough to which can be attributed a public reaction in the form of paranormal interest. It did, however, have several elements that marked the other periods of paranormal fascination; the Cold War continued, there was the Iran-Contra scandal, and the scandals of past administrations that had come to light, causing more distrust than ever in the government, and enemies of the United States were now feared to be within, rather than without. Similar to the European witch craze, the satanic panic was not the result of ignorant masses persecuting some poor outsiders due to superstitious fears; rather, it was propagated by the elite. Doctors, activists, psychotherapists, law enforcement, and media fueled the belief, distrust, and fear of a vast underground network of Satan worshippers who routinely committed heinous acts of murder, cannibalism, rape, child-molestation, kidnapping, suicide pacts, and Black Masses. Their influence reached all levels of society, including the government, and culminated with the McMartin Preschool Trials—to date the most lengthy and expensive trial in the history of the United States, and which led to every single defendant being acquitted of all charges.

The satanic panic was nearly a perfect storm of conspiratorial fears mixed with paranormal and religious beliefs and fueled by a new form of psychotherapy that would ultimately prove unreliable and downright traitorous. The satanic panic did involve one element of science, and that was the science of psychiatry and psychotherapy, though not considered a science by some. This relatively new pseudoscience was accepted as fact. But it wasn't fact; it wasn't real, and people paid dearly because of it. If the failure of this new form of psychotherapy, known as repressed memory theory, taught us anything, it is that the mind is a very fertile place with some very dark nether regions that can seemingly tap into the collective experience of generations long past. The very same heinous acts that people were accused of committing in the 1980s had been used as evidence against the Christians in ancient Rome and against the Jews and heretics by the Christian church in the Middle Ages. All of them focused on Black Masses, cannibalism, sexual rites, infant sacrifice, conspiracies, and pacts with the devil. But how did the general public, the average therapy patient, or even children come to say and believe all these things? How were they able to lob the same accusations against teachers and parents that had been lobbed at different groups throughout history? Perhaps, if this era taught us anything about psychology, it is that universals do exist in human thought—things passed down from generation to generation, culture to culture. The satanic panic revealed the darkest side of this universal consciousness and the willingness of the masses to succumb to its influence.

Malcolm McGrath, in his work *Demons of the Modern World*, indicates that while the European witch craze had a set theology such as the *Malleus Maleficarum* that reinforced the beliefs, the satanic panic seemingly did not have any theological merit at the time. He also offers the idea that the satanic panic differed from McCarthyism because there was no actual evidence upon which to base these fears.

> McCarthyism went into full swing only after real spy rings had been uncovered within the United States leaking atomic secrets to the Soviets, the USSR had demonstrated its atomic weaponry, and the United States Army had suffered crushing military setbacks to the Chinese communist army in Korea. The logic of the Satanism scare was almost exactly the opposite: the reality of the threat was assumed at the outset, and the search for physical evidence was only to follow in its wake.[39]

However, there was a social mythology regarding Satanism that went back to pre-Christian Rome, when the Christians were accused of some of the very same dark deeds.

Despite McGrath's assertion that there were no incidents of actual Satanism, the 1970s experienced a series of high-profile murder cases that were supposedly rooted in satanic ritual. These newspaper reports of satanic cult killings, sensationalized by the media, would have established the existence of these cults before the panic began. In 1973 a high-profile case garnered national attention when three members of a cult sacrificed a 17-year-old in a satanic ritual. As reported by the Associated Press, "Deborah A. Shook, 22, of Washington, NJ, took the witness stand at the murder trial of a youth she said was the cult's high priest. She told a 12-member circuit court jury that she saw Ross Michael Cochran, 17, bound to a wooden altar in the basement of a rundown rooming house last April and later wiped up the blood after Cochran had been taken away."[40] The murder took place in California, which would later become the epicenter of the satanic ritual abuse scare. Cochran was tortured and then beaten to death with a club in the forest. The article goes on to discuss other mysterious happenings in the area: "Cochran's death came about 18 months after Satan worshippers performed a series of Black Masses, cemetery desecrations and animal sacrifices around Velusia County."[41] Prosecution sought the death penalty.

Another high-profile case concerned the disappearance of eight young women who attended the University of Washington in Seattle, six of whose skeletal remains were found in two distinct locations. "A young Miami woman who recently fled Seattle fearing that a Satanic cult had targeted her

for death may be the key to the solution of a series of apparent ritualistic slayings in the Pacific Northwest, police said."[42] So there was not only a mythological base for the oncoming panic, but also a base in reality resulting from
murders, police investigations, and trials.

Mix into this cultural soup the breakdown of organized, traditional
religions and the breakdown of the family, and you have a perfect recipe for
a modern witch-hunt. The sixties had produced the counterculture, whose
religious leaning began to incorporate the occult/New Age mysticism and
was eventually epitomized by Charles Manson's cult-like family. The
Church of Satan had been founded in San Francisco in 1966, and despite
the fact that they believed in paganism and magic rather than Satan, founder
Anton LaVey made a public spectacle of performing rites and ceremonies to
specifically offend the Christian public. The satire was lost on most of the
Christian base; his words and actions, along with his book, *The Satanic
Bible*, furthered Christian fears of Satanism. Also interesting is the fact that
many of the children in the 1980s were the offspring of this counterculture,
baby boomer generation. However, when their music of peace and love gave
way to Ozzy Osbourne's Mr. Crowley—an ode to the famed occultist
Aleister Crowley—the parents began to get a little nervous. Heavy metal
music was largely blamed during the satanic panic, precisely because many
of the artists made use of the imagery and language of the Black Mass that
had been passed down through the years, and many claimed publicly that
they were influenced by such people as Aleister Crowley. While much of it
was for shock value and youth revolt, it had an unsettling effect on both
parents and media watchdog groups.

So there was an existent mythology regarding Satanism and Black Masses
that had been passed down for hundreds of years, and a mythology that was
primed for an American cultural milieu whose traditions had disintegrated
during the sixties and whose conspiratorial suspicions were largely confirmed
through the seventies. As Jeffrey Victor points out, "Threat rumors about
satanic cults are, therefore, metaphors for a dangerous heresy which threatens
the legitimate moral order of American society, and which is causing the
destruction of American values."[43] Victor also notes that during these times
of difficulty, it is often deeply held mythological sources to which we turn
for answers. "In the cultural heritage of all societies, there exists a ready-
made explanation of the origins and workings of the evil which threatens to
undermine the most cherished values of a society. Anthropologists call this
culturally inherited explanation of evil, a 'demonology.' "[44] Similar to the
Salem witch-hunt, the Satanism scare was a public reaction that turned to
long-held European mythologies to explain the cultural breakdown of

traditions. Satanism and demonology were Christian concepts that began in Europe and migrated to the United States, bringing with them a "culturally inherited demonology."

The fundamentalist Christian community was also primed for the panic, as Bill Ellis points out in his work, *Raising the Devil*. Ellis traces some of the seeds of the panic to the development of the Pentecostal movement in Christianity, which emphasized speaking in tongues while being "filled with the Holy Spirit," which, essentially, amounted to an individual being willing to be possessed by a spirit. This was an effort to gain supernatural contact with God and thereby confirm an individual's or group's beliefs. However, Ellis notes that confirming one's belief system does not have to be limited to conferring with God. Ultimately, conferring or gaining contact with demons or Satan has a similar effect; by confirming the existence of Satan, one also confirms the existence of God. This can be accomplished through various means, including exorcism and the use of spirit contact rituals such as a Ouija board. ". . . Both activities are alike in their goals—to allow participants to participate in the Christian myth directly. In most denominations, believers are passive, with acts of power—prayer, healing, the consecration of the Eucharist—reserved for priests and other institutionally designated specialists. Bible reading and reflection on doctrinal issues may satisfy many believers, but others seek a more direct experience of the divine."[45] The satanic panic was adopted and driven largely by Christian fundamentalist and Pentecostal organizations. Furthermore, Pentecostalism had its beginnings in work of Kurt E. Koch, who emphasized deliverance from demonic possession. For him, physical and mental ailments stemmed from occult and demonic influence, and thus, people had to be delivered from evil through the power of Christ in order to be healed. This is strikingly similar to some of the origins of the European witch-hunt, where people believed unexplainable disease and tragedy were the result of a witch's curse. Oddly enough, Koch was born and raised in Germany and developed his theories there, where more witches were convicted and killed during the European witch-hunt than in any other European country. Koch's focus on deliverance through exorcism opened the door to obtaining direct contact with the supernatural through both demonic and godly sources. His beliefs and teachings planted the seeds for the Pentecostal movement, which found a home in the United States.

There was a mythological, legendary, and theological source for belief in Black Masses, child sacrifice, and satanic conspiracies; the mythology had been passed down for centuries and had become firmly rooted in the American Christian consciousness. Because the things described in these rituals were so profane and so obscene, they acted as a catalyst for unquestioning belief and an assurance that there is true good and there is true evil, thus making the idea of these happenings all the more believable when the medical, media, psychiatric, and law enforcement institutions all began to say that the United States was under siege by a conspiracy of Satan-worshippers. McGrath states that there was never any evidence found indicating actual satanic practices; however, that issue will be addressed in a later chapter.

There have been many books written about this period of time and the satanic panic, largely because it seemed to be an anathema to science, modernism, tolerance, and justice, and, as such, a variety of social and legal causes for this panic have been documented. Malcolm McGrath focuses on the psychotherapeutic influences, Jeffrey S. Victor takes a look at the fundamentalist Christian right, Bill Ellis discusses the legendary lines of Satanism, and Debbie Nathan and Michael Snedeker look at the social-political climate and legal changes that led to the incarceration of innocent men and women.

While belief in satanic ritual was buried in the subconscious of U.S. culture, it needed a catalyst to bring it to the forefront and create a panic. While I have focused on scientific and technological breakthroughs as possible sources for paranormal upheaval, the catalyst for the satanic panic was different. Its origins lie in the institutionalization of beliefs based on "experts" in the field of psychology and therapy. While the JFK assassination and the conspiratorial mindset created by the flying saucer invasion called into question the idea of "expertise," the satanic panic was the ultimate betrayal of the public by a cabal of experts who institutionalized belief in a satanic world conspiracy centered around child abuse, murder, pornography, and power. This belief made careers and fortunes for those who preached its merit on the basis of their expertise; meanwhile, lives were ruined. While there were many roads leading to the panic that have been analyzed in a number of books, they all point to one catalyst that really started the ball rolling—a little book entitled *Michelle Remembers*.

Michelle Remembers was written by Michelle Smith and her psychiatrist, Dr. Lawrence Pazder. The book recounts the therapy sessions during which Michelle brought forth long-repressed memories of her abuse at the hands of a satanic cult in Canada. Michelle suddenly begins to remember these incidents following a miscarriage and quickly begins to recount strange, subjective, enigmatic episodes involving her mother and a man named Malachi. Michelle even begins to manifest physical symptoms related to the memories and spends hours in Pazder's office in tears as the doctor tries to comfort her and encourage her to continue with her memory recovery. The book, poorly written to say the least, paints a picture of a doctor-patient relationship that has stepped far over its boundaries, with Pazder accepting Michelle's story at face value, spending entire days with her, physically holding her in his arms, and Michelle contacting him while he was on vacation with his family. The doctor's conclusion that she had obviously been abused by a highly secretive satanic cult appears almost at the beginning of the book narrative, and is, itself, a fair demonstration as to the nature of human psyche to form narratives out of incoherent babble. Pazder takes Michelle's story without question because of the level of emotion that she experiences during her episodes. However, Pazder was already inclined to believe in such things, as he was heavily involved in the Catholic Church and almost immediately recommended that Michelle confer with a priest. It is also indicative of a poor relationship boundary between psychiatrist and patient in that Michelle had been treated by Pazder for many years prior to these sudden memories. Pazder had lost his objectivity, and Michelle had come to rely solely upon him. The two eventually divorced their spouses and married each other as they went on extended book tours and interviews following the release of *Michelle Remembers*.

Michelle Remembers was a commercial success and inspired attention-starved women across North America to suddenly come forth with "repressed memories" of satanic ritual abuse. The psychiatric community was quick to take up the cause and institutionalize the belief that satanic groups were organizing to perform sadistic acts on children.

Therapy aimed at recovering repressed memories of childhood abuse exploded in North America during the 1980s, conducted by a wide range of practitioners from qualified psychiatrists and psychologists to self-styled therapists with little more training than the attendance of a few workshops and seminars. Over the course of the decade, recovered memory therapy took on the appearance of a social movement. Adherents to the movement suggested that abuse and molestation of children was an epidemic in America, citing statistics that suggested that as many as 38 percent of American women were sexually abused by the time they were eighteen.[46]

Not all the memories of abuse were satanic in nature, but the ones that were captured the media attention and generated rumors, speculation, and fear. It also embedded the idea of organized satanic cults into the American psyche, thus feeding into the Christian mythology already embedded within the general population. Fundamentalist churches seized on the reports as evidence of Satan's work in the world and as a call to arms for Christians everywhere. In particular, the fundamentalist movement had survivor stories such as Mike Warnke, who claimed to have been a satanic high priest in the San Diego area and who released a book detailing his experiences, *The Satan Seller*, in 1973. Warnke claimed that drugs, pornography, murder, and mutilations were all being driven by a satanic underground cult that managed to avoid prosecution through bribes to police and public officials. Warnke's story was taken at face value until 1992, when the fundamentalist Christian publication *Cornerstone* determined that Warnke's story could not possibly be true. "After our lengthy investigation into his background, we found discrepancies that raise serious doubts about the trustworthiness of his testimony. We have uncovered significant evidence contradicting his alleged satanic activity. His testimony contains major conflicts from book to book and tape to book, it contains significant internal problems, and it doesn't square with known external times and events. Further, we have documentation and eyewitness testimony that contradict the claims he has made about himself."[47] Warnke's ministry had told an entire generation of youth about the perils and practices of Satanism. He also made a bit of money in doing so; his personal salary in 1991 totaled $303,840.[48] Having been raised in a fundamentalist Christian church, I personally remember Mike Warnke's testimony and his stand-up comedy. His videos were shown to the youth of the church for entertainment, education, and to warn about the insidious satanic underground, of which he professed to have been a part. Warnke was a major contributor to the church involvement in the satanic panic during the 1980s.

The media, likewise, needed no help in sensationalizing reports involving occult activities and Satanism. Throughout the seventies and eighties popular attention to these incidents were only increased through the theatrical release of cult-based films and books. Furthermore, there were major murder cases in which the defendants claimed they had been involved with Satanism or committed the act due to satanic influences. Among the more sensationalized were the Richard Ramirez "Nightstalker" case, the Son of Sam case, and the Matamoros Mexican murders, in which a U.S. college student on spring break was ritually murdered by a drug cartel seeking protection from spirits against capture or prosecution. Understandably, these reports generated great concern in the public that actual satanic cults were at work in the United States and internationally.

But the media interest and sensationalism regarding the possibility of satanic practices had always been there, and the Christian church had regularly been warning against the presence of evil cults all throughout the seventies, particularly following Warnke's story. What truly sparked the panic was the assertion by doctors and therapists in the field of psychiatry that these stories were, in fact, true. They then institutionalized the beliefs by making them both secular and a *cause célèbre* for championing activists and professionals trying to make a name for themselves. Furthermore, law enforcement was relying on the testimony of "survivors" such as Michelle Smith and doctors such as Lawrence Pazder for advice and education about these cults and their practices.

In short, if your local church, your local newspaper, your doctor, and the police all tell you that something is true and dangerous, are you really going to risk ignoring the warning? As Jeffrey S. Victor points out, nearly all the panics were in rural areas of the United States, rarely in the cities where people were more focused on immediate threats such as robbery, gang violence, and so on. Rather, the satanic panic effected suburbia and the quiet little towns that dot the United States and form the essence of the traditional American dream; and it was here that the fear of satanic cults—an opposition to those American dreams and values—found its home.

The institutionalization of the satanic cult myth truly coalesced around the McMartin Preschool trials. The accusations against the owner and employees of McMartin Preschool in California were first made by Judy Johnson, a woman later diagnosed as a paranoid schizophrenic who could barely form an intelligible sentence and died of alcoholism.[49] Due to changes in the existing laws and procedures for police, the job of interviewing the children was turned over to social workers and child therapists, who videotaped the sessions so that the children would not have to be put through the stress of testifying in court. However, the therapists' tactics left much to be desired by objective standards; they had already solidified their positions in psychiatric and therapeutic circles as "experts" in the field of child sexual abuse. One of the chief therapists was Kathleen "Kee" MacFarlane, who developed the idea of using anatomically correct dolls to interview the children, who had supposedly been abused, without doing any testing on the reactions of non-abused children to the dolls. She also developed and served on the board of many organizations whose designated mission was to protect children from forms of sexual and ritual satanic abuse. MacFarlane's own Children's Institute International conducted over four hundred interviews of the children who attended the McMartin Preschool and concluded that a vast majority of them had been sexually molested. MacFarlane went on to testify before Congress that there was a vast underground network in the United States that specialized in sexually abusing children and distributing child pornography—a claim that was later debunked by law enforcement.

Another key player in the McMartin accusations was Dr. Bruce Woodling, who developed untested methods for determining if a child had been sexually molested. His methods were themselves disturbing for the children to undertake. However, he was appointed chief examiner for evidence of rape in Southern California and was called in to examine the children of the McMartin Preschool. Woodling believed that by examining in very close detail marks and fissures on children's vaginas and anuses, he could determine whether or not the child had been molested, regardless of the child's testimony. According to his own testimony under cross-examination, he stated, "It is my belief that sometimes children will say that nothing happened because they have a great deal of difficulty talking about the issue..."[50] Woodling's methods were later discredited, but because the field of rape and molestation research was so young at the time, his opinions were given merit. However, it is clear that in many instances, his examinations were far worse than any imagined molestation: "At trial, he repeated his findings while the jury stared at his exhibits: jumbo photographs of the sisters' vaginas and rectums being pulled open by his fingers."[51]

Just as in the European witch craze, the true criminals dabbling in black arts were the accusers rather than the accused. What truly solidified the satanic panic, however, was the newly invented diagnosis of repressed memory disorder (RMD) and resurgence in the diagnosis of multiple personality disorder (MPD). Psychiatrists, academics, and therapists began to claim that a vast network of conspiratorial, underground Satanists were at work in all levels of society and regularly kidnapping, molesting, and sacrificing children to their dark lord. Malcolm McGrath expertly and definitively traces the progression of this diagnosis and its impact on the satanic panic, and documents the ascension of many of the RMD and MPD "experts" into positions of power and prestige in the psychiatric community. Armed with such intellectual firepower, there is hardly any wonder that people began to fear a satanic underground at work in the United States. As these "experts" began to disseminate their opinions and "information" to law enforcement, the media, and the public, cultural fears based on satanic mythology and religious theology were given the catalyst necessary to create a public panic.

These doctors became heads of organizations and hospitals. They spoke at conferences and symposiums, they offered advice to police and investigators, and they trained new psychiatrists and therapists in their belief systems. Dr. Bennett Braun and his partner, Dr. Roberta Sachs, opened a clinic in St. Luke's Presbyterian Hospital devoted entirely to multiple personality disorder. They were later successfully sued for ruining people's lives and leading them to believe, through the use of hypnosis and drug therapy, that they had been abused in satanic ritual abuse cults.

> Over the course of [Braun's] therapy, Anne's satanic cult story became increasingly detailed. She learned that her family had been part of the cult since 1604; that she had been continually raped and forced to cannibalize her own aborted fetuses; and even that, as an adult, she had been a high priestess of the cult to which she had belonged until the time she entered the hospital. Braun took pains to assure her that implausible as many of the details seemed, such as the idea that she had eaten parts of up to two thousand people a year, they would all eventually make sense. He pointed to the fact that people also denied the Holocaust at first. With Braun's help, Anne's story grew into an elaborate conspiracy theory involving AT&T, Hallmark Greeting Cards, the CIA, and eventually the FBI.[52]

Even as late as 1992, Dr. Cory Hammond, at the Fourth Annual Regional Conference on Abuse and Multiple Personality Disorder, gave a speech in which he detailed the origins of a massive satanic cult operating with impunity in the United States. He opened his speech stating, "I've finally decided—to Hell with it, if the cults are going to kill me, they are going to kill me ..." to a round of raucous applause. Hammond detailed a strange story involving satanic Nazi scientists who had been brought into the country following WWII and began to work with the CIA on brainwashing techniques.

> This group of scientists brought with them a Jewish boy named Greenbaum, whom they had spared during their experiments because he was able to tell them the secrets of the ancient Jewish mysticism called Kabala, which squared well with their satanic Nazism ... Eventually, their experiments would become a massive but secret satanic brainwashing operation headed by Greenbaum, who subsequently changed his name to Green. By the 1980s the operation encompassed much more than just the CIA, including NASA, the Mafia, and many prominent business leaders and media figures.[53]

Psychiatrists such as Braun, who diagnosed multiple personality disorder and advocated for the repressed memory movement, were actually participating in an ancient, spiritual practice. Bill Ellis, in his book *Raising the Devil*, cites the similarities between religious exorcism (particularly exorcism in the Pentecostal tradition) and the emergence of MPD and repressed memory. Known as "deliverance" in the Pentecostal tradition, exorcism had gained in popularity as a religious subject during the seventies. An exorcism seeks to identify another being (a demon), which is inhabiting the body of an otherwise normal person and causing them great distress, and then banishes the demon in the name of God. Likewise, MPD psychiatrists sought to identify other "selves" in an afflicted individual and to gradually banish those different personalities from the patient. Much like an MPD patient, the demoniac suddenly changes personalities to reveal his or her affliction. In this role, the psychiatrist acts as the exorcist as he or she confronts multiple personalities (sometimes numbering over 30 in recorded cases), identifies what caused those personalities to emerge, and then frees the patient from the control of those personalities by integrating the patient's mind back into a whole. MPD and memory repression went hand in hand because doctors believed that when an individual witnessed something too traumatic to handle, their psyche fractured and invented another self in order to repress or deal with the stress that resulted. In essence, the doctors who worked with these patients and led them down these nightmare roads were, unknowingly, steering their patients down a path of ancient spiritual myths that had been part of the European and American tradition since before Christ. The themes of ritual child sacrifice, pacts with the devil, cannibalism, and conspiracy had become part of the Western world's mythology—part of its own subconscious. Thus, when trying to understand what horrors could possibly have created these multiple personalities—these demons that dwelled within ordinary people—they plumbed the depths of their own psyches and produced the same story that has been told in differing versions for thousands of years. They mistakenly took on the role of exorcist and became entangled in a snare of belief, superstition, religion, and myth, and a lot of people paid dearly for it. The satanic panic resulted in innocent people being put on trial, families and communities being fractured, mental disorders being created through trauma, and, worst of all, memories of ritual molestation being planted in the minds of many, many children. While Satanism had been a part of Western folklore for hundreds of years, it wasn't until it was institutionalized that it became particularly dangerous and resulted in a public panic.

> Institutional mythologies like Satanism are not folklore, even though they appropriate folk ideas and practices that have been preserved in a given community because they have proved functional for that community's needs. Once appropriated by an institution for a different use, however, such ideas and practices become dysfunctional. Historically, crusades that have been based on appropriated folk beliefs have done more damage than good, whatever truth or good intentions may lie behind them. Sadly, it is easy for institutions to forget this.[54]

As the "experts" and their institutions began to pass down the "truth" about satanic conspiracies, rituals, and practices to law enforcement, the media took notice, and thus the public became informed that a vast underground satanic cult was at work in the United States. Inundated with information, survivor testimony, media blitzes, high-profile arrests and trials, and doctor testimony, the public came to believe exactly what they were told, and rumors began to circulate among small towns that cults were at work in their communities. Jeffrey S. Victor was on scene to document such a rumor panic in rural New York in 1986 and offers a unique, real-time glimpse at the way the satanic panic influenced communities and law enforcement.

The immense variety of criminal activities attributed to Satanism spanned the spectrum from graffiti to kidnapping, torture, sexual abuse, sadomasochistic rape, murder, ritualistic bloodletting, animal sacrifices, and infanticide; all were given a background narrative under the heading "Satanism." With that narrative came the belief that there was a vast conspiracy of people within the underbelly of society that caused these diverse and normally pathologically unrelated crimes to be woven into a singular, definitive problem. The institutionalization of Satanism allowed police, psychiatrists, therapists, and activists to summarily place society's ills into one overarching narrative; a narrative in which they were the key players opening the eyes of the world and saving lives. Unfortunately, while these crimes did occur, the narrative was baseless. The institutionalization of this belief narrative created and fueled the satanic panic until the accusations and stories became too ludicrous for all but the most delusional supporters. The vague definitions of "Satanism" led to the inclusion of nearly everything outside the norm of American beliefs and values.

The irony, of course, rests in the fact that a science, one that delved into the consciousness of man, became so ambiguous and decidedly dark with religious and paranormal foreboding that it became the very thing it feared—a cult whose absolute faith and belief in its own fantastical worldview superceded any objective inquiry or contrary information. The true Satanists were perhaps the very people conjuring these nightmare worlds in the minds of the trusting patients who came to them for help. The true cult was that of the believer and purveyors of this myth, who would often accuse anyone who dared to question their logic as being part of the satanic conspiracy. The darkness was not found without, in the vast conspiracy of satanic kidnappers and killers, but rather, within—in the fears, fantasies, and myths that created a universal consciousness of gothic tales and evil conspiracies.

CONCLUSIONS

Public fascination with and belief in the paranormal increases during times of social upheaval and change, and few things have caused such dramatic upheaval throughout history as development in the sciences—in particular, the major scientific revolutions that truly upended previous worldviews, such as the Copernican revolution, Darwinism, and the atomic age. These scientific revolutions caused people to question previously held beliefs and practices; in effect, they caused a form of social dissonance in which society had to either adapt their previous beliefs to conform with the new developments in science and technology or reject them completely. It was during these times that paranormal beliefs gained massive support and literally formed social movements: the European witch craze, the Spiritualism movement, the saucer panic, and the satanic panic can all be seen through the lens of social dissonance in reaction to scientific development. Of course, there are many other factors that contribute to these movements; distrust of government and government expansion, gender roles, and economic pressure all play roles in the development of these movements, and different authors assign different amounts of significance to each. What is also noteworthy is the role that societies' elite play in the different movements. The European witch craze and the satanic panic were sparked largely by the educated elite such as doctors, theologians, government representatives, and social activists. However, Spiritualism and the saucer panic began from the ground up; they were movements begun and championed by the poor and working class, and only occasionally championed by the social elites.

What is also interesting to note is that nearly every paranormal movement is somehow reflective of Spiritualism in that they all involve communing with the spirit world or, in the case of the saucer panic, other alien worlds that behave and communicate in much the same way. Both the European witch craze and the satanic panic involved a fear of those who communed with the spirit world in odd practices and beliefs, while the saucer panic produced various UFO cults that communicated with aliens in much the same way as Spiritualist mediums consulted the dead and, very often, had much the same things to say. What would appear to change the way these practices are perceived is not the kind of paranormal activity taking place, but rather the world in which it is taking place. The state of mankind changes with each new age and generation, and depending on the environment, the idea of communing with spirits can seem enlightening or frightening.

As stated in the beginning of this chapter, these paranormal beliefs never go away, but they do experience increases in public interest during times of social unrest. As society and the world change, people seek answers from a different plane of existence that cannot be found on this one. Hence, as the scientific revolutions rocked the religious foundations of many societal structures, people began to look for proof, for evidence that they were not alone and that their religious beliefs were valid and true. Faith, it would seem, was not enough in the scientific age—religion required proof to remain legitimate. The paranormal offers to some people that proof, but it is a dangerous game to play because the paranormal is the world of the trickster and it, by definition defies explanation, categorization, and study; you can be made a prince and made a fool all in the same moment. Thus, the paranormal can be as dangerous to the individual as it is fascinating; it can be a road to ruin as much as a road to revelation, as shown by the sometimes disastrous results of the different paranormal movements.

But what of today's world? This age that began in approximately 1998 and is only now beginning to fade, in which people are once again, on a large scale, fascinated with the paranormal and pursuing it both for entertainment and the conviction of beliefs. Now televised across the entire world, this ghost hunter age will be addressed. The rise in paranormal belief systems should be seen as a sign for the nation to look within itself and find what spiritual battle is, in fact, being fought.

Artist portrayal of a witches' sabbat, Francisco Goya (1789). (© M. C. Esteban/Iberfoto/The Image Works)

Dr. Jeff Meldrum examines a Sasquatch cast. (AP Photo/Jesse Harlan Alderman)

Photo of UFOs taken in 1952 by the U.S. Coast Guard. (AP Photo/Shell Alpert)

The Great Pyramid and the Sphinx. (© Joseph Callahan IV. Used by permission)

Gettysburg: America's "Holy Ground." (© Erin McCullough. Used by permission)

Gettysburg. (© Erin McCullough. Used by permission)

One of America's Gothic castles: Fairfield Hills Asylum. (© Gary Hodge. Used by permission)

The "Amityville Horror" house as it stands today, peaceful and dormant. (© Gary Hodge. Used by permission)

The Mothman Statue, Point Pleasant, West Virginia. (AP Photo/Jeff Gentner)

Artist's depiction of a banshee (1912). (© Mary Evans Picture Library/The Image Works)

CHAPTER 7

The Rise of Paranormal Television

On a cold, dark October night a farming tractor makes its way up a mountain road and turns off the pavement into a field of apple trees and corn that overlooks a valley. The tractor tows a cart loaded with bales of hay and about 30 adolescents and adults, huddled together to stay warm, smiling and laughing in anticipation. As the tractor enters the field screams and howls emanate from an acre of maize, a strobe light is flashing in the center of the cornfield, and a chainsaw can be heard revving its rusty motor.

Around a bonfire, more young people are laughing and behind them is the gaping entryway to the "Haunted Corn Maze," one of many local Halloween attractions that host thrill-seeking children, teens, and adults every year. My wife and friends and I have come for a night of fun—to be given a brief scare and some laughs and the possibility of experiencing something that is beyond our realm of normal life—fear.

Naturally, there is nothing to actually fear. We have purchased tickets to engage in a willing suspension of disbelief and allow ourselves to be startled and scared by a teenager in a mask and some creepy music. But why? Why do some people go out of their way to experience a sensation that, for all intents and purposes, should be considered unpleasant? Fear is a natural, biological response to something that is threatening and potentially harmful. It reminds us to run or fight in order to preserve our lives. It is an evolutionary response to dangerous stimuli meant to ensure the survival of the individual and, hence, the species. In the case of Halloween attractions, when someone jumps out at us from behind a doorway or from stalks of corn, we get the initial rush of adrenaline with the knowledge that, in the end, we will be safe.

If fear is the response to dangerous situations that is designed to ensure our survival, wouldn't the haunted maze be more frightening if stocked full of actors dressed as gang members, diseased and poverty-stricken third world villagers, and teenagers with driver's licenses? These present real-world fears with real-world consequences. Instead of a corn maze on the top of a rural hillside, would it not be more frightening to go to the ghetto? Naturally, we want the jolt of fear without the consequences of potential harm. So instead, we travel to a farm with corn and are frightened by actors wearing masks of monsters, ghosts, ghouls, and supernatural killers like Freddy Krueger and Jason Voorhees.

However, why would we find the prospect of ghosts, monsters, and the supernatural frightening at all? It does not represent any biological threat that humanity has ever known, so why would we seek those paranormal figures as a source of fear? Shouldn't they be completely unknown to our sense of fear? Joseph Campbell uses the example of newly hatched chicks that instinctively know to hide at the sight of a hawk or even the shadow of a hawk. "Furthermore, even if all the hawks in the world were to vanish, their image would still sleep in the soul of the chick—never to be roused, however, unless by some accident of art . . ."[1] Is our fear of ghosts, demons, and monsters actually deep-seated memories from ancient times that have left their mark on the human consciousness?

For many people, the haunted maze and other Halloween attractions encompass their experience with and use for the paranormal. It is nothing more than a fun way to have a fright around the harvest. It is something for Stephen King books and John Carpenter movies. It encapsulates a brief jolt—a moment of fun—and nothing more.

But for some others these representations of the paranormal are so much more. They, in fact, represent a worldview, an economy, a source of inspiration, a religion, a dream, and a nightmare. If religion is considered paranormal (which for this work it is), than one can instantly see the influence that the paranormal has on society and the individual. There is often resistance to classifying religion as paranormal; a more accurate interpretation is that religion is a belief system based on the paranormal. Religions are defined by the supernatural, whether it is Christ rising from the dead, Moses parting the Red Sea, or Mohammed splitting the moon. All of these events would be considered supernatural, in other words paranormal, and the belief systems that have developed from those miracles have influenced and continue to influence the world in varying degrees of peace and destruction.

The United States of America is a young nation that hosts a variety of different cultural belief systems held over from people's homelands. But the United States may be developing a mythology all on its own, and the paranormal plays a role in that mythology. The fear that the paranormal creates in an individual is not a real-world fear; rather, it is an otherworldly fear, one that is rooted in the unknown, the darkness, and the mythological divine. It is a more primal fear; not a fear of being hunted by a predator but rather a fear that has its roots in ancient man, when the world itself was the great mysterious. In her book on the history of Halloween, Lesley Pratt Bannatyne writes, "The Celts believed that the dead rose on the eve of Samhain and that ancestral ghosts and demons were set free to roam the earth ... Samhain marked the start of the season that rightly belonged to spirits—a time when nights were long and dark fell early. It was a frightening time for a people who were entirely subject to the forces of nature, and who were superstitious about the unknown, with only a primitive sympathetic magic system to rely on for comfort."[2] With only the firelight in the darkness by which to see, these peoples believed that just outside the flickering light were ghosts and demons, which were let loose during the darkest of days. This change in season also represented a time of hunger, cold, and death. While our practices of celebrating Samhain have changed over the millennia, the recognition that the darkness descending on the land is a time of an unsettling fear remains. It is a fear of the unknown. The darkness represents the great unknown and, in our efforts to conceive of that which cannot be known, the mind creates supernatural figures of frightening proportions. These ghosts, demons, and monsters are symbols, whether real or imagined, of all that cannot be known.

For many people this is the extent of their involvement in the paranormal—a scary movie or a haunted corn maze in October. It is a chance to relive primitive days through the reenactment of the old rites of Samhain. It calls forth childhood fears of the dark and allows us to experience a primitive type of fear with a fun payoff.

As we enter the Haunted Corn Maze, the air is filled with the sounds of otherworldly horror; smoke from the bonfire is wafting in the night breeze and screams from other patrons can be heard above the din of the chainsaw. But, as we enter the maze, the darkness surrounds us and there is nothing—no monsters, no ghosts, no actors. It is desolate and we are alone for a long time, merely winding our way through the annals of the corn stalks. We walk slowly, barely able to see the trail, waiting in anticipation for the coming scare. A group of kids, laughing loudly and walking quickly through the maze, catches up with us and we let them pass by so that we can enjoy the suspense uninterrupted.

There were no scares or actors for the first half of the maze. Rather, it was only darkness and the imagination of what lay behind the layered stalks of corn. That was the truest experience in the maze; the suspense and belief that behind the façade of stalks there was something alien, unknown, malevolent, and frightening waiting for us. All we had to do is walk further into the darkness, further into the unknown.

Those who pursue the paranormal are walking into the unknown. Whether "real" or not, the paranormal represents all that cannot be known about our existence. The same way that every town has a haunted house or graveyard upon which beliefs and fears of the unknown can be heaped, the paranormal, in general, is where we place our hopes, beliefs, and fears regarding the very nature of our existence. Those who use the paranormal for entertainment are subtly engaging in the fear of the existential unknown—letting their primitive selves awaken for a moment before repressing them again in their everyday normal lives.

The use of the paranormal for entertainment is nothing new. Since plays and stories first began there have been depictions of monsters, ghosts, and devils. The relevance between fiction and reality lends to an age-old question: which came first, the ghost in reality or the ghost in fiction? Could ancient man have simply imagined these beings and then cast them into the fictions that proved most entertaining and influential, like the ancient Greek and Roman gods?

The ancient gods were used to explain the unexplainable at a time when science was just on the verge of birth. The gods were a way by which the people understood their world when there was no modern science. If ghosts, monsters, and UFOs are merely creations of the public imagination, such as the ancient gods were, then what, if anything, are these creations seeking to explain? Are these merely symbols of things that the public does not understand—things such as space and time travel, life after death or the complexity of the biological world or the notion of evil? While the use of gods to explain natural occurrences such as lightning and disease were understandable for ancient man, it seems entirely backwards for modern man in this age of science and reason to focus on the paranormal to explain various experiences. It is the intermingling of the scientific world and the world of the unknown, or paranormal, that has been the cause of much of the interest generated in modern society. It is a clash between two belief systems, science and faith— faith not only in religious terms, but faith in the paranormal. The clash between science and faith has at its heart the American way of life and has found a public arena in which to wage its wars—literature, theater, and, of course, television. Similar to the "Scopes Monkey Trial" portrayed in

Inherit the Wind, in which creationism and evolution were pitted against each other to determine whether or not evolution could be allowed in schools, a similar dynamic has been played out between science and the paranormal on television.

The conflict makes for good television as man seeks answers where there have only been questions. Questions such as, Are we alone in the universe? Is there life after death? Is there true good and evil? The conflict and the interest therein has been building for centuries, and in the 1950s it finally received the ultimate medium—the television. Though humble and black and white at the start, television has morphed into a medium almost bigger than the world it inhabits. From our living rooms we watch lions on the plains of Africa, see the intricacies of ultra-slow-motion movement, and visit outer space. Our understanding and connection to the world has grown immensely. It has served our purposes for education, entertainment, economy, and imagination, and more recently, it has become the one-stop shop for everything paranormal.

Paranormal programming has grown to include everything from kids' shows in which tween contestants try to test their ghost-busting abilities in supposedly "haunted" areas, to reality shows featuring séances and demonic possession. They range from National Geographic's scientifically critical *Is It Real?* to the ridiculous and mindless *Ghost Adventures* on Travel. Most fall somewhere in the middle, trying to use science to explain or prove their findings, though never proving the existence of the paranormal nor debunking it completely. The mystery and the conflict between the paranormal and science is what draws the audience. It appears that while the intention of these programs may be to find and "prove" the paranormal, they silently acknowledge that to do so would mean the end of their programming, their jobs, and their income. Hence, it is a balance between the paranormal and the scientific that drives paranormal programming. If a show were to conclude without a doubt that ghosts are not real, they would probably lose the average viewer. It is the quiet hope that perhaps science may not have all the answers, the idea that science can't disprove everything fantastic that maintains viewer interest. Though nothing has ever been proven scientifically on any of the paranormal programs, the idea that the paranormal could be true keeps people watching.

A BRIEF HISTORY OF PARANORMAL TELEVISION

Before television there was radio, which served as the foremost entertainment medium in households until the 1950s and '60s. During this time of radio-dominated entertainment, there was a paranormal scare that swept across a portion of the United States, and suddenly normal, working-class

citizens feared for their lives and prepared to defend against an attack from
alien life forms. This was, of course, the radio broadcast of Orson Welles's
War of the Worlds, which aired on October 30, 1938.

> All across the United States, listeners reacted. Thousands of people
> called the radio stations, the police and newspapers. Many in the New
> England area loaded up their cars and fled their homes. In other areas,
> people went to churches to pray. People improvised gas masks.
> Miscarriages and early births were reported. Deaths were also reported,
> though never confirmed. Many people were hysterical. They thought
> the end was near. Hours after the program had ended and listeners real-
> ized that the Martian invasion was not real, the public was outraged that
> Orson Welles had tried to fool them. Many people sued. Others won-
> dered if Welles had caused the panic on purpose.[3]

Although the program had been buffered with warnings explaining that
the program was fictional, many people missed the announcements, and the
fact that Welles took over another radio program to expand the listening
audience further contributed to the confusion and panic that spread across
the Northeast. Following the radio broadcast, newspapers across the country
gave numerous accounts of the panic, and the incident quickly became a part
of the American paranormal landscape. However, this 1930s radio show was
not the only instance of an entertainment medium reaching, influencing,
and frightening its audience. Bill Ellis defines this as "ostension," which is
the "dramatic extension into real life" of story.[4] *War of the Worlds* was certainly an instance of ostension, and it would not be the last. The history of
the paranormal as entertainment is tainted with the belief that some of its stories are true (for instance, the Amityville Horror), and thus can lead to real-
life action by some individuals.

With the advent of the television, a new medium was accepted into households around the world, and with it came a new blending of fiction, reality,
and the paranormal. The earliest paranormal-based nonfiction program was
Arthur C. Clarke's Mysterious World, which aired in 1980 and explored paranormal phenomena such as UFOs, sea creatures, ape-men, and mysterious
rock formations. The 13-part series was introduced by Arthur C. Clarke, an
author widely known for his science fiction, and narrated by Gordon
Honeycombe. The series documented cases of paranormal phenomena, and
then interviewed witnesses and used science and technology to try to determine whether or not the phenomena could be explained. The answer then,
as it is now, was that while there were scientific theories concerning what
the phenomena might be, there was never any proof one way or the other.

All they had was witness testimony and scientific conjecture, and with only testimony and conjecture, the viewer was left with exactly what he wanted, a mystery. That was, after all, the title of the show: *Arthur C. Clarke's Mysterious World*. It would not have been a good show unless it delivered on the promised mystery. And it is this idea of the mysterious that would find its way through the eighties, nineties, and into the information age. It is the doubt that's left behind after everyone has told his or her story and modern science has offered its best explanation with no verifiable truth or law. It is exactly this rift between what has been witnessed and what can be explained by science that causes the continued viewer interest. It is the mysterious world that the viewer craves—a world without explanation. This documentary-style program set the format for such future programs as *MonsterQuest* and *Is It Real?*, in which scientists examine claims by witnesses in an effort to either prove or disprove the paranormal. Invariably nothing is either proven or discredited, at least to the viewer. The program, no matter how critical, leaves the viewer with a mystery and a dilemma—to believe the word of a seemingly reasonable, normal person or to believe science that has, thus far, been unable to prove the existence of said phenomena. The beauty of this style of paranormal programming is that science rarely stands a chance against the word of the witness or witnesses featured in the program.

The problem is a matter of timing, coincidence, and the burden of proof. Firstly, the scientists have a very limited window of time in which to try to prove or refute a paranormal claim; they must do so while the cameras are rolling. Witness testimony requires no cameras or timing. It is often a thing of coincidence; a couple is walking through the woods and spots a Sasquatch. This is a fantastic coincidence that could take decades for science to replicate, thus science is given a small window of time to explain the unexplainable. Scientific explanation is automatically given the lower hand by means of timing, and as a result, the viewer is left believing that maybe this is a phenomenon beyond the abilities of modern science. Another example would be the investigation of a haunted house. The residents of the home spend 24 hours a day, 7 days a week in the house. The probability of them witnessing a ghostly occurrence is much greater than that of a scientist or an investigator who comes to the home for a limited amount of time to gather evidence of the paranormal. It amounts to fishing in the Dead Sea.

Secondly, there is a very logical argument that is often overlooked in the world of the paranormal, and it explains why science is often so skeptical; namely, that extraordinary claims require extraordinary proof if they are to be accepted. Terence Hines does a wonderful job of illustrating this point in *Pseudoscience and the Paranormal* when he states, "The most common characteristic of a pseudoscience claim is the nonfalsifiable or irrefutable hypothesis. This is a hypothesis against which there can be no evidence—that is, no evidence can show the hypothesis to be wrong."[5] In terms of paranormal programs, this very basic logic is what imbues the documentary style program with the element of the mysterious. In the course of a typical program, seemingly normal, good people will claim to have seen something unexplainable; and science, within the time given, is unable to prove them wrong. However, Hines argues that the burden should not be on science to debunk the claim but on the witnesses and proponents to prove it. It is nearly impossible to disprove what an individual claims to have seen, or, in the case of video or photographic evidence, it is impossible to explain away every single photo or video clip. Something that cannot be explained does not qualify as proof of the existence of the paranormal. However, in the modern documentary-style paranormal program, science is left with the burden to disprove witness testimony and evidence, which is nearly impossible in most cases. Hence, the viewer is left with a mystery. It should be noted, however, that Mr. Hines does believe that science should investigate claims of the paranormal.

> First, the claim may, in fact, be true. Failure to examine it would then delay the acquisition of new, perhaps important, knowledge. Second, if the claim is false, the scientific community, which is heavily supported by the public through taxes, has a responsibility to inform the public . . . Third, several important psychological issues relate to the study of pseudoscience and the paranormal . . . Fourth, and finally, the unthinking acceptance of pseudoscientific claims poses real dangers. Believers may act on their beliefs and cause physical harm, even death.[6]

World of Strange Powers in 1985 and *Mysterious Universe* in 1994 followed *Arthur C. Clarke's Mysterious World*. However, it was in 1987 that one of the most well- known and popular programs involving the paranormal was released. *Unsolved Mysteries* takes a look at unsolved murder cases, missing persons, and unexplained paranormal phenomena, including alien abduction cases, ghostly occurrences, psychic predictions, and Bigfoot. *Unsolved Mysteries* set the standard for reenactment style programming that would ultimately influence Discovery's *A Haunting* and *Ghostly Encounters* on Biography. *Unsolved Mysteries* was narrated by actor Robert Stack and the combination of his deep, resonating voice and the genuinely eerie Halloween-esque music made for creepy viewing. The series was run regularly on NBC from 1987 to 1997. It was then broadcast by CBS for several years and then on Lifetime. Stack eventually quit the show due to ailing health, but the program ran in syndication well into 2008 when Stack passed away. In 2008 Spike Television brought the series back in an effort to ride the paranormal tidal wave sweeping across cable television; the series is hosted by Dennis Farina.

While some claim that *Unsolved Mysteries* was a documentary-style program, it used paid actors, Hollywood sets, and special effects to reenact what the witnesses or victims claimed happened. One episode even featured a young Matthew McConaughey. Furthermore, especially in cases of the paranormal, there was little to no investigation done concerning the witnesses' claims. The viewer was left with only the witness testimony acted out on the screen and perhaps a few cautionary words from Robert Stack stating that "no one knows what really happened and so it remains an Unsolved Mystery." Each hour-long program would generally feature three to five reenactments based on witness testimony. Whether it was a murder, a missing person's case, or the paranormal, the mysteries would be acted out for the camera and narrated by Stack, occasionally cutting to the actual witnesses themselves being interviewed and telling their story. This is the exact same format used by Discovery's *A Haunting*, including creepy intro music and adding special effects that are much easier and cheaper to produce in the information/technology age. Discovery even goes so far as to make a disclosure at the beginning of each episode, which states, "The events depicted in this program are based on eyewitness accounts." While this lack of critical inquiry could be seen as a drawback to the reenactment programs, they do make for entertaining and occasionally scary television viewing.

The third and final type of paranormal program is the reality-based program, which is the most widely used and most-watched program. This type of show rides the wave of the reality-television series by having camera crews follow paranormal investigators through their days as they hunt for ghosts, interview witnesses, and occasionally exorcise homes and people. The cost for producing a reality-based program is relatively low by comparison, and with some fancy editing work can be made to seem very realistic and action-packed as the ghost hunters poke and prod their way through various haunted houses with a variety of ghosts. *Most Haunted*, a British television show that featured some paranormal investigators and mediums exploring some of Europe's most famous haunted locations, inspired this style of paranormal programming. The show became a hit for the Travel Channel as viewers tuned in, not only to watch the exciting and creepy investigations, but also to watch the investigators as well. The team consisted of a psychic medium who could communicate with the dead, a historian, and several investigators, all led by the presenter and narrator, a pretty British blonde named Yvette Fielding. However, despite being quite popular with both British and

American audiences, *Most Haunted* had some setbacks in the form of purported hoaxes that were aired on YouTube. The impact of *Most Haunted*'s style, though, was huge; it has become the most replicated form of paranormal programming to this day. Employing sweeping aerial shots of eerie locales and rehearsed stock footage of the crew gathering their equipment and preparing for an investigation, the actual investigation is filmed in the reality style of programming that has become so widespread and popular in modern television culture.

However, *Most Haunted* was not the first paranormal program to employ this style and stir up a bit of controversy. Probably even more influential was the 1992 faux-documentary entitled *Ghostwatch*.[7] Presented as actual video footage of a real haunted house, *Ghostwatch* investigators filmed a small family being terrorized by the ghost of a former inhabitant. The video footage showed young girls running from their rooms as furniture was tossed about, and it even showed the possession of Michael Parkinson, a BBC presenter, by a spirit called "Pipes." There were mediums channeling the voices of spirits and further possessions of the family living in the home. Interviews with neighbors revealed a terrifying history of the house. A former resident had claimed to be possessed by the spirit of a woman, and consequently, hung himself. His 12 cats were left hungry and, eventually, fed on the body before anyone discovered it.

As discussed before, the program caused a panic and was blamed for at least one death. Once again the paranormal had managed to cross the boundary between fiction and reality by transcending the popular entertainment medium; in this case, television. And it was the second time in less than a century that a new medium had unleashed a wave of paranormal fright and reaction. Only this time, instead of Pennsylvania country folk reacting to an on-air reading of *War of the Worlds*, it was a modern, technologically savvy British public that was misled by the blending of fiction, reality, and the paranormal. It is ostension (as Bill Ellis defines it) in the truest form; the imagined, the mythical, had reached out of the television screen and become reality, and suddenly Britain, for a brief period of time, was under attack by evil, otherworldly spirits. As Terence Hines indicated in his argument for scientific inquiry into the paranormal, "the unthinking acceptance of pseudoscientific claims poses real dangers. Believers may act on their beliefs and cause physical harm, even death."

In this next section we will examine three specific paranormal programs, which can be viewed online (web addresses are provided in the Notes). We will look at the History Channel's *MonsterQuest* as the documentary-style program, Discovery's *A Haunting* as a reenactment-style program, and finally *Ghost Hunters* as a reality-based program. We will examine the motives and methods of each of these programs as they present their cases of the paranormal. Are they real or just entertainment? How close are they to the true stories? And why are they presented in their particular style? This section will serve to deconstruct and analyze these programs based on modern television media and the history of the paranormal in the United States.

THE HISTORY CHANNEL'S *MONSTERQUEST*: "SASQUATCH ATTACK"[8]

"Around the world people report seeing monsters; are they real or imaginary? Science searches for answers on *MonsterQuest*." These are the opening lines for one of the History Channel's more successful paranormal programs, which, as of this writing, is into its fourth season (It was announced in March 2010 that History had cancelled *MonsterQuest* in an effort to pursue a new direction). *MonsterQuest* interviews witnesses and scientists to examine the possibility of the existence of species that are unknown to science, such as Sasquatch, or sightings that are unknown to a particular region, such as sightings of a panther-like big black cat in rural England. In four seasons they have managed to find solid evidence for two possible "monsters": a mountain lion in North Carolina that was previously believed extinct from the area, and a shadowy underwater image of what is possibly a giant, killer Humboldt squid at a depth of 50,000 feet. They have also managed to disprove several monster theories, such as the flying rods that occasionally appeared on camera but which actually turned out to be out-of-focus insects. However, the odds are stacked against *MonsterQuest* when it comes to finding these mythical beasts; do they really hope to prove, over the course of a one-week excursion into the animal's territory, the existence of an animal that has remained hidden for centuries? The answer is no, probably not. While these beasts have had eons of time during which the myths and stories have developed, *MonsterQuest* has only one week to try to find them, albeit using superior technology. *MonsterQuest* is, therefore, immediately at a disadvantage in finding these creatures; but is finding these creatures really the point?

"Sasquatch Attack" begins in much the same way as many other paranormal programs—a presentation of evidence, snippets of witness testimony, and flashes of possible evidence supporting the possibility of paranormal phenomenon. In the case of "Sasquatch Attack" we see an insurance video of a ransacked fishing cabin in the remote wilderness of Canada and hear eyewitness testimony, speculation by amateur cryptozoologists, and a teaser of the action to come with various *MonsterQuest* crewmen coming under attack by the creature and the possibility of DNA evidence proving the creature's existence. This is the part of the program that separates it from a traditional documentary in that the program establishes a dramatic tone to maintain audience interest. It is a form of sensationalism, which, of course, is important to gaining an audience and maintaining interest. However, does it create a disparity in the authenticity of the program and the reputation of the History Channel? The History Channel has long been regarded as a source for accurate, factual documentaries regarding history, both ancient and modern; is *MonsterQuest* a break from that style of programming? Is the History Channel using its reputation in order to gain a wider viewing audience for a subject matter that is most likely unsolvable? It comes down to a matter of audience expectation and trust. The audience watching the History Channel puts more faith in the producers and editors to present a clear and truthful case than do, perhaps, the viewers of the Syfy Channel, where the term "fiction" is embedded into the concept of the channel itself.

Doug Hajicek has never had to worry about money. He is the creator and executive producer of *MonsterQuest*. As a young man he realized that the only way he could pursue his dream of making nature films was to invent something that would make him wealthy so that he would not have to worry about becoming a starving filmmaker living off charity and wild grasses for the rest of his life. So by experimenting with polymers and mixing a few different ingredients that supposedly wouldn't work, he created and developed a new form of polymer that is still in use by car manufacturers 30 years later. Following this breakthrough and the subsequent financial windfall, Doug was able to pursue his true passion without having to live a poor man's life. He became a producer of television programs, the newest of which has become a hit for the History Channel—*MonsterQuest*.

"One of the reasons that the show has been a hit is because, unlike a lot of other documentaries or paranormal shows, we don't have an agenda. Our mission is simply to find out the truth whether good, bad or indifferent," Hajicek said. He went on to reference a BBC program, *X-Creatures*, which was highly critical, if not mocking, of the Patterson-Gimlin Bigfoot video.[9] Hajicek states that it was obvious, from the narrator's tone to the efforts put forth in recreating the beast walking into the forest, that the BBC's sole purpose was to disparage the film and prove that the whole thing had been a hoax. "That really sours the audience to the whole experience. We actually hope that people learn something from our show. People want to be informed, but they don't want to be told what to think."

MonsterQuest, in fact, did not begin as a foray into the paranormal; it was originally a scientific documentary influenced by Peter Jackson's release of the remade *King Kong* film. Hajicek set out to make a documentary about the real "King Kong" that once roamed the Asian continent and may have made its way to North America by crossing the land bridge during the Ice Age. This was a large, presumably bipedal ape species known as *Gigantopithecus blacki* that weighed in at a massive 660 pounds. In the course of their filmmaking, however, they found that many Bigfoot researchers believed Bigfoot was actually an existing *Gigantopithecus*. The subsequent documentary, *Giganto: The Real King Kong*, aired on the History Channel and explored the history and fossil findings of *Gigantopithecus*. The documentary received good reviews and good ratings, so the History Channel approached Doug about doing similar, shorter features, thus birthing *MonsterQuest*.

Hajicek doesn't see *MonsterQuest* as a diversion from the History Channel's mission, but sees belief in monsters and the paranormal as a part of American history and a part of our mythic heritage. "We have this European heritage that has been repressed, we have very little culture in this country, we don't have the ancient culture that Europe or the rest of the world has and our culture seems to manifest itself because people generally do live by the rule of paranormal. You can put religion in that category, you can put a lot of things in that category, but here's the kicker . . . the paranormal is fueled constantly by experiences people are having. Here in America every third person you talk to has had some kind of experience they can't explain, they saw something they couldn't identify, saw something in the sky they couldn't identify, saw something around the corner of their house they couldn't identify, there's something going on constantly that fuels this belief in the paranormal. If it wasn't fueled it would die off." Doug makes the point that there are never reports of unicorns, so we don't talk about unicorns and they are not part of our cultural language. Instead, people are seeing giant bipedal apes roaming the forests, strange crafts in the skies, and apparitions in their attics. "Nobody claims to see unicorns," he explained, "and since nobody is seeing them, the belief is not fueled and it dies off. That hasn't happened for Bigfoot."

Doug, however, has more to base his interest in monsters on than just stories from witnesses. While filming in the Arctic during the summer, Doug and his crew landed their seaplane on an isolated lake in the farthest reaches of Canada. When they came ashore they found footprints lining the sandy beach. They were human-like and massive, and there were hundreds of them walking the shoreline of this wilderness lake high in the Arctic. They followed the tracks as far as they could and then tried to convince the pilot to take them further in search of the animal. He refused, and they were left with only the tracks leading out into the cold wilderness where no barefoot man could survive.

That was what led Doug originally to question the existence of a mysterious creature and, of course, to create *MonsterQuest*. His interest was only fueled as he began to talk to scientists, such as Jeff Meldrum, who were examining the evidence of giant footprints very carefully and putting their careers on the line to explore the possibilities of an undiscovered giant humanoid creature. But Doug was soon going to find himself the subject of his documentaries more than he cared to be.

The remote cabin in the Canadian wilderness featured in "Sasquatch Attack" isn't just a random location that the *MonsterQuest* team decided to investigate. It was where Doug would take his family and friends for some time away from civilization to fish the plentiful waters and stay in a cabin run largely by solar energy and located 250 miles from the nearest town. It was his refuge—his vacation spot, where some nights he would pull his mattress out onto the dock and sleep under the stars. "I felt safer there than I do in most hotels," he said.

The story begins rather modestly when some coworkers that Doug had brought to the cabin claimed that a good-sized branch had been lobbed at them from the forest. They couldn't see who had thrown it and none of them thought very much about it, figuring that it was somehow an anomaly of the wind moving through the trees, much like the groans of a house settling. Years later, while at the cabin with his son who had recently graduated from high school, they heard singing in the middle of the night from across the lake. "We sat there and listened to a very human-like voice singing in a language I could not understand. It sounded native but I couldn't distinguish any words; it was beautiful, almost like opera. It wasn't a bird. It was something big with big lungs that could really belt out a tune. It sounded female, big but feminine and we listened to it for nearly an hour." However, Doug still did not believe that this was anything out of the ordinary; after all, the cabin was in such a remote and strange part of the wilderness that it was like a different world and a different time. "It's like a T-Rex could come wandering out of the woods and it wouldn't surprise you." In essence the enchanting wilderness had lulled them into a dream; and in that prehistoric dream, there was a voice singing in an unknown tongue—something strange, but also familiar.

Then, while Doug and two of his friends were there on a father-daughter fishing trip, things changed and took a more dangerous turn. Following a day of fishing, they heard a loud wood-knock. A wood-knock is the act of knocking a piece of wood against a tree and is often used by apes as a warning to others. It is often cited as evidence of a Sasquatch in the area and is one of the more commonly reported phenomena in the deep northern wilderness.

Around 2 a.m. they decided to wood-knock while sitting around the fire. They received an immediate response that sounded nearly 20 yards away. "We turned white," Doug said. As the wood-knocking continued back and forth, they threw some rocks into the forest. The rocks were immediately thrown back and landed directly at their feet. They continued this strange form of communication for nearly an hour. After the rock throwing ceased they tried several other methods to entice the creature to communicate, but to no avail. They retired to the cabin and all fell asleep except Doug. "I was too wired to sleep so I stayed up and read some magazines." Before falling asleep, Doug went to the kitchen sink to wash his face. "The moment I turned the light on, screaming started at the front and the back of the cabin, things started hitting the cabin and the cabin started getting lifted and shook." He quickly blocked off the skylight in the roof, fearing that something would be thrown through the window and immediately tried to awaken his friends, but they didn't wake. And then, as quickly as it had started, it ended. "It was the scariest moment of my life." Doug's immediate thought afterward was, "we have to get some scientists up here."

Thus, this particular episode of *MonsterQuest* was born from Doug's own experiences with his friends and the experience of the cabin owner who documented the damage done to his cabin by an unknown source. During the filming of "Sasquatch Attack" the crew was lucky enough to have their stone throwing returned, and then, at one point, they were forced to hide in the cabin out of fear.

Laura K. Leuter is the president and founder of the Devil Hunters in southern New Jersey. They, like their Bigfoot-hunting counterparts, collect stories of encounters with a creature known as the Jersey Devil; they gather statistics and conduct field research in an effort to find the legendary beast. Laura and her group have been featured on a number of programs, including *MonsterQuest*, but it was the portrayal of her experience on *World's Scariest Places*, a program on Fox Family that angered her and summed up why many people may doubt paranormal programs such as *MonsterQuest*.

There appeared to be two glowing orbs way off in the distance, at the point from which we had come. We were a little baffled by it at first, and we started to check it out. We couldn't get it on the camera, and the film crew was of course playing it up like it was the best thing in the world. Finally, I had a bright idea—I knelt down and said "I'll put a stop to this" and reached into my bag, producing the night vision goggles. Through the goggles, I discovered that the light we were seeing was produced from a reflection off the headlights of Harry's jeep.

False alarm. Of course, the film crew cut that part out...Of course, before we left, they tried to stump us with fake tracks, which we picked up on instantly. The tracks in the video appeared to be made by a creature that would have had two of the same feet! Neither print resembled anything real, either. And as any Jersey Devil buff knows, the prints are usually hoof-like. This one looked like someone's hand with a few random fingers here and there. The production assistant later told us that Harry had been in charge of creating them for us.[10]

This is the fine line between entertainment and serious inquiry that Doug Hajicek and his crew have to walk, and it is the blurring of this line that causes so many skeptics to critique these programs. Are otherwise reputable scientists convincing themselves that there is a boogeyman outside in the hopes that if they believe hard enough, there will be?

"Certainly if I ever heard of a crewmember doing anything like that, I would fire them," Hajicek said. "Obviously, we have a lot of crews, but if anything like that happened I would deal with it. But I think we do a pretty good job with presenting things as they actually happened. We can't have a boring show, but we can't be fabricating things either. You can dramatize what did happen by adding music and things like that." The third season of *MonsterQuest* marked a return to the cabin in Canada and another effort to entice the creature to come forth. This time Doug went armed with a full budget of gear and complex plans that would keep the crew safe while allowing them to view what was happening outside the cabin, as well as a host of different tracking, infrared, and motion-sensitive lighting and equipment, only to turn up empty-handed. Absolutely nothing happened at the camp. "If I was going to fake something, that would have been the episode," he said. "We poured tons of money into that project and got absolutely nothing." The project was saved by a freak coincidence. The pilot of their transport plane had to touch down 150 miles away for repairs, and while there, they heard that a local woman had spotted a Sasquatch in the area. This led the researchers to theorize that the creature may have been following the seasonal blueberry harvest. Either way, it was a minimal payoff for the money and effort that had been put forth by Hajicek and his crew, and they barely came away with a show.

However, Doug feels that despite having to dramatize certain aspects of the program, *MonsterQuest* has aided the scientific community. Hajicek and his crew have developed new and interesting methods for capturing wildlife on film. He is particularly proud of capturing a glimpse of a giant squid by attaching a camera to a smaller squid, something that had never been done before. *MonsterQuest* is experimenting with new and different ways to find the truth, and while a majority of the time they find nothing but more questions, the process of attempting to answer those questions has led to breakthroughs for modern scientific inquiry. They have developed a laser camera that both films and measures an animal within a quarter of an inch. They found the elusive Greenland shark off a man's dock in fresh water, a species which grows up to 20 feet in length, and they documented evidence that mountain lions were returning to parts of North Carolina where they had been thought to be extinct. Hajicek believes that science is best benefited by thinking outside the box and trying new things, "doing things so bizarre that there was no way it would work." This is Hajicek's scientific method: try anything and everything because, who knows? Scientists can often face ridicule from within their own community by working on paranormal cases. Hajicek thinks that this is "flat thinking" and results in scientists constantly "repeating the past." Doug believes that skeptics aren't necessarily close-minded people, because they are open to finding answers for paranormal experiences as much as anyone else; their findings just differ from others in many cases. Thus, the lack of agreement in the scientific community regarding the paranormal and the numerous eyewitness statements, combined with the numerous possible logical explanations, begin to make the science of the paranormal a matter of faith. "I know that my statements about what happened at the cabin probably don't count," Hajicek said. "I'm a producer of a paranormal television show, but I can tell you that what we experienced up there was absolutely real or else someone was playing a very elaborate hoax on us. I don't know how or why someone would do that but those are the only two options. There is either an animal there or someone managed to pull an amazing hoax."

Doug related one last incident to me—one that never made the final *MonsterQuest* cut because they had all been too scared to leave the cabin, and his eldest son, who had been with them during filming, went into shock. Things such as full-sized logs were being thrown against the cabin with such force that they all figured something was going to come through the wall and kill them. "The reason that never made the show is that I was too afraid, and so was my crew, to get up and investigate because we thought we were going to be killed. That's the simple truth." Doug says that his son, Blaine, has had panic attacks since that night.

Part of the fun of *MonsterQuest*, according to Doug, is the fear of the unknown. But it is a good fear—a fear of childhood wonder, when the world was still an incomprehensibly large, alien place and monsters roamed the countryside. Hajicek only asks that his audience be as open-minded as he is. "I just ask that people look. When I interview a couple who were driving down the road in the middle of the day and saw something large and hairy walk across the road in front of them, and they're too scared to go on camera because they run a day care out of their home, did they want to see it? No, that's probably the last thing they wanted to see. But I guarantee you that from now on they'll be watching the side of the road as they're driving. Once your eyes are opened and your mind is opened to the possibility, you begin to look and realize that the world isn't completely figured out. If you never look to the sky, you'll never know what you missed."

What if the Sasquatch were found? What if tomorrow a hunter showed up with an actual body? The scientific community would obviously be in an uproar; suddenly innumerable expeditions would be made into the habitat of the Sasquatch. The body would be dissected, analyzed, and mapped down to its very DNA. Suddenly the mystery would be gone, and the answers would seem perfectly simple and logical. Men and women would shake their heads and wonder how they had missed it, Animal Planet would carry non-stop coverage, and the endless, ongoing debate would cease to be. What good would it do for the world? Or what harm? What if that never happens? What if Bigfoot is never found and all we have are giant footprints tracing the outline of a lonely Arctic lake? Would it be so bad to watch those prints disappear into the forest and never know for certain what created them? Would it be so bad to keep that childhood wonder rather than having the adult answer? This is the crux of a moral dilemma that quietly plagues paranormal programs that seek the truth—not whether or not finding the truth is possible, but whether or not it is wise to do so. What would change and in what way? These are big-picture questions, cultural and moral and ethical questions that can be overlooked in the near-sightedness of eager scientists, filmmakers, and entertainment executives. Proving the paranormal would be a moral and ethical atom bomb, but was the world better off before or after the atom bomb?

DISCOVERY CHANNEL'S *A HAUNTING*: "WHERE EVIL LURKS"[11]

The Discovery Channel's *A Haunting* was actually the inspiration for this book, as I found a regular source to quench my thirst for horror movies. The program is generally creepy and chilling—a mini horror film that is aired twice a day at 1:00 and 2:00 p.m. respectively, as Discovery regularly shows repeats to fill up daytime slots. Thanks to TIVO, I was able to quickly catch up on all four seasons. But as I watched the program I began to ask myself a few questions. I grew up with the Discovery Channel's Shark Week, stories of space explorations, and film footage of jungles, deserts, and cultures from around the world. It was a respectable, scientific, and informative source of programming. However, with the arrival of *A Haunting*, I began to wonder if we were all somehow being duped. All these people who seemed like perfectly normal, average, hard-working individuals were making claims of paranormal and supernatural events and experiences, and Discovery Channel felt these stories to be legitimate enough to air alongside their regular programming. Were all these witnesses lying? Were they all suffering from some mental disorder? Considering the reputable Discovery Channel was willing to air their stories, considering that I could find no benefit whatsoever to the witnesses in possibly putting themselves up for ridicule, and considering it seemed highly unlikely that all of them were engaged in some kind of hoax or mass hysteria, I decided to look into the matter for myself.

A Haunting began with two specials, *A Haunting in Connecticut* and *A Haunting in Georgia*, both produced by New Dominion Pictures. However, based on the success of the specials, Discovery adopted the idea for a series, and thus began a four-season run of *A Haunting* that continues into the present (It was recently renewed for a fifth season on Discovery's sister channel Destination America). "*A Haunting in Connecticut*" was based on an incident in Southington, Connecticut, involving demonologists Ed and Lorraine Warren, who tried to exorcise a house in the late 1970s that was formerly a funeral home. The owners eventually fled the house, and their experiences were turned into a book, cowritten by the family, that was released in the 1990s. The story has now reached Amityville Horror status with the release of the feature film *The Haunting in Connecticut*, released in 2009. Thus, Discovery's adoption of *A Haunting* has proven successful on a large scale, both financially and culturally.

"Where Evil Lurks" is a particularly fascinating example of Discovery's program for several reasons. Firstly, this was not Casper the Friendly Ghost—this was an entity that was frightening and destructive enough that the Shea family in Arkansas felt a serious need for help that could not be provided by any source other than the Spirit Seekers, a paranormal research group. Secondly, the way it was portrayed in the episode, the paranormal activity was witnessed by a number of different people; the incidents were not confined to one individual having an experience, but by a group of people simultaneously sharing a paranormal experience. Thirdly, the situation was never resolved. According to the program, the family fled the house in the middle of the night and never returned. This aspect of the haunting is particularly fascinating because it actually uprooted a family and caused them to flee a very large real estate investment. Anybody who has ever moved from a house knows that it is not something that is taken lightly. In the Amityville

Horror case, the family also left all their possessions behind, not wanting to stay in the home another moment. There are several similarities to be found between the Amityville Horror and the Shea home in Arkansas, but whether or not these similarities are due to an ingrained idea in the minds of the Shea family due to the infamy of the Amityville house, or because they were both supposedly occupied by demonic entities, remains to be known.

When the Sheas were searching for a new home, they found evidence of satanic rituals in an upstairs bedroom of one of the houses they looked at. Thinking it was only teenagers that had been playing a prank in an abandoned house, they decided to purchase the house and continue with their move as planned; the room became their son's room.

There are two additional influences to consider when discussing the experience of the Shea family: teens who dabble in the occult and the idea that certain regions tend to be haunted. The idea of teenagers experimenting with Satanism, which then leads to a haunting, is fairly common in stories of the supernatural, similar to the desecration of Native American burial grounds. Teenage experimentation with the occult is often a form of rebellion against traditional adult values, but according to paranormal investigators, such activities open portals through which evil entities can enter the earthly plane. Often, the teenagers get more than they bargained for with their occult "play." But the idea of ritualistic Satanism having taken place in the Shea house offers an explanation as to the haunting that followed.

Also, inherent in the story is the land itself being susceptible to haunting. The introduction to each episode of *A Haunting* sets up any given regional area where a haunting has occurred as a place inanely haunted by otherworldly spirits. "The Ozark River Valley once stood as a gateway to the West, a last outpost of civilization before the wilderness beyond. But nestled amid this lush countryside lies a different kind of portal, a crossroads between life and death where the mortal and the eternal collide." This idea that certain regions of the United States are naturally haunted and pocked with portals to eternal realms is a staple of *A Haunting* and reveals the inherent opinion of the program that these stories are to be believed without the need of further evidence. It creates a sense of place and history that is associated with a sense of horror, similar to Steven Spielberg's *Poltergeist*, for which the cause of the haunting was the desecration of gravesites. Thus, it appears that the United States is dotted with supernatural areas that cannot be explained, and "when doors are opened, nightmares become reality." This point is reiterated when Mrs. Shea, while checking out books on the supernatural, talks with a local librarian and finds out that their new home has long been known as a "haunted house."

The Shea family's nightmare begins shortly after moving in. There are sounds of a baby crying when their baby was gone, voices in empty rooms, feelings of being touched by unseen hands, and the appearance of a frightful, reaper-like face in the darkened screen of the computer when Mrs. Shea sits down to type. The final straw comes when Mrs. Shea and her oldest daughter, Tory, are involved in a car accident, which almost claims Tory's life. *A Haunting* implies that this accident was the work of whatever evil forces lurked in the house. The reaper entity had appeared the moment that Mrs. Shea veered off the road.

As Tory recovers at home following the accident, the Sheas finally reach the end of their rope and seek help. They contact the Spirit Seekers, a paranormal research group headed by Alan Lowe. A historical researcher and two clairvoyants, who can communicate with and sense the presence of spirits, join Alan. The group begins to monitor the house using video and audio equipment, and the clairvoyants walk throughout trying to find pockets of psychic activity. Their search comes to a head in the son's bedroom where the satanic symbols had been found. Violet senses myriad different spirits and then, finally, one frightening demonic entity, which has likely been causing all the Sheas' troubles. The Spirit Seekers then perform a séance ritual and use a Ouija board to communicate with the entity. The Ouija planchette moves without anyone touching it. It spells the name SETH and indicates that this being was never human, thus eternal and demonic. The planchette then begins to move rapidly across the board and then stops and points to a television monitor that is trained on the upstairs hallway. The group lets out a collective gasp as a dark figure is seen ambling down the hallway toward Bridger's room.

This is essentially the epitome of a paranormal experience: a dark, frightening figure on camera witnessed by a variety of people. It is a shared experience rather than one individual's story of feeling "like I was being watched" or seeing a figure from the corner of one's eye. This should be the defining moment of paranormal research and programming. If this figure is on tape and can be seen by multiple people, then it would seem to constitute some of the best evidence ever gathered of ghostly and demonic entities. However, this is not the case.

A Haunting is based on witness testimony and only witness testimony. Unlike *MonsterQuest* or other documentary-style programs, *A Haunting* does not offer up evidence or proof of the stories they present. They offer only the story of the people involved as it was told to the producers. Thus, Discovery has already examined the stories and assigned to them a notion of belief. Larry Silverman is the executive producer of *A Haunting* and, while he declined a request for an interview for this book, he was previously interviewed by *iamlegend*, a blogger who regularly posts for The Haunted Report, a weekly report specializing in the haunted house/horror film market. Silverman states that *A Haunting* seeks "to figure out how to tell someone's story and still structure it in a way that is like a traditional Hollywood horror film, but not do anything in which we are making anything up ... We have to submit to Discovery an annotated script, which means everything in the script has to have a source. Whether or not these things actually happened to these people, we don't know. We decided early on that we weren't going to question, we were just going to tell the story as they said it happened."[12]

A Haunting certainly imbues its stories with a horror film quality. Ghostly figures pop onto the screen, demonic entities manifest in dark rooms and in reflections in mirrors, people and things levitate, frightening sounds are heard, ghostly winds blow through closed rooms, and mysterious lights appear down hallways. Alan Lowe, head of the Spirit Seekers, who attempted to rid the Sheas' home of its demons, feels that the special effects in the horror film that depicted the Sheas' experience served a two-sided purpose. "The facts were accurately presented, although some parts were dramatized. This was necessary, in part, in order to impart to the audience the creepy feeling that the home had. I was hesitant about participating in the program in the beginning, for fear of how it would be handled. I was pleasantly surprised that the producers attempted to present events as accurately as possible, while still making the program entertaining to watch."[13] Thus, *A Haunting*, like all other television programs, must remain entertaining to ensure viewers; however, they must balance entertainment with accuracy. Scenes are dramatized using special effects but, as Silverman claims, the stories themselves remain true to the witness testimony. "We turn down a lot of stories," Silverman said, "where people say something happened someplace but it's just anecdotal."

A Haunting, unlike documentary-style programs, is a show. There are sets, art directors, sound stages, special effects—in essence, it is a production. Silverman readily admits that he is a fan of the horror genre, and that the tried-and-true techniques used in creating horror and suspense in film have been recreated in *A Haunting*. However, at what point do the lines between truth and fiction become so blurred that one leaks into the other? Discovery Channel is known for producing the highest-quality nonfiction programming, and viewers essentially expect that something aired on Discovery will be factual and reality-based. While New Dominion Pictures tries to balance between witness testimony and entertainment, sometimes one can get lost in the other. As illustrated before, the culmination of "Where Evil Lurks" lies in the Ouija board scene in which the demon spells out its name and then manifests itself on camera. Alan Lowe was present during this séance and witnessed the events for himself, but they differ slightly from the witness statement given on *A Haunting*. "In the scene with the Ouija board, the planchette did move on its own and point toward an investigator holding a camera. The dark figure seen moving along the upstairs hallway was seen by Violet, who is psychic, and portrayed as she described it." The subtle difference lies in the fact that Lowe seemingly asserts that Violet's gift of being a psychic enabled her and only her to see the figure on the camera, but the Sheas state that they also saw the figure moving through the hallway during an on-air interview. While this is a fairly minor discrepancy, and could, in fact, just be a miscommunication between the different stories being told, it calls into question the most frightening and solidifying piece of the story—a shared paranormal experience between two distinct groups of people, the Sheas and the Spirit Seekers.

Despite this discrepancy between stories and the artistic license taken by the producers, *A Haunting* is still based upon individuals and families who are willing to go on national television and tell a story that may have social and economic consequences. As Doug Hajicek asserted about Sasquatch witnesses, these people don't want to see anything, but they do; they see something they can't explain and begin looking for answers. "Belief in the supernatural is not a matter of faith, but simply a result of being open to the truth. The Spirit Seekers have had some extremely skeptical investigators with no real religious faith; however, they were open-minded and curious. Once a person experiences a paranormal event, it then becomes necessary to understand it as much as possible. When all other explanations fail, people are often convinced that the supernatural is real," said Lowe. Or as Silverman puts it, "If we were just a bunch of writers sitting back saying, 'Okay, what do you want to do this week?' it would be one thing, but we're at the mercy of the stories we find."[14] The question of the paranormal often boils down to the chicken and egg scenario; do programs such as *A Haunting* and groups such as the Spirit Seekers exist because people are having experiences they cannot explain, or are people seeing things that do not exist thanks to the effects these programs and groups have on their imaginations?

The Sheas' story ends a little differently from many others. The family, unable to rid the home of its portal to hell, flees the house in the middle of the night, leaving their possessions behind. In a final scene, Mrs. Shea and Tory are confronted with the demon Seth as he approaches them down the hallway from the son's bedroom. It is a spectacular and frightening finish. It leaves you with the conclusion that it must be real; why else would a family abandon their home? But we have only the witness testimony to go on. However, with regards to the blurring of reality and entertainment, let's take a look at the similarities in this passage from Jay Anson's book, *The Amityville Horror*, a nonfiction work that has been hotly contested as a hoax and was turned into a major motion picture. "On the top step stood a gigantic figure in white. George knew it was the hooded image that Kathy had first glimpsed in the fireplace. The being was pointing at him!" At this point the Lutzes fled the Amityville Horror house and left all their possessions behind.

Witnesses are actively seeking out New Dominion to give credence to their stories, to establish a shared reality through television for these experiences, which they cannot explain; but their story has to be one that is presentable in *A Haunting*'s format. New Dominion and its producers are not writing these stories but simply giving them an entertaining medium through which the world can hear the stories. With all the stories being presented through the wide variety of paranormal programs, or even just the stories on *A Haunting*, it would be foolish to assert that every witness is lying or that every witness is delusional. Perhaps there are those who are looking for their 15 minutes of fame, but what about the witnesses that do not reveal their identities? What are they to gain from sharing these strange, otherworldly experiences? Perhaps it is what Bill Ellis describes as an individual seeking a "belief language" for an experience they cannot explain. Programs such as *A Haunting* help individuals reconcile the real world with the supernatural. The particular format of *A Haunting* allows the witnesses to speak unchallenged by the slew of skeptics that would probably otherwise make them appear to be crazy or liars. It allows them to share more openly experiences that they cannot explain any other way than by assigning them a supernatural quality. The openness of *A Haunting* validates their feelings, their fears and experiences, and allows them to share with the world and be accepted by it through the medium of television.

A Haunting does not hide the fact that it dramatizes the stories for entertainment's sake and does not challenge the witnesses' testimony. However, there seems to be no end of witnesses coming forward to share their experiences. While the format does not seemingly fit with Discovery's long-standing reputation for science-based, nonfiction programming, the fact that there is a segment of the population claiming to have these experiences should be enough to foster some inquiry from serious, scientific-minded people, as well as interest from people that just like a good, creepy story with the possibility that it may be real; that the world is actually full of doors, that when opened, make nightmares reality.

SYFY'S *GHOST HUNTERS*: "WAVERLY HILLS SANATORIUM"[15]

Ghost Hunters can be seen as a merging between the ancient and the new, the past and the present, the spiritual and the material—the ancient belief in ghosts and demons meets *Keeping Up with the Kardashians*. This reality-based program is the culmination of the paranormal in the twenty-first-century United States. The program follows The Atlantic Paranormal Society (TAPS), which is headed by Jason Hawes and Grant Wilson, as they investigate properties rumored to be haunted (when they're not snaking sewer pipes for Roto-Rooter). The style of *Ghost Hunters* may have less to do with fascination with the paranormal than with the voyeuristic thrill of watching the team's personal interactions with each other. Indeed, they have become stars. At a recent lecture given by Grant and Jason, a majority of the questions and comments revolved around the various TAPS members who have come and gone, and there was much fan adoration. A quick visit to their website reveals a slew of advertisements for TAPS clothing lines, TAPS bumper stickers and vanity plates, message boards, and TAPS magazine subscriptions. The places they investigate are largely commercial entities such as taverns, hotels, museums, and historical sites; these places are shown on their website as being haunted, and in this paranormally charged marketplace, "haunted" spells money for these businesses/places, an aspect of the paranormal that we will explore in later chapters. Though they do claim to investigate residential homes, they also claim that much of what they investigate is confidential. The two would not reveal the experiences that led them to believe in ghosts and to form a society that seeks them out.

They have guests that appear on their program to aid with the investigation ranging from fellow investigators that may be local to the area, to WWE professional wrestling stars that walk around the haunted area with EMF readers, searching for voices, sounds, and bumps in the night. Grant and Jason even own an inn located in New Hampshire, which is supposedly the site of paranormal activity. The program is aired on the Syfy channel, a channel that has "fiction" in its name, so how seriously are we supposed to take the *Ghost Hunters?* Alan Lowe of the Spirit Seekers even expressed some concern over programs such as *Ghost Hunters*: "People often seek out Spirit Seekers after seeing a paranormal investigation program, and are relieved to know that we can help them. However, I am suspicious of these programs and their dedication to truth. There are often scenes of 'paranormal' activity that could easily be staged. I think many in the audience may believe they are fakes and can become more suspicious of serious investigators." This statement essentially gets to the heart of the interest and suspicion surrounding *Ghost Hunters*. It is filmed in a reality format, but since it's on television, anything can be edited in or out and anything can be staged (audiences have been burned before by "reality" shows), so people who don't truly want to believe in ghosts remain skeptical. Let us begin by analyzing the "Waverly Hills" episode.

After the usual opening and introduction of the investigators, including an ECW wrestler as a guest investigator, the team assembles outside the sanatorium to discuss the game plan for moving ahead with the investigation. The team has been here before and has had experiences. The sanatorium is located in Louisville, Kentucky, and the team immediately establishes a haunted history to the building. "Over 68,000 people died here" after it was built in 1910 to house tuberculosis victims. It is sacred ground. The narrator adds that the bodies were carted out of the building through the "body chute" to be disposed of. This is a fairly typical investigation site for *Ghost Hunters* and a traditional "haunted house." A history of death under terrible circumstances and the desecration of dead bodies is a common theme in the notion of haunting. The most haunted places in the United States are traditionally places where people died under violent or otherwise horrible conditions such as Gettysburg, the bloodiest battle site of the Civil War, and the Lizzie Borden House, the site of the infamous axe murder of a family. Incidentally, both these places are now historical sites where people can pay an admission and tour the areas. So the Waverly Hills Sanatorium already meets the standard for a traditional haunted house: a history of death under terrible circumstances, and an old, abandoned place where Americans lost their lives, only to be sent down the body chute.

The investigation begins at night. The lights are turned off so that the haunted house notion is accentuated. Night is the traditional time for spirits and ghosts. Owen Davies discussed the influence of the darkness in the seventeenth- and eighteenth-century notion of ghosts. "The night was popularly thought to be the conducive time for devils, fairies and evil spirits to emerge from the depths of hell or the bowels of earth. From a religious perspective of inversion, if God, the angels and the saints were radiant, casting light wherever Christianity was practiced (as iconography depicted them), then it stood to reason that darkness, by contrast, was the natural home of the ungodly and the damned."[16]

In the American tradition we can find similarities between the methods and practices of *Ghost Hunters* and a story from *Scary Stories to Tell in the Dark*, a collection of folklore retold by Alvin Schwartz; a book commonly brought along for sleepovers and campouts. The story "The Haunted House" is about a preacher who spends the night (not the day) in a haunted house to try to end the haunting. While there, he encounters the ghost of a girl who was murdered. The girl leads the preacher to a treasure that he can donate to the church if the preacher can help her bring her killer to justice. She gives the preacher a bone from her finger to put in the collection plate. Whoever the bone sticks to is the killer. When the preacher passes around the plate at the next service, the finger sticks to a man who then confesses to the murder. The preacher is rewarded with a fortune for his church, justice is served, and the spirit of the girl can finally be at peace. Schwartz writes in the notes, "The tale of a person who is brave enough to spend a night in a haunted house, and who is often rewarded for his bravery, is told again and again around the world."[17] Coincidentally, the TAPS team is seeking out the ghost of a boy named Timmy who is said to roam the halls of Waverly Hills. They leave a ball for him to play with to see if the ball moves. TAPS takes the role of the preacher, bravely going into haunted houses to put tormented spirits to rest, tempting them into manifesting themselves so as to communicate with them and perhaps enact some kind of justice.

The ball does move, though very slightly; but it was left in the middle of a hallway that may have had an angled floor and possible airflows moving through the corridor. Still, they assign the movement of the red rubber ball to a ghostly presence. Speaking of red rubber balls and ghostly children, Stanley Kubrick's film, *The Shining*, probably solidified the creepy notion of ghost children and bouncing red rubber balls. Thus, whether purposefully or inadvertently, *Ghost Hunters* touched upon one of the most well-known and influential horror movies in Hollywood history by incorporating a large mansion-like facility, a terrible history, ghosts of children, and bouncing red rubber balls; and the intertwining of fiction and reality create a general sense of history and horror for the viewer.

Meanwhile, down in the body chute, two investigators, a pretty young girl named Kris and her male counterpart, Dustin, make their way into the darkened tunnel. They see something, and both jump in fright. They quickly speculate that they may have seen something paranormal (this entity was not seen by the viewers), and they exit the tunnel with a bit of excitement. Once again, *Ghost Hunters* is tapping into the traditional American haunted house motif; two young people, a young couple, if you will, enter the haunted house as an adolescent rite of passage. Traditional ghost stories and legends often center on youth challenging themselves to face the fear of the unknown, either staying in a haunted house, or walking through a graveyard at night or into a haunted wood. These traditional legends and stories, often passed down through storytelling, have inspired what are now known as legend trippers, people who actively seek out paranormal legends and haunted places in order to test their resolve against the unknown. Legend tripping has become a new rite of passage for some youth, and Kris and Dustin are completing their legend trip in exploring the body chute of Waverly Hills Sanatorium. There is also a sexualized aspect to the traditional adolescent rite of passage; a young couple, alone, in the dark, with the fear of the unknown stretched out before them. It is often places like this, places of dark history and death and rumor, where small-town youths will drink alcohol or experiment with drugs or explore their sexuality. "Witches, were-wolves and the like at first seem incongruous with the desire to get high, but in fact, both are means of escaping from the symbolically sterile world governed by school, parents, and police ... The illicit nature of the sexual adventure is the key: authority figures such as parents, teachers, and other chaperones are united in trying to keep the sexes apart, thus essentially castrating them until the age of socially recognized maturity."[18] The experience of the young "couple" is that of being alone, away from reality and in a threatening place. But it is their rite of passage to brave the unknown realm that is in opposition to what the conventional world has to offer, and their being together entices the audience into thinking that maybe they will break those old social mores of sexuality and experiment. Of course, Kris and Dustin are adults, not adolescents, and while they are not a couple, the program is tapping into our childlike wonder and that need for rebellion, escape, and the possibility of sexual exploration.

The rest of the investigation is studded with similar experiences, subjective jolts of fear, cold spots, feeling that someone or something has touched one of the investigators, highlighted with ECW star, Elijah Burke, shrieking, throwing his hands in the air, and running away. He claims that he felt something touch his face. The investigation is followed by an analysis of the recordings made during the investigation. We watch as the investigators pore over hours of digital recording, infrared recording, and night vision video, occasionally stopping to point out something in the background or a sound that was previously missed. *Ghost Hunters* also features an interactive website where viewers can join the ghost hunt online and hit the "Panic Button" if they spot something the team missed. According to the team, "millions of people" must have been watching and interacting with the show.

Finally there is "the reveal," where Jason and Grant present their findings to the owner of the establishment and make a determination as to whether or not the facility or home is haunted. It is interesting that they chose "the reveal" to head this part of the program. The *reveal* is a term used in magic when a magician, in essence, tips his hand and shows the audience how the trick was accomplished. The incorporation of this term as a title heading for

Ghost Hunters adds an element of trickery to a program whose actions and investigations are already suspicious.

The more interesting human story aspect of this program is at the end of the Waverly Hills investigation, when the audience finds out that many of the investigators were actually auditioning their ghost hunting skills in an effort to be a part of the TAPS team. This allows the drama of competition for inclusion on the team to play out over the next several investigations and also sets the stage for personal dramatic interactions between the TAPS members and the trainees. TAPS is a club, and the newbies are trying to earn their way into the club and onto the show, striving for that little bit of reality television fame.

During the second half of this episode, the team investigates a private home in Massachusetts. This is actually a bit unusual for the program. In the past eight seasons only a small percentage of investigations were performed on private residences. The vast majority of the investigations are done on either historical sites or commercial estates, which get free advertising as being haunted and will reap the benefits (to be discussed later), while the *Ghost Hunters* get a big, spooky haunted house to investigate.

The Massachusetts home was the site of a suicide, and the woman's daughter is seeing a man with "a boo-boo on his head," and she can "see his brain." The child reports this even though she has never been told of the house's history. Over the course of the investigation, they record electronic voice phenomena and an image on the thermal camera that appears to be the upper torso of a man. During the reveal they disclose to the homeowner that her home very well may be haunted and counsel her on how to handle her child's reports. The homeowner seems genuinely pleased to be housing a ghost, even though it is the ghost of someone who died a violent death.

Once again, this is the typical haunted house scenario; the scene of a violent death, a tortured soul still roaming the bedrooms and hallways, and a mother who is gaining a certain level of excitement by staying at the house. Her bravery is being rewarded by both her opportunity to be on television and now her excitement; she will probably also claim some local fame as the owner of a haunted house. This is not to say that this woman is in any way lying or manipulating in an effort to achieve her 15 minutes of fame. Rather, the point is that both the *Ghost Hunters* and the people claiming these places to be haunted are playing roles set forth by archetypes in fiction and film. An archetype is a base story or character upon which many other stories or characters are modeled. *Ghost Hunters* and the people that contact them are, most likely, not doing this on purpose; it's just that the archetypal story of the haunted house and the characters that explore it has ingrained itself into the American consciousness and is unknowingly being played out on television on a national scale. This is not to imply that hauntings are not "real" but instead to illustrate how much fiction has fed into reality and vice versa. The investigations play out like the preacher going into the haunted house in *Scary Stories*. He goes in to rid the house of a presence that is trapped there due to a violent and untimely death. His bravery is rewarded with a treasure he finds for his church. TAPS is being rewarded in a different way; they have achieved fame and money and have "millions of people watching." They claim to receive over 1,500 requests for investigations a month.

Also being played out is the adolescent legend trip; an act of bravery that is rewarded through respect, admiration, acceptance by peers, and, last but not least, providing some excitement and mystery in a world that seems all too real and knowable.

Ghost Hunters is entertaining to watch, though it probably always comes with a bit of suspicion or disbelief as to what we, the audience, are actually witnessing. Are we being duped by a giant, innocent prank being played out on television? Are we merely witnessing full-grown adults scaring themselves in big, dark mansions, or are we actually seeing people experience something beyond their reasoning and knowledge? This quandary forms much of the appeal for *Ghost Hunters* and for all paranormal programming, no matter the format. There have been instances in paranormal programming where fraud was discovered and brought to the public's attention; however, to assume that all the witnesses that come forward in programs such as *MonsterQuest* and *A Haunting* are all collectively lying or are delusional is foolish and reductive.

The archetypes of haunting stories and stories of mythical beasts are played out by the witnesses, the investigators, and the producers in these programs. These archetypes have been passed down from traditional oral stories, to the theater, to the written word, to radio, and then finally to television. The idea of the unknown and mysterious has ingrained itself into the mythos and folklore of the American landscape, and such haunted sites and forests have become proving grounds for both individuals and television networks. These shows are popular. They are designed with entertainment in mind but also, for the most part, to contain the element of truth. Without this element of truth, these stories would be mostly boring versions of Hollywood horror movies; but instead, the public finds them fascinating, waiting to see what science won't be able to explain next.

These haunted sites and stories of mythical monsters connect us to the past. They feed the collective gothic narrative of the United States. Whether in the history of an asylum where tens of thousands lost their lives to an epidemic, or in the stories of Native American tribes that describe a great "hairy man" that roams the forest alone, these paranormal experiences connect our modern world to one that has faded into history. Perhaps these hauntings are the effect of a social conscious that doesn't want to forget our varied and sometimes tragic history. If that is the case, then these television programs are giving voice to that collective conscious and highlighting histories that may have otherwise remained in obscurity. Whether the story of an asylum, a mythical beast, or simply the history of an individual home, these programs give voice to these places, albeit in an entertaining and spooky format.

CHAPTER 8

The Paranormal Reality

There is a reality to what is seen on the programs just discussed. The paranormal world exists outside the television; it exists within the general population, within people who have individual experiences that are outside the realm of their personal understanding. Many of these people, in their search to find answers, turn to certain groups, whether paranormal investigators or support groups, to find absolution and comfort in the fact that other people have had similar experiences. Bill Ellis describes a "belief language" and asserts that when people have undergone a strange experience for which there is no word or expression by which to describe it, that experience becomes a major source of stress. Ellis describes the Newfoundland legend of the Old Hag. The Old Hag was a witch that would sit on a person's chest at night and cast a spell on them. This legend, it is thought, was developed from people experiencing sleep paralysis, a sleep-state in which the mind and body are asleep but the person's eyes are open, and occasionally they see visions. This is often interpreted as an Old Hag experience, or in the case of American cultural language, as an alien abduction experience.[1]

One of the more famous cases of an alien abduction experience came in the form of Whitley Strieber's book *Communion: A True Story*, in which he describes experiences over the course of his life that he fears may have been caused by "visitors." While initially derided by much of the scientific and psychology community, now, 20 years later, Strieber's account appears to be a diary of understanding what it means to be human rather than what it means to be alien. Strieber never states explicitly that the visitors are from another planet. In fact, he offers up many different possibilities, including that they are all in his head. That being said, Strieber certainly believes that he is having experiences for which there is no explanation he is aware of, and therefore they are strange, frightening, and confusing to him. Strieber seeks answers to these experiences and eventually comes in contact with a group of people who have had similar experiences; they are an alien abduction support group that would meet regularly to discuss their lives in the wake of the unexplainable and paranormal. Strieber describes a particular meeting: "I found that my experience had many similarities to those of the support group. We have almost all seen versions of the same creatures. Some of these are small and quick, wearing gray or blue uniforms. Others are taller, graceful, and thin, some with almond eyes and others with round eyes."[2] Strieber refers to this support group as the hidden choir. "The purpose of the colloquy was not primarily to discuss the details of being taken, but rather the experience of coping with it, of trying to live a normal life without knowing for certain what is real, of facing the risk of personal and public ridicule, of finding one's way in a strange world that has suddenly become very strange indeed."[3]

Strieber masterfully describes the difficulty facing a person who experiences something that is incomprehensible and unexplainable. It is a frightening notion that you and you alone have experienced something that appears to be outside the realm of normal accepted reality, and without any cultural belief language with which to describe this event, you may turn to previously held notions of alien abductions, ghosts, demonic possession, and unknown creatures.

Perhaps the most interesting aspect of Strieber's work, and certainly one that pertains to the exploration of the paranormal in American culture, is the fact that he uses these paranormal, alien experiences as a way to better understand himself and mankind. He reflects on philosophical notions of time and memory and battles with the confusion that can often surround our interpretation of our individual lives and histories. "I wrestled with the notion that something might have been happening in my life—real encounters—that were having a tremendous, hitherto unconscious effect on me. Certainly I had acted as if this were true before any conscious memories had emerged. The conscious memories didn't really come before the first week in January of 1986. Yet, as early as the summer of 1985 I had become nervous about 'people in the house,' even to the point of buying expensive burglar alarms and, in October, a shotgun."[4] Strieber's feeling of something else being with him, haunting him as it were, manifests itself in the form of fear and anxiety. His fears that the unknown may, at any time, enact forces upon him causes a snowball effect of ever-increasing fear and anxiety and, for the unknown entity, a greater and greater power.

In this chapter we will see the reality of the paranormal experience that exists outside of the television screen. For every paranormal story told on television there are literally thousands that go untold. The fantasy of television can often blur truth, reality, and entertainment, and paranormal programs such as *Ghost Hunters* and *A Haunting* are subject to producer and editorial revision, rendering us a few steps further from the true story. Here, however, is merely the story of a paranormal investigation team and one of the many families they have helped over the years. There are no television cameras or producers. I personally met and talked with each of these individuals and can firmly say that they truly believe they are experiencing something outside the realm of normal, everyday life.

THE CONNECTICUT PARANORMAL INVESTIGATORS

I found the Connecticut Paranormal Investigators through their website, www.ctparanormal.org. There are many websites advertising many different paranormal research groups in Connecticut (which incidentally is considered one of the most haunted states in America); however, CPI's site differed from the rest. While most websites were cluttered with cartoon-like images of ghosts and links to larger, televised organizations such as TAPS, which is featured on *Ghost Hunters*, this site seemed far more serious and independent. In trying to find an organization to partner with for research I had begun to examine the tip of the iceberg in paranormal studies and organizations, a vast, often inter-connected network of believers and skeptics, investigators and mediums. They all advertised their skills and recent investigations (some notably near to my home), and each had descriptions of different kinds of paranormal occurrences: strange lights, voices in the dark, objects moving on their own, apparitions. It became difficult to choose which organization to contact. I was looking for the "real deal" when it came to paranormal investigators. I wanted to get away from the hype of the television *Ghost Hunter* world and find the guys who actually worked the beat, so to say. I hoped, through this organization, to meet someone who was actually the victim of a haunting. I wasn't looking for some-one who was being haunted by Casper the Friendly Ghost, either. I didn't want to find someone who thought that their haunting was fun or a means of adver-tising their business. I wanted to find someone who was actually scared; who did not want there to be such a thing as ghosts but who was forced to come to that conclusion only through his or her experiences. In other words, I was looking for someone I could trust wouldn't be selling me a ghost story but rather someone who was trapped in one and in need of real help.

And that is how I found Connecticut Paranormal Investigators. When I read the caption on their website I was intrigued and fairly sure I had found the right people. Their homepage reads,

> Are you experiencing paranormal activity? Worried about making that call for help? Don't be. Almost every phone call we receive starts out the same ... Your going to think I'm crazy, but ... If you are having problems dealing with paranormal activity make that call. Don't put yourself or your family through the trauma of dealing with something you can't control. CPI has years of experience dealing with the unexplained and is here to help. We not only investigate. We will work with you on ways to rid your home or business of this problem. There are no guarantees, but our track record speaks for itself.

I guess what I was really looking for was the movie version haunting, an *Amityville Horror* or a *Poltergeist*. I wanted a reluctant hero who didn't see the paranormal as a way of making a quick buck and a name for him or herself. This organization did not glorify the paranormal; instead, its investigators were reaching out and trying to help people who were being set upon by things and forces they could not explain. Their site dealt largely with negative or demonic entities. They were concerned with the effects of the paranormal on children, and their site contained several warnings about the influence the paranormal can have over a family with small children or adolescents. In essence, their organization saw dangers in the paranormal and wanted to help people who had reached their limit in dealing with the unexplainable.

I met Bob Baker and his partner Richard at a Ruby Tuesday's in Connecticut. They were waiting for me in a large black van. Bob was a tall, kind, gentle-looking middle-aged man with his hair swept back from its widow's peak and wearing traditional suburban yuppie attire, a sweater over a collared shirt, jeans, and loafers. He talked very calmly and quietly as we made our introductions. Richard was far more animated. He vigorously shook my hand and talked rapidly and close to me with a deep, grainy voice. He was excited to talk about the spirit world, Christianity, demonic entities. His belief is stitched on his shirtsleeve, but there is something about Bob's faraway look, a quiet disturbance, that intrigues me and makes me wonder what he is hiding. He seems to know more than he cares to share and allows Richard, the animated, charismatic character, do much of the talking as I record our conversation over the music playing in the restaurant and simultaneously take notes.

Bob and Richard have been working in the paranormal world for some time now. Each had previously trained and worked for other organizations around Connecticut. The world of paranormal investigative teams is a bit like the religious community; they all believe the same things, but their methods and dogmas differ from team to team, causing teams to split up and certain individuals to branch off to their own practice. Bob and Richard had both been members of teams in the past but had left for a variety of reasons. Bob and Rich stuck to their ideals and eventually formed their own group. "We've been so busy lately," Bob says. "You wouldn't believe the number of cases we're working on. Some real bad stuff, too."

"Bad stuff" is one of CPI's specialties. What sets them apart from other investigative teams is that a large amount of their work focuses upon evil entities and demonic presences. CPI works with Bishop Robert McKenna of Stepney, Connecticut. Bishop McKenna, an Orthodox Catholic bishop, is one of the leading authorities on demonology and exorcism, having performed over 125 exorcisms in his time. To show me how close they are with the bishop, Bob and Richard each show me a Class 1 precious medal given to them by the bishop. Bob's is a medal of St. Valentine from AD 435 that has a piece of the saint's bone and a small section of his clothing held in a 24-karat gold locket. Richard's is similar but is that of the first American saint, Elizabeth Seton. I had expected a paranormal research team to be run by some former Generation X goth kids, but these were two serious professionals supporting families with their day jobs and investigating on the side. "We do not charge for our services," Bob says, "and we generally don't accept gifts either. We don't want people we help to feel obligated." Richard almost immediately offers to send my wife and me medals bearing the image of St. Benedict to protect us. I kindly accept, knowing that it will thrill my deeply Catholic wife.

I explain to them my project, examining the rise of paranormal beliefs and television programs, and each say they are not surprised, considering the number of people who contact them every week looking for help with the paranormal. When I ask their opinion about such programs, Bob rolls his eyes. "Some of the stuff they do is good and they raise awareness about ghosts and demons, but what they do is dangerous for the people actually living in the home. They come into a home where there may be negative spirits and entities and get everything riled up, challenging the spirits, and then turn off the cameras and leave the next day. Well, what happens the next day? Just because a spirit doesn't reveal itself while the cameras are rolling doesn't mean that it's gone and won't become angry after the investigators leave. The homeowners have to live with that and it can be dangerous." Bob explains that they spend weeks and even months trying to rid a home of negative spirits or helping lost souls travel to the other side. "It's a lot of work and time; it's not just one night and you're done."

As I was a bit confused regarding the difference between negative entities and lost souls that need to "cross over," they explained: a ghost is the spirit of a person who was once alive. These spirits are generally not negative and can be confused as to where they are. Many have been killed unexpectedly and do not realize they are dead, while others may be afraid to cross over into eternity—afraid to own up to their earthly deeds. CPI helps them cross that plane of existence into eternity with God. They tell me about helping a young boy cross over into the light. He was a lost spirit who had died suddenly, and he was looking for his mother in their former home. They contacted the spirit and gently ushered him from one plane of existence to another.

Then there are negative entities, or demons. These are evil spirits that were never alive and whose sole purpose on earth is to terrorize the living. "They hate us [humanity] and they prey on the weak and the sick. They're cowards who will come at you when you are most vulnerable." Richard explains that probably 90 percent of their cases are demonic in nature. "It's exhausting and never easy. Sometimes we just hope for a regular case with a regular ghost." I ask why there are so many demonic cases. Bob looks at me and says, "It's the end times, people don't believe in good and evil anymore and they are completely free to do whatever they want."

"The greatest trick the devil ever pulled was convincing the world he doesn't exist?" I asked, quoting Kevin Spacey from *The Usual Suspects*.

"Exactly. You said it," Richard says.

They explain that a demonic presence must be invited into the home, but people rarely realize what they are doing. They warn of Ouija boards (which are warned against on their website) and divining rods and séances. "People don't realize how old Ouija boards really are. They think it's a game and suddenly they're in over their heads. They're gateways to hell." They also warn of drug abuse and satanic music.

Christianity is a major part of CPI; however, they do not limit their efforts to Christians only. "You have to have some kind of spiritual faith, Christian, Hindu, Muslim, but you need something," Richard explains. "Otherwise, we can't help you. We use God to help us rid these homes of negative presences; but if you don't believe in God, how can we possibly help you?" It was an interesting point they made. If you are calling paranormal investigators because you believe there is a spirit in your house, how can you logically argue that there is no spirit world and no God? "It doesn't matter what your religion is," Richard emphasizes. "But you need to have faith because it is the only thing that will get you through this."

I'm intrigued with the adventure of it all, Richard's enthusiasm and Bob's sly, quiet knowing. They tell me they have a case they're working right now dealing with a negative presence. They have been working on it for weeks, and the homeowner has agreed to let me interview her. After all this talk about demons and exorcisms, I am admittedly nervous. I don't know if I believe in the paranormal, but I also don't want to push boundaries that aren't meant to be pushed. "You will stay with us the entire time," Bob says. "You can never be alone in the house. If you feel afraid or sick at all or see something you can't handle, we'll get you out immediately. Bring a camera and you can do the investigation with us." I, of course, agree to the terms, but first they have offered to meet with me a second time to show me the evidence that they have collected over the years. Numerous photos and videos, electronic voice phenomena (EVP) and recordings of a woman alone in her house being tormented by some unseen entity. We agree to meet again at Bob's house within a few weeks to review their evidence before scheduling an investigation on which I can accompany them.

Almost as a side note, as we gather our checks and prepare to part ways, I ask them if they believe in UFOs. They nod deeply, stating they absolutely believe in them, but not as alien life forms. Rather, they believe UFOs are evil entities that are preparing humanity for something. They tell me to watch *UFOs: The Hidden Truth* on YouTube when I get home.

I return home and immediately go online to find out what possible link there could be between UFOs and demonic entities. What I find is a school of thought about UFOs based on the story of Noah in the Bible. This school of thought believes that in the days of Noah, fallen angels (or Lucifer's minions, demons) bred with human females and caused the earth to become so evil that God destroyed all but Noah's family, whose lineage had remained unblemished. The prediction for the final battle between God and Satan says that the days leading up to Armageddon will be like the days of Noah. Based on this reasoning, it is asserted that UFOs are actually demonic entities that are psychologically preparing the way for Satan to try to claim humanity as his own. UFO abductees often exhibit signs similar to demonic possession and report sado-masochistic sexual manipulation, and UFOs often cause poltergeist-type activity in the home. As Whitley Strieber wrote, he had the feeling that "there was someone in the house," but he could not find that entity (interestingly enough, Strieber is featured in *UFOs: The Hidden Truth*). UFOs, according to this train of thought, are not beings from another world, but evil spirits that are preparing the world for the return of true evil. As skeptical as I am, the idea is frightening, and my childhood memories of church, the End Times, and stories of demons come flooding back to me.

Two days later I received the precious Catholic medals in the mail from Richard. There were two sets of two, one for myself and one for my wife. He wrote in a steady, intense hand on a card, "St. Benedict holding the cross in one hand and the holy rule in the other. The Latin words mean, 'May His Presence Protect Us in the Hour of Death,' and on the reverse side of the cross, the initials mean "Be Gone Satan!"

I brought my wife with me to look at CPI's library of paranormal evidence. She's a psychiatric nurse and has been working in an acute psychiatric hospital for five years. I wanted someone on "my side," if you will, so that I would not feel outnumbered. I also wanted her opinion regarding the stability and sanity of those with whom I was working and what it was we were looking at. Besides, she wanted to personally thank Rich for the medals and, being that they shared similar religious views, wanted to talk with him.

We met Bob and Rich at Bob's house—a big, beautiful suburban home tucked away in community of other big, beautiful suburban homes and in view of a pond with a fountain spraying water into the air. Rich was already there; his Chevrolet Avalanche parked in the driveway looked brand new and just reinforced my opinion of him as an outgoing, charismatic 25-year-old in a 57-year-old body. Rich gave my wife a big hug and Bob introduced himself. The home was warm and roomy, more *Seventh Heaven* than *Ghost Hunters*, but on the dining room table Bob and Rich have assembled several lap-tops with speakers and editing software, digital voice recorders, infrared digital cameras, and plain old-fashioned pictures. Rich and Erin quickly seated themselves on the couch and got acquainted, talking about religion and spirits and viewing film pictures of sinister faces reflected in windows and mirrors, apparitions that looked like fog dancing across the floor of an empty house, and the ever-present spirit orbs that hover in a room.

I sat down with Bob, eager to see what he had to show me and eager to find out a bit more about him, as he was the quieter, more scientific of the two. He showed me a picture taken at a wedding of him and several relatives standing together for the typical wedding photograph. In the middle of the picture, highlighted against a woman's dark-colored dress, was a small dot of light. "See this orb right here?" he said. "It's a demon." Straining to see it, I was a bit disappointed in what he claimed to be a demon. It seemed a far cry from what I had come to expect. I had read about orbs, which have often been proven to be dust particles captured by camera or tricks of light off the camera lens. Even the *Ghost Hunters* on television didn't put much stock in orbs. Bob could see that I was not yet buying into the idea. "I'll show you," he said. He digitally zoomed in on the picture, getting closer and closer to the orb until it appeared to take on a form of its own. "Do you see the face?" he asked, and indeed I did. It was a face like a jack-o'-lantern; a grimacing, menacing, smiling face that appeared to have pointed teeth. It seemed to be in motion, caught by the camera as it circled the wedding party. Then he showed me another picture of an orb and focused in the screen. It was the same grotesquely grimacing face as in the previous photo, but this was at his home and taken years before the wedding. "This," he said to me, "was the demon that I saw when I was child. It took a human form and stood down the hallway from my room smiling at me with that very same face. I could see its eyes and I could see its teeth, and I was terrified. That is why I do what I do today."

This was what Bob had been holding back; this was what kept him drawn in contemplative silence. Terror had beset him as a child, and it would not let him go.

Being a ghost hunter or paranormal investigator can be like standing in the middle of a war zone, a spiritual war zone that tolls casualties of the soul. If you lose control of yourself and surrender to fear, that fear will haunt you until you break physically, emotionally, and mentally. "I hope to one day write a book about it," he said.

I began to ask Bob about how belief plays into the paranormal. What I wondered was: if I'm sitting alone in my house and a book that appeared otherwise stable fell off its designated shelf, should I think "ghost" or just odd coincidence? Do the people who tend to believe that it was a ghost lead themselves down a dangerous path of skewed perception, thinking that everything in their life is somehow being influenced by the spiritual world?

Bob explained that acknowledgement of entities empowers them; they play off fear and belief. Those who don't believe in God or Satan are more easily susceptible to Satan's works, as he can sneak into your life through the auspices of anonymity. Those who don't believe in God are already susceptible to evil's influence; however, those that do follow God are targeted by evil in an effort to break them down when they are at their weakest. And those who only believe in the spirit world but not in God are essentially playing with fire and opening themselves up to a myriad of forces beyond their comprehension. These are the people most susceptible to negative entities and hostile hauntings.

To give me an example, he pulls up video on one of the laptops. Erin and Rich join us as Bob explains the situation. Tim, we shall call him, and his girlfriend were self-described Satanists, practicing and worshipping the anti-God. One night Tim saw something rise up from his neighbor's chimney and flow into his body. He had, in essence, become possessed by a demon. He invited Bob to come to his home and try to help him. As Bob interviewed Tim he became aware that there was definitely something wrong. Tim didn't appear normal. He kept nervously walking around the room, refusing to look at Bob, and becoming more and more agitated. When Bob explained to him that the only way he could be helped was to turn to God, Tim refused and stated that he didn't believe in God. Bob apologized and told Tim that he would not be able to help him with this problem. The video on the computer, however, showed something very interesting. The camera was set in a corner of the room so that both Bob and Tim were visible during their conversation. Every time that Tim turned away from Bob, his eyes became big, black holes, which would then disappear when he faced Bob again. Erin and I watched the video several times over trying to see if it was somehow a glitch in the digital video recorder or some kind of play of light, but there was nothing we could find (not that we are experts, but just using common sense). It didn't happen to anyone else in the video and it did not happen just once. It happened several times over and from different positions where Tim stood. It didn't appear to be a play of shadow and light; rather, his eyes appeared to become deep, black holes, larger than his normal eyes. They seemed to create a cavity where once there were windows to the soul. Erin and I could not explain it rationally. "A demon's eyes are black," Bob told us. "Tim had invited us there hoping that the entity would attach itself to us and leave him, but it didn't. He will be stuck with this for the rest of his life unless he gets help, but we can't help him. The worst part, though, is that Tim and his girlfriend had a young child together." I could see Bob's child-safety consciousness shining through and began to wonder if maybe his profession as a child-proofer for new parents could be the result of his encounter when he was young.

Bob and Rich went on to show us numerous photos. Some were like seeing the man in the moon—it's there if you want it to be, but I couldn't call it reality. Others were not so easy to dismiss; reflections of men in mirrors that were clearly not there, sinister faces appearing in windows and corners of rooms. They played for us electronic voice phenomenon (EVP) they had recorded in the house of a particularly distraught and haunted woman named Billie. EVP are voices and sounds that are recorded in empty rooms by voice recorders. Paranormal investigators believe that these recorders can pick up sounds and whispers not detected by the human ear or sounds that are whispered when no living person is there to hear them. Bob and Rich had left this recorder in a particular room of Billie's house and then had left the room. What it recorded varied between what sounded like a car passing on a nearby highway to what sounded like multitudes of people crying and one particular bloodcurdling scream that erupted from nowhere and disappeared just as quickly. Some sounds I chalked up to passing traffic; others I chalked up to "I don't know what that was, but it didn't sound good."

The saddest and most chilling piece of their evidence was a recording that was made of Billie herself sitting alone in a dark room of her house (her son had moved out because he couldn't stand living in the house any longer). Billie is drinking and smoking a cigarette in the living room and she talks in the darkness to no one in a dead monotone voice. She sounded like the loneliest of the lonely, sad and intoxicated and barely alive anymore. But she spoke to something. "Was that you in the sunroom? I'll put a paper bag on your head and cut out some eyeholes so we can talk. How many of you are there? Who is Nightmare Man? I don't do anything because of you." It sounded like the sad ramblings of a schizophrenic, but there were certain phrases such as "Nightmare Man" and her inquiry as to the number of them that particularly stood out as perhaps something more than mental illness. It was like the time Jesus asked the name of the spirit that had possessed the man at Gerasenes, and it replied, "We are Legion, for we are many."[5] That demon may have been Legion, but this one was Nightmare Man.

During our drive home Erin and I discussed what we had seen and heard. I was particularly interested in her take on the recording of Billie. Erin had told me stories before from her work at the hospital, about children who see demons and witches coming after them, children scrambling on the ground and pointing to the ceiling, screaming in terror while there was nothing visible to any of the doctors, nurses, and mental health workers. She had described to me a young girl who, while talking with Erin, began trembling because there was a demon behind her, talking to her. These stories had always fascinated and frightened me and immediately conjured up the film *The Sixth Sense* in which a young boy could "see dead people." But this wasn't a film; it was real and documented, and nervous, frightened parents had turned to psychiatry to quiet their restless, haunted children.

But I wondered, what if they can just see something that we can't? What if these kids do have a sixth sense, like a dog that knows when its owner is about to have a seizure or the famous cat that stood outside the door of elderly nursing home residents just before they were about to die? What if psychiatry and drugs were just putting to sleep this part of the brain that allows them to see? Reality is basically the agreed-upon perception shared by the majority of the world, and the majority of the world appears to believe that visible ghosts and demons are not a part of reality. However, there are always people who have a different perception; people who think, function, and act differently from the majority—does this make their "reality" and experiences any less real?

"The strangest thing," Erin said, "was that she [Billie] appeared to be responding to external stimuli. She doesn't sound schizophrenic, she certainly sounded depressed, but not psychotic or schizophrenic. It's hard to say one way or the other."

Either way, if CPI could help her, who's to argue?

The night before I was to meet CPI at an investigation site, I was plagued by grotesque, somewhat vile dreams. Had all the research and curiosity caught up to me? Should I actually be worried? Everything that Bob and Rich had discussed with me had been serious, but serious in a cosmic, spiritual war sense. They operated in secret in a world that most people couldn't imagine, wouldn't believe, or would simply choose not to enter. Either way, that morning I was plagued by those dreams and one other rather mundane question: what do you wear to a paranormal investigation? For one, I wore the medals that Rich had sent me. I have said since the beginning of this work that I don't believe one way or the other regarding the paranormal. I consider it journalistic integrity to not have all the answers but just to report—but better safe than sorry.

Interestingly enough, my visit with CPI and a family that had been plagued by paranormal events occurred around the same time as a new horror film was being released, entitled *The Haunting in Connecticut*. It was based off Discovery's *A Haunting* episode by the same name. The episode that appeared on Discovery was, by my own admission, fairly freaky. The Snedekers move to a house in Southington, Connecticut, that was the site of a former funeral home, only to beset upon by demonic forces so powerful that one of the investigators working with the Warrens quit the investigation after having a terrifying encounter with a fully formed demon. These demonic forces terrorized the family, forcing one older son into a psychiatric institution and terrifying two of the younger boys with late-night encounters with ethereal voices and haunting visions of the dead. After an exorcism by two priests, including Bishop McKenna, the Snedekers moved out, and in 1992 helped coauthor a book with the Warrens and horror novelist Ray Garton. They promoted the book on television talk shows and the house became an instant Amityville Horror, Connecticut style. The Snedekers no longer live in the home; they have moved to Tennessee to avoid the press. However, the current owners are not too happy with the infamy. They constantly endure onlookers and trespassers trying to get a view of a ghost or trying to get a piece of the house as a keepsake. The new owners have experienced nothing unusual and feel that the whole story is absolutely false, but still they must deal with the trespass of those who believe.

So much of the paranormal is a combination of what you expect and what you don't. The house we were investigating was not a sprawling Gothic mansion nor was it an isolated ancient farmhouse; but rather, it was a small cape located in a small suburb of Hartford on a steep hill lined with similar houses. It had a small, shrub-lined front yard; chopped wood was piled by the driveway, which held a late-model Infiniti J30. The back was a multilevel wood deck surrounding an aboveground pool. I really hadn't expected a Gothic mansion, knowing how Hollywood loves to increase the amperage on any and all subject matter, but this was still not the typical haunted house. It wasn't the Amityville Horror house with windows like eyes staring out into the night or the Connecticut Haunting house, formerly a funeral home housing the dead. In fact, strange as it may sound, it seemed a bit small to house spirits; I mean, they at least need room to haunt, right?

Outside the house was a small, thin, scruffy man smoking a cigarette and walking a pint-sized dog in the yard. I introduced myself and told him I was there to meet Bob and Rich. He showed me inside and introduced himself as Joe, one of the owners. Inside I am greeted by the small yapping barks of four Chihuahuas and by Joe's wife Kathy, who greets me at the door. Kathy is short and blunt, with an animated look to her that you can read like a book. She is of a particular breed of people who wear their emotions on their sleeve; one can see her thoughts splash across her face, but always with a tenacity that says she is ready to fight for those thoughts. A person who isn't concerned what the world may think of her. I shake her hand and she smiles at me; her teeth are decayed and some are missing, but she is genuinely happy to see me and open with her home.

The inside is surprisingly roomy and immaculately cleaned, decorated with an art deco flash mixed with a real-world, blue-collar sensibility. At a time when oil concerns are at their highest, the living room has a wood-burning stove that heats the house and would probably be featured in a *Better Homes* magazine. Perhaps Joe and Kathy have shocked my stereotype mindset with the interior of their home, but I find myself constantly taking note of all the little details and intricacies of their furnishings: marble countertops, hardwood floors, free-standing shelves with pictures in custom frames. I keep waiting to turn the corner and see two sober intellectuals reading Kant, but Joe and Kathy are more Lynyrd Skynyrd than Bach.

Bob is seated at the dining room table with his laptop flipped open, examining a photo taken of an orb that manifested in a picture directly above their newest team member—a pretty, mystic-looking woman named Rose who has a shock of white in her otherwise auburn hair. Bob introduces me to her and tells me that she is "clairvoyant"—in other words, she has a special sensibility regarding the spirit world. Bob sits me down and shows me several pictures of the manifesting orb. "You can see it gathering energy from around the room," he says as he points out smaller dots of light that seem to be moving in the direction of the orb. "It needs to gather energy to manifest itself." He then focuses in on the orb and again points out the face and what appears to be an arm. "This is a demon," he explains, "that's what we have here in this house."

Richard, on the other hand, is playing with the dogs, giving them treats and trying to calm their jitters. Joe and Kathy are standing in the kitchen talking with Rose, and I overhear a bit of conversation that catches my attention—something about one of her daughters being diagnosed as schizophrenic. I explain to Joe and Kathy why I'm here and what I'm researching and then begin to inquire about their story. I begin asking them about their daughter who was diagnosed with a mental illness. "She doesn't actually have schizophrenia," Kathy said. "She called me weeks ago from her father's house and told me that she stopped taking her medicine a long time ago. She told me that she isn't sick; it's just this house that is the problem. She hasn't heard any voices since she left."

The story of Joe and Kathy's house, Bob assures me, is very typical of a negative presence that has attached itself to a family. Joe and Kathy tell me that they themselves have never experienced anything out of the ordinary. "We hear creaks and knocks sometimes but just figured it was the house settling," Joe said. The children in the house had been the most greatly affected, and that was what led to Kathy contacting CPI. It began with Kathy's eldest daughter, Erica, who was from her first marriage. The problems started about nine years prior, when Erica was sleeping in the upstairs bedroom. She began hearing voices telling her to do things, and she believed that her stuffed animals were coming to life and telling her to kill her youngest siblings—two infant boys from Joe and Kathy's marriage. The voices persisted to the point that Erica had pushed the infants' cribs to the window of the second floor and was prepared to throw them out until she was found and stopped. In another incident she placed the two boys, toddlers at this point, in the middle of the steep road running in front of the house and positioned them in such a way that it was nearly impossible to see them. Again, she was found and the boys were unharmed. After that she was evaluated for psychological problems, but all the while she insisted that the voices were coming from the house and from her stuffed animals. She was diagnosed with schizophrenia and sent to live with her biological father, where she remains today. "Negative presences prey on the weak, and often that is the children," Bob explained.

Following the trouble with Erica, their second daughter, Ashley, moved into Erica's old room. Ashley was Kathy's daughter from a previous marriage whose father had passed away. At about 4 years old Ashley began to wake in the night screaming that there was a man in her room. Joe and Kathy would tell her that it was only a dream, but she repeatedly insisted that there was a dark shadow man in her room. When this "dream" persisted, Kathy began to open herself up to the idea that maybe it was the girl's biological father looking in on her from time to time; but Ashley was frightened and said that it wasn't her father, that her father wouldn't scare her like that. Ashley eventually moved to a room downstairs, but the figure kept returning to loom over her bedside during the following years. Finally, one night she went to the kitchen for a glass of water and the figure stood before her, cloaked in black shadow. It spoke and told her its name.

"What was its name?" I interrupted.

"We can't say the name," Kathy said. I looked to Bob, "You should never speak its name because that calls it forth and gives it power."

"We told her to never say its name," Kathy said, "but she did tell me what it was at the time."

The next day Ashley left a note for Kathy explaining that she couldn't take it anymore, that she couldn't live in this house with the shadow man. Ashley was beginning high school by this time, and she went to stay with a friend. Kathy was now at her wit's end and frightened. It wasn't just the girls—the two boys were also affected. The door to their room would refuse to open, despite there being no locks on the door; a large burn was found on the wall above their bed, but there had been no smoke and no fire and the boys claimed to know nothing about it. Joe explained that he had to replace a section of the wall and paint the room again because of it. The boys would frequently claim that in their nightmares predatory animals would come to speak with them. Wolves and sharks would show the boys their teeth and tell the boys they would eat them. During one afternoon BBQ with family and friends, Toby refused to show off his newly acquired swimming skills because the shark in his nightmare said he would kill Toby if he went in the water.

More frightening yet was 3-year-old Alex's wandering onto the roof in the middle of the night. He claimed that a voice had told him to go out onto the roof in the middle of the night while everyone was asleep. It told him to go to the highest point, which was probably about 35 feet off the paved driveway. Alex went but became frightened, and instead walked the roof to the back of the house where the pool and patio were located. There he managed to hang from the gutter and drop down about six feet to the ground. He stayed locked outside for a couple hours until he was finally heard by the family. When they found him he was trying to stack patio chairs up so that he could climb back on the roof. Kathy showed me exactly where he touched down from the roof, just outside the sliding glass doors. I couldn't imagine the fright a parent would feel knowing that their toddler had been wandering the rooftop at three in the morning.

Amidst all of this, the family was deteriorating. One daughter had already left and was diagnosed as being mentally ill and the other daughter with similar symptoms was afraid to stay in the house any longer. The boys were experiencing frequent nightmares and dangerous nighttime wanderings, and on top of all that, Kathy and Joe were fighting. "You should have seen them," Bob told me when Joe and Kathy stepped outside for a cigarette. "When we first arrived here they were nearly ready to kill each other." It seemed a far cry from what I saw now, though Joe and Kathy did seem to have the potential for an abusive relationship. "That's what a negative entity tries to do," Bob explained, "they try to tear the family apart, break everyone down; and it just feeds off that negative energy and gets stronger and stronger." The house looked calm and serene to me, not the home of bedeviled stuffed animals, shadow men, and knockdown, drag-out marital disputes, but that is what Joe and Kathy's family had been, until CPI came along.

Like many victims of the paranormal, Kathy had thought her family was falling apart, going insane. When she turned to a friend for help, the friend researched online and contacted Bob. As Bob had indicated previously, he has heard the same story many times before. "This is their MO," he said. "They function the same way every time, and their goal is chaos."

After meeting and interviewing the family, CPI called in Bishop McKenna to perform an exorcism on the house. Few people realize that exorcisms can be performed on places as well as people. While Bishop McKenna has performed exorcisms on people in the past, he no longer does so and will only do properties. Following the exorcism, the house was blessed and CPI brought the family together and taught them prayers of protection. "We were never religious before," Kathy said. "But now we pray together as a family." I asked her if she ever believed in the paranormal prior to these events. "Not really," she said. "It wasn't anything that really crossed my mind." Since the intervention of CPI, the activity in the house is nearly gone, but it has taken over a year of working with the family. Bob even commented that he felt like a member of the family because he had spent so much time at the house and knew the family so intimately. Indeed, exorcisms, prayer groups, and fearful children breed intimacy much more quickly than the run-of-the-mill visit, and the family is quite grateful. "We used to fight so much," Kathy said. "We didn't even realize that the stress of it all was tearing us apart, but we're much better now." They had recently called Bob and Rich when the negative energy in the house seemed to be rising again. They wanted it stopped before it grew any stronger.

I, of course, want to the see the bedroom(s) where all this had taken place. Bob indicates that they felt the spirit had been emanating from the master bedroom upstairs where they had previously recorded electronic voice phenomenon. Directly across the hall from the master bedroom was the children's room where both daughters and the boys had previously slept. I keep my digital voice recorder that I have been using for the interview on, and together all of us make our way up the steep, wooden stairs to the second floor and a thin, hardwood hallway that runs perpendicular to the staircase. The bathroom, located in the center of the house, had been torn out to be remodeled. Bob explains (and I am aware from watching paranormal programs) that often a disruption in the structure of the house can lead to a resurgence of activity because the energies are disrupted. In any case, Joe proudly shows off the new bathtub system he has personally installed and the new shower walls made of faux stonework.

We enter the master bedroom, and immediately I can feel a change; there's a sensation of entering a tunnel, as if the walls are closing in. It is a claustrophobic feeling, which is amplified by the rather gloomy, Gothic nature of the room. It is at least 15 degrees colder; a chandelier is suspended over the king-sized bed. The wall is dappled with small mirrors in a puzzle-like framework and the ceilings slant downward at the edges. This part of the house appears much older than the rest; the walls are not the standard sheetrock so common in newly built homes, but rather a hard, textured plaster that probably adds to the ambiance of the room. There are several wall lights, like candles, and a small television area complete with loveseat and chair in a section of the bedroom that is much wider than the rest. It could easily pass for a hotel room charging $200 per night, but there is genuinely something creepy about the room, and I feel it immediately upon entering. Whether it's the textured, angled walls, the chandelier, or the wall-mounted electric candles, the room appears to actually be something out of a haunted house movie, part of an old, Gothic mansion rather than a suburban homestead. As we all gather in the bedroom I notice an eerie feeling that there is someone standing behind me. It is something that persists throughout our time there. I realize that it very well may be caused by what is known as the "funhouse effect." The style of the room plays with your peripheral vision and constantly alerts your brain that there is something at the periphery and makes you want to spin around to find it, only to find that there is nothing there. Rose has an electromagnetic frequency detector, and she scans the room and the closets, occasionally getting spikes in the readings. It is in the small, deep closet that pushes behind the wall to the edge of the house where Bob believes the entity emanates from. From there it works its way throughout the house, including the room across the hall where the boys currently sleep. I wander into their room. There is a set of bunk beds decorated with baseball logos, but the similar lighting and wall/ceiling structure again give me that eerie sense of being followed. I could understand, being young and impressionable and possibly afraid of the dark, how this room could affect a child. Hell, it was affecting me.

We gathered again in the master bedroom in a circle. We each pulled our precious medals or crucifixes from beneath our shirts, and Rich led us in a prayer, blessing the house and the family. Then Bob and Rich went from corner to corner, room to room with holy water blessed by the bishop, sprinkling droplets anywhere an entity could hide and warning away any evil spirits. I followed them throughout the house with my voice recorder and Rose followed with the EMF. We wandered to the basement where we were hit with the smell of dirty laundry and cat litter, the boxes of which sit beneath the stairs. To the right is a two-car garage filled with bikes and toys and tools and to the left there is a large room furnished with a bed, couch, computer, and television. I walked into the room with Rose and looked around. It was dark and gloomy, far from the light above ground, and there is something odd about the bed. It is a full-sized bed, but the head of it sits in what appears to be an old fireplace; an alcove of the wall made of wood and brick and surrounded by darker recesses of the room that go farther back. For some reason, to me it looks like an ominous altar, and my mind immediately begins to wonder about the history of the house. Who was here before? Who is here now? As much as we like to pretend we know people, we are often wrong; and as forthcoming and kind as this family has been to me during my visit, I know little to nothing about them. It is an odd feeling when you're unsure as to what the truth is, especially when you're walking through a stranger's house.

When Bob and Rich are finished blessing the house, they anoint Joe and Kathy with oil, a right bestowed upon them by the bishop. I ask about the history of the house; who was here before? Is there any reason for the haunting? The house was built in the 1950s and occupied by only one family prior to Kathy buying it. So what is the source of the haunting?

"It could be anything," Bob said.

"Yes, but I get a sneaking suspicion that it comes from that house over there," Rich adds. I look at the house next door, a replica of the one I'm standing in. However, the owner, as Joe explains, has a habit of smoking too much marijuana, retreating to the backyard, and engaging in Native American tribal rituals, banging on drums and chanting. "He could have summoned something accidentally and not even know what he's doing."

According to many of the paranormal programs, it wouldn't be the first time that someone had accidentally summoned bad spirits through dabbling in ancient practices. Many ancient religions used to chant and summon demons to sic on their enemies. Something from another world could have been sent to this house through a ceremony that the reefer-smoking neighbor did not fully understand. I am struck by the connection to the ancient ways and customs, good or bad.

CPI had been working with this family for over a year. When they first began, things were bad; the children were frightened, the parents were fighting, and there was a general negativity to the house. After initially quelling the negativity and educating the family on the paranormal and negative forces that can breed in such an environment, things began to calm down. But it took a long time, and the truth is that it may never end. "If something has attached itself to you," Bob said, "it will follow you wherever you go until it is either fully defeated or attaches itself to another person." So CPI's purpose with this family is ongoing. They are always on call for Joe and Kathy; when things start to slip downward into chaos, they come and investigate, counsel them, and bless their house and their family. This is the way in which the reality of the paranormal differs from what is shown on television and what the *Ghost Hunters* do weekly; theirs is not a one-night investigation, but potentially a lifetime commitment. They are spiritual family counselors as well as paranormal investigators; they try to bring people back from the edge of chaos, and whether or not the forces at work in these families are empirically "real" takes a back seat to the real good that they do. Joe and Kathy's family is closer and more at peace with each other than they had been previously, and when they need counsel, Bob and Rich hop in their van and make the hour-plus drive to be with them and lead them toward tranquility.

Can it be proven scientifically? Probably not. But CPI claims positive results across the board, and Joe and Kathy are just two of their testimonials. Bob and Rich see themselves as being on the front line of a spiritual war over people's lives; the negative wants to pull people into chaos, and CPI is there trying to help people stay at peace both physically and spiritually. Perhaps the most eye-opening aspect of working with CPI was realizing that, unlike the movies and television programs, it is not places that are haunted, but rather people.

Not long after this writing, Richard left the Connecticut Paranormal Investigators. Bob cited differences of opinion between him and Rich; while Rich largely handled the religious aspects of their investigations, Bob felt that lines had been crossed. "Instead of calling clergy in on a case, he would want to handle that end of the case himself; and in some of the cases dragged the case out for weeks or months at a time. I decided I no longer wanted to be part of that. This was needlessly making people deal with their paranormal problems much longer then was necessary."

Bob also severed ties with Rose, the medium, indicating that he believed she had been making things up during the investigation. This has always been a problem with mediums, and has occasionally resulted in embarrassing moments on such popular programs as *Most Haunted*. The paranormal community is notoriously polluted with infighting, rivalry, philosophical disagreements, and nearly incestuous relationships between different organizations. George P. Hansen cited a "fluidity of belief"[6] and attributes the difficulty in remaining cohesive and organized as an effect rendered by the ambiguity of the paranormal. "Historically, many groups that attempted to engage paranormal phenomena became unstable."[7] As Bob said, "This is so much the norm in the paranormal community. If you haven't thrown out at least half a dozen members, you better start doing background checks."

However, Connecticut Paranormal Investigators remains stronger than ever and began receiving national attention when it was featured on Animal Planet's *The Haunted*. In one of the more chilling episodes, Bob reveals the supposed voice of a demon on a digital recorder that clearly states "Get out" in a very threatening voice. They were featured a second time on the same program, and Bob reports that CPI remains busy working in Connecticut. Joe and Kathy have reported no further problems.

CHAPTER 9

The Paranormal Economy

There is a money-making industry behind belief in the paranormal, and it is one that touches the imagination of people from every walk of life—believer and skeptic alike. The paranormal economy is most obvious in the film, television, and book industries. Films such as *E.T.*, *The Exorcist*, and *The Sixth Sense* topped the box office around the world. Perhaps even more importantly, these films have become a part of the fabric of American culture and have made alien abductions, demon possession, and ghosts everyday forms of entertainment, thus making them part of our cultural language. Furthermore, films claiming to be based on true stories such as *The Exorcist*, *The Amityville Horror*, and, more recently, *The Haunting in Connecticut*, have become legendary and are part of the American mythology. Much to the frustration of skeptics and ghost hunters alike, the films are accepted by audiences as representations of actual events. However, it may not be that filmgoers actually believe that events such as the Amityville Horror actually happened; their belief may be spurred from a desire to believe and a conscious effort not to look skeptically or scientifically at the real truth of the film. Audiences expect Hollywood to dramatize and embellish. Simultaneously, the rumors surrounding these films had spread through communities, largely among the adolescent population who were eager to imbue their widening world with a sense of supernatural wonder. It is part of the fun of both the film experience and the maturing process. In essence, the films and the stories they tell become part of the American folklore and legend history. Jan Harold Brunvand writes in *The Vanishing Hitchhiker: American Urban Legends and Their Meaning*,

First, it is simply traditional to listen to and appreciate a good story without undue questioning of its premises. Second, "belief" in an item of folklore is not of the same kind as believing the earth is round or that gravity exists. A "true story" is first and foremost a story, not an axiom of science. And third, the legends fulfill needs of warning (don't park!), explanation (what may happen to those who do), and rationalization (you can't really expect sensational bargains not to have strings attached); these needs transcend any need to know the absolute truth.[1]

Take, for instance, the story of the Amityville Horror, which is widely believed to be a "true" story: The Lutzes purchase at a bargain price a home in which a multiple murder was committed (we know from records; that much is actually true). However, upon moving into the home the family is set upon by demonic forces. Add to this fact that, according to the book written by Jay Anson, "It seems the Shinnecock Indians used land on the Amityville River as an enclosure for the sick, mad, and dying. These unfortunates were penned up until they died of exposure. However, the record noted that the Shinnecocks did not use this tract as a consecrated burial mound because they believed it to be infested with demons."[2] There are some lessons to be learned from the Amityville Horror: beware of houses where a murder has been committed (an age-old belief), beware of houses that are being sold dirt cheap, and respect the former lands of Native Americans and their belief systems. This is not to say that the Amityville Horror story was not true, although there is much debate about its merits; but this shows how certain stories can become folklore if presented with the right ingredients, drama, rumor, and publicity (the Amityville Horror house made headlines across the United States).

These stories work their way into the American culture, particularly through the youth. Stories about *The Texas Chainsaw Massacre*, *The Amityville Horror*, and *The Exorcist* are told among adolescents as true stories, and thus, they create a tendency towards belief in the paranormal from an early age. As a preteen I recalled hearing a story in my hometown of Brookfield, Connecticut, about a boy who had become possessed by demons and murdered his family. The boy was supposedly still living in the town. My best friend remembered the incident well as his family had just moved to Brookfield because it was a safe town. When the murder and subsequent story of demon possession hit the newspapers, his mother was rather distraught. Only at the age of 30 did I finally research the story to find out what really happened as presented in the book *The Devil Comes to Connecticut*. It was a bit different from the rumor I had heard. The boy did not kill his family; it was a member of his family that had killed someone else. However, it did make headlines across the nation because it was the first time a plea of "Not Guilty by Reason of Demonic Possession" had ever been used in court. The plea was rejected, and the accused was found guilty and sentenced to 20 years. However, that story and its subsequent rumors have endured in Brookfield. The story was told on Discovery's *A Haunting*, and there are rumors of a movie deal, thus regenerating the cycle of occurrence, rumor, and publicity; and in the end, money is made on the back of a legend.

Books make up the other major money component of the paranormal. Stephen King is one of the most celebrated and widely read authors in history. His books have been turned into films; some have been box office hits and memorable horror films such as *Carrie* ($33 million), *The Shining* ($44 million), and *Misery* ($61 million), while others have been flops that were quickly forgotten—films such as *Dream Catcher* and *Salem's Lot*. However, his stories of the paranormal have made him one of the wealthiest authors in history, topped only by J. K. Rowling with her Harry Potter series. The paranormal provides readers with a fantasy background for escape in much of the popular fiction. The current trend shows that the vampire books and the increasing number of zombie novels are ranking high on the bestseller lists, influencing the youth and introducing them to paranormal ideas, and subsequently being turned into hit movies, such as the Twilight series.

Aside from the traditional horror fiction market, there has been major growth in the nonfiction market in recent years. The emergent popularity of ghost hunting programs on television has brought about an increased interest in nonfiction books that tell stories of hauntings or how-to books for amateur ghost hunters. New Page Books was launched in 2000 from Career Press as a line of books devoted solely to spirituality, history, science, and the paranormal. Some of its major titles include *Flying Saucers and Science*, *Witness to Roswell*, and *2013: The End of Days or A New Beginning*, a book concerning the Mayan calendar and a global transformation. Some Christian publishers such as Anomalos Publishing have also found a niche with readers searching for answers to the paranormal within a biblical context. *The Omega Conspiracy*, written by Dr. I. D. E. Thomas, asserts that UFOs are actually demonic harbingers preparing the world for the return of the Nephilim—the Nephilim being a race that was created when the "Sons of God" reproduced with the "Daughters of Men" to create an evil race that God subsequently washed from the earth with the great flood. Other titles such as *Nephilim Stargates: The Year 2012*, *The Return of the Watchers*, and *The Emerging Brave New World* have found a home and a willing audience through this Christian publishing company. These books assert a Christian viewpoint and biblical answer for questions concerning UFOs and aliens, thus blending one of the world's largest religions with one of the most debated paranormal phenomena. It is a powerful mixture, and the authors' ability to tap into the Christian background of the American public carries a strong influence in the public and among believers. Amazon's ability to hold a near infinite number of books, and the development of print-on-demand technology has allowed for a large number of obscure publishers to increase their sales and reach buyers across the world. By and large the Internet has been a boon for publishers of paranormal nonfiction and theory.

This, however, does not sit well with the other side of the paranormal aisle at your local Barnes & Noble. For every paranormal book, there is a book positing the opposite, skeptical viewpoint. These books are also well received by the public. Carl Sagan's works all made the *New York Times* best-seller lists. His work is largely scientific and skeptical of the paranormal. Often it is the scientists and skeptics that attract the larger publishing houses as the authors can be touted as leading thinkers and scientists in their respective fields. Careers have been made on both sides of the book aisle—both debunking the paranormal and advocating for it. While the debunkers may get the bigger publishing houses in the nonfiction market, the number of books proclaiming the validity of the paranormal, both fiction and nonfiction, vastly outnumber them. It would seem that scientists face an uphill battle, and the numbers are against them. They face cries of elitism when trying to disprove or even debate the paranormal, and their work is often thankless despite the fact that they want to believe. Carl Sagan writes, "I would be very happy if flying saucer advocates and alien abduction proponents were right and real evidence of extraterrestrial life were here for us to examine. They do not ask us, though, to believe on faith. They ask us to believe on the strength of their evidence. Surely it is our duty to scrutinize the purported evidence at least as closely and skeptically as radio astronomers who are searching for alien radio signals."[3] Scientists feel it is their duty to debate paranormal claims, but it doesn't get them invited to many parties.

The scientific debate aside, the point is that both belief in the paranormal and skepticism of the paranormal have a large stake in both the book and film industry. Any follower of horror or science fiction films can surely attest to the marketing and money-making potential inherent in the very suspension of disbelief that analytical scientists decry. While books, television, and film are by far the largest industries that find the paranormal profitable, there are other, more obscure ventures that are profitable, particularly in the tourism industry. The U.S. fascination with the paranormal has many places in which it can thrive—places that open the door to exploration, wonder, mystery, and fantasy.

IF THESE WALLS COULD TALK

Ted and Carol Matsumoto run Captain Grant's Bed & Breakfast, located in Preston, Connecticut, just outside of the tourist destination of Mystic. They have owned and operated the inn for 14 years and have developed a bit of a reputation, but not just for Carol's delicious blueberry pancakes and homemade syrup. Captain Grant's has established a reputation as being a haunted house, and people are more than willing to pay to sleep beneath the ancient wood beams that traverse the ceiling.

If a location has the right to be proclaimed as haunted, it is Captain Grant's. It is a time capsule of American history. Built in 1754 by Captain William Gonzales Grant, it housed three generations of the family long after Grant died at sea. It served as a garrison during the Revolutionary War and protected runaway slaves during the Civil War. Some of the most heart-wrenching times in U.S. history flowed through this house.

What's more is that it lies in the middle of a triangle of lost souls. Across the street from Captain Grant's is St. James Cemetery—a quiet, small patch of land that pushes far back into the forest and is barely visible from the road. The names and dates here are old and all seemingly familiar. It is the resting place of the young—sailors and fishermen—who lost their lives at sea, soldiers who died in battle, and those who were struck down by disease. The ages on the stones are a reminder that more than a century ago life was much more fragile, and much more dangerous. Just up the street and within sight of the house is St. James Church; a fine-looking façade with a history as long and varied as Captain Grant's. Its inception was during a time of great conflict for the Church of England, and the building of St. James was not without strife and public difficulty. Unfortunately, the church has occasionally encountered bad luck; it was split apart by a hurricane in the thirties and burned to the ground in the sixties. It has been twice rebuilt as a religious landmark. However, the most interesting and haunting area is the abandoned cemetery that lies across a field behind Captain Grant's. Surrounded by a crumbling stone wall and covered by trees, you could easily trip on one of the sunken tombstones before realizing that you were in the midst of the dead. The grass and shrubs are tall and overgrown, the stones have sunk into the dirt—sometimes only a few inches of the stones are still showing. The sepulchers seem to blend with the landscape as if they had been formed during the glacial age. Only when you look closely can you see that they are man-made. The abandoned cemetery, known as Cemetery 17, looks as if it has become a part of the natural landscape. Truly, it is ashes to ashes, dust to dust.

In the middle of this triumvirate of lost and forgotten souls is Captain Grant's Bed & Breakfast. My wife and I spent our first anniversary in the Adelaide Room, supposedly the site of the most paranormal activity. We spent a lovely night there without incident except for a very friendly cat that found its way in from the hallway and spent a large portion of the evening with us. In the morning we ate breakfast with Carol on the veranda, served with her finest antique silver and her very own homemade pancakes and syrup (if it sounds like I'm plugging the place, I might be just a little). This gave me a chance to speak with Carol and find out her history with Captain Grant's old home.

While they do not advertise the bed and breakfast as being haunted (they have previously lost bookings from religious groups who believe that all ghosts are demonic), Carol is the first to tell you that the place is haunted and that she has had many experiences of her own in the 14 years that she has operated Captain Grant's. She showed me two photographs that were taken on the property. The first is in the second floor hallway, just outside the Adelaide Room. It is a white glowing mist that appears to have arms and legs, like a tall, lanky man walking across the hallway. It could be a spot on the lens or an error in the film development, but Carol claims she saw this materialize out of thin air. The other photograph shows the backyard of Captain Grant's—bordered by a large fence-like structure. Carol explains to me that there has never been a fence in the backyard since she has owned the place, but it appeared in this photograph. It looks plain as day, solid and physical.

Of course, no haunted house would be complete without its ghost stories. Ted told me of a New York City detective who stayed one night and woke up the next morning, angry with Ted and Carol for making so much noise in the attic above his room the night before. Ted explained to him that he and his wife weren't even in the house the night before and then showed the detective the attic, which was so cluttered with building materials that no one could possibly have been walking around up there. The detective came back the following Halloween to participate in the annual Halloween party held at Captain Grant's. He became a witness and a believer. Then there was the shower rod in the Adelaide Room. No matter how hard the couple tried to secure it to the wall, it would repeatedly "fly off" as if someone had knocked it from its perch. Ted finally had to bolt it to the walls. More recently there had been a ghostly experience that lost Ted and Carol a member of their staff. Amy, one of their cleaning persons who had been skeptical about the haunting, was in the Adelaide Room fixing the blinds when a young girl appeared and walked right through her arms. Amy was so hysterical that she had to be sent home; she never returned for work again.

Stories like these, and others, draw a large number of customers to Captain Grant's Bed & Breakfast, and the location is well known among paranormal investigators. Ted and Carol claim that "quite a few people come for the ghosts, a lot of ghost hunting and ghost hunting training" takes place at Captain Grant's. Naturally, Ted and Carol aren't going to let this economic resource go untapped. They host an annual Halloween night that attracts tourists, researchers, and people who have had ghostly experiences. They begin the night with a flashlight tour through St. James Cemetery and end the night with cider, a big bonfire, and personal stories of ghostly encounters. In the morning they tour the abandoned gravesite out back. They are sold out every Halloween.

Stephen King writes in *The Shining*, "... every big hotel has got a ghost. Why? Hell, people come and go. Sometimes one of them will pop off in his room, heart attack or stroke or something like that. Hotels are superstitious places. No thirteenth floor or room thirteen, no mirrors on the back of the door when you come through, stuff like that."[4] Indeed, it would appear that hotel builders build and design with a reverence for superstition and the paranormal and, over the years, certain hotels have gained reputations and notoriety through paranormal experiences. Strangely enough, Stephen King wrote *The Shining* while staying in room 217 of the Stanley Hotel, which is listed as one of the most haunted hotels in the United States. The made-for-television version of the film was subsequently shot there. The number of "haunted" hotels, inns, and B&Bs appears to be growing as more and more people "come and go" through the years.

Hotels and B&Bs often harbor storied pasts of violence, suicide, romance, and mystery. The Lizzie Borden House in Massachusetts, where Lizzie Borden allegedly took an axe to her father and stepmother thus inciting the trial of the century, is now a B&B for $200 a night. The Hotel Coronado in San Diego is supposedly haunted by a woman who was found dead on the beach from a gunshot wound after her lover did not meet her at the hotel. The Lizzie Borden House, the Coronado, and the Stanley are all listed on Forbes's Top 10 Haunted Hotels.[5] While these represent some of the most elite and storied places across the United States, Canada, and Britain, they are, by far, not the only game in town. The fact that a publication such as *Forbes* even has such a list should be testament to the new popularity of haunted hotels. And *Forbes* isn't the only list; *USA Today* and the Travel Channel all have similar lists, but often with different hotels. In other words, there are many supposedly haunted hotels, and apparently they don't mind the attention and free advertising that comes with their reputation. As in the case of Captain Grant's, ghosts are good for business.

The paranormal has had a love-hate relationship with tourism over the centuries. In the sixteenth and seventeenth centuries, places reputed to be haunted were avoided out of fear; however, in the Victorian era, with the rise of Spiritualism, "haunted locations were advertised as tourist attractions in Victorian travel guides, such as Harriet Martineau's *Guide to the Lake District* (1858), and in attempts to attract English middle-class visitors to Scotland by advertising places mentioned in the hugely popular Scottish novels of Walter Scott."[6] This mirrors the fact that fans of the hugely popular Stephen King are attracted to the Stanley. So are we living in a modern Victorian era? With the phenomenal growth of the Internet, hotels are able to market their "haunted" status to potential customers, and with the rise in the popularity of paranormal programming, there are more and more hotels claiming to be haunted, and more and more people paying to stay overnight. While it is difficult to estimate the revenue produced by people interested in staying in haunted hotels, based on the increased popularity of paranormal television programs, many of which feature the above-mentioned hotels, it is safe to say that these rumors of ghosts and hauntings are certainly not hurting their business.

Staking claim in this new tourism fad are also bars, taverns, and restaurants. The paranormal program *Ghost Hunters* regularly investigates hotels, bars, pubs, tourist sites, and museums that were formerly residences of historical figures, as well as general points of interest in the American landscape. In his book, *Ghost Hunters*, John Kachuba and a demonologist investigate a supposedly haunted coffee shop. Bill Ellis outlines the legend of the Fast Food Ghost that is seen in a local McDonald's or Pizza Hut or whichever establishment happens to be in the area where the legend is spreading. However, hotels have a special place in the paranormal heart of the United States. Perhaps it is because hotels, especially older ones, have a natural storied past because they have seen so many people's lives over the years. If their walls could talk, what kind of stories would they tell? Throughout the hundreds of years that some of these hotels have been in business, thousands, if not millions, of people have come through the doors and spent a small portion of their lives in these rooms. They are vestibules of time. Moments of life, death, love, and hate have played out repeatedly over the years, making hotels largely haunted, if not by ghosts, then by the history of all those who have come before.

In *The Shining*, a little boy keeps having recurring visions of all the tragic, violent, and untimely deaths that have occurred in the Overlook Hotel. In the basement, his father finds remnants of the past—receipts, pictures, and newspaper clippings from the decades during which the hotel was open for business. During its time of abandonment, however, there are only empty spaces where the history and life that had come and gone through its walls lay dormant. Unfortunately, the effect of the Overlook on King's characters is negative and maddening, but for the rest of the nation it appears that the prospect of ghosts roaming legendary hallways and stalking storied rooms is a draw that is helping to drive a new tourist economy.

> It was a living sound, but not voices, not breath. A man of a philosophical bent might have called it the sound of souls. Dick Hollorann's Nana, who had grown up on southern roads in the years before the turn of the century, would have called it ha'ants. A psychic investigator might have had a long name for it—psychic echo, psychokinesis, a telesmic sport. But to Danny it was only the sound of the hotel, the old monster, creaking steadily and ever more closely around them: halls that now stretched back through time as well as distance, hungry shadows, unquiet guests who did not rest easy.[7]

Punderson Manor sits atop a hill overlooking a large pond in Ohio's Geauga County. It is a large English Tudor surrounded by a golf course and a state park that bristles with tangled roots from small, twisting trees and thickets that line the pond. Inside, a grand spiral staircase, a chandeliered dining room, a bar room, and numerous books and leaflets outlining the manor's haunted history can be seen. A young black girl who drowned in 1977 is sometimes seen emerging from the dark pond outside the manor; a woman is seen descending the spiraled staircase at night, a disheveled bearded man appears at the foot of guest beds only to disappear into the walls, and a ghostly image of a man hanging from the chandelier remains for three hours during the night, finally fading with the onset of morning. These are some of the stories that make up the history of (or the haunting of) Punderson Manor.

Upon our arrival my Uncle John, a deputy for the local town of Burton, tells us stories of how the park rangers and police patrol the grounds at night to watch for possible or potential suicides. "There's something about the place," he says, "people go there to off themselves. No one knows why." He then tries to bribe the manor staff for a key to our room so he can play a hoax on us during our three-day stay. Uncle John may have been pulling our leg with his stories of suicides, but his stories came from a true place—a part of human nature that inherently blends reality and fiction, eventually creating a legend and assigning mythical importance to an ancient place. I could only find two stories about suicides that were associated with Punderson Manor; one concerned a former owner who supposedly used a bathtub to float into the middle of the lake and then pulled the plug, and another story was of a man who was prevented from killing himself through police intervention. Such stories, however, are common to state parks, as they tend to be secluded areas, and there are often cars there after dark.

Over the years Punderson Manor has added new facilities to the original Tudor-style building. There are updated rooms in the new section, a part of the manor that hasn't yet had time to develop its own haunting stories. However, it's easy to see how the original building developed its history and inspired stories; it is in a quiet, secluded location surrounded by thick brambles and a dark, heavy forest, which also surrounds a nearby pond; inside are the spiral staircases and vein-like hallways that lead to octagonal sitting rooms filled with old books and furniture. The psychological effect of the old construction is enough to keep you looking over your shoulder, but there is something more in the hallways, rooms, and dining halls; there is some sense of life and history that manifests when you are alone in the corridors. Like King said, it is the sound of "the old monster creaking steadily and ever more closely . . ." It creeps into our stories, our legends, and our knowledge of all the history that has come before us.

Bill Ellis dissects the haunted history of a set of ruins known as Gore Orphanage in nearby Huron County, where an orphanage was supposedly burned to the ground in a fire, claiming all its children. While the ruins were actually that of Swift Mansion, Ellis describes the significance of this place to the development of oral history and legend.

> Although literal-minded historians might conclude that the Gore Orphanage legend is a collection of alcohol- or drug-induced visions and borrowings from other adolescent legends, in fact the Swift Mansion was the ideal place for urban history to resurface in oral tradition. Already associated with the tragic deaths of children and with the return of their screaming, restless ghosts, its secluded nature and the ominous sound of the road's name suited it well for the purpose. But by transforming a real fire into a legendary one, teenagers simultaneously changed history into archetype.[8]

THE GHOST TOUR

At the Queen Anne Hotel a crowd of about 30 people is gathering in the lobby. They talk in small groups, relax in ancient, high-backed chairs, and admire the craftsmanship and artistry of the antique woodwork that can only be found in buildings that predate the twentieth century. My wife and I tour the lobby, noting the ornate woodwork and the quality of work that cannot be found in modern hotels. The Queen Anne began as an orphanage and over the course of a century became a high-end Victorian hotel. Not only did it become a high-end Victorian hotel, but it gained a reputation for being haunted; and the 30 people milling in the lobby (ourselves included) have come to find out more and go on an official walking ghost tour of San Francisco to see all the legendary haunts of the Golden Gate city.

A woman announces that anyone taking the ghost tour should meet in the main dining room—an open, carpeted room with flowing window curtains, a chandelier, and tables with coffee and tea. We take our seats at a round table covered in white cloth and make small talk with other couples around us. The guide enters and introduces himself to us. His name is Jim Fassbinder—a tall, charismatic man whose height seemed far greater with his top hat, cape, goatee, and long, wavy hair. He has dressed the part for the paying audience; he looks like a gothic, ghostly crypt keeper or perhaps a ringleader at a circus of the macabre. He speaks with a mysterious booming voice and informs the audience that he is more than just a tour guide; he is, in fact, a paranormal investigator—a member of several different paranormal organizations and a bit of an actor. His charisma and storytelling ability are put to full use to entertain the crowd. He gives us several guidelines during the tour, along with instructions not to use flash photography at certain locations because the present owners, who are quite wealthy, have come to regard the tour past their homes as an invasion of their privacy.

We actually begin the tour at the Queen Anne Hotel. Jim gives a history of the location, including the reports that have developed over the years of ghostly encounters, glowing orbs, and general bumps in the night. We are then invited to explore the hotel on our own and take as many photographs as we please.

The Queen Anne seems amazingly compact and complex at the same time, and it is easy to see how one could see ghostly figures and hear whisperings. Its ancient rooms and doors, long narrow hallways and odd corners are the perfect combination for dark imaginations and experiences. Jim then gathers us together, and we begin walking the steep inclines of San Francisco for the next three hours. Jim is never without witty comment or an entertaining story. His tour doesn't consist of just ghost stories; rather, it includes stories of San Francisco, the history of a beautiful city. The haunted tales serve as the vehicle for the drama of the city to unfold. Along the way, he reveals the most frightening aspect of the tour—the real estate prices! We stop at places of history and legend; houses that make up the dark side of San Francisco, including a house where a famous stabbing occurred, the place where a woman discovered her husband's body in a barrel, and the home of Mary Ellen, the Voodoo Queen of San Francisco—a slave woman who became the richest, most powerful person in San Francisco in the eighteenth century—some say through the black arts, voodoo and blackmail.

The tour was fascinating. It was an oral history of San Francisco, a three-hour trek through some of its most historical and legendary haunts. Anyone who has attended grade school has heard of Harriet Tubman, but who has heard of the slave who took over San Francisco, utilizing the most devious business skills ever known in corporate America? All the places on the tour are currently occupied by private, mostly wealthy citizens or, in some cases, a business that wants nothing to do with the paranormal. But, how much of this dark history would be lost without the ghost tour? Not too many people want to advertise that their home was the site of a famous double murder, but these events, however gruesome, are part of the city's history. The city is more than just the stone it is built on, and the ghost tour serves as an oral history that can be passed down to the next generations through the tourism industry.

San Francisco's haunted places are not limited to just the houses on the tour. The city itself, much like many other cities across the United States, has an abundance of reputedly haunted areas that double as tourist attractions. San Francisco, for example, has Alcatraz, an abandoned army hospital, the Golden Gate Park, and the Bay Bridge, where a headless man supposedly appears beside cars. Indeed, the city seems littered with haunted landscapes; a walk near the Golden Gate Bridge would reveal a hidden history that manifests itself in eerie ways. Small mounds of earth reveal dark stone doorways behind grassy overgrowth. They were used as storage bunkers for munitions during the wars that found their way to the West Coast. The hills are steep and guarded over by tall trees like sentinels, and a fog rests near the pathways and ammunition bunkers. It all makes for a haunting experience with or without macabre stories.

This is not unique to San Francisco, though. Across the United States, cities are developing ghost tours as part of their tourism industry. They combine the history of the city with the supernatural to generate business and revenue. The city of Savannah posted revenue of $1 million in 2007 on ghost tours alone,[9] and towns such as Salem, Massachusetts, have their entire tourist industry based on the paranormal. Even tried and true tourist areas have been exploring the paranormal as a means of generating more revenue. Gettysburg, aside from being one of the most visited historical places in the United States, is also considered to be the most haunted place in the United States and boasts several ghost tours to spice up the family experience. Some cities, such as New Orleans and Salem, also include vampire tours, and many of these paranormal tours have been featured on the Travel Channel and the Syfy Channel. There are also extensive websites dedicated to ghost tours and brochures advertising ghostly adventures.

All in all, the paranormal has built up the tourism industry in major cities and tourist destinations. The obvious appeal is the mystery and spooky, macabre fantasy. Rarely are any of the tours in bright, happy locations with happy ghosts; they are, instead, the sites of famous murders, mysteries, and executions. However, it is the fascination with these macabre events that is preserving these sites and histories. Cities and tourist locations are using mystery and the burgeoning fascination with ghosts to generate new interest and the money necessary to continue their historical missions and preserve these sites. The difference is fairly easy to understand; which sounds more interesting to the average tourist—a tour of classical architecture in a city or a ghost tour of a city with supernatural legends, murders, and stories? More and more often, the ghost tours are winning out.

THE SCIENTISTS

For being one of the world's leading and most recognized UFO researchers, Stanton T. Friedman is surprisingly a devout humanist. Talking with Mr. Friedman, I noted immediately that his assertion that alien life forms are visiting earth went hand in hand with the belief that we, as humans, could be so much more than we are. Researching the UFO phenomenon is like researching the future path that humanity should take, but more than likely will not.

Friedman has become the face of the UFO movement, and with good reason. Friedman boasts an impressive education and background, which makes him a credible researcher and formidable debater. He received both his bachelor of science degree and his master of science degree in nuclear physics from the University of Chicago. He then went on to work for several companies, including General Electric, General Motors, and Aerojet General, developing nuclear propulsion systems for rockets and spacecraft. Many of these projects were classified at the time, and Friedman was in the unique position to have top-secret clearance. However, in the late 1950s, at the height of the flying saucer invasion, he became casually interested in flying saucers, largely because of the scientific implications of space travel. "I thought, maybe if UFOs were real, they were using nuclear power for their craft."[10] Thus Friedman began his study and interest in the flying saucer phenomenon, and he became not only a believer, but a lecturer, author, and expert on the subject. Using his background in nuclear physics, Friedman postulates that it is possible and, indeed, evident that earth is being visited by extraterrestrial life forms that are much more advanced than we are.

Mr. Friedman has made a career out of studying flying saucers. He is careful to distinguish between flying saucers and UFOs; a UFO is only an unidentified flying object and, in reality, could be anything ranging from a meteor to an earth-bound aircraft. But flying saucers are unique to the UFO phenomenon in that they always remain unidentified and the definite shape of the crafts is indicative of design rather than some kind of natural object. Since his entry into the study of UFOs, Friedman has lectured at over six hundred colleges and universities around the world and appeared on numerous television programs, including several appearances on *Larry King Live*.[11] He even has his own holiday in Fredericton, New Brunswick: August 27 is Stanton Friedman Day. He was recently the subject of a short film entitled *Stanton Friedman Is Real*,[12] which provided a behind-the-scenes look into Friedman's world. Although some may doubt his findings, few doubt his integrity and tenacity. With his trademark beard and winged eyebrows, Friedman has managed to become a major player in an overlooked industry—the UFO industry.

"I don't get paid when I go on the Larry King show," he says. "I have to wake up at 4:00 a.m., catch a flight to Los Angeles, take a car over to the studio, and do the show. They pay for the flight and the hotel stay, but I'm not being paid directly. It's not easy or fun. If I'm lucky I'll stop and have lunch with my daughter who lives out there. Then I take a flight back home; it's not all that glamorous."

However, Friedman does get paid for his books and lectures. He is, by all accounts, prolific on the lecture circuit, and at 73 years old, shows no signs of slowing down. Upon discovering how much universities were willing to pay for a guest lecture in the 1950s, which is when Friedman began lecturing, he was amazed and, by his own admission, thought, "Well, maybe this is something I can support my family with." However, it should not be assumed that the prospect of making money indicates fraud; if this were the case, there wouldn't be an honest person alive—scientist, ufologist, or otherwise. Money is not indicative of fraud, but it is indicative of an industry. There is money to be made through the research and belief in UFOs, and Friedman has made a career out of tapping into that industry.

He has been called "the flying saucer physicist" and has been referred to as an evangelist for flying saucers, but at the basest and most cynical viewpoint, he is ultimately a salesman. This does not mean that he doesn't believe in what he's selling; by all accounts Stanton Friedman is an honest man. And it doesn't mean that he does not know nearly everything about his subject material; few people have spent as much time researching presidential and government records as Friedman has. But in order for him to subsist and continue his work, he must ultimately sell. He is selling himself to those who believe or want to believe and to those who need reassurance that their beliefs are valid. Liberal individuals will say that all beliefs are valid, but not so in the scientific community. The primary difficulty facing those who believe that the earth is being visited by extraterrestrial beings is not the public scrutiny, because, as Friedman often illustrates, a majority of the public is open to this idea. Their greatest hurdle in trying to find legitimacy for their beliefs comes from the scientific community. While Friedman insists that many scientists actually agree that there are alien life forms visiting our planet, they are surely the unspoken, invisible minority because, by and large, the scientific community appears to reject this theory. It is not only the research scientists in related fields, such as astronomy and physics, but the attack-dog skeptics who have devoted their lives to destroying this belief. People such as Philip J. Klass can be unscrupulous in their attacks on citizens who may have experienced something they do not understand or who genuinely claim to have had an experience with a UFO. Thus, many people may be hesitant to come forward with their experience.

Furthermore, in a technocratic society where much of an individual's credibility is based on the degrees conferred upon him or her by higher institutions (apparently, as proof that said individual is intelligent, capable, and sane), someone who lacks degrees and experience in "science" may feel woefully inadequate to defend his or her beliefs against the skeptics. This is where people like Stanton T. Friedman or the late J. Allen Hynek become such valuable resources for those who have either had an experience with a UFO or those who believe that extraterrestrials are visiting earth. His experience, intelligence, degrees, and ability to take massive amounts of data and turn it into theory renders a sense of legitimacy to the community of believers. He is unafraid to debate the skeptics and scientists who might otherwise use their technical experience and prestige to browbeat the average Joe or Jane.

While it is wrong to assume legitimacy based on educational merit, it is, unfortunately, the result of a society focused on the sciences and technology. How can one presume to have seen a flying saucer without the proper education as to what the planet Venus looks like when the earth is at a particular point in its rotation? Using information and sciences largely beyond the experience and grasp of the average individual, an astronomer or physicist can come up with a complex equation of numerous natural phenomena combined with unreliable witness testimony to explain that the craft following your car down a dark, deserted road a mere 50 feet off the ground was actually the planet Venus seen in a particular light. Without similar scientific expertise to offer a rebuttal, the average Joe is left looking the fool, having been roundly put into his place by the intelligentsia.

Friedman is able to play the game on the skeptics' terms. He can talk the talk, understand the data, and, using formidable debating skills, can offer a counterargument to the establishment claims. And, frankly, he has plenty at his disposal. Friedman debates even the technology and science behind the ability of flying saucers to travel such great distances. Many skeptics point out that even if life does exist on another planet, it would be too far away for those beings to travel here. However, Friedman refutes that argument; simply because man doesn't understand yet how it can be done doesn't mean that interstellar travel isn't possible (even as I write this, the scientific world is buzzing from the report that a neutrino may have surpassed the speed of light in the CERN particle collider; though it has yet to be verified, it would mean a revolution in physics—something that was once thought impossible has happened). One of Friedman's favorite lines is, "Progress comes from doing things differently in an unpredictable fashion."[13] And, indeed, he has history on his side to prove his point; it was thought that man would never fly and that landing on the moon was impossible. Friedman even coauthored a book on this very premise, entitled *Science Was Wrong*, detailing the scientific establishment's lack of imagination in the past.

Part of Friedman's salesmanship is his coining of certain phrases, usually humorous, that he uses as talking points—the way a politician sticks to his stump speech. Friedman has been doing this for a long time, so naturally he has an inventory of preset answers. He uses terms like "nasty, noisy negativists" to describe the rabid skeptics; he defines SETI as "Silly Effort To Investigate." He has the ability to use talking points and frame the discussion on his terms and therefore is a difficult target for skeptics and a ray of light for the believers. Friedman is certainly not the only accomplished and educated ufologist, but he has certainly managed to corner the market on selling himself and his message better than anyone else. In a world where those who are confronted with the paranormal are looked upon as fools by the establishment, Friedman comes to their defense, rhetoric blazing.

During our interview Friedman rehashed many of his traditional lines, but in his defense, my questions weren't that profound. There are only so many times one can answer a question such as, "Why don't the aliens just land on the White House lawn?" before it becomes boring to answer. However, it was his answer to that very question, no matter how well rehearsed, that reveals Friedman's hopes for humanity embedded in his study of ufology. His answer was simple: "Why would they?" In Friedman's view, man has squandered his potential and is still holding himself back. He lists a series of humanitarian failures—from wars to starvation and poverty. He cites the millions killed in World War II alone, and the use of nuclear weapons on our own species, which raises the obvious question that if human scientists came across a particularly violent and intelligent species in nature, would they just walk up and say, "Hello"? Probably not. Like much of the paranormal, Friedman's research has led him to the big questions—the questions that define our existence.

> Who are we? This question has bedazzled scholars for millennia. Are we the masters of all we can see? Is there a God providing hope and perhaps fear for all of us? Or are we casting God in our image to justify our ways? These may seem to be strictly religious questions, but they are not. Many wars have been fought over interpretations of God and the Universe and governments for or by the people, and the need to fight Evil and do Good. The other guy is always the evil one, isn't he? And God is always on our side, right?[14]

Perhaps this is why ufology and skepticism can often take on the appearance of religious fervor, if not actually become a religious belief—because the study of these phenomena will ultimately point to the truth of our existence. What you believe, or what you want the truth to be, may define what side you end up on in the debate over the paranormal. Science takes a back seat to these deeper questions, though science indeed frames some of the debate. Friedman's assertion that progress is made through doing things differently in an unpredictable way could also be applied to the social sciences, because, thus far, it appears we have reached a less than testable, perfect theory for governance and maintenance of humanity. As Mr. Friedman mourns the squandering of potential, perhaps he hopes that something new and different may eventually save us. We are quite young as a species, and if there are alien civilizations that predate us, then it means they have been able to not only survive an alien world and its environment but also survive each other. Mr. Friedman sells a dream and tells people that it is possible and, like so many other dreams before it, could eventually come true. With that kind of message, is there any wonder that he has been able to support his family financially throughout the years? The more the world spins out of control, the more his message resonates. He is salesman, preacher, politician, and scientist supported by the people, for the people . . . and for the aliens.

Reading Dr. Carl Sagan's book, *The Demon-Haunted World: Science as a Candle in the Dark*, reminds me of a conversation I had while bartending a restaurant located in a secluded and wealthy area of Connecticut. After overhearing that I was a graduate student, a retired couple at the end of the bar started discussing with me the merits of education and reading; I will call them Joe and Mary. After a few martinis Joe leaned over the bar and, in a whisper, said to me, "You see, well, my wife and I are intellectuals." Confused and wondering if this "intellectual" thing was a paying job, I pushed him for a little more information. He continued, "Don't you think that we"—myself included now; I assume because I was in grad school—"as intellectuals are under attack in this country?"

I looked around, still a bit confused, and asked, "Under attack by whom?" Gesturing as if to refer to the rest of the world or at least the rest of the people in the room, he said, "All these dumb people!" I could only smile and agree and say, "You know, I do feel that I'm under attack by dumb people." The sarcasm was lost on him, thanks to the martinis, and at the end of the night I still received a generous tip.

In a society that is both knowingly and unknowingly mired in belief systems based on faith, the skeptic can often find himself frustrated, angry, elitist, and a bit vindictive. One can hardly blame him when the price of such unfounded and unproven beliefs can exact such a tremendous toll. From the Associated Press, 2009:

> A jury has found five New Zealanders guilty of manslaughter in the death of a family member during an exorcism ceremony to drive a "makutu" or Maori curse from the woman. Nine family members of the victim, Janet Moses, 22, performed an exorcism on her in October 2007, forcing water into her mouth and eyes to flush out the demons and lift the makutu. Moses drowned and a 14-year-old girl the group also believed was possessed suffered serious eye injuries as people picked at the demons they saw in them, the High Court hearing was told.[15]

The power of belief has compelled some of humanity's worst atrocities, all in the name of some unproven, unknown entity. Skeptics, on the other hand, take the world for only what can be seen and proven with empirical evidence. It can be a noble position at times, while in other cases skepticism can become the very thing it claims to rebuke—blind faith. Either way the skeptic's position can ofttimes lead him or her to being the lonely nerd sitting by him- or herself at the lunchroom table. In other words, the skeptic can be a bit of a downer.

Carl Sagan is, perhaps, the most famous skeptic in recent history. His ability to render science interesting for the masses made him a great spokesman, similar to Stanton Friedman. And like Stanton Friedman, he attended the University of Chicago and worked on serious scientific programs, largely with NASA. Friedman and Sagan sparred occasionally regarding the question of alien life forms visiting earth. Friedman coauthored a book about the Betty and Barney Hill abduction while Sagan worked to debunk the story. However, they remained mutually respectful, and Friedman actually wrote an article on Sagan after his death, praising his ability to bring science to the masses.

While Sagan did work with NASA, much of his fame and fortune came from engaging with the paranormal. He was the preeminent skeptic; the intellectual who used science to trump the faith and folklore of the masses and assure the world that the modern scientist had everything well in hand— that life and the cosmos could be boiled down to a chemical equation or quantum physics. Unfortunately for the skeptic, those chemical equations and quantum physics are written in a language that is largely unreadable to the average Joe or Jane. This leaves the skeptic/scientist in the position of being the sole possessor of the knowledge of the mysterious workings of the universe; it puts the skeptic in an elitist position, which means he or she can often have difficulty reaching the masses.

It is difficult to draw a line through the sand as to which side has benefited more from paranormal's economic potential. Certainly, those who teach and write about the paranormal have a very large group of customers willing to buy books, DVDs, and attend lectures. Indeed, most of the world is comprised of religious people who believe in a supernatural explanation for existence, and thus, are inclined toward paranormal belief. However, the skeptic enjoys a level of prestige that is often lost on those who follow belief and faith over empirical science. That prestige comes with the various merits and degrees bestowed upon these men and women by universities and colleges. These are men and women who are adept and trained in the sciences. They have been trained to see the world through the prism of known science. If they form any differentiation between the known and the unknown, it is a difference between the observation of a known and understood natural occurrence and a yet-to-be-understood natural occurrence, but still a product of nature and the physical forces that operate therein. As Edward Bulwer-Lytton wrote in his short story, "The Haunted and the Haunters," "Now, my theory is that the Supernatural is the Impossible, and that what is called supernatural is only a something in the laws of nature of which we have been hitherto ignorant. Therefore, if a ghost rise before me, I have not the right to say, 'So, then the supernatural is possible,' but rather, 'So, then the apparition of a ghost is, contrary to received opinion, within the laws of nature—i.e., not supernatural.' "[16] Scientists, therefore, are not averse to the unknown—in fact that is their bread and butter—but they tend to be non-accepting of supernatural theories.

For the intellectual skeptic there is a niche market, though not as sizeable as the market for believers in the paranormal. Prometheus Publishers publishes books almost entirely devoted to skepticism and disputing the paranormal. It also has a monthly magazine entitled *The Skeptical Inquirer*, which offers articles and investigations of paranormal phenomena that are almost always roundly debunked. Run by the Center for Skeptical Inquiry, both Prometheus Books and *The Skeptical Inquirer* regularly produce and sell to their growing audience.

Sagan, like many skeptics will readily admit, wants to believe in the paranormal but can't, due to that pesky little rule called the scientific method; "I had been interested in the possibility of extraterrestrial life from childhood, from long before I ever heard of flying saucers. I've remained fascinated long after my early enthusiasm for UFOs waned—as I understood more about that remorseless taskmaster called scientific method."[17] Sagan hoped to find extraterrestrial life and was instrumental in setting up SETI (Search for Extraterrestrial Intelligence), which uses a radio telescope to broadcast into outer space the Arecibo message, which he cowrote with Dr. Frank Drake, in the hopes that it will be heard by intelligent life forms and translated, so that contact can be established.

Sagan was highly successful in his public career. Along with his extensive work in the sciences, he is most widely known for bringing science to the masses through his writing and television work. His book *Cosmos* became the best-selling scientific work ever published in English, and he had many notable follow-ups, including a Pulitzer Prize for *The Dragons of Eden*. However, one of his greatest successes was his novel *Contact*, which imagined the consequences if the Arecibo message was ever received by intelligent beings and contact were established. The book was a best-seller and was eventually turned into a movie starring Jodie Foster. It remains one of the most imaginative and realistic portrayals of contact with extraterrestrial beings ever written. Unfortunately, Sagan passed away before he was able to see the film on screen. Sagan was popular with mainstream audiences and fostered his own catchphrase of "billions and billions" and was an occasional guest of late-night talk shows. He had a certain charisma that many in his profession lack—he had a passion for the sciences but was able to popularize it and elevate the average Joe to the level of informed, scientifically aware, above-average Joe.

Friedman and Sagan are complimentary opposites, but both are ultimately humanist in their aspirations; they are/were men on a mission to change humanity for the better. One of the reasons that these two men make such an interesting dichotomy is that their pursuits are not limited by their respective viewpoints; Friedman believes that earth is being visited by extraterrestrial beings but Sagan did not. Each offers evidence, each has impressive scientific background and education, and each is an engaging public presence with the conviction of an evangelical preacher and the swagger of the consummate politician. However, they are bound to each other by an underlying ideology: that humanity is descending into calamity. Friedman writes,

> I should think it would seem strange to the visitors that 30,000 children will die every day of preventable disease and starvation, and that we apparently can't afford to spend enough money to make a dent in the tragic statistic. We know we are fouling our waterways and the skies above, but we certainly don't seem to be able to get together with others on the planet to solve what are planetary (rather than national) problems. Certainly, despite all the jokes about aliens landing and saying 'Take me to your leader,' we know there is no leader of the planet to whom to be taken.[18]

Similarly, Sagan writes,

> I have a foreboding of an America in my children's or grandchildren's time—when the United States is a service and information economy; when nearly all the key manufacturing industries have slipped away to other countries; when awesome technological powers are in the hands of a very few, and no one representing the public interest can even grasp the issues; when the people have lost the ability to set their own agendas or knowledgeably question those in authority; when, clutching our crystals and nervously consulting our horoscopes, our critical faculties in decline, unable to distinguish between what feels good and what's true, we slide, almost without noticing, back into superstition and darkness.[19]

Sagan wrote this hauntingly prophetic passage in 1996—before the Internet had become a life-changing force, and before the world was forever changed on 9/11.

Both men had a vision—a message in their work; and this is why they are so strangely connected. Perhaps it is why Friedman felt it necessary to pen an article praising Sagan's work when, in life, the two had been so at odds with each other. They are each sending a message through their opposing viewpoints: humanity is on the wrong track, and continuing on this path will inevitably lead to destruction. We are capable of so much more, and yet, each and every day we prevent ourselves from truly advancing. In this way they were like evangelical preachers, and in this way they were perfect embodiments of what the paranormal represents—a warning to us to change our ways, lest our society be destroyed. Each of them urges us to return to a value system, one that values life, nature, possibility, and science, and each of them believes that man is capable of so much more. The way a preacher warns mankind of the error of his ways and encourages him to aspire to divinity, likewise, Friedman and Sagan admonish mankind to aspire to divinity. They urge us to become god-like through an understanding of the sciences, reaching for the stars, communicating with superior beings, and embracing benevolence for all mankind. Perhaps this is why their message resonates so well with the public and why they were each embraced by the media; they are not necessarily selling aliens or science but are rather selling an ideology that man faces ruin and must act in order to save himself. It is an ideology buried deep in their respective viewpoints, but one that is, nonetheless, communicated to the listening audience. Friedman and Sagan are like two sides of the same coin; balanced on edge, they face different directions but are made of the same metal.

CHAPTER 10

Based on a True Story . . .

Hollywood loves to claim that paranormal movies are "based on a true story," but how true is that statement? Our history of film provides many "true stories" that are verifiable and absolutely true to the best of the director's and actors' knowledge. However, there are other so-called true stories that are not necessarily "true." As discussed in "Paranormal Hoaxes," one of the hallmarks of the paranormal is the blurring of the boundaries between fact and fiction, empirical evidence versus interpretation. The difficulty with "true" paranormal stories is the difficulty in verifying the phenomenon that is central to the film. The phenomenon is what the audience links most directly with the "true" statement in the title. Normally, there is very little doubt that a particular individual existed, or that a certain house was the site of some grisly murders, or even that there was an individual missing for a long period of time, only to show up again with no recollection of where he had been, as in the case of Travis Walton in *Fire in the Sky*. For instance, *The Amityville Horror* is one of the films that worked its way into the pantheon of the American paranormal experience; most remember it as being lauded as a "true" story. It is true in that there is a house in Amityville, New York, that was the site of some grisly murders. The house was bought by the Lutz family, who then abandoned it approximately one month later claiming that the house was haunted. Ed and Lorraine Warren, who investigated the house, confirmed the haunting. There was much media sensation surrounding the claims, a book was written, a subsequent film was produced, and the legend of the Amityville Horror was born. So many people descended upon

Amityville that the town eventually had to change the name of the street where the house was located to keep people from trespassing.

All of that is absolutely, empirically true. It all happened. But what of the phenomena claimed by both the Lutz family and the Warrens? This is where "truth" becomes blurred. There is no way to verify the phenomena other than taking their word for it. The story is "true" inasmuch as it is the story they told and attest to be true. When asserting that a book or film is a true story, the author, director, and producers are, in effect, telling the audience that they accept the witnesses' testimony as truth. The audience is not allowed to make a decision one way or the other; the "truth" is told to them. However, the audience appears to be willing and able to believe this truth.

When we enter a movie theater, we pay a fee that allows us to willingly suspend our disbelief for a short period of time; it is essentially why we go to movies. While watching *Star Wars*, I accept the fact that the *Millennium Falcon* can move freely through the universe at remarkable speed, defying all physics known to man. I accept it as an act of my willing suspension of disbelief, so that I can enjoy the movie without bogging down my brain trying to figure out the physics of it. But no one ever claimed that *Star Wars* was a "true story." When a film claims to be a true story and we enter the darkness of the theater—the place where we traditionally suspend our natural inclination to disbelief—are we somehow more vulnerable to believing the story at face value? Or are the "true" stories being told resonating with audiences because they confirm their already existent beliefs or because they have had similar experiences themselves? Based on the reactions that some of these films have elicited from audiences, the answers to both these questions seem to be an emphatic "Yes."

In middle school I recall hearing for the first time (that I can remember) about the film *Texas Chainsaw Massacre*. One of the kids told me that it was a true story, and I was willing to believe him. For some reason, the belief in a massacre in Texas involving a chainsaw made sense to me and seemed to resonate with some deeper horror that I had only just begun to realize. For years I walked around with the presumption that the *Texas Chainsaw Massacre* was a true story, precisely because I didn't feel the need to dig any deeper. It wasn't until my college years that I finally did some research on the story and found that it wasn't true in the least. It was very loosely based on Ed Gein, a Wisconsin grave robber who eventually turned to murder. He committed monstrous acts but murdered only two people, and neither involved Texas or a chainsaw. In the case of *The Texas Chainsaw Massacre*, the "true story" aspect was probably for promotional gains; however, the story became legend—one that school kids were telling each other and readily accepting.

When *The Blair Witch Project* came out, many people were tricked into believing in the Blair Witch legend, which was entirely fictional. Some were even tricked into believing that the footage was real. Once again, it was entirely promotional; as yet, the Blair Witch seems to have made no steps toward becoming an American legend. But there are films that have. There are films that, through their assertion of being true stories and the audience's willingness to believe that they are true, have become a part of the American cultural landscape—a movie mythology. The films that will be examined in this book claim to be true stories and, in fact, have a basis: the stories are real in that they were played out on a national media level and there were real people behind these films attesting to their truth. Additionally, the audience's reaction attests to a certain truth in their perception of the films—everything from fainting in the theater to protests of criminal acts were associated with these films. *Fire in the Sky*, *The Amityville Horror*, and *The Exorcist* all managed to become part of the American movie mythology. The stories are told around campfires and in schoolyards, debated on television by skeptics and believers, and they have found a widespread audience more than willing to suspend their disbelief.

THE EXORCIST

William Friedkin's *The Exorcist* is the "big daddy" of all horror films. It is widely considered the most frightening film of all time. It was an international blockbuster, an Academy Award contender (losing Best Picture and Director awards to none other than *The Godfather*), and it was controversial to say the least. Some derided *The Exorcist* as a pandering to the Dark Ages, as religious pornography; film critic Jon Landau wrote,

> The audience knew instinctively that *The Exorcist* is nothing more than a religious porn film, the gaudiest piece of big budget schlock this side of Cecil B. DeMille (minus the gentleman's wit and ability to tell a story), and an assault on their sensibility at the most basic levels of shock and surprise. If it hadn't made me angry, I might have been content to acknowledge that by virtue of its sheer outrageousness it may very well be a good bad movie, even an entertaining one, and let it go at that.[1]

Other critics lauded the movie as one of the finest ever made.

> *The Exorcist* is one of the best movies of its type ever made; it not only transcends the genre of terror, horror, and the supernatural, but it transcends such serious, ambitious efforts in the same direction as Roman

Polanski's *Rosemary's Baby*. Carl Dreyer's *The Passion of Joan of Arc* is a greater film—but, of course, not nearly so willing to exploit the ways film can manipulate feeling.[2]

However, more often than not it is the audience, not the critics, that propels a film into the pantheon of classics; and stories of the audience reaction to *The Exorcist* were as extreme as the film itself.

Peter Travers and Stephanie Reiff authored the book *The Story behind The Exorcist*, and were allowed by William Friedkin to tag along for the making of the film. Thus, they have recorded the most in-depth look at the making of the film, including the audience reaction upon the opening of the film.

> But what of the reports of vomiting and fainting? Surely these people were not reveling in the voyeuristic pleasure. Nor were the people who were running to their priests for reassurances that the Devil was really only found in artistic representations. One had only to pick up a copy of a daily newspaper to read the accounts of construction workers in Texas demanding an exorcism for a building site formerly inhabited by the members of a pagan church, or young girls staying up all night to say the rosary, or even, the young men in Boston parading naked in front of the screen shouting they were the Devil.[3]

However, contrary to the media hype, there appear to be few, if any, verifiable accounts of such extreme reactions in the theater. Part of this hype may have been inspired by audience reaction to Alfred Hitchcock's *Psycho*, and the stories of people fainting and vomiting in the theater may have been influenced by many of the grindhouse films that were released to low-rent movie houses in the late sixties through the early eighties that would sometimes advertise as having EMTs on hand upon the release of the film because it was so graphic and horrible. Travers and Reiff's reporting of the incidents may have been just more hype; they had been given full access to the directors, writers, producers, and studios of a film that had been kept under tight wraps, it was only in their best interest to keep the hype going.

All these rumors, however, did inspire a great amount of public interest, and there were, in fact, lines going out the theater doors for *The Exorcist*. From the *Christian Science Monitor*, circa 1974, "He was standing in line for two hours on one of New York's stinging cold days waiting for *The Exorcist*... He was joining the 4 million people already paying $10 million to see the film, queuing up for hours in line winding around city blocks, often in awful weather, to see an occult thriller supposed to shock audiences into nausea, fainting or more severe forms of physical and mental illness."[4] There was also a dramatic increase in public interest in exorcism; the Catholic Church was inundated with requests for exorcisms and questions from a frightened public concerning Satan. Unfortunately, the church was largely unprepared and at odds with itself regarding Satan and exorcism. The Second Vatican Council had just recently convened and had modernized many of the Catholic rituals and was reexamining whether or not Satan was an actual being, thus virtually fracturing the religion itself. Some critics even say that the Vatican II did away with the notion of pure evil. Then suddenly *The Exorcist* is released and a religion in flux is forced to confront its very own demons.

This is one of the many "truths" of *The Exorcist*. Much of the Catholic faith was in question at the time, and *The Exorcist*, for many, was an affirmation of their belief system—an affirmation of true good and true evil—and it ultimately struck a chord in a nervous community. It was not a modernist film, but rather, a film that harkened back to the Dark Ages—to primeval beliefs in spirits, demons, devils, and God. It was a refutation of the modernist social and religious changes of the times. The religious aspects are some of the truest in the film and generated the greatest reaction from the audience. Naturally there was shock and horror and outrage at the graphic nature of the film, but it was the religious context of *The Exorcist* that drove it straight into the hearts and fears of the audience.

William Peter Blatty released his novel, *The Exorcist*, in 1972; it was the story of a young girl living in Georgetown who became possessed by a demon and required an exorcism by a local Jesuit. Blatty had formerly been a seminary student and was very familiar with the inner workings of the church, particularly the Jesuits, one of the most educated and devout factions of the Catholic faith. While *The Exorcist* is a work of fiction, it was inspired by an exorcism that Blatty had read about in a newspaper in 1949, in which a 12-year-old boy was exorcised over the course of several months. The boy, whose identity has always been protected by the Catholic Church, by Blatty and subsequent authors, was originally from the Georgetown area, but the exorcism was performed over the course of one month in St. Louis, Missouri. The actual case was not quite as extreme as the film; there was no 360-degree rotation of the boy's head, no projectile vomiting, no levitation, and no murder (although one of the first priests to attempt the exorcism was badly injured when the boy slashed him with a piece of metal he had somehow removed from the hospital bed), and no "Captain Howdy," the name Regan gives to the demon before it possesses her. The exorcism was largely performed in a Catholic hospital with the priests returning night after night to confront the boy, who, for all intents and purposes, behaved perfectly normal during the daylight hours. The exorcist, Father Bowdern, kept a diary of the events and thus made it the first documented exorcism in U.S. history.

While there may not have been any instances of the more memorable moments of *The Exorcist*, there were reports of objects moving across the room, the bed shaking when the boy was on it, numerous violent acts by the boy, and a rather weak case of the boy speaking in unknown languages. Some of this is refuted even by the Catholic Church. Thomas Allen, journalist and author, wrote a full account of the boy's exorcism in his work, *Possessed*, which was subsequently turned into a film by the cable network Showtime. Allen's report is based on Bowdern's diary, which he acquired through another priest who was present during the exorcism. He writes,

> The Roman Catholic Church has never said whether demons possessed Robbie (fake name), despite what seems to be enough ecclesiastical evidence to render a verdict... Archbishop Ritter, following Church procedure, appointed an examiner—a Jesuit professor of philosophy at St. Louis University—to investigate the case. The examiner had the authority to interview participants under oath. According to a Jesuit who is familiar with the results of the investigation, the examiner concluded that Robbie was not the victim of a diabolical possession. Buttressing that report were statements by psychiatrists at Washington University. They said they saw no evidence of the supernatural or preternatural.[5]

Furthermore, the origins of the possession are different in the actual case as opposed to the film. The actual case was tied to the boy's aunt, a woman who was heavily into Spiritualism and trying to contact the spirits of the dead. She encouraged the boy to use an Ouija board and used it with him. After she passed away, the 13-year-old boy was devastated and attempted to contact her through the board. When the phenomena began, the family thought it was actually the boy's aunt trying to communicate. This has led to some speculation of an inappropriate relationship between the two, whereas in the film, Regan was a seemingly innocent victim of a spirit predator, rather than a sexual predator.

So how is *The Exorcist* a true story? Well... it's not. It is based on a fictional novel that was based on an article that William Peter Blatty read while attending seminary. Blatty did speak with Father Bowdern, but according to Blatty,

> I got in touch with the exorcist and presented my credentials to try to convince him that a great apostolic purpose could be served if this was

a nonfiction book written by him . . . He said instantly that he was not interested in writing the book, for he had taken a vow of silence on the subject . . . The exorcist wrote me and implored that I not write anything that would connect the victim in the case to the material in my novel. I thought he was going far, far overboard, but I decided to change the character from a boy to a girl.[6]

Blatty then began to research exorcism in general to create a suspense/ horror tale around the phenomena; and when he teamed with William Friedkin, they attempted to add as much truth as possible to the film.

So what was true? On a very basic level, *The Exorcist* is based on an actual exorcism that took place on a 13-year-old boy in St. Louis in 1949 and was reported by the *Washington Post*; the story inspired William Peter Blatty. Regardless of whether or not one believes in demons and the devil, exorcism is practiced to this very day, and Blatty's book was based on one of the very few recorded exorcisms. As indicated before, the exorcism of this 13-year-old boy did not manifest such grotesque phenomena as shown in the film *The Exorcist*; this has caused some of the priests involved to question the legitimacy of the boy's possession. However, it was rumored during that time that another exorcism had taken place years earlier on a farm in Iowa—one in which the full spectrum of manifestations had become horrifyingly real.

Father Theophilus had hardly begun the formula of exorcism in the name of the Blessed Trinity, in the name of the Father, the Son, and the Holy Ghost, in the name of the Crucified Savior, when a hair-raising scene occurred. With lightning speed the possessed dislodged herself from her bed and from the hands of her guards; and her body, carried through the air, landed high above the door of the room and clung to the wall with a tenacious grip. All present were struck with a trembling fear.[7]

This account came in the form of a pamphlet written by Celestine Kapsner and was originally published in German. The exorcist was Father Theophilus Reisinger. There were further phenomena that are quite similar to the special effects generated in Friedkin's film: "As a result of these disturbances, the woman's face became so distorted that no one could recognize her features. Then, too, her whole body became so horribly disfigured that the regular contour of her body vanished. Her pale, deathlike and emaciated head, often assuming the size of an inverted water pitcher, became as red as glowing embers. Her eyes protruded out of their sockets, her lips swelled up to proportions equaling the size of hands."[8] There are also stories of "pails of vomit" and several different languages used by the one possessed.

Father Nicola, an American theologian and priest, was on hand for the filming of *The Exorcist* as a spiritual advisor. He has become one of the world's foremost authorities on exorcism. In 1973, Nicola stated, "When I read *The Exorcist*, it struck me immediately that everything in it could be documented from one case or another of diabolic possession. Amazingly, it was 80 to 85 percent accurate from the one case in 1949 on which Blatty based it."[9] More recently Nicola stated in Matt Baglio's work,

> Whenever I express a fear and unwillingness to act as exorcist, I get letters from people assuring me that they have successfully cast out demons and that, as long as one relies on the power of Christ, there is no need to fear the demons. It is my conviction that they are thinking of something entirely different from what I am. Solemn public exorcisms are rarely performed in modern times in the Western world. When they are performed, they are as gruesome and ugly as anything in the world.[10]

Director William Friedkin was focused on maintaining a stark realism in his work, and in order to reach that level of realism, he not only incorporated phenomena from previously documented exorcisms, but also had on staff an actual exorcist who could guide and direct them.

It is interesting to note Nicola's participation in the making of this film at that particular time in the history of the Catholic Church. As indicated before, many felt that the Vatican II had modernized the understanding of religion and, particularly, the devil; and meanwhile there was a priest advising on a Hollywood film that depicted the devil as a true, personified being that was at work in the modern world. Nicola's interest in the film could have been two-fold. He worked to maintain the realism of the film in order to ensure that the ancient Catholic rite was presented in a manner appropriate for the church, but also to assure that the public or the new church did not quickly forget these ancient rites. The issues between the new church and the International Council of Exorcists will be addressed in a later chapter, but suffice to say, there could have been motivating political factors that contributed to Nicola's participation.

There are other levels of truth to the film that add to the disturbing effect the film has had on the audience; one of them that still, to this day, has not been replicated. Special effects are regularly used in films and often contribute to our willing suspension of disbelief. Special effects remind the audience that what they are viewing isn't real. However, in the case of *The Exorcist*, even the special effects are so close to reality that the audience rarely receives the reminder that special effects are being used. This is because many of the special effects are not that "special." The film depicts the room in which the demon resides as being ice cold, the priest's breath visible with every word. That is because it really was that cold on the set. Friedkin brought in massive air conditioners and lowered the temperature of the set to 30 degrees in order to achieve a "real" effect, rather than a special effect. During a disturbing scene in which Regan is throttled up and down in her bed, there is nothing more than a pulley system rigged to Linda Blair's back that jerks her up and down, back and forth. It provided a more realistic vision of someone being moved against her will.

Friedkin insisted on shooting the opening sequence in Iraq, much to the disappointment of the producers because of the cost; but Friedkin insisted that it could not be in Arizona or Mexico or any other desert. It had to be in the cradle of the world, a place ancient and barren. Also, the statue of the demon that Father Merrin sees in Iraq is the image of an actual demon called Pazuzu. According to the *Encyclopedia of Demons & Demonology*, Pazuzu is an "Assyrian and Babylonian Demon god of the first millennium BCE, who sends diseases, pestilence, and plagues into households."[11] Friedkin's adherence to reality causes a level of discomfort that is unlike nearly every other horror film ever made. Perhaps *The Exorcist* taps into some kind of deeper, shared knowledge—something passed down from ancient times. The average viewer probably knows nothing of Pazuzu, but there is something about the demon's image that arouses discomfort. For some reason, the demon, which is accurately represented in the film, appears as something foreign, grotesque, and evil, yet stirs something in our collective consciousness that is familiar. Suddenly, the demon is no longer wandering the barren plain of the Iraqi desert but has taken up residence in a Georgetown home, inside an innocent little girl. The very notion of it is the true power of the film—this ancient evil is not banished to some foreign desert but is actually right next door.

The Exorcist stands to date as the most horrifying film ever made. It doesn't ask for the viewer's willing suspension of disbelief because the assumption of the film is that the viewer already believes—already knows deep down that it's true. At least, that appears to be the formula that Friedkin and Blatty were using, and it worked. *The Exorcist* took the world by storm. It was a world that had lost itself in its modern ideas. Louise Sweeney's article for the *Christian Science Monitor* in 1974 was entitled "Occult Interest Suggests Technology Faith Shattered." In this article she writes, "A cultural paradox is at work in America today: the stainless-steel society glistening with technology and bristling with scientific rationality suddenly reverts to the occult. Why?"[12] This is a question that she asks several different psychologists and theologians, and they are the very same questions being explored today in this very book. Perhaps *The Exorcist*'s lasting power comes from the fact that we have failed to find the answers to these questions, or, perhaps, we are no different than the men and women who roamed the earth in the Iraqi cradle of life who feared Pazuzu and wore amulets to protect themselves from his evil. Perhaps we are still those people despite our "stainless-steel" society. Perhaps the truth of *The Exorcist* is a truth about the nature of man rather than the nature of Satan.

The Exorcist's power ultimately rests within the audience. Its effect at that particular time in history can attest to that very power. *Newsweek* ran two cover stories, lines for theaters wound around city blocks; there was a surge in occult interest, in Catholicism, and in requests for exorcism. People were frightened. Fear is the most difficult emotion for a film to manifest, and therefore represents one of the greatest artistic feats of the film industry. If you want to make the audience cry, you can usually kill one of the main characters or the family dog; if you want to make them laugh, simplistic physical gags or toilet humor will usually do the trick. But the art of eliciting fear is something entirely different. The audience is not in any danger—they are sitting in a theater surrounded by people; there is nothing in their vicinity that should create an emotion of fear. Fear is an emotion that is brought about by some kind of perceived threat. Thus, the audience must perceive a threat on screen. If the audience has been masterfully drawn in to the film by the director and actors, then they come to identify with the characters in the film and fear on their behalf.

However, with certain films, that fear is extended outside the theater because the threat represented on screen is something more real, something more true. Alfred Hitchcock's *Psycho* terrified audiences nationwide with its infamous shower scene. Suddenly people were terrified of roadside motels that they had previously frequented. Steven Spielberg's *Jaws* had much the same effect; people were afraid to go into the water, and fisherman were killing sharks by the boatload. In these two particular cases there was an empirical basis for the films; people are murdered (daily), sometimes in motel rooms and sometimes by mentally deranged maniacs; and shark attacks do happen every year and, while rare, they can represent a frightening possibility for surfers and swimmers. But where does this leave *The Exorcist*? The public reaction was much the same as that of *Jaws* and *Psycho*, and the film has demonstrated long-term effects on audience perception and reaction. The film was re-released in 2000 and included scenes that had originally been cut from the film, much to Friedkin's dismay. *The Exorcist*'s re-release coincided nicely with the sharp upturn in public interest in the paranormal, upon which this book is based.

Both *Psycho* and *Jaws* represented the possibility of film becoming reality, and thus they had enormous audience impact. *The Exorcist*, however, is not about something that we know to be empirically true. *The Exorcist* renewed an ancient fear, something that we do not deal with on a day-to-day basis, something that we do not read about in daily newspapers or that has an annual week devoted to it on Discovery Channel, such as Shark Week. It tapped into an audience reality that may not be an empirical reality. It touched different aspects of the audiences' religious-cultural experience and thus elicited real horror—the horror of a true evil that exists in the world, the horror of supernatural entities bent on our harm. The truth of *The Exorcist* is that whether real or imagined, the film tapped into a primal, ancient fear that rests in the collective human conscious.

THE HAUNTING IN CONNECTICUT

My original intention was to dissect the story of *The Amityville Horror*, as it has become one of the "true" stories that has made its way into the American cultural mythos. However, the story has been told, retold, and debated so many times that any further analysis of the film seems pointless. Furthermore, it is a film that belonged to a past generation. It was remade in an attempt to gain a younger audience, but the film—starring Ryan Reynolds, normally a comedic actor—was pretty much laughed right out of the theater, and the old line about it being a "true" story did not seem to resonate with the younger generation. That being said, *The Haunting in Connecticut* did seem to stoke the paranormal fires of the newer generation. Of course, being a resident of Connecticut and not living too far from the town of Southington, perhaps I just paid closer attention. The film enjoyed moderate success and better DVD sales, but also garnered quite a bit of attention in the media due to the true story factor.

The Haunting in Connecticut and *The Amityville Horror* are similar in several respects, nearly making them interchangeable: each haunting resulted in the family abandoning the home; each investigation involved Ed and Lorraine Warren and the exorcism of a demonic presence; each haunting involved a fair amount of media attention; and neither home experienced any difficulties when the new owners moved into it. And, of course, both were turned into books, cowritten by a horror novelist, and were subsequently turned into films. The Connecticut case also had the further distinction of being featured on Discovery Channel's *A Haunting* under the same title, thereby giving more credence to the "true story" than it would probably have had otherwise. Therefore, I have chosen to use *The Haunting in Connecticut* rather than the Amityville story for contemporaneous purposes.

First, let's start with the story as told by the Snedeker family through the book, *In a Dark Place*, which was coauthored by Ray Garton and the Warrens.

In 1986, the Snedekers moved to Southington, Connecticut, so their son, Philip, could continue to receive daily cobalt treatments for lymphatic cancer at John Dempsey hospital, which is part of the University of Connecticut. Philip was 14 at the time; though his name is listed as Stephen in the book, we will refer to him as Philip. Carmen's husband, Allen Snedeker, was not the children's father and was not living at the house a majority of the time during the two-year haunting. Instead, he continued to work in upstate New York, staying in motels and living with his family on the weekends.

The house, which was formerly a funeral home, is still standing on Meriden Avenue in Southington, though the current owners don't seem to appreciate the newfound fame as they are constantly questioned about whether or not their house is haunted. The new owner, Susan Trotta-Smith, stated in an interview with the *Record-Journal*, "We've lived in this house for ten years. Our house is wonderful. This is all Hollywood foolishness. The stories are all ludicrous."[13] Similar to the Amityville Horror house, the new owners have experienced none of the reported phenomena but are plagued with sightseers, trespassers, and paranormal investigators. This could be due to the entire thing being a hoax or it could be due to the exorcism that was supposedly performed on both residences which expelled the entities; take your pick as to which is the truth.

The Snedekers only lived in the lower half of the house. The house was divided into two apartments for rental. Carmen claims that she was never informed of the history of the house, but it became apparent when they took a look in the basement and saw that many of the tools and the equipment used for preparing bodies were still in place. According to Carmen and the book, Philip immediately began to complain of hearing voices in the basement and seeing visions. He claimed that the house was evil. Naturally, the parents thought this to be his imagination. That was, until Carmen began experiencing the haunting herself, along with her other children, a niece who stayed with them during her parents' divorce, and, supposedly, a neighbor. The story tells of a black dog constantly barking at the house, mop-water turning blood-red, apparitions of dead, naked beings, a green-glowing woman seen in the vacant upstairs apartment, the house shaking, and ghostly sexual molestation.

For whatever reason, despite his insistent fear of the basement, the Snedekers forced Philip to make the basement his room; however, the book indicates that he slept on the couch in the living room most nights until his brother moved into the basement with him. It is then reported that both boys began to see visions of dead people in the room and hear whisperings. They slept with the lights on, which apparently prompted Allen to remove all the lights due to the electric bill climbing ever higher.

However, that is where the similarity between the actual purported story and the Hollywood film end. The film postulates that séances were held in the funeral home and that the funeral home owner never actually buried the bodies. Rather, the bodies were hidden in the walls of the house, which Philip burns down at the end of the film. There was also very little involvement from a priest, though the book vaguely details an exorcism held at the home, which concludes the haunting.

Philip's cancer went into remission during the two years at the home, but he was then institutionalized for sexually assaulting his own cousin, who was living at the home. Carmen Reed and the book insist that Philip's cousin, Trish, was constantly being sexually assaulted by the ghosts; the implication is that Philip became possessed by the entity and then committed this act. In fact, there is a lot of ghost rape in the story of the Snedeker haunting, including rape of Carmen and even Allen. When the Warrens were eventually called in to investigate, Lorraine used her psychic abilities to determine that the house had been the site of ritualistic necrophilia, which had then caused a demonic infestation; "hands—rough, male hands that reached down to fondle the dead bodies, to touch their most private parts in horrible ways . . . fingers closing over limp, dead male genitalia . . . entering the cold, dead private places of women . . ."[14] Following the release of the book, Carmen and her family appeared on an episode of *Sally Jessy Raphael* entitled, "I Was Raped by a Ghost." The Warrens brought in their investigative team for an extended period of time, including their nephew, John Zaffis. It is during this time that Zaffis claims he was attacked by a demon, while everyone else in the house was sleeping in a demonic-induced trance. Zaffis writes in his foreword to *The Encyclopedia of Demons & Demonology* by Rosemary Ellen Guiley, "One of the demonic cases brought me face to face with genuine evil: a reptile-like entity that manifested in an infested home, a former funeral parlor in Southington, Connecticut, and came at me down a staircase. The intensity of the evil was astonishing. I had never before experienced anything like it, and I have to admit, I was so shaken that it was several days before I could return to the case."[15] As indicated before, the investigation concluded with the Warrens obtaining an exorcism of the property from a priest and the haunting ended.

The haunting story, as told by Ray Garton's *In a Dark Place*, tells of a highly sexualized haunting that stemmed from sexual abuse of dead bodies in the care of the funeral home owner. However, the film uses scenes of old séances centered on a child medium and on bodies improperly disposed of in the actual walls and foundation of the house. It tells of a priest who warns them about the dangers of the house and warns them to "Get out now!" The film is a long way from the story told in the book. It even caught the ire of Lorraine Warren herself, who said, "Imagine, if it had been done the right way, it could have been something that could more or less educate the public on what happened. They chose not to."[16] However, leading up to the release of the film, several other revelations were made concerning the supposedly true story.

Joe Nickell investigated the case following the release of the book *In a Dark Place* and reached radically different conclusions regarding the family's experience. He appeared on the *Sally Jessy Raphael* episode to offer his take on the haunting. "On the *Sally* show, I appeared with the Warrens and the Snedekers as well as several of the latter's skeptical Southington neighbors. Ed made veiled threatening asides to me (not aired) and, offstage, swore like a sailor. During the taping, the Snedekers sat on a brass bed while telling their story of demonic sexual attack."[17] The Snedeker family made the rounds on the talk show circuit, from *Maury Povitch* to *A Current Affair*. Nickell brought out the landlady and neighbors who refuted the story. "Long before the *Sally* show, in response to the Warrens' shameless media exploitation, the Snedekers' landlady—who had served them with an eviction notice for failing to pay their rent—had responded to the supernatural claims. She and her husband, she said, had owned the property for two and a half years and experienced no problems with it."[18]

Even more damning were the accusations from Ray Garton, primary author of *In a Dark Place*, which surfaced after the release of *The Haunting in Connecticut*.

They couldn't keep their stories straight, for starters. The family was a mess, but their problems were not supernatural and they weren't going to get the kind of help they needed from the Warrens. At the time I was with them, Carmen was running some kind of illegal interstate lottery scam that I don't think I was supposed to find out about, but when I did, she repeatedly urged me not to mention it in the book and not to tell anyone. Their son, around whom their entire story centered, was nowhere to be found. I never met him. I was allowed to talk to him briefly on the phone, but as soon as he started telling me that the things he "saw" in the house went away after he'd been medicated, Carmen abruptly ended the conversation. The Warrens repeatedly told me they had videotape of actual supernatural activity shot in the house and they were going to show it to me while I was there, but they never did. They said they couldn't find the tape. I never saw the inside of the house (the former funeral home in the story) because the people living there at the time wanted absolutely nothing to do with this circus, and they claimed there were no problems at all in the house. The Warrens explained that this was because the house had been cleansed by a priest who had performed an exorcism, but to the best of my knowledge, the Catholic church has absolutely nothing to do with the Warrens in any official way, and there are questions about the legitimacy of the priests who work with them. Since writing the book, I've learned a lot that leaves no doubt in my mind about the fraudulence of the Warrens and the Snedekers—not that I had much doubt, anyway. I've talked to other writers who've been hired to write books for the Warrens—always horror writers, like myself—and their experiences with the Warrens have been almost identical to my own.[19]

When the film was released, Carmen Reed was interviewed on a number of different news talk shows, and she claimed that she had "always" been sensitive to spirits.[20] Carmen Reed now markets herself as a "Spiritual Advisor" and has a website advertising her abilities and retelling her story in the Southington house. "As an intuitive child, I always had an imaginary friend named Jaco. He was and still is my spiritual guide. I could always see into someone's spirit and know whether they were good or evil. The priests call that the gift of discernment. I always look for the good, in most there is more good than evil, but sadly that is not true for all people."[21] Naturally, such an assertion begs the question of why it took her son being placed in a psychiatric institution before she was aware of any demonic or spiritual activity in the home (though she does claim that she can use her "gift" at will and often does not).

Perhaps the only "truth" touched upon by the Snedekers' story as told in the book, *In a Dark Place*, has to do with Carmen's concern for her son's new friend and his sudden interest in heavy metal music. At the time of the supposed haunting of the Southington house, the nation was awash in fears of satanic cults and the influence of Satanism in heavy metal music. Known as the satanic panic, parents feared that their children were being led down destructive paths through listening to this new form of music. Rumors of Ozzy Osborne biting the head off a bat at a concert and reports of teenagers committing suicide or murder under the influence of these musicians spread rapidly across the nation. Likewise, these fears were projected in the story of the Snedeker haunting. Carmen laments Philip's new friend "Cody," whose parents aren't home very much and who introduces Philip to heavy metal music. Under Cody's influence, Philip begins to listen to the music day and night, reading heavy metal rock magazines and isolating himself from the family. "By Christmastime, Stephen [Philip] had obtained a battered old leather jacket on the back of which he put a skull and crossbones and the logo of some heavy-metal group that combined an upside-down cross with a bloody dagger."[22] This was the quintessential image of what every parent in the 1980s feared: their child increasingly isolated, increasingly rebellious, and spurred on by music that celebrated Satan. During the eighties, the fear of your child becoming a Satan-worshipping monster was in the back of every concerned, middle-class, suburban parent's mind. In the book, that is eventually what Philip becomes—a loner, listening to satanic music, who eventually makes a deal with the devil and gives himself over to the evil presence lurking in the basement and eventually goes on to sexually attack his own cousin and succumbs to insanity. "Stephen [Philip] was his own company. He stayed downstairs when he was home, the electric squeals of his heavy-metal music muffled by the closed and latched doors. Sometimes he could be heard, alone in his room, laughing . . ."[23]

Each time the story is retold we are driven further from the truth. Garton claims to have made up a large portion of the book *In a Dark Place*. For an author of Garton's talents, the book is poorly and hastily written, similar to Jay Anson's rendering of *The Amityville Horror*. The film *The Haunting in Connecticut* deviates even further from the truth by adding séances, bodies hidden in walls, priests, and a fire that destroys the house. *The Haunting in Connecticut* is the grossest rendering of Hollywood truth to date. The assertion of truth in the film amounts to a family who said they once lived in a haunted house, and nothing more. To that end, Hollywood could probably make any haunted house story a "true story" because there is no limit of people who claim to have had experiences in a haunted house. However, the Southington house had gained a bit of fame in the 1980s when the story was first reported in the papers; then the book was written and the family began to make the rounds on the talk show circuits. With the story having been told to the media in the past, the film appeared to have a stronger base in reality, but that reality was not reflected in the film. It deviated so far from the story that it is more fiction than fact. Given Garton's damning testimony that he made up much of the book because the family couldn't keep their story straight, it would appear that even the "true" story is a far cry from reality.

FIRE IN THE SKY

On November 5, 1975, Travis Walton was reported missing in the small town of Heber, Arizona. He was reported missing by his friends and coworkers who had been working with him that day on the Mogollon Ridge of the Apache-Sitgreaves National Forest. They were loggers assigned to thinning the mountains under a Forest Service contract that would allow for better growth, watershed, and land usage. Although Travis was reported missing, he was not reported lost or injured; rather, the six men with him that day reported that he had been abducted by a flying saucer. What happened after that became national news and sparked a multiday search; it also became one of the best-documented and most controversial UFO abduction cases in history, and in 1993 became the film *Fire in the Sky.*

But first, it began as a real incident. Here are the facts of the incident. On November 5, Travis Walton was reported missing. The six men who reported him gone—Allen Dalis, John Goulette, Dwayne Smith, Kenneth Peterson, Steve Pierce, and Mike Rogers—claimed that a UFO had struck Walton with a "ray." The Associated Press reported on November 11, 1975, "Walton disappeared last Wednesday after leaving work with six other woodcutters in the Apache-Sitgreaves National Forest. His six companions said Walton jumped from their truck when he saw a light overhead and followed it down the forest road. Moments later, the men said, the light ray struck him and he vanished."[24] The men's explanation was obviously met with skepticism from authorities; an immediate search of the mountain range began, but no trace of Walton was found. The men were all subjected to a lie detector test administered by Cy Gilson, which they all passed with the exception of Allen Dalis, who angrily quit the lie detector test halfway through, therefore rendering the results inconclusive.

The men were largely suspected of murdering Walton; however, five days after the incident Travis Walton called his brother Duane from a payphone outside Heber, Arizona. Walton was taken to his brother's home in Phoenix, but not before contacting Ground Saucer Watch—a UFO research organization that had approached Duane and warned him of possible dangers coming from the government and shadowy organizations. However, upon making contact with GSW, the Waltons decided that the organization was a sham and returned to Duane's house. Travis's brother "fended off the media by telling them I had been taken to a hospital in Tucson."[25]

Walton then began to work with the Aerial Phenomena Research Organization (APRO) with financial backing from the *National Enquirer.* APRO and the *National Enquirer* funded the testing by doctors and psychologists to evaluate Walton's condition. Travis met with the local sheriff who had originally been given the report on November 11 and sat down with reporters from the *National Enquirer* on November 13. Travis claimed that he had been held against his will on a UFO and examined by creatures.

"I looked frantically around me. There were three of them! Hysteria over-came me instantly. I struck out at the two on my right, hitting one with the back of my arm, knocking it into the other one . . . The one I touched felt soft through the cloth of its garment. The muscle of its puny physique yielded with a sponginess that was more like fat than sinew."[26] Travis claimed that while aboard the UFO, he had been able to move around the craft and encountered two "humans"—a man and a woman—and at one point found himself in a room in which he could see nothing but stars and could control the rotation of the craft by the use of a device.

Travis originally scheduled a lie detector test with Cy Gilson but aban-doned the appointment. Instead, Walton was administered a polygraph under the guidance of Dr. James Harder, one of APRO's scientists and a pro-fessor of civil engineering at the University of California. The results were inconclusive; "The theory behind a lie detector is that people register stressful physiological responses when they lie. He noted that I was still extremely agi-tated when talking about my experience. He counseled that, if a test was per-formed, the results should not be taken too seriously."[27]

However, Travis was given a polygraph at a later date by Cy Gilson and passed. All seven men were given a polygraph before the release of the film *Fire in the Sky* nearly 20 years later and, once again, all passed, including Allen Dalis, whose results had originally been inconclusive. That is where the indisputable facts end; Travis was reported struck by a beam of light from a flying saucer by his six coworkers and subsequently disappeared, a five-day search of the mountains involving helicopters, men on horseback, and vehicles found no trace of him, Travis reappeared on November 10 claiming that he had been taken against his will aboard a UFO, and all seven men, for all intents and purposes, passed multiple polygraph tests. But for many, this does not equal the truth, and Walton's experience to this day is highly controversial and derided by skeptics offering any number of theories that range from LSD-induced psychosis to a hoax engineered by Mike Rogers in order to get out of his logging contract. Walton was personally attacked by any number of skeptics.

While we accept that "based on a true story" entails undisputed facts mixed with personal accounts which can generally not be verified, how does the film *Fire in the Sky* stand up to the actual story?

First and foremost, there are people missing from the film. *Fire in the Sky* only has five other workers with Walton, whereas in reality there were six. Ken Peterson refused to sign the permissions to be portrayed on film and the studio went ahead with the filming without him. They also cut out Walton's brother-in-law, Grant, who originally received the phone call from

Walton and left out Walton's eldest brother, Don, in favor of the intimidating Duane. The film only lightly touched upon Travis's strange experience with GSW in a short scene right after he is picked up by his brother Duane and his girlfriend, and it left out much of the story of the *National Enquirer*'s involvement as well as the involvement of APRO, which are considered to be some of the most controversial parts of Walton's story. Obviously, being backed by the *National Enquirer*, a national tabloid known for its sensationalism and occasional fiction, would stir suspicion of a hoax for monetary gain and fame. Of course, a film must be cut for length purposes, but it would seem that this would be an important aspect to leave uncut. The film also portrays the men as being pushed by law enforcement into taking a polygraph test to prove their story and their innocence, when it was the men who actually requested a polygraph, knowing full well that no one would believe their story. The majority of the film rests largely on the ambiguity of whether or not Travis was abducted by aliens or murdered, so skewing of the motivations for the polygraph may have been a tool for building suspense in the film. Many people in 1995 were probably unaware of Walton's story, so the murder suspicion was a useful vehicle for the plotting of the film.

However, the film does not completely buy Travis's story and there are many allusions and knowing nods to the skeptics' arguments. Firstly, there is the tabloid that the sheriff finds in the workers' truck. Some skeptics claim that Walton was fascinated with UFOs and that recent television programs depicting true stories of alien abductions had led him to commit a hoax for the fun of it. Most notably was the 1975 made-for-TV movie *The UFO Incident*, based on the story of Betty and Barney Hill and starring James Earl Jones. Skeptics also support this idea due to the ease with which Travis's mother accepted the story and believed that aliens had taken Travis. The skeptics' viewpoint is largely represented by James Garner's character, Sheriff Frank Watters, who is never convinced of the UFO story.

But it is not the small things left out or the little things placed in the film that differentiate it from the "true story"; rather, it is the fictionalization of Walton's experience that marks the biggest departure from the real story.

Travis Walton himself feels that his character was misrepresented in the film; he was portrayed as a young, carefree, harmless troublemaker with nothing more on his mind than riding his motorcycle and marrying the girl he loved, who happened to be his best friend's sister. While Walton did marry his friend's sister in reality, he claims that his more serious, intellectual side was completely overlooked. Walton expressed his concern in a letter to the producers, "In earlier versions of the script there were scenes and dialogue that displayed the more philosophical, thinking side of my personality . . . But now with all the chopping and shuffling involved in the rewrites, a critical factor has slipped away. Inadvertent as this may have been, in this script I have become not much more than a one dimensional character, a wild, irresponsible risk seeker."[28] This was certainly true about all the characters in *Fire in the Sky*; each is nearly a cardboard cutout of a character: the bad boy, the boss, the local sheriff, the religious man—though no one can really blame Walton for the director's ineptitude. Travis spends a fair amount of time discussing his interest in philosophy and learning, repeatedly attesting to his intelligence in his book to the point where it becomes obvious that Walton is suffering from small-town paranoia—trying to show people that he is more than just some back-woods bumpkin. He even directly addresses the issue in the beginning of his book, pointing out that small towns are derided in the media as being backwards and filled with uneducated people. "I have news for them. I've seen both sides and I can tell you that rural communities have no corner on tunnel vision."[29] It is true that many people living in the metropolis of the modern city regard places such as Snowflake, Arizona, with a certain disdain, but Walton does an impressive job in the beginning of his book explaining the small-town mentality and showing that the "educated elite" in the cities are sometimes just as dumb and backward as the rural folk they ridicule. Certainly, human prejudice and stupidity knows no particular location. But Walton should not be so paranoid, because his book is quite well written and a testament to his intelligence, compassion, and wisdom. Whether or not you believe his story, the book is a fantastic account of some deeper human truths as well as a great look inside the Hollywood machine that can turn a true story into a fictional story at the drop of a hat and the word of a producer.

But the greatest fictionalization of the story comes in the portrayal of the UFO and Travis's experiences inside the craft. First, the scene in which the characters see the UFO was changed. The craft appears huge, as if it takes up the entire sky, and it swirls with a lava-like red glow. While this special effect made the craft appear more frightening and primal, the actual craft measured approximately 20 feet across and about 8 feet high and glowed bright yellow.

More importantly, however, were Travis's experiences inside the craft. While the scenes portrayed in the film were some of the few parts of the film actually praised by the critics, they were a far cry from Travis's original story. The creatures in the film are grotesque, the craft itself is dirty—a floating gothic garbage dump. The creatures are portrayed as malevolent and powerful, and Travis is subjected to torturous experiments with medieval instruments in a dingy and dark operating room. The reality of Travis's story, however, is quite the opposite. While he did feel somewhat powerless in the craft and, obviously, completely out of his element, he actually felt that he could easily overpower the creatures physically and that they were, in fact, afraid of him—the way the trainer at a zoo might be afraid of the tiger he is training. While they were superior in their technology and intelligence, they were inferior as far as physical ability. When Travis began to resist them, they quickly exited the room and left him alone, just as a trainer may leave an agitated animal that could easily cause great physical harm. His description of the creatures is uncanny:

> Their bald heads were disproportionately large for their puny bodies. They had bulging, oversized craniums, a small jaw structure, and an undeveloped appearance to their features that was almost infantile. Their thin-lipped mouths were narrow; I never saw them open. Lying close to their heads on either side were tiny crinkled lobes of ears. Their miniature rounded noses had small ovals. The only facial feature that didn't appear underdeveloped were those incredible eyes! Those glistening orbs had brown irises twice the size of those of a normal human eye's, nearly an inch in diameter! ... But strangely, in spite of my terror, I felt there was also something gentle and familiar about them. It hit me. Their overall look was disturbingly like that of a human fetus![30]

Furthermore, the craft itself was not a dirty, dingy, floating Gothic castle, but rather a well-lit, clean, and seamless craft—smooth and quiet and utterly beyond Travis's understanding.

After Travis became aggressive with the creatures, they promptly left, and Travis found himself able to wander around the craft. He did not see the creatures again but instead found four humans, three men and a woman, who were attractive, tall, and physically well built, wearing some form of spacesuit. None of them said a word to Travis, but led him calmly to a room in another area of the craft, and laid him on a table; he has no memory of what happened after that. The next thing he remembers is waking up on the side of the road in Heber, Arizona.

Walton's story obviously differs greatly from the gothic horror depicted in the film; however, it should be noted that it is the gothic motif of UFO abduction stories that contributes to the overall fascination with the phenomena, though to date there has not been an abduction report that resembled anything close to what was portrayed in the film sequence. But how does Walton's experience stack up against other abduction claims?

The late Budd Hopkins was one of the world's most recognized authorities on UFO abductions; his life was dedicated to telling individuals' stories about their experiences. He authored several books and works with psychologists and psychiatrists to uncover these stories, which often go unreported. One of the hallmarks of the UFO abduction experience is the inability to recall the events surrounding the abduction; thus, hypnosis is used to help the individuals recall their experience. What generally happens, and what Budd recorded, is that the individuals will see the UFO, usually in the form of a light or a craft, and then suddenly find themselves back in the same place, unharmed, but with several hours having passed of which they have no recollection. This fact prompted Hopkins to title one of his books *Missing Time*. However, in the days, weeks, and months following the sighting, these people will find themselves in the grip of an unknown and inexplicable fear or depression, prompting them to seek help from either a psychiatrist or a ufologist, or, in many cases, simply bury it deep inside and never talk about it.

That is what generally happens, but not always. There are several things that distinguish Walton's experience from the vast majority of reports. Firstly, Walton is able to remember part of his time in the craft without undergoing hypnosis. However, the totality of Walton's memory for the five days that he was gone is only about 45 minutes; but it is still a remarkable incident in UFO history. Secondly, the majority of UFO abduction reports come from the individual abductees themselves and are nearly impossible to authenticate and verify. In Walton's case, however, there were six eyewitnesses who saw the craft and saw it render Walton unconscious, there was an immediate police report, a massive manhunt, national media attention, and several polygraph tests, thus making it, by far, the most documented alien abduction case in history. It should also be noted that Walton's experience is one of very few cases, if not the only case, in which the individual was shot with some kind of "ray" (it is difficult to say whether or not something is "the only" case due to the number of different stories and the inability to verify those stories).

What is truly remarkable, however, is not how Walton's case was unique in ufology, but rather how it was similar. One of the arguments for the reality of the alien abduction experience is the similarity of the reports, particularly the descriptions of the alien beings. Walton described the beings as humanoid creatures under five feet tall with large eyes and some kind of clothing or jumpsuit. They did not speak but communicated nonverbally (many claim that the aliens communicate with them telepathically during the experience). However, one of the most uncanny and intriguing aspects of abductee stories is the way they describe the flesh of the alien creatures. Walton described the creatures' flesh as "white, marshmallowy-looking."[31] Hopkins, in his book, *Missing Time*, writes,

The list of examples can be extended many times over, but centrally important is the sense one has of honest, frightened people trying to be as precise as possible about what they saw. They were taken by humanoid creatures whose skins were whitish-gray in color and disturbingly soft looking, like a mushroom, or a marshmallow, or like putty. These three images denote consistent textural, coloristic, and kinetic qualities, all apart from the repeated description of the figures being between four and five feet tall.[32]

It is also interesting to note that other abductees have claimed to believe that the smaller alien creatures were, in fact, afraid of them and they also describe the creatures as wearing some kind of clothing or suit. The metaphoric descriptions of these creatures by the abductees are the most chilling and believable aspects of the abduction stories because they are not horrific, nightmarish, grandiose, or something out of *Star Wars*, but rather they are so *plain* . . . and therein lies the horror.

Furthermore, Walton's description of being rendered powerless and examined in a medical fashion, and his description of the inside of the craft, is strikingly similar to many other reports from around the world. Many abductees report "experiments" being performed on them, medical tools being used, and in some cases actually having minor surgery performed on them.

Obviously, Walton's story, along with the countless others, are very difficult to believe, and many skeptics have offered explanations as to the Walton case being a fraud, but they run into difficulty. One explanation is that the men were all using LSD when they witnessed the UFO, and Travis merely wandered off into the woods and then popped up again five days later after going on a bender. Firstly, Travis claims that he never in his life used LSD and did not drink. Secondly, it is difficult to envision seven men having the same, simultaneous, drug-induced hallucination and then being clear enough to talk to the police a couple hours later and pass polygraph tests. This theory also does not account for Travis's missing five days; no one saw him, no one served him in a bar or saw him on the side of the street—he was nowhere to be found. Some claim that he was hiding, but why? And from what?

Another popular theory among skeptics is that Walton's friend and boss, Michael, invented the story as a way to get out of his contract with the Forest Service through the "Act of God" clause. Common sense dictates, however, that this would be the stupidest story to tell in order to invoke such a clause; it is impossible to prove and nearly as impossible to believe, and proving it legally would mean having to prove the existence of aliens—a fairly large order for any defense attorney. Also, Michael never tried to invoke that clause with the Forest Service contract. While some people have tried to use the paranormal in legal matters, the paranormal is a notoriously bad defense. In Connecticut in 1983 a man pled innocent of murder due to demonic possession. The judge promptly threw out the plea.

Lastly, there is the matter of publicity and money; Walton's tale was all a hoax to generate publicity and, in turn, money. Walton did, in fact, accept the *National Enquirer's* help in exchange for his exclusive story, and he did immediately seek out UFO organizations rather than heading straight for the local hospital and the local authorities. If Walton wanted to be believed, this was the worst way to go about it, because these actions call into question his integrity upon returning to Snowflake, Arizona. Hindsight may be 20/20, but Walton claims that he and his brother took these actions to protect him from the media and allow him ample time to recuperate after the ordeal; unfortunately, from an objective, commonsense standpoint, it smacks of hoax. Travis claims that he was not wise to the way that this incident and his subsequent actions would be viewed, but it is difficult to simultaneously accept that people in Snowflake are as wise and open as the rest of the world while he invokes the "I didn't know any better" excuse. That being said, the story was backed up by several polygraph tests administered to everyone involved, which repeatedly showed that they were being truthful.

Travis did make money on the incident... eventually. It was 20 years after the incident that the film was finally made, and while Travis did enjoy a bit of fame—appearing on television specials devoted to the paranormal—he also enjoyed a great deal more ostracism and humiliation, as well as personal attacks in the media from skeptics and believers alike. He lost touch with nearly everybody involved, and he and his best friend, Michael, had a falling out that lasted two years. Travis never became wealthy or even particularly well off, and despite his expense-paid trip to Oregon to see the filming of *Fire in the Sky* and hobnob with the B-grade actors, he never really took much away from the incident. Overall, the results of this incident left him as powerless on earth as he was in the spacecraft. Therein lies the difficulty with the hoax theory... nothing was gained and much was lost. Travis lost his ability to control his own fate and destiny. If it were a hoax, he would have been much better off to admit it early on and return to a somewhat normal life that was within his grasp and outside of the targets of many of the skeptics, believers, and slanderers that continue to sight Travis in their crosshairs. Regardless of the reality of Walton's story, questions could and should be asked: "Was it worth it?" Was the truth, one way or the other, worth it? Judging by the tone of his book, *Fire in the Sky: The Travis Walton Experience*, it seems he may answer in the negative.

Walton's experience runs the full gamut of the paranormal experience turned Hollywood. Stories are coopted, names are changed to protect the innocent, drama flares, and special effects are exaggerated. What's more is that his story encompasses a wide range of intersecting agendas, viewpoints, and emotions. His story shows the paranormal at its most extreme. The stakes of his story were high—the only verified and witnessed UFO abduction in history, and all the players came off the benches to have a swing at it, which is why it persists today. His story shows the collision of paranormal groups and believers with skeptics, with the media, and with a small-town population; the equivalent of four cars smashing into each other while speeding through the same intersection. One of the reasons that Walton's story is important, whether or not it is empirically real, is because it gives us a once-in-a-lifetime opportunity to see all these factors collide and collude and ultimately show the chaotic, ambiguous nature of the American paranormal experience.

In his assessment of the state of horror fiction and film from 1950 to 1980, *Danse Macabre*, Stephen King wrote, "Terror often arises from a pervasive sense of disestablishment; that things are in the unmaking."[33] Horror films, the genre of which these three films certainly occupy, try to create this terror. Nearly every film that uses the paranormal falls into the category of horror with the exception of the fairly lame and unwatched films about angels and ghosts who try to make people fall in love. If the essence of terror is that "things are in the unmaking," then the "true" story is an easy shortcut to reach that terror. Typical horror films aim to create this apocalyptic fear through fiction, but what if it isn't fiction? What if it is true? Good horror films can often comment on society while inspiring fear. "I believe that the artistic value the horror movie most frequently offers is the ability to form a liaison between our fantasy fears and our real fears."[34] However, the "true" horror film takes the horrors of fantasy and tells us that they are real and true and something we should fear. But why do we believe what they say? Why are we willing to accept a little girl possessed by demons, a house that is haunted by evil spirits, and beings from another planet that abduct and perform experiments on a young man? Why do we tolerate the "true" label and let these stories sink into our collective mythology? The films may be touching something more primal in our humanity—the sense that things *are* in the unmaking, that there *are* things more powerful than mankind and that our technology *cannot* save us. In a world where there is more than enough to fear from violent crime, terrorism, nuclear war, and so on, many of us find our true fears are more spiritual than physical; the fear that our construction of the world is an illusion, a façade over something greater, more powerful, and more sinister. Perhaps H. P. Lovecraft's tales meant a bit more than just fantasy/fiction—indeed, they ended up forming their own mythologies. Likewise, the "true" horror film forms its own mythology, passed down from generation to generation, talked about over campfires and in schoolyards. The legends of the terror live on and this may, perhaps, be the most "true" part of these tales—their ability to strike the heart of the viewers and cast upon them their spell for generations. Not because we are told they are true, but because we feel that they are true.

CHAPTER 11

A Lack of Faith

Gallup reported in 2011 that approximately 92 percent of surveyed Americans believe in God.[1] However, ReligiousTolerance.org noted that only about 40 percent of those actually attend weekly church services.[2] That leaves 62 percent of a population that has belief and faith in a spiritual world that exists beyond our common reality but do not practice any ritual or dogma to celebrate it. Religion, by its very essence, is related to the paranormal. Religious belief is, by definition, paranormal. In the Christian religion, believers accept by faith that God, in human form, was born of a virgin, completed numerous miracles in his lifetime, had thousands of followers, and was then crucified and rose from the dead. Paranormal is defined as that which is outside of normal accepted reality and is without explanation. The story of Christ certainly fits the mold.

Christianity also postulates absolute evil and absolute good, defined as Satan and God, and that both are at work in this world. Thus, miracles and disasters, charity and murder, being born again and possessed by demons are all at work in the real world, and it is the believer's role to play an active part in one of those two sides. Thus, there are religious services and black magic rites, calls for prayer and witches' spells. The world is a spiritual battleground of opposing forces, and we are right in the middle.

More importantly, however, is the nature of religious belief, which binds it to the paranormal. It is the belief that there is a reality beyond the one we see before us—as if our day-to-day reality is a veil that can be lifted to reveal the ultimate truth. If there is a spiritual world and an afterlife, then our limited, mortal world is merely a prelude to the grand truth. As people seek out this truth in their lives, many will find the church, while others will pursue alternative avenues such as New Age practices and mysticism, cults, ghost hunting, and, sometimes, witchcraft and Satanism. These are all forms of faith in an ultimate reality that is separate from the earth. If 92 percent of the population readily admits to there being a spiritual realm, then 92 percent can readily take the next step to belief in ghosts, demons, UFOs, and Bigfoot. The terms of many Christian faiths, in fact, enforce the belief of demons, witchcraft, ghosts, and UFOs. They are part and parcel of the same ideology; the belief in something more than the material world.

The belief in the spiritual world is far more ancient than dogmatic religion, thus making the paranormal far more ancient than modern religion. But as religion developed, so did paranormal beliefs; and as science developed, religion and the paranormal sought to reaffirm that their faith was true. The paranormal and religion were formed, not by what was known and understood, but by that which was not understood and outside the realm of human knowledge. However, as scientific and technological knowledge increased, religious beliefs either faded or had to be reinvented to accommodate this new knowledge, a process that still continues today. Copernicus's assertion that the earth revolves around the sun rather than vice versa set off a firestorm of religious upheaval and anger. However, in the aftermath of his discoveries, the religious world had to adjust its thinking and rationale. These discoveries also resulted in a power upset for the religious world, in that their assertions of the natural scientific realm were suddenly banished and the church had to relinquish some of its powerful hold over society.

Something quite similar occurred, and is still occurring, with Darwin's *On the Origin of Species*, perhaps the most significant and influential work on the religion-science dichotomy in history. Over one hundred years later, science and religion are battling over the teaching of evolution and creation in the classroom. The church has been scrambling to find new ideas in order to adapt to the overwhelming evidence that is presented in support of evolution. Hence, the intelligent design theory has been put forth as a means of incorporating both belief in a creative power and evolution.

Evolution has, rather quickly, become accepted as scientific fact; however, it still remains a theory open to change. The difficulty with a scientific "fact" is that the rapidly changing world of science offers a litany of theories that are quickly labelled as fact, sometimes by the media and sometimes by the scientific community itself, but are then proven untrue and are quickly revised. In this technological time, these facts and subsequent revisions occur so rapidly that faith in science can often be fleeting and difficult for the public. Religion, on the other hand, has remained fairly consistent over thousands of years with minor revisions being made to the overall idea that there is a God and his spirit is at work in the world. It is much easier to have faith in an idea like that than in quarks, quasars, antimatter, and dark matter.

Likewise, paranormal beliefs that posit a world of truth beyond the one we know have had to change and adjust throughout the years. But the seemingly acausal belief that there is something unseen is much more familiar and easier to believe than much of what science can offer, largely because the belief that there is something greater than ourselves is an intrinsic feeling. As man grows and develops in the world, both ancient and modern, he looks upon reality and senses that there is something more than what is seen, that in all this complexity there must be a benevolent order that precedes it all. Some believe that order to be physics and others believe it to be spiritual; either way, both are searching for that underlying truth. With every genome that is sequenced or galaxy that is discovered, the scientist seeks to unravel the underlying order to the world. Likewise, the believer seeks the spirit and tries to find the intricate dance of day-to-day life in the conjuring up of ancient rituals that have been passed down through thousands of years.

THE MAGICAL AND MIRACULOUS ORIGINS OF FAITH

The idea of gods—of forces greater than our own—probably originated with the very first lightning strike. Natural forces, which were well beyond their level of comprehension and technology, beset early humans. Hence, the unexplainable became the magical or miraculous. Forces were controlled by gods rather than weather patterns and by spirits rather than plate tectonics; the world was a place of action and movement that was beyond the comprehension of man. These things inspired fear and a belief (rightly so) that there were forces at work greater than man's that could not be comprehended or explained. Paul Kurtz writes in his work *The Transcendental Temptation*, "The fundamental premise of those who believe in a magical-religious universe is their conviction that there are hidden and unseen powers transcending the world, yet responsible for what occurs within it . . . Ancient peoples were troubled by seemingly inexplicable occurrences. At first they attributed them to animistic causes, believing that material objects and animals have an inner spiritual consciousness like ourselves, which was separable from the body and had causal efficacy."[3] Hence, if everything had a soul similar to our own then it would behoove early man to try to appeal to those spirits in order to ensure his own survival, in that the effects of appealing to the gods or spirits could be experienced in the real world. Max Weber writes in *The Sociology of Religion*, "The most elementary forms of behavior motivated by religious or magical factors are oriented to this world . . . Even human sacrifices, uncommon among urban peoples, were performed in the Phoenician maritime cities without any otherworldly expectations whatsoever ... Thus, religious or magical behavior or thinking must not be set apart from the range of everyday purposive conduct, particularly since even the ends of the religious and magical actions are predominantly economic."[4] In other words, magical-religious thinking and practices were used to appeal to the unseen forces to ensure good hunting, a good crop harvest, rain, warm weather, and so on, so as to better ensure survival. As society and technology developed—the domestication of animals, irrigation of crops, and better soil utilization—people were less dependent on magical-religious beliefs to ensure their survival. However, people were still faced with a litany of unexplained phenomena such as earthquakes, volcanoes, disease, famine, and war. Religious appeals were used to a great extent to ensure victory in war and deliverance from famine and disease.

"In these cases, religious behavior is not worship of the god but rather coercion of the god, and invocation is not prayer but rather the exercise of magical formulae."[5] During the earliest stages of religious development, the one who was best able to coerce the gods was the shaman, a charismatic and liminal figure in the group who was closely associated with the spirit world. "In their initiations shamans may spend long periods alone in the bush. They seek visions, sometimes facilitated by illness or fasting, which can involve death, dismemberment and rebirth. Shamans' ventures into the bush and mystics' retreats into the desert are examples of journeying into the wilderness. Shamans and mystics put themselves outside society, at least temporarily. Shamans contact ancestors and other spirits in séances; they serve as a bridge between this world and the next."[6] Being the tribe's connection to the spiritual world, the shamans held great power and respect and were allowed a greater freedom to act outside the norms of tribal life. However, the shaman did have to produce magical-spiritual-economic results. The shaman had to be able to produce rain, game, crops, and good weather through his interaction with the spirits. Thus, the shaman had to develop certain rites and rituals in order to ensure his effectiveness. "Every purely magical act that had proved successful in a naturalistic sense was of course repeated in the form once established as effective. This principle extended to the entire domain of symbolic significances, since the slightest deviation from the ostensibly successful method might render the procedure inefficacious. Thus, all areas of human activity were drawn into this circle of magical symbolism."[7]

This development elicited two results: firstly, the development of dogma, a set of rituals and behaviors meant to elicit good favor in the spirit world, and secondly, it gave the shaman more control over the tribe or people; if the shaman performed a rite and there were no results, he could say it was because the people of the tribe had somehow offended the spirits through particular behaviors. Thus, the shaman's negative results could be scapegoated onto the people. The shaman could much more easily coerce the people than the gods. Dogmatic rituals and behaviors allowed the shaman to rise to a position of great power and set the groundwork for the enormous power that priests, rabbis, imams, and churches in general would wield throughout history.

In essence, one's connection to the divine or spiritual world was demonstrated by one's ability to control and manipulate forces of nature—in effect, to work miracles. It was the greatest of these miracle workers, men who not only influenced the natural world but seemingly controlled it, who inspired the major religions. Moses, Jesus, and Mohammed each enacted such incredible miracles at their very command that they superceded all other mystics, shamans, witch doctors, and wizards before them. The miracle is the proof of divinity, and that divinity would not have been believed without it. Thus, religion is based on the power of an individual to coerce and manipulate the natural world through unknown or supernatural abilities, i.e., a connection to God.

Who would Moses have been, and of what use would he have been to the Israelites, if he had not been able to call down God's wrath in the form of the 10 plagues, or if he had not been able to part the Red Sea? Who would Jesus have been had he not healed the blind and raised the dead? Who would Mohammed have been had he not split the moon? They would merely have been another mystic, another shaman for the people. It was their connection to God and their ability through God to work miracles that made them divine, and subsequently, drew people to follow them, spawning three major religions of the world. Religion is built on the belief that there is a spiritual world and that man can interact with, influence, and be influenced by that spiritual world. It is something unseen by the human eye, yet it can be felt, and, on rare occasion, manifested. This belief system comprises belief in the paranormal. If communication with the God of Good can influence the world and the people in it, then certainly communication with Satan can do the same through the presupposition that the spiritual world can interact with the corporeal world. Thus, witchcraft, magic, soothsaying, Satan worship, and other nefarious activities are a direct result of the rise of religion. If influence on the spiritual world can be used for good, then it can also be used for evil. Our world is caught in the middle.

But alas, we don't see many miracles these days as told in the Bible. There have been no seas parted, moons split, or water turned to wine. Today's miracles, along with today's expectations of the divine, have shrunk considerably. Modern man no longer expects that God will move a mountain or split an ocean. The church does not seek such miracles on its own behalf, either. Religious expectations are much different today than in previous days. We no longer rely on divine intervention to be sure that we are fed; in fact, we recognize that divine intervention has little to do with whether or not there is an earthquake, disease, drought, rain, flood, good crop yield, or availability of meat. We have taken the divine out of the equation through science and technology. We no longer seek out priests, rabbis, and mystics to intervene on our behalf for survival (though we often do in cases of disease). This is what Weber calls the "rationalization of the world." Science and technology have replaced what used to be mystical intervention with the divine. We are no longer mystified by unseen maladies like disease. We know them now. We intercede on our own behalf. This has led to a great "disenchantment" with religion, and this disenchantment has been growing for some time; in essence, much of the magic is gone. "The rise of Protestantism was one step in the global rationalization process, and its contrasts with Catholicism are instructive. Catholicism has the stronger mystical component, whereas Protestantism largely disavows mysticism and monastic orders. Protestantism has no priests who serve as mediators between God and humanity. In the Catholic Mass with transubstantiation, bread and wine become the body and blood of Christ, but in Protestantism, they are only symbols."[8]

Science and technology have brought about this rationalization. This, of course, isn't meant to be critical, merely factual. The more that humanity has come to understand the world around them and the way it functions, the less inclined they are to accept supernatural explanations. Oddly enough, the abatement of the supernatural has not led to a decline in religious beliefs. Paul Kurtz ponders this absurdity and offers several ideas ranging from genetic predisposition to the idea that we are all a lot happier living an illusion; but all, by his own admission, seem to come up short. The magical-religious belief system carries on despite scientific evidence that has rendered much of it false. Logically, it doesn't make sense, and it has infuriated those scientists and skeptics who insist upon a logical world. Erich Fromm writes in his work, *Psychoanalysis and Religion,*

> While we have created wonderful things, we have failed to make of ourselves beings for whom this tremendous effort would seem worthwhile. Ours is not a life of brotherliness, happiness and contentment, but of spiritual chaos and bewilderment dangerously close to a state of madness—not the hysterical kind of madness which existed in the middle ages, but a madness akin with schizophrenia in which the contact with inner reality is lost and thought is split from affect.[9]

It would seem that Kurtz and others feel that the disenchantment, the rationalization, the scientific understanding—in effect, the "wonderful things"—would satiate our lives, create contentment and comprehension, but they have not. Instead, man is left at odds with himself in relation to the material understanding of the world. Fromm posits that the soul is unfulfilled despite whatever technological advances may be made—the world and the soul are at odds.

And why wouldn't they be? There is an intrinsic feeling that there is something more both within us and without; yet we are being told there is not, and our world functions as if there is not. Humanity is not logical, and logic is not the answer to all of man's ills. That must come from somewhere else, whether it is religion or paranormal beliefs. This may be the answer to the persistence of religious belief systems in the face of scientific development and technological breakthroughs; it is that they are *only* scientific developments and technological breakthroughs. Fromm writes,

> Self-awareness, reason and imagination have disrupted the "harmony," which characterizes animal existence. Their emergence has made man into an anomaly, into the freak of the universe. He is part of nature, subject to her physical laws and unable to change them, yet he transcends the rest of nature. He is set apart while being a part; he is homeless, yet chained to the home he shares with all creatures. Cast into this world at an accidental place and time, he is forced out of it, again, accidentally. Being aware of himself, he realizes the powerlessness and the limitations of his existence. He visualizes his own end: death. Never is he free from the dichotomy of his existence . . .[10]

It is this dichotomy between the material and the immaterial that leaves open the door for magical-religious belief and thought, and they are not without merit.

The divide between the material world and the soul, the scientific community and religion is wide, but it doesn't necessarily have to be. Fromm's statement that man was "cast into this world at an accidental place and time" is interesting in that it appears he is speaking in scientific terms of evolution and the universe. The world exists without meaning—everything being a beautiful accident. Kurtz posits that mankind invents illusions to avoid this difficult, existential fact.

> We live our brief lives in a particular slice of space-time history and in a specific sociocultural context. A relatively minor planet in one galaxy among billions, we are only an infinitesimal part of the total cosmic

scheme . . . The world viewed from our individual vantage point is often ambiguous. The entire universe confronts us with its enormity, inviting us to unravel its secrets, yet resisting any easy interpretation into its mysteries. Yet since the inception of philosophical reason and science, we have made significant headway in this adventure.[11]

We may have made significant headway in the understanding of the *function* of the universe—the "how"—but not so much in the *reason* of the universe or the "why." That is perhaps one of the ambiguities that Kurtz mentions and is one of the torturous dichotomies that pervade humanity. But could there be a possible reconciliation between the two through the theory of chaos?

MODERN MIRACLES AND CHAOS

I spent my first year of college at a Christian college. At my parents' urging I attended Eastern Nazarene College in North Quincy, Massachusetts. I was only there for one year, but it was a year that profoundly changed my views on God and Christianity. Until that point I had been raised in the First Assembly of God Church, a traditional Pentecostal church. However, during my first semester I attended a course on astronomy. The professor began the course by asking us, "How many of you believe that God led you here to this school and to this class?" Being good Christian youths, we all raised our hands. "Now, how many of you were brought here through a miracle in which you were transplanted from your ordinary life, across time and space, and basically 'miracled' into this classroom?" Not one raised their hand. The realm of miracles had changed.

The Bible claims that God is all-knowing, all-present, and all-powerful. God can move mountains, but has anyone ever seen it done? The miracles that are described in the Bible—the parting of the Red Sea, turning water into wine, the raising of the dead, the sun standing still—are no longer witnessed by mankind. Our miracles today are different. They are smaller; in essence, less miraculous. Or are they? No one today has witnessed the deliberate moving of a mountain by God. However, we witness on a daily basis the literal moving of mountains by construction and road-building teams. This amazing feat of human ingenuity is actually the result of a mistake made by ninth-century Chinese alchemists looking for an elixir for immortality and instead developed gunpowder. Thousands of years of coincidences, interactions, loss, failure, success, and curiosity have led man to the point where he is literally able to move mountains at his command. It did not happen overnight, but considering all the things that could have occurred in those centuries, the fact that it happened at all is a miracle.

In fact, the chances of life occurring on this floating rock in the middle of space are so infinitesimal, that it alone can be considered miraculous. Ancient man was right to assume that there was something greater than himself—the mistake may not have necessarily been to personify that assumption, but to make it dogmatic. There are certainly forces greater than our own at work in the universe.

John Briggs (a former professor of mine) writes in his work *Seven Life Lessons of Chaos*, "The scientific term 'chaos' refers to an underlying interconnectedness that exists in apparently random events. Chaos science focuses on hidden patterns, nuances, the 'sensitivity' of things, and the 'rules' for how the unpredictable leads to the new. It is an attempt to understand the movements that create thunderstorms, raging rivers, hurricanes, jagged peaks, gnarled coastlines, and complex patterns of all sorts, from river deltas, to the nerves and blood vessels in our bodies."[12] In essence, the study of chaos is attempting to understand the underlying order behind these seemingly chaotic events, the events for which early man had no explanation other than belief in a god or gods. Early man recognized that there was some existing order that lay behind these chaotic processes, and attempted to explain and simplify this understanding through personalization of the order in the form of a god or gods. Shamans and witch doctors attempted to understand this underlying order and influence it to the benefit of the tribe. In chaos, the most minor of actions can influence the largest of events. It is often characterized with the expression, "A butterfly flaps its wings in Brazil and creates a hurricane in East Asia." In chaos the very subtle can influence the cosmically large. That is why large systems are so subject to chaotic change; the subtle, in great numbers, influence the larger systems, which then interact and influence each other in a myriad of interactions based on billions and billions of smaller subtle actions. But acting beneath all of this is an underlying order, which is not necessarily supernatural, but its effects are, nonetheless, miraculous, not merely coincidental. It is this underlying order of interacting systems, of "coincidences," that led to the Chinese inventing gunpowder, which, through many, many years and interactions, became capable of moving a mountain that previously blocked a roadway. God at work.

One of the more commonly heard miracles these days involves the mysterious curing of a dreaded disease such as cancer. Take, for instance, a cancer patient named Tommy, 53 years old and father of two, recently divorced. Tommy has an inoperable brain tumor and doctors have given him zero chance of recovery. Tommy's friends and family are praying for his recovery, but things look dismal. Tommy has never really been one for church, and has led a less-than-admirable life; indeed, his family has also never really been believers, but now they turn to God for help. Three weeks later, the tumor is gone, the doctors are baffled, and Tommy goes on to live a long and productive life.

On the other hand we have Mandy, a 14-year-old girl diagnosed with a similar tumor. She is young and innocent, and her family attends church regularly. Within four months she has wasted away to practically nothing, is delirious from the disease, sickened, weak, and bald from the chemotherapy. Then she dies.

Tommy's case would be considered by the religious to be a miracle, but to the scientific community—a mystery. Mandy's case, however, is justified by the religious as being God's ultimate plan, while the scientists bemoan their inability to treat such an innocent victim. If the traditional Christian notion of God were true—that he is a human-like sentient being that exists with his hand guiding the course of human endeavors, these cases would not really make much sense. Religious people justify this by intimating that God works in mysterious ways and that his plans are not ours to know. But what of that plan? What is the ultimate plan that God has in mind for this world, particularly if he plays an active role in the day-to-day happenings? This is a question that theologians have struggled with for centuries.

What if this underlying order, the "interconnectedness" of the world, is the plan by which the religionists view the miracles and tragedies of the world? The events and intricacies that led to Tommy's miraculous recovery would be so infinite that it would be beyond both comprehension of man and science as well as the spiritual understanding of the religious. Likewise, Mandy's death would be the result of millions of intricacies and events that make up part of that underlying interconnectedness of the world. Both miracle and tragedy can be understood through the interaction of an infinite number of people, places, things, systems, and natural occurrences. In either case, it is seen as an act of God in accordance with his plan.

Would Tommy's case be any less miraculous, however, because it was not divinely ordered by a sentient being that watches over the world? In fact, it would seem even more miraculous. Tommy's recovery would be the result of the influence of powers and systems well beyond the comprehension of man. It would be, in effect, a miracle generated by all of life, time, and power; the act of something omnipresent and omnipotent.

When God appears to Moses at the burning bush and Moses asks for his name, God replies, "I am who Am." I am "all being"; I am everything in relation to everything else simultaneously in the great seemingly chaotic system. "But there is profound irony in this name. It expresses the process of being rather than something finite that could be named like a thing. The meaning

of the text would be accurately rendered if it were translated 'My name is
NAMELESS.' "[13]

Using this understanding of the miraculous, is it not possible that the paranormal could be a result of such processes? If something like cancer can mysteriously disappear from a patient whose death sentence has been announced
by the best medical minds, then why couldn't an image in the form of a ghost
or UFO or hairy ape-like creature appear visible to an individual? Within all
chaotic systems there are aberrations—anomalies that are produced from
the interactions within that system. Could not the vision of a spirit be such
an aberration? Could psychics not occasionally be right? As early shamans
tried to influence the massive systems around them, they found both success
and failure. Upon success, the shaman would try to repeat what he had done
that had led to the success, thus leading to the earliest form of dogmatic ritual. However, if the shaman's repeated rituals did not again produce favorable results, then the shaman was able to cast blame on the conduct of his
tribesmen rather than admit his impotency in the face of the Great Mystery.
Religion was born of the unknown chaotic systems and their underlying
interconnectedness, and man's attempt to control those systems. Likewise,
man tries to call up spirits, predict the future, and signal UFOs through ritual
and dogma. The influences of such actions and rituals will probably never be
fully understood, but it doesn't necessarily make such things supernatural,
but rather, natural in the grandest sense of the word.

RELIGIOUS VIEWS OF THE PARANORMAL

I have little to no doubt that some ideas in the previous section will be
contested by both sides, but that is part of the beauty of ideas, and I welcome
an open discussion that will hopefully bring people together to discuss differing notions of God and reality.

But there exists a modern church, one that has been built through thousands
of years of culture and society, miracles and paranormal events. The modern
church is one that both fully engages in the paranormal, and yet sits on the side-
line, hesitant about entering the paranormal fray. As mentioned before, the
Christian church has undergone many changes throughout history as it has
tried to adapt to the ever-emerging scientific discoveries, and it will, no doubt,
have to defend itself again in the future. The church and the paranormal have
a long, parallel history that is the result of the same cause—the miraculous and
mysterious. Whether it is a thunderstorm that lights up the sky for early man
or a ghostly apparition that appears before a stay-at-home mom, the belief system remains similar: there is something more than our concrete reality,

something beyond our vision and understanding. In that regard, religion, and particularly the Western-dominant religion of Christianity, has formed the basis of much of the paranormal belief systems. Ideas about angels and demons, heaven and hell, ghosts and chariots in the sky, have come from the Christian tradition. Therefore it is necessary to our understanding of the paranormal to understand the exact viewpoints of the modern church with regard to these subjects.

SID ROTH AND THE MESSIANIC MESSAGE

I happened upon Sid Roth's program, *It's Supernatural,* while flipping through the television channels one day. The show appears on the Inspiration Network, a network whose mission is "to impact the destiny of people and nations for Christ through media." This is not a channel I would normally stop at, but the title of the program caught my attention, and I began to watch. Sid Roth was interviewing guests regarding Christian perceptions of UFOs and discussing the theories regarding the Nephilim—the fallen angels and demonic entities that were put forth by I. D. E. Thomas in his book, *The Omega Conspiracy.* Sid was raised an Orthodox Jew and then converted to Christianity and began his ministry known as Messianic Ministries, which focuses on trying to convert Jews to Christianity. Sid's personal history in dealing with the occult is what led to a conversion in his life; it sounds similar to Saul's miraculous conversion while on the road to Damascus. "When I was 29 I got involved in New Age. I got in over my head. It was called the occult back then, now it's called New Age, but it's all the same, it's really Buddhism . . . I got in over my head and almost lost my mind, and I was rescued by Jesus. I lived the life of the movie *The Exorcist.* I had something evil inside me." It wasn't until Sid recognized this evil and the way that it was destroying his life that he finally cried out for Jesus and was converted. "I had separated from my wife and daughter; life was too hard, I pretty much threw in the towel . . . I woke up the next morning and there was a presence in my room of love that I had never experienced in my entire life. It was so tangible and so real, and I had a knowing inside me that Jesus was my messiah and he was stronger than the evil inside me and that the evil inside me was gone. Then I heard the audible voice of God for the first time in my life and it said 'return to your wife and daughter'; I did and God restored my life, my mind, and my marriage."

Since that time Sid has been actively engaged in his Messianic Ministries and has actively pursued trying to keep people away from the occult/New Age movement, which he says is very dangerous. "The occult is a counterfeit, a good counterfeit, of something authentic. Anything authentic has a good counterfeit, and that's where most Christians get caught. My experience is that anyone who has been in the New Age and has become a Christian has a special discernment for those working with New Age powers ... I can just walk into a room and feel it." Sid's focus is on converting Jews to Christianity and away from the New Age/occult practices. Sid states that a Jew, more than any other ethnicity or faith, requires a supernatural sign in order to be moved by God and cites the biblical book of Corinthians where it says, "The Jew requires a sign." "I was hungry for the supernatural before I met Jesus, and I was hungry for the supernatural after I met Jesus. Hence, the show, *It's Supernatural.* Most people don't know the reason for the show's name; but the reason is that the best way to reach a Jew is to make the supernatural the platform, because the Jew requires a sign. If you look at the leadership of the cults and the occult in America, you'll find an amazingly high percentage of Jews. Why? We have a zeal for God but not according to knowledge." Sid believes that Jews are more often drawn to the devil's counterfeit supernatural because they have a special yearning for the supernatural; and since they do not have an intimate knowledge of Jesus, they have no positive direction in which to steer that drive. Robert L. Snow, former police officer and author of several books, including *Deadly Cults: The Crimes of True Believers,* writes, "Interestingly, studies have also found that cults are more appealing to certain groups of people. For example, research has shown that the percentage of Jews in cults is far higher than the number of Jews in the general population. Estimates of the proportion of Jews in cults range from 20 percent to 50 percent."[14]

A quick reading of the Old Testament will show that the Jewish people were often skeptical and required repeated instances of supernatural evidence to be convinced of God's presence. Various miracles were performed in order to keep God's chosen people following Moses through the wilderness; the parting of the Red Sea, manna from heaven, a pillar of cloud by day and a pillar of fire by night, and various supernatural actions that interceded on behalf of the Israelites as they battled enemies and sought their promised land. Sid's belief is that this long tradition of supernatural signs and intercession is at odds with modern Judaism's nonacceptance of Jesus Christ as the Son of God. This leaves a divide in the Jewish desire for the supernatural, and the satisfaction of that desire on earth through the purported miracles of Jesus. Since the Jewish faith rejects the notion of Jesus as the Son of God, they are left waiting for a supernatural sign from God, a manifestation of God on earth—and they have been waiting a long time. Naturally, some will seek out other sources of supernatural evidence and beliefs and become drawn into the New Age belief systems to satisfy that need.

While Moses conferred with God on Mount Sinai, the people grew restless waiting for him. They sought out Aaron, whose staff God had caused to blossom, and he instructed them to build and worship a golden calf. When Moses finally came down from the mountain, he was so angry that he broke the stone tablet, which contained the words of God. Moses himself had to demonstrate great supernatural powers, not only to the Pharaoh, in order to secure the release of the Jews, but to the Jewish people themselves in order that they would follow him.

Likewise, Sid claims that his ministries contain that element of the supernatural that will cause the Jewish people to rise up and follow Christ, rather then continue waiting for the Messiah or getting immersed in New Age occult practices. "I will reach more Jews doing *It's Supernatural* and not platforming that I'm Jewish and believe in Jesus and you're Jewish and you too can believe in Jesus. I do lectures around the country and around the world for that matter about the supernatural, and many that attend the lecture will be healed. I recently had a lecture in Brighton Beach where 400 people received the Lord. They didn't receive the Lord because I was a great evangelist, but because in the middle of my talk someone in a wheelchair stands up and starts walking, and her attendant grabs the mike and says, 'I've never seen her walk before,' and then it was easy to say, 'The God that just did this, how would you like to know him?' " Sid claims that miracles occur at his lectures, enabling him to lead Jews to Jesus. He also claims that his ministry would not be possible without the supernatural.

Sid believes that the resurgence in belief in the paranormal is consistent with the approaching return of Christ, and that the devil is increasing his efforts to lead people to their spiritual and physical deaths through drawing them into a counterfeit supernatural belief system. He cites Deuteronomy, chapter 18, which states, "Let no one be found among you who sacrifices his son or daughter in the fire, who practices divination or sorcery, interprets omens, engages in witchcraft, or casts spells or who is a medium or spiritist or who consults the dead. Anyone who does these things is detestable to the Lord . . ."

"It is an abomination for anyone to be involved in the New Age; but it is worse for a Jew because a Jew is under a covenant with God, a gentile is not." According to Sid and his ministry, the paranormal, as we know it today and as discussed in this book, is a counterfeit designed by the devil to entrap the human soul; and the New Age, which often has paranormal links, is a new version of the occult. The recent increase in paranormal and occult belief patterns has been exacerbated by the modern church's rapid slide toward rationalizing its traditional beliefs. "Religion [today] is just fumes, it's not the authentic anymore. They found that by eliminating the supernatural, speaking in tongues, etc., they can grow and they get extremely large. You don't see praying for baptism in the Holy Spirit in public anymore, you don't even see a message on speaking in tongues in a charismatic church because they think they can't reach nonbelievers with messages like that. So the church is holding back on the supernatural; the devil is not holding back in the New Age so it's a pied piper. It's a no contest . . . if the church ties one arm behind its back, what do they expect?" Sid refers to these churches as "seeker-sensitive," in that they downplay the supernatural to appeal to a wider audience.

Sid's message is one of return; return to the traditional, supernatural beliefs upon which the church was founded. The steps that modern churches have taken toward minimizing belief in the Holy Spirit and miraculous healings and so on are costing souls in the ultimate fight against Satan. To be fair, however, the modern church is between a rock and a hard place when it comes to the miraculous and supernatural in that it has repeatedly been burned through false ministries headed by con men who have fleeced believers for their money while claiming miraculous healing abilities. The hypocrisy is also found in charismatic church leaders, as newspapers discover their sexual exploits; and all the while, science continues to gain more and more insight into what was previously considered supernatural. The church has had to move toward the rational and push the supernatural to the sidelines of their ministries in order to win new believers. Sid, however, thinks this is a grave mistake; to him, the paranormal resurgence is a call for the church to return to its traditional values and belief systems so that people actively seeking the supernatural will seek it through the church rather than through the occult, New Age, or paranormal. The stakes for people's belief could not be higher because of the ability for belief to drive the course of human history.

"It's sort of like Adolf Hitler. Do you really think that *nut* could have mobilized the entire nation without supernatural help? He had supernatural charisma." In the case of Hitler, the people believed his cult-like charisma and the people followed. It was, perhaps, the greatest display of evil the world has ever known, and the Jewish people were its greatest victims.

CLIVE CALVER AND WALNUT HILL COMMUNITY CHURCH

Reverend Clive Calver is the head pastor of Walnut Hill Community Church, which is, essentially, one of the seeker-sensitive churches that Sid Roth indicated was leaving behind the supernatural traditions upon which the church was founded. There is no altar call at the end of the service, no public speaking in tongues with interpretation following, no laying on of hands and anointing in oil for healing; rather, it is a church that is focused on expressing Jesus's love and devotion in the community. Clive is not your typical small-town preacher, either. Born and raised in Great Britain, he obtained his degree in theology from London College of Theology, was president of World Relief for seven years, and the head of the Evangelical Alliance of the United Kingdom. He has authored 20 books on the subject of Christianity, has appeared on CNN, BBC, and ABC, and led the Youth for Christ movement in Britain. He is an imposingly brilliant man, his office more like a library than a traditional office, and his stare is one of unhindered intelligence and education. I immediately felt like the dumbest person in the room.

Clive is the culmination of the modern church leader: educated, worldly, experienced, focused on community and world outreach, and focused on showing Jesus's love to others through charity rather than condemning to hell those who don't believe. The Protestant separation from the Catholic Church was one of the biggest steps toward religious rationalism in the history of religion. It took away much of the magical symbolism that distanced the believer from God. No longer was a priest needed for confession, no longer was the bread and wine transubstantiated into the actual body and blood of Christ, no longer were dogmatic rituals the basis of worship. A new, freer, more accessible God had arrived onto the scene, and today's evangelical churches are the spawn of that reformation.

Likewise, much of what Calver and his work are about is also what they are not about; they are not about the televangelist nightmare that has caused so much damage to the evangelical Christian religion. He is not causing people to pass out with the wave of his hand, and people in wheelchairs who have been unable to walk are not standing up in front of television cameras, nor are there any other innumerable frauds happening that have previously been wrought upon the Christian religion by the Jerry Falwells and Pat Robertsons of the world who have been so divisive. Several weeks before we met, a massive earthquake had struck Haiti, killing over 200,000 people and wounding many, many more. Reverend Pat Robertson commented on his television program that the earthquake was the result of a contract that the Haitian people had made with the devil in order to get out from under the control of the French.[15] I asked Calver about that statement. "You know, I don't normally utter obscenities to someone who is interviewing me, but the idea that God sends an earthquake to punish people in that way without the warning beforehand would be ridiculous, if you want to be theological about it. I don't think that has any connectedness at all. I think if you want to see where God was at work in the earthquake, it was in the response—the rescuing."

However, it is the notion of the devil, the idea of true and pure evil, which remains an inherent difficulty for Christianity and has led to much debate over the nature of evil and its personification in Satan. Recent modernist ideas about the nature of humanity and evil have allowed belief that there is no such creature as the devil, and that evil is merely a lack of God's love in the person who is committing the evil act or that evil acts are merely part of the range of human behavior. The denial of a true devil has left open the possibility of other denials within the Christian belief system. However, blaming the devil for things such as the Haitian earthquake is just as devastating to the church's message. Calver says, "There are two dangers that face the church when they're encountering these issues, one is to disbelieve in the devil and his existence. The second is to magnify his power and influence much further than they should." Calver cites the much-publicized rites of exorcism used by the Catholic Church and made famous in *The Exorcist* as an exaggeration of the devil's power. "I've watched an 18-year-old girl pulling her face off because of the stuff [occult] she's been engaged in and then how she was seeing herself. I've seen the results of the trickery that the devil has been engaged in, and if the church believes its own message, then you don't need to go stomping around for three or four hours to release someone. If they want to be free from occultic involvement, you can see that happen in a moment; in the name of Jesus they can be released. You exult Jesus and dismiss the devil." Calver points to the actual Greek texts of the Lord's Prayer and cites a fallacy in the line "deliver us from evil." "It's just not there in the Greek. The actual line is 'deliver us from the evil one.' So the *force* of evil has more to do with George Lucas and *Star Wars* than it does with any theology. Scripture has always been up front and personal about a personal devil and recognizes the existence of a power of evil. Not as powerful as Jesus, but no less real."

The question of true evil is one that arises, unfortunately, almost daily in the news media as we hear of horrifying crimes committed by human hands that seem beyond the capability and understanding of the public. It is precisely this lack of understanding that has led to belief in a supernatural evil entity, and this evidence is something that the church has to face. That evil exists is not debatable; however, what is debatable is whether or not that evil has a root cause in a spiritual entity. Carl Jung wrote, "Evil is terribly real for each and every individual. If you regard the principle of evil as a reality you can just as well call it the devil."[16] And in the novel *The Brothers*

Karamazov, it is written, "I think that if the Devil doesn't exist, but man has created him, he has created him in his own image and likeness."[17] It is this image of man, the reflection of man, in these horrifying acts of evil that lends itself to the belief in a pure force of evil. When humanity is confronted with the horrific acts that history has recorded, whether through a political movement such as the Nazis or through an individual such as Jeffrey Dahmer, there is an inherent disconnect between the way that the modern, well-adjusted person visualizes humanity and the ghastly image that is being reflected in that mirror. So a reason is found, whether empirically real or psychologically real (as in Jung's statement), and that reason is called the devil. The devil accounts for that gruesome image that glares at us from the mirror where there should be an image of civility, love, and respect. Evil, whether personified in Satan or not, is still an act of man against man. The mission of Satan is to destroy and cause chaos and death . . . and so far, so good. It is the difficulty that the average person has in trying to reconcile the nature of man with the incredibly cruel things that are witnessed on a daily basis that causes the suspicion of some greater force at work. Of all the possible explanations for evil—sociological, genetic, behavioral—none of them seem to account for the *degree* of evil that is witnessed. "Yet there is no convincing evidence that any somatically rooted instinct is the cause of spontaneous destructive aggression in man. Even if such evidence existed, it would not explain the human violence and evil that go well beyond the bounds of defense of life or territory. Nor would it explain the range of different forms that evil takes in different circumstances."[18]

"When you have stood as I stood in a church in Rwanda where 22,000 bodies are buried outside, and you've encountered a 17-year-old kid who is jamming an AK-47 up your left nostril, you look into his eyes and you know. When you've watched what the machetes have done when they've hacked their way through families . . . I don't believe it's just distorted human nature. The obscenity is the degree." Similar to Sid Roth, Calver points to the likes of Hitler as evidence of Satan's work on earth, and he extends that belief to apartheid, social injustice, and poverty. "I believe there is a personal force of evil and that because it is personal, it's more than just this vague, nebulous concept or force."

That evil is not just found in psych wards and third world countries. It comes home to roost. Most religious leaders will tell you that it is nearly impossible to deal in the spiritual realm without having to face the negative side of this realm, as people in their congregations will sometimes find themselves faced with negative forces that seem otherworldly and outside their direct influence. Calver related how a family at the church felt that there was a negative presence in their home, something that had not previously been there. Clive offered to come to the home to see if he could sense anything (the Bible talks of the ability for followers of God to have spiritual discernment); however, after a routine walk through the house and the basement, Clive could not sense anything out of the ordinary. "They were solid, stable members. I was amazed that they thought there was anything at all . . . It's very rare that you get something evil attached to an inanimate object. Have I seen it? Yes. I've seen it in a prayer cup from India which infected a home . . . one or two things like that." As a brand-new pastor at Walnut Hill and with a very public and credentialed background, Clive felt some pressure to find something to exorcise from the home. But he could find nothing. "I'm feeling total, dead loss. There's nothing in this place at all, so why on earth did they think there was. My young protégé was looking very disenchanted and disillusioned, so I asked if we could go outside . . . I had to do something—I had to look intelligent. I got three quarters of the way around the house, and it kind of hit me like a brick wall . . . the neighbor's house where the owner had hung himself four months earlier. There is a presence of evil that can permeate people or even an inanimate object when it's really coming from personal distress."

Calver's experience on the world stage gives him a unique perspective concerning American views on the spiritual world and the occult. Coming from Great Britain, which was, in his words, built upon a tradition of witchcraft, and then migrating to the northeastern United States, which, he claims, is also a hotbed of Wiccan activity, gives him an unparalleled outsider view of the United States. "I think it's important to distinguish between the paranormal and the occult. I think the rest of the world looks [at the United States] with an incredulity at such things like 'was God an astronaut,' but it also looks with incredulity at the materialist image here that sees everything in terms of the material and doesn't recognize that there can be factors that go beyond that." Calver recalls a time in the United Kingdom when he was actually called into a psychiatric hospital. "They had a patient, who, I think by this time, they believed was enmeshed in the demonic, and they asked me to come in to pray. I respected the fact that they respected the fact that the church had a role, and also that the church wasn't saying that there was no place for these guys [psychiatrists and doctors] because as for me, I'll pray for someone and then send them to the doctor."

It is precisely this level of interaction between the spiritual and the scientific that has been gaining ground in Europe as the churches begin to interact more with doctors, particularly psychologists and psychiatrists, and vice versa, when no appropriate answer can be found. In his book *The Rite: The Making of a Modern Exorcist,* journalist Matt Baglia follows an American priest to the Vatican to become trained as an exorcist. While this may sound archaic, exorcism has recently been moving to the forefront of religious thought and experience. Baglia describes a place where people regularly line up for exorcism and blessing, "For thirty-six years, the Passionist priest Father Candido Amantini performed exorcisms there until he died in 1992 . . . It was rumored that he saw around sixty people every day, and while not everybody needed an exorcism, he tried to at least give them a simple blessing or even just a reassuring pat on the back."[19] The practice continues to this day, with Father Amantini having been replaced by Father Tommaso. But the spiritual now interacts much more with the scientific, each trying to maintain a mutual respect. "Numerous mental illnesses can also be mistaken for demonic possession. For this reason, exorcists should insist on a full psychiatric evaluation before proceeding . . . Typically, though, an exorcist will have a team of individuals (a psychiatrist, psychologist, and perhaps a neurologist) whom he trusts to help him with discernment."[20]

Of course the difficulty in such an interaction comes from the deep-seated skepticisms of the scientific world and the overzealous religious believers. One side is often hard-pressed to meet the other halfway. There are, however, psychiatrists, even in the United States, who do acknowledge the possibility of possession and will work with the church. Some psychotherapists and psycho-dramatists will also employ "exorcisms" as part of a role-playing method with their patients in order to give a name to the affliction and force the patient to battle through it (it should be noted that these are not supernatural acts, but merely role-playing).

The ultimate goal for both doctor and pastor is to alleviate suffering. Doctors can and do alleviate physical suffering; but sometimes an individual's suffering is something that is not physical, and it may not be psychological or even emotional. It may be something else—something spiritual—and in this case, sometimes the best help comes from those who work within the spiritual realm; pastors and priests and evangelists who seek to heal something that cannot be stitched or set. Their operations are far more difficult, confusing, and intimate than any bodily surgery.

FATHER BOB BAILEY: ST. MARIA GORRETTI

The Catholic Church is the granddaddy of modern religions that have any basis in the paranormal, particularly when it comes to witchcraft, exorcism, demonology, ghosts, devils, Halloween, and the magical-religious experience. Spawned of ancient Judaism, and the father of Protestantism, it is one of the most mystical of the major belief systems. The priest acts as the gate-keeper to the divine; there are blessings and rituals designed to turn wine to blood and bread to flesh, there is holy water, corpses of saints that never decompose, and magical symbolism from rosaries and crucifixes to pictures and precious medals containing the remains of saints. The follower of the Catholic faith is immersed in a world of spiritual dogma and mysticism. In its long history, Catholicism's belief in the spiritual world of demons and witches has resulted in some of the darkest times in human history: the witch-craft trials both in Europe and America, the Inquisition, and numerous cruel acts performed in the name of the church and the magical-religious belief sys-tem it proclaims. Certainly, there have been few belief systems more powerful and influential in the history of the world than that of the Catholic doctrine.

This is not to deride the church as being evil; but the past examples are com-monly acknowledged instances in which a magical-religious belief system, coupled with a lack of scientific or technical knowledge, has led to the very evil that the church was trying to defeat. In essence, a belief system could quickly turn dangerous without the intercession of science. As man has progressed, so has the church. However, science and the average person on the street no longer believe in witches on brooms, pacts with the devil, curses, and cultic coven meetings in the forest by firelight (or do they?). The modern church has also largely disregarded demonic possession and exorcism. Modern achieve-ments in the fields of medicine and science now allow for diagnosing and treat-ing mental illness, so that much of what would have been interpreted as demonic possession is now known to be the result of psychiatric problems. The practice of exorcism has come to be seen as archaic and silly. Additionally, there have been some highly publicized cases of exorcism that resulted in the death of the person who was supposedly possessed; cases such as that of Anneliese Michel in 1976, in which the court determined that Anneliese was starved to death over the course of the year-long exorcism. The bishop who had originally approved the exorcism had to recant and admit that Anneliese was not possessed. Hence, the church, in acknowledgement of their flawed his-tory in this respect, has changed in recent years and has dispelled some of the magical-religious thinking.

As stated earlier, the Protestant Reformation was probably the biggest step toward rationalization and modernization of religion in its history; however, the Second Vatican Council, held in 1962, resulted in a virtual crisis of Catholicism, as many priests and worshippers refused to accept the changes to the Mass and the sacraments. The goal of the Vatican II was to bring the church into the modern era and make it more accessible to modern man. Changes such as the Mass no longer being said in Latin made the services more "seeker-sensitive," to use Sid Roth's terminology. However, there were some deeper, more intimate changes, including changes to the exorcism prayers known as the *Rituale Romanum*, and a redefinition of evil and hell. On June 19, 2002, the *Los Angeles Times* reported John Paul II's redefinition of hell, which was really the result of the Vatican II's changes. John Paul II stated that hell should not be seen as a fiery underworld, but rather as a state in which individuals "freely and definitively separate themselves from God, the source of all life and joy." Logic dictates that if hell is only a moral state of mind, then evil itself is merely a behavioral condition and Satan a myth. "This denial of hell and the devil is no more evident than ever before when viewed in conjunction with the latest change in the rite of exorcism decreed by the Vatican."[21] There exist entire churches and groups of believers that ceased to follow the official Catholic Church following the Vatican II; they continue to practice the Mass, sacraments, and rituals as they had been practiced for centuries as they wait for the church to come back around to its traditions. "It has been, however, during the past 40 years that the Catholic Church has undergone some of the most radical and revolutionary changes in her history: changes that have left members of the church confused, frustrated and bewildered. Observing the devastating effects of these changes, many Catholics have asked themselves, 'What has happened to the Catholic Church?' The spiritual crisis of our day, the appalling decline of morals and universal loss of faith can be directly traced back to the Second Vatican Council (1962–1965). This council, better known as Vatican II, directly attacked the heart of the Catholic faith—her immutable doctrines, the Holy Sacrifice of the Mass and the Seven Sacraments."[22]

Father Bob Bailey is the head of St. Maria Gorretti in Pawtucket, Rhode Island. Ordained in 1993, Father Bob has never known life outside of the Vatican II reformations; and while many of the reformations of that council have dismissed much of the magical-religious aspects of old Catholicism, Father Bailey's personal interest drove him toward the paranormal. He is a modern clergyman living in a modern world of technology and science. He has a Facebook page, a Twitter account, and his own website. He emails, texts, and chats on his cell phone; today's priest may not be the archaic, disconnected, lonely friar lost in his religion as some may speculate. Bailey is quite at home in this modern world and has found a balance between the modern world and his Catholic life. But part of that modernization involves a disconnection between today's priests and the priests of centuries before, particularly when it comes to dealing with the paranormal, the demonic, and exorcism.

The modern Catholic Church, Father Bailey states, does believe in the devil and demons. "We believe in personified evil, namely in fallen angels (demons) and the chief of them, which is Lucifer or the Devil. We clearly teach that there is personified evil . . . There is evil that exists in the world but we also believe in a personified evil. Exorcism is a part of our faith, but it is rare. There are different forms of demonic influence, the most severe being demonic possession."

Despite demonic possession being a rarity, the requests for exorcisms in the past two decades have skyrocketed. In 2000, Pat Burnell authored an article for the *National Catholic Register* in which the exorcist of the Archdiocese of New York, James LeBar, stated that he had seen a "large explosion" of cases in New York since 1990. "Ten years ago I had no cases and now I have 300."[23] And Tracy Wilkinson of the *Los Angeles Times* wrote in 2005, "In Italy, the number of official exorcists has soared over the past 20 years to between 300 and 400, church officials say. But they are not enough to handle the avalanche of requests for help from hundreds of tormented people who believe they are possessed. In the United States, the shortage is even more acute. The largest number of cases, however, is coming from Europe and Africa."[24] This may not be due to the devil being more active in these areas; rather, it may be cultural in nature. In Italy, for instance, the vast majority of people are devout Catholics, which would predispose them to belief in exorcism as a means of addressing a mysterious ailment (such as mental illness). It leaves open a big chance for misdiagnoses based on religious beliefs. Priests here are routinely instructed to consult psychiatrists before exorcising someone. In Africa, however, the issues may be related more to traditional African belief systems, which involve a number of spirits, both good and bad, that are able to possess individuals. That, coupled with belief, past and present, in witch doctors and other forms of mystical experience, which the Christian faith deems occult, could contribute to more cases of possession being reported. The other contributing factor is that these societies accept the existence of a spiritual world, whereas parts of Europe and the United States are far more materialistic and scientific in their beliefs and are less likely to believe that something is the result of spiritual intervention or demonic possession. That being said, there are still cases of demonic possession that come to the church from around the world.

One of the major contributing factors to the church shying away from exorcism has been the rather new understanding of mental illness. In ancient times a variety of different mental afflictions were treated as demonic possession. The understanding of mental illness, however, has cast the idea of demonic possession into a whole new light. These days we are more able than ever before to diagnose and treat these disorders, so demonic possession has largely been cast aside as an archaic, ignorant, and medieval definition of mental illness. However, there are psychiatrists and doctors who believe in the phenomenon of demonic possession and have reached those conclusions by working directly with those believed by the church to be possessed. Scott Peck, psychiatrist and author of the best-seller *The Road Less Traveled*, worked with former Catholic priest Malachi Martin in examining cases of possession. His last book before his death in 2005 was entitled *Glimpses of the Devil: A Psychiatrist's Personal Accounts of Possession, Exorcism, and Redemption*, in which he argues that demonic possession is a reality above and beyond the scope of psychiatry. Richard E. Gallagher, a graduate of Yale University School of Medicine, serves on the faculty of Columbia University Psychoanalytic Institute and is a privately practicing psychiatrist in Hawthorne, New York. In 2008, Gallagher released an article entitled "Among the Many Counterfeits: A Case of Demonic Possession," in which he claims to have personally witnessed the possession of a woman named "Julia" who had previously experimented with Satanism. "Sometimes objects around her would fly off the shelves, the rare phenomenon of psychokinesis known to para-psychologists. Julia was also in possession of knowledge of facts and occurrences beyond any possibility of natural acquisition. She commonly reported information about the relatives, household composition, family deaths and illnesses, etc., of the members of our team."[25] Gallagher also reported that Julia was able to tell the difference between holy water and tap water, had a hatred for and used vile language toward the clergy that were present, had the ability to speak in foreign languages previously unknown to her, and in one instance she levitated six inches in the air for approximately 30 minutes. "Julia at first had gone into a quiet trance like state. After the prayers and invocations of the Roman Ritual had been going on for a while, however, multiple voices and sounds came out of her. One set consisted of loud growls and animal-like noises, which seemed to the group impossible for any human to mimic. At one point the voices spoke in foreign languages, including recognizable Latin and Spanish."[26] This exorcism was conducted in the United States, not in Italy or Africa. Gallagher goes on to discuss the different kinds of mental illness that often mimic possession and points out the intricate differences that can be looked for in order to determine actual demonic possession. He states that possession is an extremely rare event.

Before moving forward, it should be noted that not every exorcism is performed due to demonic "possession." Full-blown possession is the rarest of cases involving demonic influence; there are actually four stages, ranging from the least severe, for which perhaps only a simple blessing and prayer of cleansing may be needed, to the most extreme case (possession), for which a performance of the *Rituale Romanum* may be necessary. Infestation is demonic activity in a particular location such as a "haunted house" and would generally be associated with a prayer of deliverance. Oppression is when an individual is actually being physically attacked by something demonic. Some have had scratches appear on their skin, some have been shoved down stairs, and others have reported that they were forced out of bed. Obsession is when the demonic force is at work on the individual's mind, causing them to think and imagine awful and terrifying things that often cause the person to believe they are going insane. I cannot help but recall a patient I worked with at a psychiatric hospital, a very kind and good-natured young man, who would cry because of the thoughts of terrible evil that were going through his mind. They would come upon him like attacks, and he was so sad that he was "going crazy" (this is not to imply that this individual was experiencing some kind of demonic attack, but simply to say that this really does happen to people outside of their wanting it to and it can be a very, very distressing affliction and very difficult to cure).

Lastly, there is full-blown possession, in which the demonic entity can exhibit control over the individual's thoughts, behaviors, and actions, causing him or her to say and do what the demon wants; it can also result in paranormal manifestation, such as speaking in unknown languages, having knowledge of secret things, and vomiting up objects that were never ingested. Possession occurs during moments of crisis; the demon does not, however, take up residence inside the individual. A demon is a spirit and, subsequently, comes and goes as it pleases, but can directly control the actions of the individual when it pleases.

The goal of the devil and his demons is to destroy God's creation, and God's greatest creation is man. Both Sid Roth and Clive Calver cited Hitler as a prime example of evil at work in the world, and one could certainly speculate (and many have) that Hitler was under demonic influence. His actions resulted in such great loss of life that if the devil's goal is the destruction of God's creation, then WWII was his greatest victory. But such massive displays of evil should not overshadow the suffering of a lone individual. We disregard the nature of evil when we rationalize suffering and turn it into statistics, as Jeffrey Burton Russell points out in *The Devil*.

> Numbers only disguise reality. Six million Jews exterminated by the Nazis become an abstraction. It is the suffering of one Jew that you understand, and your powers to extrapolate beyond that are limited. That is why Milton's Satan can seem so proud: the evil he personifies is disguised by abstraction. Ivan's one tortured child alone in the

darkness reveals the true nature of the spurious glory of Satan, a glory that we feel only if we allow our minds, borne aloft by abstract considerations, to forget the suffering of the individual.[27]

Evil is experienced on an individual basis—the suffering of one is the suffering of many. "The Jew in the gas chamber; the heretic at the stake; the lonely old man mugged in the city street; the woman raped; that one of these, just one, should suffer is intolerable. That one should suffer imposes the absolute obligation of trying to understand and so grapple with the problem with evil."[28]

That evil exists is undeniable. While the Second Vatican Council changed the official Catholic position, the actual practice of Catholicism remains very similar to the church before the Vatican II. The Catholic religion does appear to believe that there is an ultimate force of evil known as the devil who is at work in the world. The exorcist is the representative of the Catholic Church whose job it is to understand and grapple with that devil. Exorcism may sound archaic, but it is alive and working today. "Nowhere is the shortage of exorcists seen as more serious than in the United States, where skepticism about the practice abounds. There are fewer than a dozen official exorcists at U.S. dioceses, and it is a topic that most American priests seem to avoid."[29]

In 2005, in response to the numerous and growing reports of possession and requests for exorcism, the Vatican, for the first time, sanctioned a year-long course in exorcism at the Regina Apostolorum and ordered that every bishop appoint an official exorcist. This may sound odd, but until 2005 there was no training whatsoever for exorcists. Not only was there no training, exorcism was, and still is, looked upon by some priests as a silly and archaic ritual that is not fit or appropriate for the modern world. Despite the church's belief in true evil and its personification in the devil and his demons, exorcism and exorcists were still very much out of the ordinary and out of the loop.

Father Gabriele Amorth is the Vatican's official head exorcist and founder of the International Association of Exorcists. He laments that exorcists were not consulted when the rites of exorcism were officially changed under the Vatican II's new measures.

As the various parts of the Roman Rite were gradually being reviewed in keeping with the requests of the Second Vatican Council, we exorcists waited for Title XII to come up, the Rite of Exorcism. But it was evidently not considered a thing of relevance because years passed and nothing happened. Then suddenly, on June 4, 1999, the ad interim Rite appeared to be tried out. It was a real surprise to us that we had not been consulted beforehand even though we had our requests all prepared well in advance of the revision of the Rite.[30]

Not only were the exorcists not allowed their input into the changing of the official rite, their work is rarely recognized by the church. A convention of exorcists held in Rome under Father Amorth was denied reception by the pope. "Here were 150 exorcists from the five continents, all priests appointed by their bishops in conformity with the norms of Canon Law which state that these priests must be prayerful, knowledgeable and of good reputation, the cream of the clergy, in short ... here they were asking to take part in a public Papal Audience and being thrown out."[31] Amorth states that exorcists are "barely tolerated" by their bishops and feels that the modern church has fallen under the fraud of the devil, who has a large portion of the church convinced that he does not exist.

> We have a clergy and an Episcopate who no longer believe in the Devil, in exorcism, in the exceptional evil the Devil can instill, or even in the power that Jesus bestowed to cast out demons. For three centuries the Latin Church—in contrast to the Orthodox Church or the various Protestant professions—has almost totally abandoned the ministry of exorcism. So because they no longer perform exorcisms, or study them, and never having seen them, the clergy no longer believe in them. And they no longer believe in the Devil.[32]

However, Father Bailey, for his part, believes in the devil, his demons, and the ability to cast them out. "I am not an exorcist at this point, but my bishop has given me permission to give deliverance over people. Say there is an oppression or obsession or a presence attached to someone, I can do a deliverance. There is also exorcism over place. But I don't use the 'E' word very much because when people hear the word 'exorcism' they think of *The Exorcist*, so I kindly use 'deliverance over place,' if there is some kind of infestation in a house." Father Bailey has even enjoyed a bit of fame and screen time on television. As a fan of the show *Paranormal State* on A&E, Father Bailey noted that the head of the program, Ryan Buell, had posted a blog lamenting that he didn't have any clergy willing to work with him. Father Bailey reached out, and Ryan asked him to assist during a cleansing they were doing on the East Coast. He also performed deliverance on a home in Enfield, Connecticut, with the Connecticut Paranormal Investigators for the program *The Haunted* on Animal Planet. However, he confirms that he has never had any training and that most priests actively avoid the topic of exorcism and the paranormal. "We've never been trained; seminaries don't teach it. There may have been [training] years ago, but right now ... we touched on it in my seminary a little bit ... we are told there is evil, there is a devil, and there are demons, but as far as dealing with it using our Priesthood, no—there's nothing like that." Another issue is that many priests have a fear of confronting something unknown and demonic. "It's not for everybody, even priests; but if it's something that you're meant to do, it won't scare you. I have absolutely no fear of it."

Exorcism and dealings with the demonic and paranormal are a form of ministry in the Catholic Church. The ultimate goal is not to defeat Satan, because only God is capable of that; rather, it is to show the glory of God to the individual who has been affected, who has been touched by evil. "An exorcism is tantamount to a miracle—an extraordinary intervention of God," stated Father Gabriele Nanni, "it is not that we poor men are so powerful to be able to banish the devil. It's that God gives us the power."[33] Father Bailey has created his own ministry, known as the Paranormal Warriors of Saint Michael, to work with the issues of the demonic and paranormal. He has constructed a website and is reaching out to other clergymen. "What I'm trying to do now is establish a national clergy network of priests and ministers who would be willing to work in the area of the demonic and be of help to paranormal groups who encounter that."

Father Bailey thinks that demonic activity in the world is on the rise, mostly due to people's inability to recognize or accept its workings. "There's such a vacuum; people not practicing their faith, people getting into different types of occultism, even fooling around with it. I know in Africa and other places the instances are rising so much that there are more instances where exorcists are needed . . . I think Pope Benedict has really talked about that." Father Bailey hopes to one day go to the Vatican to participate in the schooling to become an exorcist.

"I think that it's a natural thing, to have an interest in something other-worldly. Before, it was not something people talked about, but now it's something that is out there. I think that because there is that vacuum, people are looking for answers, for life after death, and the paranormal is a way for them to find answers." Father Bailey is not averse to dabbling in paranormal things. He regularly visits Salem, Massachusetts, around Halloween and also indicates that there is a difference between the demonic and ghosts—a stark difference between the Catholic view and the Protestant view. "We would believe that there are souls there. As far as ghosts, we don't have a clear-cut theology on that, but if you look at the scriptures, there was a belief in ghosts in the time of Jesus. When he was walking on water or when they saw him [after crucifixion], they think he's a ghost, and Jesus never says that they are wrong to think that. He says 'touch my hand, know that a ghost does not have flesh and blood.' He says that; he doesn't say that there are no ghosts. So from that we can infer." Father Bailey points out that there are different kinds of spirits or ghosts, as well as "damned souls"—those who have died and been damned to hell and have not yet gone on to their "reward," and for some reason are allowed to roam. "I think that ghost hunting is one thing, but I'd like to give the message to paranormal groups that you have to go into it realizing that if you're doing it for years you're probably going to run into something negative . . . at that point you should seek out some help."

Deuteronomy warns against the use of mediums, spiritists, and occultists, so I questioned Father Bailey as to how he could justify use of mediums when performing an investigation or deliverance. "The way I read it in the Old Testament is the Witch of Endor, who conjures up Samuel, who was dead. There's a big difference. The Witch of Endor conjured up something that wasn't there; when paranormal investigators go in or even myself, we're not conjuring anyone up at all, we are trying to establish communication with something that is already there. The Witch of Endor was a medium and a cultist . . . I'm 100 percent against Ouija boards and séances, because it's calling something up that is not there . . . it's different to bring something up, because there is danger. We're dealing with something that is already there, and we're not doing it for kicks, we're doing it to try to help."

The Catholic Church, despite its official theology, seems divided on the subject of the paranormal, the occult, and practices such as exorcism. The church must maintain a belief in evil and in Satan, in his ability to work in the world, and also in a spiritual world that occasionally crosses over to our own. The church is confronted with one aspect of the paranormal or another on a daily basis; the spiritual realm, after all, is its bread and butter. However, it is also confronted with a modern world in which psychology, science, and technology have replaced many previously held belief systems that used the spiritual world to dictate the physics of existence. Priests are, by no means, uneducated in the sciences; they are extensively educated and have specialties such as law and psychology. They are not blind believers in archaic rituals but have a theology, a belief, and dogma, which shape their everyday practice. The Catholic Church is as divided on the subject as the public is; and often-times, those in the church who pursue the paranormal are relegated to the edges of acceptance, just as in the public setting. They are tolerated, but per-haps not taken seriously. The Vatican II's influence has been monumental on the church and on the world; it was the Catholic Church's attempt to recon-cile its theology with science and technology. This has left little room for ancient rituals such as exorcism and scholars of demonology and the paranor-mal. While they remain liminal figures in the Catholic Church, the exorcists do exist, and lately, they have been working more and more. Despite a church that is divided on the subject, more and more people are battling inner demons and seeking out God; ancient belief systems are at work in the modern world, like ghosts that haunt a Gothic castle.

WHAT DOES THE PARANORMAL MEAN FOR RELIGION?

It's no real surprise that church attendance has dropped off over the past few decades; however, belief in a spiritual world has not. More people are open to the idea of a spiritual world but have no tradition by which to practice it. As indicated before, 92 percent of Americans believe in some form of God, but only 40 percent regularly practice any type of faith. This leaves open the possibility for the influence of New Age ideas, occultism, and interest in the paranormal. As Father Bailey said, people are looking for answers; and even as early as 1950, Erich Fromm wrote that,

> If the churches were the representatives not only of the words but of the spirit of the Ten Commandments or of the Golden Rule, they could be potent forces blocking the regression to idol worship. But since this is an exception rather than the rule, the question must be asked, not from an antireligious point of view but out of concern for man's soul: Can we trust religion to be the representative of religious needs, or must we not separate these needs from organized, traditional religion in order to prevent the collapse of our moral structure?[34]

Few in the clergy would argue the fact that the moral structure of the United States has collapsed; on the contrary, the United States is often seen as Satan's playground. Fromm sees this as a failure of organized religion, which has repeatedly sold its soul to secular politics and dogmatic delusions. Has the modernization of the Christian faith caused people to be drawn away to the New Age and the occult? Have the seeker-sensitive churches lost their hold on the supernatural fascination of man and allowed people to seek that supernatural elsewhere? Looking at it from the paranormal viewpoint, the answer is an emphatic "yes."

For Pacific Coast Native American tribes, the sighting of the Sasquatch was a warning to return to their traditional values or face destruction of the society. Likewise, the paranormal today is a call to the religious to return to their traditional beliefs, values, and practices or face fading into obscurity or indifference. The world has witnessed a new explosion of belief in the supernatural and paranormal, and as people look for answers, they are not looking to the church. However, it is the Christian church and its belief system that has created and fueled these beliefs. In essence, the world of the paranormal revolves around the spiritual world that religion has dominated for past centuries. As the public interest in the supernatural grows, the church is urged to respond in kind with the supernatural. Preachers and priests are confronted with the paranormal every day, and many do not have answers, so they turn to the world of science to try to answer spiritual questions. The traditionalists, however, see this as a fallacy. The rise in the number of people claiming possession and requesting exorcists has forced the Catholic Church to reengage an ancient practice that was all but dead to its clergy; Messianic Ministries uses the supernatural to show Jews the way to a Christian God; and community preachers are called upon to cleanse homes of evil presences and confront witchcraft in suburban neighborhoods. All of it beckons to the church. All of it shows that something along the way has been lost that needs to be regained. The paranormal pushes the church away from the scientific rationalization of the twentieth century and back to its original roots and values. Because there is no scientific explanation for these phenomena and because the questions people ask are spiritual rather than rational, the church must turn its gaze backward to its older rites and traditions.

The United States is greatly influenced by its organized religions; the fact that these religions are being pushed toward the more traditional values of the past may point to an upcoming trend in society—a relinquishment (or abandonment) of the modernist ideas and a return to traditional values. Traditions develop to ensure a society's survival through repetition of effective rituals and patterns. Modernists often deride traditional values as being outdated or archaic; but in light of the current moral state of the nation, it would appear that modernism has largely failed people's expectations or has failed to appeal to their spiritual nature. Man's ancient quest for and interest in the supernatural has not gone away with the introduction of modern thought; it has simply changed its face. The desire is still there, but the knowledge that used to be provided by religion is gone as the church has modernized itself to suit science and, for the most part, minimized the supernatural. The church has had to cede many of its ancient beliefs to science, but the reason may be because the church was trying to offer a religious explanation for everything in nature, essentially sticking its nose where it didn't belong. The motion of the earth around the sun, or vice versa, has no place in religious thinking and belief, but the church put it forth as dogma until science rendered them inaccurate. The church's repeated forays into areas that should be reserved exclusively for science (which has proven them wrong again and again), does not necessarily negate its spiritual beliefs. Unfortunately, these repeated embarrassments over the centuries have resulted in a church that is striving to avoid the sensationalism and spiritualism that once drew supernatural seekers to organized religion.

There have always been skeptics and zealots, but it is the church's responsibility to try to navigate the middle road while keeping their values and traditions intact. Far too often the church has given in to zealotry or overstepped the bounds of its purported goal. Now, however, it seems the pendulum may have swung in the opposite direction; modernist thought has transformed the traditional church, be it Catholic, Protestant, or Evangelical. The result is a society that has largely foregone the traditional organized religions in favor of New Age and occult representations of the supernatural. In 2008 the American Religious Identification Survey estimated that there are 340,000 practicing Wiccans in the United States, though they note that it is difficult to obtain accurate numbers, as many practicing Wiccans and pagans are fearful of revealing their beliefs. According to the survey,

> Specifically, the number of Wiccans more than doubled from 2001 to 2008, from 134,000 to 342,000, and the same held true for [other] neo-pagans, who went from 140,000 in 2001 to 340,000 in 2008. Experts say the growth reflects not only an increasing number of neo-pagans, but also a rise in the social acceptability of paganism. As a result, more respondents are willing to identify themselves as followers of some pagan tradition. They also note that identification surveys do not fully measure the influence of neo-paganism. Many people use two or more religious identifiers—calling themselves Unitarian and Druid, for example—while others might adopt certain neo-pagan practices without calling themselves neo-pagan. The upshot is that neo-pagans—such as Wiccans, Druids, Asatruar (from Heathenism), and various Reconstructionists—and neo-paganism have pushed further into the mainstream. Some scholars credit the Internet and its ability to connect pagans of different tribes who would previously have remained unknown to each other. Whatever the reason, pagans have grown increasingly more organized and more visible, and today are widely recognized by religion scholars and sociologists as a group with staying power.[35]

The rise in the belief and interest in the paranormal has a serious effect on religion, and churches everywhere must eventually address it because the public is yearning for it. Regardless of whether the various religious organizations may feel they have lost their way, the paranormal represents a calling to believers to return to the traditional values and beliefs that birthed the religion. In the words of Father Vince Lampert,

It is almost like people want to believe in the extreme ... I am happy to pray with people; but if I tell them that they need to start going back to the Church and taking advantage of the sacraments, they look at me like I am crazy for actually suggesting that they practice their faith. And I know if I told them to go out and do the extreme, "Go stand on your lawn and swing a dead chicken around your head and you'll be fine," they would do that.[36]

CHAPTER 12

Is Satanism Real?

"The Rise of Paranormal Television" discussed the Discovery Channel's program *A Haunting*, and in particular looked at the episode entitled "Where Evil Lurks." In this episode, a family moving into a previously vacated home finds evidence of a satanic ritual in one of the upstairs bedrooms; candles and a pentagram painted in red mark the site where surely a group of Satan worshipers had performed a ceremony and ultimately opened the door to hell, allowing demonic entities to enter into our reality. This satanic ritual is ultimately blamed for the haunting of the house by a demonic entity. But, is it real? Does the belief in and practice of Satanism actually exist, with all its evil implications?

On the surface, this would seem to be an easy question to answer. Many people presuppose the existence of groups that worship Satan and practice evil black rites due to the popularity of the concept in books, film, media, and folklore; but the truth is that Satanism both conforms to this stereotype and radically rejects it. Satanism is far from an established religion with a solid set of beliefs and practices. Unlike the various denominations and practices of Christianity that all worship the same God who is thought to be an actual, living spiritual being who is at work in the world, the practice of Satanism is not as cohesive in its beliefs and practices. It may be that the very nature and inherent assumptions in the name of Satan and Satanism contribute to a nebulous spectrum of beliefs and practices. Satanism, by its very definition, will defy institutionalization and categorization, because it is a rejection of that which forms the basis of Western knowledge, beliefs, morality, and culture. The word *Satan* literally means in the Hebrew translation "adversary," and it is the adverse nature of Satanism that can be seen as its root ethos.

It stands, in certain sects, as an adversary to life, goodness, and decency, while in other sects (and certainly the most organized), it stands as an adversary to the Christian base of the Western culture and to the belief in anything greater than the body. Satanism ranges from religious atheism to the reinterpretation of religious texts to the criminal and insane; all of these are as old as belief itself. For every belief, there has been an adversary; and Satanism is the latest and, thus far, the most lasting of those adversarial beliefs.

In the past, nearly any religious belief system that went against accepted Christian doctrine was dubbed as "Satanism" or "witchcraft" (terms that were synonymous during the Middle Ages and the Renaissance, but now are very different); thus, believers in paganism and various other minor religions, including Judaism, have been accused of everything from cannibalism to kidnapping and infanticide in order to justify the rooting out and destruction of these believers. The fear of satanic rites, as defined by the *Malleus Maleficarum* in the 1600s, has fueled innumerable prosecutions and executions for witchcraft and for the attendance of witches' sabbats, where one cavorted with the devil and performed some of these abominable rites. However, these fears were the consequences of the institutionalization of folklore by the church and the aristocracy during the Renaissance and resulted in the European witch craze and later during the American satanic panic of the 1980s. The fears were unfounded, spurred by the panicked reactions of a Western culture dominated by Christian tradition and immersed in a history of folklore that believed in the existence of those who worshipped the very evil that would negate their existence. If we understand the devil, as defined by Christianity, as the ruler and creator of all things evil then the worship of the devil amounts to insanity. For according to Christianity, the devil desires the destruction of mankind and the overthrow of God's kingdom; he desires all that is evil and sick and terrible in the world and ultimately seeks to claim the souls and lives of those who are willing to follow him. Any rudimentary understanding of the Christian devil would reveal that those who follow him are doomed to a tortured existence and the fires of hell. So why would anyone knowingly worship such a figure? It would be moral, spiritual, and physical suicide and pursued by only the insane. But it is pursued.

There are those who knowingly worship the embodiment of evil, and sometimes they become evil and commit evil acts. However, there are others who do not worship Satan as the Prince of Darkness but, rather, see him as the savior of mankind, and still others who see Satan as merely a symbol upon which to rest their atheism. The organized Satanists are small, nebulous groups of people—a far cry from the myth of an international, highly organized, wealthy secret society propagated during the satanic panic—and they largely wish to remain anonymous, rightly fearing a long history of persecution. In the physical world we are told that for every action there is an equal and opposite reaction; perhaps the same can be said for the spiritual realm as well. There is both good and evil as evidenced in everyday life regardless of spiritual beliefs. There is both God and devil, right hand and left; and for every belief system there is an opposite belief system. Christianity exists as a dichotomy between good and evil, God and Satan; and thus, Christianity, by its very nature, must have its detractors—its opposites—and it is these opposites that the masses have mythologized and feared for centuries.

There are some aspects of Satanism that rightly deserve to be feared; however, there are Satanists who exist and practice as law-abiding believers of a different religion, albeit one whose title immediately inspires long-held folkloric beliefs that are part of the Christian European heritage. Unfortunately, the various manifestations of witch trials have served to root out from society those who were deemed as "other," whose beliefs and practices went against the norm. Therefore, they were assigned heinous, barbarous acts of satanic ritual, which gave the accusers false justification for the persecution and murder of those outsiders. This ranged from the Jews to Zoroastrians and, in the early Roman Empire, to Christians themselves. The truth of Satanism is that it both exists and does not. It does not exist as it has been purported by witch-hunters and fanatical evangelists throughout the centuries, but it does exist as a small belief system at odds with Christianity. The difficulty with Satanism, as with many other aspects of paranormal belief, is that Satanism defies institutionalization; whether that is due to its adversarial nature or to the influence of and rejection by the mass Christian populace, its pockets of believers find difficulty establishing cohesion.

There are three types of Satanism that will be examined; Satanism as defined by Anton Szandor LaVey and the Church of Satan (symbolic Satanism), which does not believe in Satan as defined by the church but believes in man as god; Theistic or Spiritual Satanism, which believes that Satan is a spiritual entity that is, in fact, good but has been demonized by the church; and what will be referred to as folkloric Satanism, which encompasses the traditionally feared acts of heinous satanic rites. Folkloric Satanists are those who do sacrifice humans to the devil in rituals that they have garnered largely from popular culture and misinterpreted pagan belief systems. They capture headlines, adding substance to fear and creating a hostile world for those who merely believe in an opposite biblical interpretation than what has been put forth for centuries. We will examine this type of Satanism first in order that the myth may be dispelled by the truth.

FOLKLORIC SATANISM

In 1985, Sean Sellers murdered a convenience store clerk and, one year later, murdered his mother and her husband in their sleep. Sellers claimed that the murders were the result of his heavy involvement in Satanism; he believed that he was actually possessed by a demonic alter ego named Ezurate when the murders were committed. "In the months before his first murder—which consummated his effort to break all 10 biblical commandments—Sean became consumed by Satanist ritual. With Richard and the eight or so members of their ad hoc coven, he took over an abandoned farmhouse and used it as a place of worship."[1] He was sentenced to death in 1986, and, at 17 years old, became one of the youngest people ever to be given the death sentence. In 2005, three members of a heavy metal group, called the "Beasts of Satan," confessed to having killed three people in satanic rituals; two had been committed in 1998 and a third in 2004. "The verdict comes amid growing concern in Italy that young people are turning to Satanism and the occult."[2] In 2010, six members of a satanic cult in Russia were convicted of murdering, dismembering, and eating four teenagers as a part of their satanic ritual in June of 2008.

> The self-styled devil worshipers, which included a young teenage girl, lured three girls and a boy aged from 15 to 17 to the spot by plying them with alcohol and inviting them to sit round a bonfire. They then killed them in a sacrificial ceremony, stabbing them 666 times each in homage to the so-called Number of the Beast. Prosecutors say the young killers then dismembered their victims' bodies and cooked certain body parts such as the hearts and the tongues before consuming them. They buried the rest of the remains in a giant pit, which they marked with an inverted cross—topped with a dead cat. Investigators say the sect was formed in 2006 and gleaned its knowledge of Satanism from the Internet, initially killing cats and dogs before graduating to homicide.[3]

When the majority of the public hears the word "Satanism," these are primarily the images and stories that they envision, and with good reason. Clearly such incidents, while rare, do occur and certainly capture mass media attention; furthermore, they are generally committed by adolescents or young adults, a fact that prompts immediate reaction by fearful and concerned parents. Truly, these are the images, actions, and fears that have been passed down through folklore over many centuries; they are images and actions of the adversary, and we fear those who would embrace it and seek to undo the laws and accepted morality of our civilization.

The satanic panic of the 1980s in the United States was a false witch-hunt. The belief that a highly organized and secretive religious group was transcending all societal barriers and conducting rituals such as those mentioned above, thousands of times a year, was the result of the institutionalization of satanic folklore, and it fostered public belief and panic. It has been proven time and time again, both in the court of law and in the investigations of modern writers, that there was no reality to the satanic ritual abuse claims made by therapists and housewives. The entire mass panic has been dismissed so thoroughly that some intellectuals claim there is no form of Satanism that exists that would ever embrace the characteristic violations and abominations that make up satanic legend and folklore. Jeffrey Victor writes, "Almost all teenagers who even profess to be Satanists lack any elaborate belief system focused upon Devil worship. Instead, they have fabricated a deviant ideology in order to: justify their underlying personality dispositions to express aggressive hostility; or to justify rebellion from adult social restrictions; or obtain public notoriety."[4] Essentially, Victor is saying that the Satanism that many rebellious youths express is merely the reenactment of folkloric beliefs and legends—what Bill Ellis calls "ostension." Youths reenact the rumors they have heard about satanic rituals or the images they have seen in the cover art of certain music albums in an effort to rebel or obtain public notoriety. Even a quick video search of "Black Mass" on Google will yield more than enough videos and images to fully engage any interested person.

However, can it merely be ostension that warps a person to the point where he or she is willing to kill and consume another person in an effort to appease a god or gods? There must be a line that gets crossed between role-playing and rebellion and ritual sacrifice and murder; at some point a person actually begins to *believe* and to act on that belief. Satanism, as it is feared in folklore, does exist, as is evidenced by the several examples in this chapter; but not as a formalized, dogmatic religion, because it cannot exist as such. Law and society would not allow for the existence of such a religion. Therefore, such practices will never be codified into a solid belief system because, by its very nature, the rituals and practices must be garnered from folklore and legend. An organized belief system that advocates and uses such rituals cannot exist; but there can be small, separate groups that seek to be an adversary to morality, religion, civilization, and life. There exist within every social system anomalies that seek to undo that very system; these anomalies come in various forms such as right-wing extremist militia groups, home-grown Islamic terrorists, and, in some cases, Satanists that carry their belief, like the aforementioned, to its extreme conclusions. Merely because it is not an accepted belief system does not mean that it does not exist; folkloric

Satanism does exist in the adversarial outskirts of our society. Whether the Oklahoma City bombing or the Sellers murders, those belief systems exist in various forms and do get passed on to others through literature, oral legends and folklore, and pure imagination.

The fanatical belief that wells within the rare Satanist who acts out his belief through murderous rituals or criminal activity has its roots in the fundamental Christian belief system, and is, therefore, more easily adopted by a disturbed individual as a belief system. Folkloric Satanism operates within the confines of Christianity; it is not atheism or the belief in a different god. The folkloric Satanist believes in the Christian God but seeks out Satan to reject that God and acquire power through evil. In essence, the folkloric Satanist desires evil and worships the Christian embodiment of evil. It is not a belief system that exists outside of the framework of Christianity, but rather, is a part of it. For this reason, we find that such satanic rites as practiced by folkloric Satanism are largely found in countries that are predominantly Christian; the United States has a history of such practices, as do Latin America, South America, Italy, Africa, and parts of Western Asia. It is the nations with predominate Christian beliefs that will, by their very nature, produce an adversarial element that seizes upon the established religions in an attempt to shock, horrify, and defy the beliefs of the majority as a means of expressing their antisocial sentiments and murderous desires. However, there does exist actual belief on the part of the folkloric Satanist, and this belief is fueled, in part, by the predominant Christian belief system of that individual's community. Christianity is used as a fuel for the rites and practices that horrify and offend and, ultimately, lead to destruction.

The Black Mass is perhaps the most recognized, stereotypical, and feared rite of Satanism. Anton Szandor LaVey remarked in his *Satanic Bible*,

> No other single device has been associated with Satanism as much as the black mass. To say that the most blasphemous of all religious ceremonies is nothing more than a literary invention is certainly a statement which needs qualifying—but nothing could be truer...No "decent" person could fail to side with the inquisitors when told of these blasphemies. The propagandists of the church did their job well, informing the public at one time or another of the heresies and heinous acts of the Pagans, Cathars, Bogomils, Templars and others who, because of their dualistic philosophies and sometimes Satanic logic, had to be eradicated.[5]

The Black Mass was and is meant to offend, not only Christian sensibilities, but the very essence of humanity. It has its origins in the folklore and rumors that were used against various religious and cultural groups throughout history including the Jews, pagans, Zoroastrians, and, ironically enough, the Christians. However, upon the acceptance of Christianity by the Roman Empire, the need to demonize nonbelievers and create converts led to a mythology built around some of the most heinous acts imaginable, such as child-eating, bestiality, and any number of other abominations. The *Malleus Maleficarum* began the codification of rumor and folklore into an institutionalized belief system near the dawn of the European witch-hunts, and it included much about infant devouring and murder. The preceding witch-hunts begat dark tales told by accused witches (under torture, of course) that described the sabbat. They included everything that would be vile and detestable and offensive in a society run by the church.

> The Devil usually appeared in the shape of a goat, ugly and smelly, though at times he was said to arrive as a toad, crow, or black cat. He presided over the sabbat while sitting on a throne. The Devil turned into a foul-smelling goat, and the witches took off their clothes and paid homage to him by falling to their knees and kissing his anus... Unbaptized infants were offered up as sacrifices. New witches were initiated by signing the Devil's Black Book in Blood, renouncing their Christianity, taking an oath and trampling on the cross... There followed a great feast, with much drinking and eating, although demonologists often noted that the food tasted vile, and that no salt was present, for nothing evil could abide salt.[6]

The idea of these Black Masses and rituals were carried down through the ages and were used to demonize Jews, the Gauls, and the "witches" during the witch craze. The mythology of a Black Mass continued through the nineteenth century and into the twentieth century. Jeffrey Burton Russell cites the influence of the decadent Romantics at the turn of the century—an artistic and philosophical movement that "was characterized by estheticism, sensuality, and fascination with such psychosexual aberrations as incest, sadomasochism, bestiality, and prostitution."[7] Russell also cites the influence of media surrounding such figures as Madame Blavatsky and Aleister Crowley, who created their own cults such as the Theosophical Society and the Hermetic Order of the Golden Dawn. These figures and their secret societies took on mythological status in Christian and secular rumor mills. Aleister Crowley, in particular, was vocal about his philosophy "do what thou wilt" and seemed to take sport in using biblical mythology such as the number 666, the mark of the beast, as way to shock the masses into believing him to be the embodiment of evil. Russell also cites a particularly popular book in Europe entitled *Là-Bas* by J. K. Huysmans. "...his [Huysmans's] initial plan was to write a novel based on the historical figure of Gilles de Rais, a fifteenth-century child molester and mass murderer whom the Decadents found fascinating. Interest in Gilles led Huysmans to medieval witchcraft and demonology, then to the black masses of the reign of Louis XIV, and finally to curiosity about contemporary Satanism."[8] Huysmans's research brought him into contact with a disgraced priest named Boullan, who had actually sacrificed a child he had fathered with a nun. He sacrificed the child in a Black Mass that he later recorded in his journal, *Cashier Rose*. Boullan and another occultist named Louis van Hacke tutored Huysmans in the black rites, which he chronicled in his novel. The novel took on cult status and was very popular among the decadent Romantics; however, disgusted by what he had created, Huysmans converted to Catholicism and left the decadents. Here's a taste of *Là-Bas*, otherwise known as *The Damned*.

> Durtal felt himself shudder. A whirlwind of hysteria shook the room. While the choir boys sprinkled holy water on the pontiff's nakedness, women rushed upon the Eucharist and, groveling in front of the altar, clawed from the bread humid particles and drank and ate divine ordure. Another woman, curled up over a crucifix, emitted a rending laugh, then cried to Docre, "Father, father!" A crone tore her hair, leapt, whirled around and around as on a pivot and fell over beside a young girl who, huddled to the wall, was writhing in convulsions, frothing at the mouth, weeping, and spitting out frightful blasphemies. And Durtal, terrified, saw through the fog the red horns of Docre, who, seated now, frothing with rage, was chewing up sacramental wafers, taking them out of his mouth, wiping himself with them and distributing them to the women, who ground them underfoot, howling, or fell over each other struggling to get hold of them and violate them. The place was simply a madhouse, monstrous pandemonium of prostitutes and maniacs. Now, while the choir boys gave themselves to the men, and while the woman who owned the chapel, mounted the altar caught hold of the phallus of the Christ with one hand and with the other held a chalice between "His" naked legs, a little girl, who hitherto had not budged, suddenly bent over forward and howled like a dog.[9]

Another influential work in the continuity of the Black Mass myth was the novel *Messes Noires (Black Masses)* by Jehan Sylvius, published in 1929. The cover was an illustration of a Black Mass, complete with a sacrificial woman, pentagram, candles, and Satan himself in the form of a man with the head of a goat. There were also films that incorporated the Black Mass and ritualistic sacrifice. As early as 1922, Swedish director Benjamin Christiansen released the grotesque silent film, *Haxan*, which depicts witchcraft lore through the ages, acting out every rumored ceremony to the utter disdain of the audience.[10] "In the 20th century, the Black Mass became a staple of Devil worship novels and films. One of the most influential fictions was the 1934 novel *The Devil Rides Out* by Dennis Wheatley, with a black magician character, Morcatta, modeled on Aleister Crowley. The novel was made into a film in 1968 by Hammer films of England during a time of occult revival and the birth of Witchcraft or Wicca, as a religion."[11] There was also the later influence of *Rosemary's Baby* and *The Exorcist*, which both, in their literary form, depicted Satanic ritual similar to the sabbat and the Black Mass.

However, despite its popularity in collective fears of Christians, the Black Mass, in its definitive and formal manifestation, has rarely (if ever) been practiced, as it must be presided over by a defrocked priest. Anton LaVey even denied his ability to practice the Black Mass (and also denied that he would even if he could), though he did offer a vivid description in *The Satanic Bible*:

> The popular concept of the black mass is thus: a defrocked priest stands before an altar consisting of a nude woman, her legs spread-eagled and vagina thrust open, each of her outstretched fists grasping a black candle made from the fat of unbaptized babies, and a chalice containing the urine of a prostitute (or blood) reposing on her belly. An inverted cross hangs above the altar, and triangular hosts of ergot-laden bread or black-stained turnip are methodically blessed as the priest dutifully slips them in and out of the altar lady's labia. Then, we are told, an invocation to Satan and various demons is followed by an array of prayers and psalms chanted backwards or interspersed with obscenities ... all performed within the confines of a "protective" pentagram drawn on the floor. If the Devil appears he is invariably in the form of a rather eager man wearing the head of a black goat upon his shoulders. Then follows a potpourri of flagellation, prayer, book burning, cunnilingus, fellatio, and general hindquarters kissing—all done to a background of ribald recitations from the Holy Bible, and audible expectorations on the cross! If a baby can be slaughtered during the ritual, so much the better; for as everyone knows, this is the favorite sport of the Satanist![12]

LaVey writes this passage with deep sarcasm, as he regards the Black Mass as simply a tool used by the church during the Middle Ages to stir fear of the devil in the populace.

The Black Mass has become a catchall term for any perceived satanic rite, as it has been understood and feared through folklore and popular conception. The "satanic rites" that have resulted in murders throughout the years have not shown any cohesion of philosophy or dogma. Sean Sellers shot his parents and a store clerk in an effort to violate all the Ten Commandments; there was very little ritual about it. While the highlighted incidents in Italy and Russia were more ritualized in practice, they still only employed some of the peripheral practices of the Black Mass. The Black Mass has come to represent nearly any ritual done in worship to the devil as a means to embrace evil and blaspheme both life and the church and is embraced and utilized by individuals who have embraced a Christian belief system, but in the same way that Christianity is utilized as a motive for bombing a federal building or that Islam is used as motive for terrorism.

Just as there are those who reject life, for whatever rationale, through suicide, there are those that will reject a belief system through embracing its exact opposite. The Black Mass or any of the anomalous "satanic rites" that have been practiced throughout history is a form of suicide, as it rejects not only Christianity and goodness, but life itself. It is a celebration of murder, cannibalism, infanticide, sexual perversion, and the inversion of all things that society embraces. To say or suppose that it does not exist is a fallacy. There certainly does not exist an organized or cohesive belief system or cult that utilizes folkloric Satanism, but these rituals and beliefs do rear their ugly heads now and again. Folkloric Satanism is born out of a belief and acceptance of the Christian God, and within a very few select members of a given society, that very acceptance generates an adversary tendency toward rebellion, rejection, and, ultimately, suicide.

These satanic rites were born out of the dualistic nature of Christianity that posits both good and evil: for there to be good there must also be evil and vice versa. The folkloric origins of the sabbat and the Black Mass were conceived in the imaginations of people who believed that if there are rites that exist to celebrate God and goodness, there must ultimately be rites that celebrate its polar opposite. These rites are the manifestation of the darkest recesses of our psychology and our dualistic philosophy, passed down from generation to generation in the form of folklore and legend and acted out by those who reject society, God, and life. To deny its existence, or to posit that it is only the result of disturbed individuals finding a religious excuse to perpetrate crimes, is to ignore the power of belief and the depths of human psychology in relation to belief. Anyone can commit murder, and thousands do on a yearly basis, but murder as a part of the satanic ritual is a very rare and isolated incident. It is the result of belief systems, legends, folklore, and religion passed down through cultural ages. It is ritualized for a reason, and that reason is to make a formal statement of rejection and an offering of sacrifice to the darkest recesses of the mind, spirit, and body. It is suicide on a variety of different scales, and it is a path that ultimately leads to the destruction of the self. If we are to suppose that Satan is real, then this is his ultimate prize, the destruction of human life and instilling terror in humanity. Those who turn to Satan to find power through evil are ultimately deceived by the very deity they worship.

Sean Sellers was executed on February 5, 1999, at the age of 30, after having tried numerous attempts to save his own life through appeals and pleas for redemption. He appeared on numerous talk shows to testify to the reality of Satanism during the satanic panic of the 1980s. He tried to obtain clemency based on his supposed religious conversion to Christianity and attempted to appeal the death sentence by claiming that he was suffering from multiple personality disorder. He attempted to appeal his case to the Supreme Court, but they denied him a hearing. In the end he was not believed by either the courts or his surviving stepsiblings and was given the lethal injection on February 5 in an Oklahoma state penitentiary.

ANTON SZANDOR LAVEY AND THE CHURCH OF SATAN

On April 30, 1966, the date of the pagan spring festival known as Walpurgisnacht, the Church of Satan was born in San Francisco, California. Its founder, Anton Szandor LaVey, became known as the Black Pope, an image that he relished and made frequent use of in promoting his new church and religion. LaVey was the consummate showman; having worked in the carnival business for many years, he knew how to entertain, mystify, and shock audiences, but he was also a surprisingly brilliant, creative, and well-read individual. The night he was to open his church, LaVey shaved his head—an homage to magical belief systems that believe the shaving of the head gives the magician greater power—and purposely altered his appearance, pointing his goatee and arching his eye brows, to give him a truly Mephisthophelean visage. He dubbed the year 1966 as Anno Satanas—the first year of the reign of Satan on earth. "It has become necessary for a NEW religion, based on man's natural instincts, to come forth. THEY have named it. It is called Satanism. It is that power condemned that has caused the religious controversy over birth control measures—a disgruntled admission that sexual activity, for fun, is here to stay."[13] The Church of Satan was a product of the times, and while the roots of its beliefs date back to pre-Christian antiquity, it was coalesced in the counterculture drama of the 1960s. As LaVey points out in his hugely popular *Satanic Bible*, the liberalization of both society and, in turn, the church, opened the doors for the Church of Satan to exist and take hold of popular imagination.

In recent years there has been an attempt to humanize the spiritual concept of Christianity. This has manifested itself in the most obvious non-spiritual means. Masses which had been said in Latin are now said in native languages—which only succeeds in making the nonsense easier to understand, and at the same time robs the ceremony of the esoteric nature which is consistent with the tenets of the dogma. It is much simpler to obtain an emotional reaction using words and phrases that cannot be understood than it is with statements which even the simplest mind will question when hearing them in an understandable language.[14]

The Church of Satan has probably been the most influential force in the world of Satanism; it has inspired numerous copycat religions, followers, dissenters, and, unfortunately, the occasional monster than any other satanic undertaking in history. The time was right and so was the place. The counterculture-laden San Francisco was its birthplace, a city that had come to epitomize the rejection of traditional values and embrace a new world. The Church of Satan and *The Satanic Bible* have been widely misunderstood by those who have not read the book or investigated the religion. Part of this was LaVey's intention—to inspire fear, disgust, and shock in the Christian community—and part of it was the tragedy of its name, the Church of *Satan*.

LaVey used the public shock and subsequent media coverage to grow his church, performing a live Black Mass, complete with nude female altar (minus the baby-eating), before the cameras in a mockery of the Christian faith, which was the subject of a documentary film called *Satanis: The Devil's Mass*.[15] LaVey's notoriety also netted him limited Hollywood attention, playing the devil in *Rosemary's Baby* and in Kenneth Anger's *Invocation of My Demon Brother*, as well as in several European films. All of this was to great effect; LaVey shocked and outraged the moral majority. But after his initial media blitz in the late 1960s and early 1970s, according to the Church of Satan, LaVey wanted to "stop performing Satanism and start preaching it."[16] Thus, he began to curtail his media efforts, eliminated an element of membership that was not fully devoted to or understanding of his philosophy, and changed the administrative setup of the church. LaVey's reaffirmation of the church's beliefs actually caused some members to split off and form their own versions of satanic churches, but LaVey was undeterred in demanding commitment to the beliefs that he put forth in *The Satanic Bible*. According to the church's website, "With his intensely elitist attitude, Anton was incensed to see his creation degenerating into a 'Satan Fan Club,' where the weakest, least innovative members were buoyed up with time and attention at the expense of the most productive, most Satanic members."[17]

As indicated before, the Church of Satan suffered from its name probably more than anything, as the use of the term "Satan" immediately called forth the old folkloric understanding of Satanism and the Christian belief system. While LaVey used "Satan" to, in effect, create the media uproar that he rode to international fame, he also used it for its original meaning, "adversary." The Church of Satan was truly an adversarial religion that, unlike folkloric Satanism, operated outside the bounds of Christian thought. In fact, the Church of Satan does not believe in God nor does it believe in Satan. Rather, the Church of Satan is a humanistic belief system that believes man *is* god, and at his full, god-like potential, he is able to cause events to occur in the world and influence nature to comply with his will.

> Most Satanists do not accept Satan as an anthropomorphic being with cloven hooves, a barbed tail, and horns. He merely represents a force in nature—the powers of darkness which have been named just that because no religion has taken these forces out of the darkness. Nor has science been able to apply technical terminology to this force. It is an untapped reservoir that few can make use of because they lack the ability to use a tool without having to first break down and label all the parts, which make it run. It is this incessant need to analyze which prohibits most people from taking advantage of this many-faceted key to the unknown—which the Satanist chooses to call "Satan."[18]

The Church of Satan acknowledges that there is an unseen magical force in the world that can be manipulated for both good and evil; science cannot define it, and Christianity begs for its mercy. When death or disease befalls one of its followers, they state that it is "God's will," i.e., this unnamable force has allowed the death or misfortune and there must, therefore, be a good reason for it. The Church of Satan rejects the prostration of man before God, which it sees as neither all-powerful nor all-good. The presupposition that God is good causes the believer to embrace and excuse the misery that befalls him or her as being part of some strange divine will that supercedes man's understanding and judgment. The Satanist rejects this, believing that no God exists but rather that man is his own god, able to move and manipulate the unseen force in this world through the use of ceremony, belief, and ritual. The Church of Satan is essentially the celebration of mankind as both beast and god among beasts; it embraces our basest instincts and desires toward carnality, greed, and power. Its roots are in the magic rituals and beliefs of primitive paganism that preceded Christianity and embraced sexuality, animism, nature, and spirituality. It sees the seven deadly sins as mere pragmatism and views the church as a slavery of mankind. "Better to rule in

Hell than serve in Heaven" the saying goes. For the Satanist, hell is here on earth, and he or she reigns supreme. He advocates pure freedom from guilt, morality, taboo, and fear of divine retribution; with absolute freedom, the Satanist becomes a god among servants, able and willing to go where others fear to tread.

However, the Church of Satan's notoriety derived more from its rituals displayed before cameras than from its Nietzschean philosophy. LaVey recognized man's need for ritual and formed his own "Satanic Mass" by which to tap into the need for ritual. Unfortunately for LaVey, his penchant for showmanship may have overshadowed his atheism. His rituals before the cameras involved him donning a devil's costume and acting out some of the rites that had caused fear throughout the centuries. Designed to shock the Christian majority and mock the Christian religion, his media presentations played into the popular fears of folkloric Satanism. While denying the ability to perform an official Black Mass, LaVey did perform a version of the Black Mass before cameras. While it was meant as a mockery, very few, it seems, got the true message and instead believed that LaVey was the embodiment of evil, worshipping Satan as defined in the Bible. As described in the *Alton Evening Telegraph*, "LaVey appears before his satanist congregation dressed in a sorcerer's costume. Instead of invoking a spiritual blessing, the high priest waves an obscene object in the air and calls down "demons" into the service . . . While members come forward and confess their desires, a nude woman lies on the stone altar—a form of the devil worship which has shocked even the police vice squad of California."[19] LaVey used the imagery of feared Black Masses to inject the shock and outrage he desired into the public mind. While LaVey never strayed from his philosophy when talking with the media, the images conjured up through descriptions of his rituals were enough to inspire fear, shock, and outrage—precisely what LaVey wanted, but perhaps with unintended consequences.

The symbolism that LaVey chose also played into fears of folkloric Satanism; in particular, his personal trademarked creation of the Sigil of Baphomet. As described by Owen Davies,

> Still, the one occult symbol depicted in the *Satanic Bible*, which also appeared on the cover—the Sigil of Baphomet—was crucial to its commercial success. The symbol consists of a goat-headed Satan framed within a pentacle, surrounded by two concentric circles containing five Hebraic figures, which, as LaVey explained, constituted a Kabbalistic spelling of "Leviathan" . . . The key significance of the Sigil of Baphomet, from a publishing point of view, is that in the popular

imagination it conjures up expectations of Devil worship, black magic, and sacrifice . . ."[20]

Thus, the symbolism, ritual, and name of the church called to mind the darkest recesses of human actions, that of folkloric Satanism; and, for some misguided individuals, like Sean Sellers, that idea fueled their depravity.

This is one of the inherent difficulties in a belief system that appeals to the darker side of humanity: it can and will be coopted by those who wish to justify their criminal behavior or psychoses. Owen Davies, in his work, *Grimoires: A History of Magic Books*, described such an incident when Eliphas Levi, a former priest and expert on the occult during the mid-1850s, met another priest looking for the *Book of Honorius*.

> For Levi the evil hold that malign grimoires could have over the weak or unstable was brought home to him by his encounter with a young priest who inquired of a bookseller where the master of magic (Levi) lived. An appointment was arranged and the priest said he desired to obtain the *Grimoire of Honorius* and would pay as much as one hundred francs for it. When Levi queried whether he intended to practice forbidden black magic, the priest merely smiled sarcastically. It transpired later that the priest was Jean-Louis Verger, a troublesome and mentally unstable young man who, in 1857, murdered the arch-bishop of Paris during service.[21]

Similarly, LaVey had to face down accusations and deranged people as he formed his church. *The Los Angeles Times*, in an interview with LaVey, cited,

> Within the past week there have been two revolting news stories in Santa Ana and Salinas, Calif., each involving murders woven with hints of human sacrifice and cannibalism, each done by alleged group worshipers of Satan. One suspect admitted receiving counsel from the "chief devil" in San Francisco. The "chief devil" has not yet been publicly named, but the suspect's attorney has affirmed that it is not LaVey. No matter, LaVey, as California's best known Satanist, is still getting it about the head and ears pending official clearing up of cases that LaVey says he finds "damn sickening."[22]

LaVey addressed the issue of weak-minded or unbalanced people flocking to his belief system: "This really is an elitist movement, and we're very fussy about who is coming in and whom we traffic with. We have to guard ourselves against the creeps, and we've screened out a lot of people who turned out to be bad apples. Mostly they turned out to be people who were disappointed when they didn't get the orgies and all the nefarious activities they were looking forward to."[23] LaVey's nude woman as an altar certainly had mass appeal, but LaVey was looking for the strong of mind, spirit, and character, rather than the delusional, drug-addicted, or psychotic. LaVey's belief system is ultimately fueled by a Nietzschean belief in the "über manch"—the superman who is god over the earth and subject to no one. Those who practice folkloric Satanism or perform rituals in worship of Satan are not truly following LaVey's philosophy; they are worshipping Satan instead of worshipping themselves.

While LaVey did not believe in a god-like entity known as Satan, he did believe that the world could be influenced through the manipulation of unseen forces. His rituals (the ones that were not for the sole purpose of mocking Christianity) were based on a learned combination of pagan practices, Egyptian mythology, folklore, and magical rituals that had been practiced in the past by such notable figures as Aleister Crowley (though their philosophies were different). In essence, the ritual magic of LaVey's practices can be related to the chaos theory metaphor: a butterfly flaps its wings in Brazil and causes a hurricane in East Asia. This saying has lately been coopted into pop culture, and its author, Edward Lorenz, lamented that it was drastically misunderstood.

> Translated into mass culture, the butterfly effect has become a metaphor for the existence of seemingly insignificant moments that alter history and shape destinies. Typically unrecognized at first, they create threads of cause and effect that appear obvious in retrospect, changing the course of a human life or rippling through the global economy... Such borrowings of Lorenz's idea might seem authoritative to unsuspecting viewers, but they share one major problem: They get his insight precisely backwards. The larger meaning of the butterfly effect is not that we can readily track such connections, but that we can't. To claim a butterfly's wings can cause a storm, after all, is to raise the question: How can we definitively say what caused any storm, if it could be something as slight as a butterfly? Lorenz's work gives us a fresh way to think about cause and effect, but does not offer easy answers.[24]

The ultimate point of the butterfly metaphor is that causality cannot truly be known due to the interaction of a multitude of different influencing factors, thus rendering everyday occurrences, such as weather, a mysterious force. In fact, taken to its ultimate conclusion it renders all of life's interactions mysterious forces. LaVey's magic is intended to manipulate this mysterious force through rituals and sending out energy so that life will conform with the

Satanist's will. It is not necessarily supernatural, but it is certainly far from scientific. But the basic belief is that life's various forces can be manipulated to produce intended results. This is, in essence, the practice of magic, and if successfully completed, can render the practitioner a god.

One such instance—LaVey's use of a curse—is highlighted on the Church of Satan website. LaVey was involved in a relationship with Jayne Mansfield, an actress known for her cleavage and platinum blonde hair, who made history by being the first mainstream actress to do a nude scene on camera. According to the Church of Satan,

> LaVey and Mansfield hit it off immediately, each fulfilling a diabolical need in the other. Jayne became passionately obsessed with Anton, calling him several times a day from wherever she traveled, eventually applying for a driver's license just to be able to drive to San Francisco unescorted by her persistently ubiquitous lawyer/boyfriend, Sam Brody. Jayne's commitment to LaVey, and her dedication to the satanic philosophy, continued until her death in June of 1967. The auto crash in which she died also killed Sam Brody, whom LaVey had formally cursed in response to Brody's jealous threats and attempts to discredit LaVey. The night of Mansfield's death, LaVey had been clipping a Church of Satan news item from the German magazine *Bild-Zeitung*. When he turned the item over to paste it in the press book, LaVey was shocked to see he had inadvertently cut a photo of Jayne on the opposite side of the page, right across the neck. Fifteen minutes later, a reporter from the New Orleans Associated Press bureau called Anton to get his reaction to the tragic accident. Jayne had been practically decapitated when she was thrown through the windshield of the car.[25]

LaVey's ceremonies, whether to curse someone or cause them to become enamored with another individual, were designed to influence and shape the seemingly random forces in the world. His magic was not supernatural, but its invocation sure looked like it.

LaVey felt that ceremony and ritual were necessary to cause the magician and others to enter a trance-like state of consciousness so that they could properly focus their minds and energy on the task at hand. This hypnotism through ritual is not unlike many, if not most, other religious ceremonies. LaVey referred to it as an "Intellectual Decompression Chamber," though he adds that the practicing Satanist recognizes that this is his intended goal in order to expand his will; whereas, the typical religious practitioner believes that he is experiencing God. Religious ceremonies and imagery are designed so that the participant enters a trance-like state in order to be prepared for a mystical encounter with the supernatural. Thus, we have the crucifix, the Catholic rosary, the Pentacostal singing and speaking in tongues, the Buddhist "Ohm," and various other keys to the transcendental experience. LaVey's ceremonies were merely different in that they utilized satanic, sexual, bestial, and magical imagery (including the use of alcohol and other drugs) to induce the participant into a state of mind where he or she would reach a transcendental moment. For the Christians, this may be a moment when God "speaks" to them or when they "feel" the love of God; for the LaVeyan Satanists, this is the moment at which they experience the freedom of being completely unbound by law and morality, history and religion; it is that moment when they realize themselves as gods and thus urge the world and the forces therein to conform to their will.

LaVey's Satanism, at its philosophical base, is one of celebration of self, and it is precisely this characteristic that makes his use of the term "Satan" so appropriate for his church. LaVey was often questioned as to why he didn't just call his philosophy Humanism rather than Satanism. He addresses that question in his *Satanic Bible*; "Humanism is not a religion. It is simply a way of life with no ceremony or dogma. Satanism has both ceremony and dogma."[26] But there is more to LaVey's philosophy than simply rejecting Christianity that forms the basis of his true Satanism. Mythologist Joseph Campbell defined the religious experience the world over as "... the birth of spiritual man out of animal man. It happens when you awaken at the level of the heart to compassion, shared suffering: experienced participation in the suffering of another person."[27] Hence, in the Christian tradition, believers concentrate on the image of Christ suffering on the cross because it represents both God willingly experiencing man's suffering through Christ's crucifixion, and it represents the suffering of all man; it is an image of divine compassion, and when we participate in that compassion, we are touched by the divine. However, LaVey posits that the individual self is divine, and his philosophy is one that focuses on the desires of the self, rather than focusing on compassion and the suffering of others; namely, the desires and gratification of the flesh are to be provided by the world. Thus, the Satanist attempts to manipulate the physical world to comply with his or her desires, rather than manipulating him- or herself in order to appeal to some higher, supposedly benevolent good. LaVey's use of the term *Satan*, defined as adversary, could not be more fitting; because at its philosophical base, it truly is the adversary of the Christian God. LaVey lists numerous rejections of the church and its beliefs (as well as other religions) based on historically demonstrated hypocrisy, greed, prejudice, and numerous other scandals and rationalizations that have formed the church as it is today. However, it is the base of his philosophy that truly makes LaVeyan Satanism satanic; it is the adversary of compassion, the glorification of self, and a return to our basest animal urges—preservation of self and satisfaction of desire. LaVey's magical rituals are testament as he gives instruction for three types of satanic ritual concerning sex, destruction, and compassion. Sex and destruction are obviously for fulfillment of lust and anger. The ritual of compassion, however, is also twisted around so that it becomes self-serving: "The compassion, or sentiment, ritual is performed for the purpose of helping others, or helping oneself. Health, domestic happiness, business activities, material success, and scholastic prowess are but a few of the situations covered in a compassion ritual. It might be said that this form of ceremony could fall into the realm of *genuine* charity, bearing in mind that 'charity begins at home.' "[28] Even the ritual of compassion is ultimately self-serving.

To say that LaVey's philosophy and, subsequently, the philosophy of the Church of Satan is dangerous would be unfair. On the whole, it represents a philosophy based on existentialism, paganism, and pragmatism; and while some of it may appear detestable to certain people, LaVey's logic is sound, even though it is animalistic in nature. Essentially, it rejects the irrational nature in humanity in favor of a nature aligned with logic, but still quenches man's need for the mysterious through its magical rituals that supposedly tap into that mysterious force that moves the cosmos.

However, it *is* fair to say that *The Satanic Bible* is a dangerous book. Without careful guidance from someone who understands the satanic philosophy *en toto*, the book can become a lighted match near a gasoline tank. LaVey's philosophies have been coopted by the weak-minded, delusional, or racist as cause to commit acts of murder and other criminal activities. Sean Sellers meditated on *The Satanic Bible* before murdering his parents. Such an act is probably most attributable to the idea that if you consider yourself a god among men, then you are not confined by the law and morality of men. Furthermore, there is LaVey's instruction that the Satanist should "Hate your enemies with a whole heart, and if a man smite you on one cheek, smash him on the other! . . . Give blow for blow, scorn for scorn, doom for doom—with compound interest liberally added thereunto! Eye for eye, tooth for tooth, aye four-fold, a hundred fold!"[29] In the hands of a 16-year-old disturbed young man, who probably considers his parents his worst enemies, this can make for dangerous motivation. Furthermore, LaVey's rabid exultation of the strong conquering the weak has been used by neo-Nazi organizations as justification for their racism and totalitarian ambitions. LaVey's philosophy ultimately taps into the "law of the jungle" mentality; it is social Darwinism taken to the extreme.

To his credit, LaVey did try to purge his church of those whom he considered weak, delusional, or undesirable, much to the dismay of some of the members who were forced out.

LaVey also addresses the notion of human sacrifice in his bible, citing that since man is god, then to sacrifice a man would be akin to killing a god, and thus, the self; "Inasmuch as gods are always created in man's own image—and the average man hates what he sees in himself—the inevitable must occur: the sacrifice of the god who represents himself. The Satanist does not hate himself, nor the gods he might choose, and has no desire to destroy himself or anything for which he stands! It is for this reason he could never willfully harm an animal or a child."[30] He also points out that the practitioner who would engage in human sacrifice is probably not so disinhibited as to masturbate in front of his devotees in order to achieve the same kind of magical energy. While LaVey generally deems human sacrifice unnecessary, he does add, "The only time a Satanist would perform a human sacrifice would be if it were to serve a twofold purpose; that being to release the magician's wrath in the throwing of a curse, and, more important, to dispose of a totally obnoxious and deserving individual."[31] It is in this area where LaVey shows some hypocrisy; he states to the media that he finds the satanic sacrifice of humans that have been conducted as "damned sickening," yet believes that it is justified if the sacrificial person has done wrong to the magician. Therefore, his requirements concerning when it is necessary or appropriate for a Satanist to perform a human sacrifice is entirely subjective. By his own standards regarding choice of sacrifice, those whom he found "damn sickening" may have been following his very instructions (although it should be noted that the murders he was referring to were conducted in the folkloric Satanism paradigm). It appears that LaVey simultaneously approves and disapproves of human sacrifice; and despite his outline for what makes human sacrifice acceptable in his philosophy, those requirements are highly subjective and, therefore, could extend to nearly every adult.

In spite of some of the more shocking and dangerous aspects of his philosophy, under LaVey's guidance, the Church of Satan, while surely arousing attention during instances of supposed satanic murders, could probably have avoided any direct influence in some of the criminal and disturbing instances in U.S. history, had his *Satanic Bible* not been published for the masses. It sold hundreds of thousands of copies, but, as indicated before, in the wrong hands it can be a dangerous tract. Similar to Levi's experience with the priest seeking the *Grimoire of Honorius*, LaVey's own grimoire fueled the evil and dark intentions of some very disturbed individuals.

Today the Church of Satan is still active and growing. Its current leader, Peter Gilmore, has been interviewed on the History Channel, which did a documentary on the Church of Satan. It has numerous magazine publications, including adult magazines, and many musicians, artists, book publishers, and paranormal research groups listed as members and affiliates. The church, however, has largely been quiet in modern days and has spawned several offshoot organizations such as the Temple of Set, which was founded by LaVey's own daughter. As in any religion, there are fractures and denominations, but nearly every form of Satanism considers LaVey's *Satanic Bible* required reading.

The founding of the Church of Satan can be seen as an important cultural moment in the history of the United States, and while the History Channel did do a documentary on the church, its influence will probably go largely unrecognized. The birth of the Church of Satan was, as Christian evangelists like to say, a sign of the times. It was the counterculture revolution, and San Francisco was the focal point of a new era that would begin with peace and love and end with death and hypocrisy. The "freedom" of the hippie culture eventually devolved into the Manson murders and gave way to a darker, more sinister side of the cultural revolution. LaVey and the Church of Satan were essentially ahead of the curve. Recognizing the gathering darkness, LaVey sought to tap the well and codify a belief system around it. The hippie generation eventually came to symbolize nothing more than self-indulgence to the point of self-destruction and hypocrisy. LaVey, however, sought to avoid those pitfalls through establishment of a religion that embodied the darker recesses where the baby boomer generation would eventually find themselves. The emergence of LaVey and the Church of Satan was, if anything, prophetic of the direction that the nation was heading. As LaVey wrote in the prologue to *The Satanic Bible*, "The twilight is done. A glow of new light is borne out of the night and Lucifer is risen, once more to proclaim: 'This is the age of Satan! Satan rules the Earth!' The gods of the unjust are dead. This is the morning of magic, and undefiled wisdom. The flesh prevaileth and a great Church shall be builded, consecrated in its name. No longer shall man's salvation be dependent on his self-denial. And it will be known that the world of the flesh and the living shall be the greatest preparation for any and all eternal delights!"[32]

THEISTIC OR SPIRITUAL SATANISM

Theistic Satanism, unlike LaVey's Satanism, believes in an actual deity known as Satan. Similar to LaVeyan Satanism, however, Theistic Satanism belief has spawned a number of different doctrines with varying beliefs, similar to the Christian church's fractioning into Catholicism, Protestantism, and the various subsets thereof that may choose a different style of worship or focus of belief. Theistic Satanism, as indicated before, believes in Satan as a god among many gods. It does not deny the Christian God's existence, but feels that God is merely one of many who has cunningly coopted his worship the world over in an effort to glorify himself. The Church of Azazel, based out of New York City and largely centered around Diane Vera and her extensive webpage devoted to Theistic Satanism, writes,

> The workings of Nature do not suggest a cosmic God who is interested in any kind of personal relationship with us humans. Therefore, a god who does want lots of human attention is unlikely to be the cosmic God. For this reason, the Christian god—a self-described "jealous God" who wants to be worshipped by everyone in the world—is unlikely to be the true cosmic Creator, or a true cosmic anything. Yahweh seems to be, most likely, a spirit (or perhaps a cluster of spirits rather than a single spirit) who was once just a local tribal war god of the Israelites, but who then got greedy and started demanding the attention of more and more people.[33]

Satan, on the other hand, has not had the same thirst for attention, but has, in fact, been the liberator of mankind. Followers of Theistic Satanism, as defined by the Church of Azazel, celebrate the gods that have brought mankind knowledge and freedom, as they are truly the ones who love humanity and desire it to advance. They celebrate these gods that have brought knowledge and understanding to humanity, even at great cost to themselves. Some of their spiritual deities include: Prometheus, who stole fire from the gods and gave it to man; Lilith, Adam's first wife who refused to submit to Adam's will and was, therefore, banished from the Garden of Eden; Ishtar, whose descent into the underworld caused all sexual activity on earth to cease, but whose return heralded the return of sexuality; Pan, god of nature whose image was coopted by Christianity as the devil—half goat, half man, and representative of the natural desires of the flesh; and Lucifer-of-Sophia, whom the church believes is the muse of enlightened spirituality. Together, these five are called the Rising Gods of the Modern West.

However, it was Satan who ultimately convinced Eve to eat the forbidden fruit in the Garden of Eden, namely, that of the Tree of Life and the Tree of Knowledge of Good and Evil. In the Christian tradition, this is seen as man's downfall, which culminated in his being cast out of paradise. However, the Theistic Satanist takes a paradoxical view. Firstly, the fruit of the tree was the fruit of Life and of Knowledge of both good and evil; these are essentially what make us human, give us free will, and enable us to become more divine through our action and knowledge. While Adam and Eve may have led untroubled lives of leisure under the graces of God until they took of that fruit, theirs was essentially a life of ignorant slavery bound to God's favor. It was not until they partook of the forbidden fruit that they truly became human and distinct from God. When they were cast out of paradise, Adam and Eve became truly human—subject to mortality, morality, free will, and strife. The taking of the forbidden fruit essentially enabled man to become divine in his own right; it enabled him to harness nature, to grow in intelligence, and to determine his or her own path, something that was impossible in the Garden of Eden. The Garden was, essentially, a fool's paradise.

In essence the gods of the Church of Azazel represent the gods that would have aided mankind on his journey after being cast out of Eden. Nature had to be domesticated for food and shelter; man had to reproduce to ensure population growth; technology was necessary to ensure man's dominance over nature and development; and women had to take their rightful place as independent heads of clans and cultures. The development of spirituality throughout the world was a way to organize civilizations and pass on knowledge. However, it was Satan who first freed man from Eden and who is, therefore, the focus of worship in the Church of Azazel.

Conversely, it is the Christian or Abrahamic God who seeks to restrain and enslave humanity to a life of devotion and worship and restraint from the very freedoms that make man a somewhat divine being—freedoms such as sexuality, technology, science, and spirituality. The Church of Azazel cites the story of the Temple of Babel as an example of God's thwarting of man's technological achievement. As mankind sought to build a tower to reach heaven, God confused their languages so that they could not complete the work. The Bible itself states that God is a jealous god, and the tower of Babel is representative of God preventing mankind from attaining god-like power and stature. Thus, the Church of Azazel worships and gives thanks to the muses of civilization, the gods that have enabled man to grow and truly develop, and rejects the Christian God as petty, jealous, and guilty of atrocities against those for whom his altruistic love did not extend, for example, the enemies of the Israelites in the Old Testament.

Diane Vera is the founder of the Church of Azazel, which she operates mostly online from her home in New York City. She also organizes the NYC Satanists, Luciferians, Dark Pagans, and LHP Occultists, which meet in person once a month. Diane is, at once, both a very public and very private individual. Her writings regarding her satanic beliefs are extensive, to say the least. A quick search of her name will bring up various interconnected websites devoted to polytheistic Satanism and the beliefs thereof, as well as links to her own Church of Azazel website and various other satanic organizations and chat rooms. However, simultaneously she is a very private individual; her beliefs are there for the world to see, but not her face. There are no pictures of her available on any of her many social networking sites; rather, her image is always represented by a satanic symbol such as a pentagram or the Church of Azazel symbol. There is virtually no personal information about her, and the route to obtaining an interview with her requires that you contact her through chat rooms or social networking sites, which (for me, at least) have been largely unsuccessful. It is fairly simple to understand her unwillingness to make herself available to the public, as Satanists of all types are routinely derided and verbally attacked by the Christian right and politicians. It could also draw the attention of those who seek to practice a much more sinister form of Satanism. While Vera has worked over the years to set up an actual church building in the New York City area, she has been unsuccessful due to a lack of attendees, as her audience is largely diffuse and spread throughout the country. On her website in a written history of the Church of Azazel, she recounts an attempt at forming a meeting of Church of Azazel members in 2009:

> The January 2010 meeting of the Church of Azazel proto-congregation was attended by a total of 12 people—the largest number of people ever to attend any of Diane Vera's Meetup group meetings up to that point. However, among those people in the NYC metro area who had a strong interest in the Church of Azazel (and who also had the necessary background to appreciate the Church of Azazel paradigm), too many had difficulty attending meetings regularly. In some cases, this was because they lived outside the city and had to travel two or more hours to get to meetings.[34]

She also attempted a meeting of Lilith devotees, which had only 15 people who were able to attend.

The Church of Azazel has been an online phenomenon, a fact that Vera cites as the main reason that Theistic Satanism has become recognized in the satanic community. Until the advent of the Internet, it was primarily LaVey's Church of Satan and *Satanic Bible* that held sway over those interested in the occult and Satanism in general, while those who did, in fact, believe in a god known as Satan were relegated to the outskirts of the community. "When this website first went online in fall 2002 C.E., we Theistic Satanists were still a despised minority within the public Satanist scene. But we have grown rapidly and now seem to be the majority—at least in online forums, though we still have some catching up to do in terms of real-world organization and in terms of being noticed by scholars of new religions."[35] In essence, Theistic Satanism provided believers with the spiritual and supernatural qualities of traditional religion combined with the rejection of Christianity and the humanism of Anton LaVey's Church of Satan. While LaVey's Satanism and magical practices were designed to elevate man to god-like status and enable man to create change in the world, Theistic Satanism acknowledges that there are gods that supersede humanity and can influence humanity to their desires, thus satisfying man's (seemingly instinctual) desire for the supernatural and mysterious. Theistic Satanism draws upon pagan magical traditions, Western mythology, and Christianity in order to understand history and religion in a new way. They have, in essence, reached back into the building blocks of Western civilization to find their gods and assert that Christianity became the dominant Western religion only through force and the systematic takeover of pagan traditions. Their supernatural beliefs appear quite similar to those of the Hermetic Order of the Golden Dawn, a famed group of pagan worshippers who made headlines in the early 1900s, and whose most infamous member, Aleister Crowley, went on to be dubbed "the wickedest man alive."

The Hermetic Order of the Golden Dawn believed in a pantheon of different gods or supernatural forces that were at work in the world and that these gods could be called upon through ritual and magic. At the height of its popularity, the Golden Dawn boasted such influential members as authors W. B. Yeats, Arthur Machen, and Algernon Blackwood, all of whom became classic authors; Yeats was considered to be quite possibly the greatest poet of the twentieth century. The Hermetic Order of the Golden Dawn was highly influential in the occult world and celebrated similar gods as Theistic Satanists, such as the nature god, Pan. However, Golden Dawn never explicitly acknowledged Satan as a god. The Church of Azazel, while recognizing and revering several gods, shows its devotion to Satan as the ultimate deity.

An interesting side note to the Church of Azazel is its political beliefs, which Vera lists as being inherent to membership in the church. The Church of Azazel is a politically left-wing organization, devoted to keeping the Christian fundamentalist right as far out of politics as possible in order to ensure that any and all religions are allowed to practice their faith unimpeded by paranoid religious fanatics that associate any form of Satanism with folkloric Satanism. This is an interesting facet of Theistic Satanism as opposed to LaVeyan Satanism, which has been coopted by far right-wing and neo-Nazi organizations, and largely advocates for a military state.

The Internet has been a boon for many belief systems, and Theistic Satanism and those who believe in it have taken full advantage of this ability to reach a wide variety of people across the globe. Their reach has been fairly extensive, although "churches" still remain just online communities, chat rooms, blogs, and videos, for the most part.

A much more visible individual in the Theistic Satanist community is Melissa Hudson, or, as she is more commonly known online, Venus Satanas. Venus is a Theistic or Spiritual Satanist who began her immersion into satanic beliefs in 1992 at the age of thirteen when she read *The Church of Satan* by Blanche Barton. "I realised that there are people out there that worship Satan, and Satanism seemed like the path for me. I was attracted to it for its self-empowering qualities, and how Satanism lets you live your life the way you want." Raised by her grandparents, she had never been indoctrinated into any traditional religion. "We were sent to nice schools and we got a decent education, but they never forced Christianity on us, so when I found Satanism, it wasn't out of rebellion." Her grandmother actually encouraged her to research the subject and helped Venus write a letter to an organization in Florida, who then referred her to a group that accepted teenage members, known as the Order of the White Wolf. She sent them some of her artwork, and they hired her to design the cover of their magazine, though they could only pay her in music CDs by bands dedicated to Satanism. "I used those recordings in a private ritual that I made, so that I could create a pact with Satan and dedicate myself to the path of Satanism."

She has since become a frequent and popular online presence in the satanic community and a highly motivated entrepreneur who seemingly understands the value of spectacle and showmanship that LaVey advocated and Vera avoids. She has over 15,000 fans and followers of her blogs, videos, and chat rooms. There are numerous online videos of her discussing the merits and particulars of Theistic Satanism; she has an attractive and enchanting video presence that she utilizes quite well and probably attracts a number of male followers. She has come to occupy a niche in the satanic community; she is a leader and professor of Spiritual Satanism with a flare for marketing. Her online website enables individuals to enjoy a live, intimate striptease pole dance from Venus to the music of Valgud, a satanic band that operates out of Texas; it also enables people to talk with her and other members of the community. Spiritualsatanist.com offers both free and premium memberships that come with a variety of perks, though it should be noted that the site is primarily geared toward Satanists. Venus, as Melissa, is also a talented artist who focuses on nature portraits and sells her work and prints online. Interestingly enough, her artist profile lists her art career as having begun in 1992, the same year that she became a Satanist.

But Venus is not just a showgirl; she uses her natural ability and tendency toward spectacle and showmanship to grow her belief system, find followers, and broaden the community of online Satanists. Her beliefs are explained and are as prevalent as Vera's, but visitors to her site have the added delight of basking in her dark sensuality as she explains the finer points of satanic belief. She is truly a fine hybrid of LaVey and Theistic Satanism.

As a whole, Satanism exists as a chaotic and decentralized belief system. Venus explains it well in one of her many online tutorials, "In Satanism, it is a chaotic approach. You have to make your own path; you have to blaze your own trail." I had the opportunity to chat with her and some of her fellow Satanists in their chat room. There were individuals from many different belief systems, with varying theories, but who came together to discuss their philosophies and educate each other. Venus is on the chat room 24/7. She has truly made a life of her belief; "the Internet is face-to-face for me. I don't see cyberspace as some kind of imaginary reality. For me it is real, and I speak with my fans every day." The Internet, in its ability to connect billions, has enabled Satanists, occultists, pagans, Wiccans, and various other independent and alternative religions to find others with common interests and beliefs. Their numbers are scattered; their church is digital.

Outside of her online presence, Venus leads a normal life a bit different than what one would imagine a Satanist might live (influenced, of course, by the popular media portrayals). "Outside of the Internet I live a pretty normal life. I have three cats, my husband who loves me—and he's not a Satanist, though he's been involved with the occult for over 30 years. Nowadays, I enjoy playing with my cats; I enjoy taking care of my garden; I look forward to when my husband comes home from work and I can give him a kiss and a hug." And when asked about her online dancing . . . "He likes that I dance; it keeps me in shape, gives me energy and makes me happy so he does not mind at all." Overall, her marriage and life sound like a success story weaved from alternative sources; a marriage based on mutual acceptance of alternative beliefs with entrepreneurship and a little eroticism thrown in to boot. When viewed through only the medium of a computer, Venus can appear to be that dark, foreboding, witch-like figure that has come to stereotype practitioners of the occult—people who largely seem to enjoy the dark side of life. "For me, Satanism is something that I can use to manifest my dreams and desires. Satan is a god of this world, so I have come to respect nature, animals and wildlife. I enjoy the sunrise and I look forward to the night. I am not depressed in any way; I've always been a happy person, and I enjoy laughter and I like to feel comfortable that there are those who are into black metal who might be obsessed with those things, and even though I like black metal, I don't really get into their scene. I'm 32 now and I've grown out of those things, pretty much."

While Satanism today surely exists, it does not exist as a centralized belief system with dogma and founding texts. It is marked by diffusion, infighting, individual philosophies, and ever-present and oppressive stereotypes. They assign themselves satanic names in an apparent effort to undercut their traditional Christian names and preserve online anonymity. Despite Theistic Satanism's belief in a number of gods and goddesses that inhabit and walk the earth, Satanism is marked by darkness rather than light. Satanists live in the shadows and use folkloric symbols and ideas to create the illusion of evil, even within organizations that claim no evil practices but simply celebrate Satan as the greatest friend to mankind. Today's Satanists, fully able to exist in a world where they are free to practice without fear of state or religious intervention, appear unable to break away completely from the Christian symbol of Satan as an evil entity that represents the darkness and malice in the world, despite member protests to the contrary. Its members are, on the whole, fringe members of society living their lives outside the "norm" of American life. But it appears they prefer to embrace the darkness of the Christian idea of Satan rather than embrace him as the bringer of knowledge (light) to man in his various manifestations of Prometheus, Lucifer, and Lilith. Their belief system, in all its various incarnations, is primarily one of rejection: rejection of God (light) in favor of the adversary (dark); rejection of traditional values in place of moral relativism; rejection of society for the individual; and rejection of compassion for the self. Satan, is, after all, the adversary.

However, there exists duplicity in the idea of adversary and rejection—in the idea that those who reject have thus been rejected. The murderous and illegal practices of folkloric Satanists need to be put aside, as they cannot exist within the framework of any civilization as an accepted form of religious practice; however, the symbolic Satanists and the Theistic Satanists are almost forcibly drawn down the dark path (or Left Hand Path) of life because of the duality that is inherent in the dominant Western religions such as Judaism and Christianity. Such duality would not be found in the Eastern religions such as Buddhism and Hinduism, where the darker recesses of humanity are embraced as part of the experience of God. Take, for instance, the Hindu goddess, Kali:

> The temple image displayed the divinity in her two aspects simultaneously, the terrible and the benign. Her four arms exhibited the symbols of her universal power: the upper left hand brandishing a bloody saber, the lower gripping by the hair a severed human head; the upper right was lifted in the 'fear not' gesture, the lower extended in bestowal of boons. As a necklace she wore a garland of human heads; her kilt was a girdle of human arms; her long tongue was out to lick blood. She

was Cosmic Power, the totality of the universe, the harmonization of all the pairs of opposites, combining wonderfully the terror of absolute destruction with an impersonal yet motherly reassurance.[36]

Both good and evil, destruction and creation, exist as one cosmic force of God in the Hindu tradition. Western culture is one of duality and opposites, where one side can only be embraced in opposition to the other, thus a "Right Hand Path vs. a Left Hand Path." Satanists exist at the periphery of a culture that is steeped in the Christian tradition; their embrace of the dark side of life leaves them in opposition to the Christian's symbol of the light of God. This does not necessarily have to be the case, but it does exist as the paradigm in which our Western culture operates.

To the Western Christian who does not possess knowledge of the Hindu religion, the image of Kali and those bowing before her would most likely represent devil worship; but to the Hindu it is the same as worshipping the God of the Cosmos—the same God that is responsible for light is responsible for dark. This has been one of the central difficulties of Western theology since its maturity during the Middle Ages—the question and problem of evil in the world when a benevolent and loving God is the ruler of all things. Theologians have wrestled with this question and continue to wrestle with it today because evil and darkness do exist. In the Hindu tradition darkness is not separated from light, while Christianity has divided the two to represent God and Satan as polar opposites. At the basis of Satanism there exist difficult theological questions: God created Satan; did he therefore create evil? God allows Satan to operate in the world, so is Satan a servant of God meting out punishment, or does this benevolent God not care about the destruction Satan wreaks? In the book of Job, Satan and God strike a bet like two rival businessmen dealing in souls, and God allows Satan to ruin Job's life in an effort to prove that Job loves God and would continue to serve him despite loss. This hardly seems the act of the God Christianity touts. But the existence and practice of Satanism ultimately calls into question the dualistic nature of Western and Christian thought.

If practicing Satanists (with the exception of folkloric Satanists) appear to reject society, it is because they have to due to the dualism inherent in Western culture. Therefore, they change their names, get tattoos, wear dark clothes, and rejoice in things that push away from the "light" and the "good," even though they do not necessarily advocate evil. If Satanists largely appear to reject society, it is because they have been rejected and are unable to exist outside the Western paradigm. LaVey made a spectacle of his satanic belief in an effort to shock the United States, but later in his career he ceased this kind of showmanship in the hopes of developing a true following of philosophic devotion. Today, Vera and Venus, likewise, are more content to follow their philosophic ideals and reach out to people who cannot seem to find acceptance in or accept the Christian philosophy. One member I chatted with was a 17-year-old girl who had become disenchanted with Christianity and was looking for a new path; she came to Venus's chat room in an effort to have some of the bigger, more spiritual questions answered that sometimes get overlooked in the dogmatic, theocratic Christian denominations. She is free to follow her path and try to find acceptance in a different paradigm.

Theistic Satanism, overall, is a benign, polytheistic belief system that embraces the old gods of the ancient pagans, as well as the deities represented in the Bible. They exist on the outskirts of traditional society and, therefore, are easy targets when the United States goes on one of its recurring witch-hunts. With the exception of people like Venus, who make themselves public figures, Satanists adopt false names for the sake of anonymity and tend to avoid publicity of any kind. Christianity holds no meaning for them, and they are, therefore, free from the constraints that have largely shaped the Western world. "Satanists in general have strayed from the typical, traditional Christian views on demons," Venus says. "We have had good relationships with Satan and with demons so we have come to our own understanding of these things, and you may find that in general, our beliefs and ideas on demons aren't the same as what Christians teach. I try to be respectful of other religions, regardless of that. I understand that religions are supposed to be meant to help people to live up to their potential, and to do good things in life."

CHAPTER 13

The American Gothic

The ground of Gettysburg is mottled with long brown grass that lies on its side in crests and valleys so that it resembles a fast-flowing river. Frogs and cicadas in the nearby swamp raise a buzzing din that can be heard from the visitors' center all the way to the High Water Mark. Giant rocks pepper the fields, left behind by the retreating glaciers of the Ice Age 13,000 years ago like gravestones planted in the ground for a time of death and loss that was certain to come. This is the site of the greatest battle of the Civil War and the deadliest battle in U.S. history, and a symbol of the American struggle for unity and independence. It is also the most haunted place in the United States.

Every year ghost hunters flock to this battlefield, upon which so many died in the throes of agony and emotion, to investigate the inns, battlefields, forests, and restaurants. Some of the most celebrated ghost videos and pictures have come out of Gettysburg, where people report that at night soldiers appear and then disappear, walking through the fields and up and down the stairs of the inns.[1] It is a place with history, and places with history have ghosts.

Actually, it would seem that history is a prerequisite for a haunting. Contemporary places do not have the aura of the past and are, therefore, not usually associated with hauntings. "In a setting where legends of the romantic past are expected, personal contact with the supernormal is sanctioned, even encouraged."[2] Ellis refers to these places as "holy ground," a title that contemporary places cannot claim. While there have been ghost sightings in supermarkets, supermarkets are not generally considered haunted. Why? Because there is no history—they are not "holy ground" where generations have come and gone, where the drama of life has unfolded decade after decade, century after century. The supermarket does not fit with our narrative of a haunted place. Our narrative is the way in which we experience the story of our society. The supermarket may not be a haunted place, but Gettysburg certainly is, regardless of the reality of ghosts. A place is not necessarily haunted by spirits, but it is most certainly haunted by its past.

In his book *Projected Fears: Horror Films and American Culture*, Kendall Phillips defines the term *gothic* as being "the tension between the known and the unknown."[3] It is a tension between the light of day and the dark of night, between the known present and the unknown past, and between the mundane of everyday life and the horror of nightmares. In visiting haunted places such as Gettysburg, there is a knowledge, which we seek to gain. Why is it not enough that we read and study about the battle in books? Why is it not enough to have learned the dates and the places and the people? Why do we feel the need to actually walk the ground and see the grass and rocks—hear the frogs and cicadas? Precisely because it is holy ground, the ground where lives were lost, dramas played out, and blood spilled. We walk there because we seek to know more; we seek to have a connection with that history, and the paranormal can give us that connection.

"At its core, the problem of both the living and the dead is their inability to reconcile the known and the unknown, and this problem is only resolved as [we] learn to embrace the unknown and thereby find peace."[4] There is always a disconnection between the past and the present. As people age and pass away, so does their direct knowledge of historical things. As the generation that fought World War II passes away, so do the direct experiences of one of the greatest and most influential times in human history. They possess a knowledge that cannot be found in books or videos. They have experience—direct knowledge—and those who do not are automatically once-removed from that history. As time progresses and the knowledge of that war relegated to books with generational gaps, the readers become even more removed from that direct history. That is why we seek out the holy ground—so that we can walk in footsteps that we did not create before they are washed away by the tide of time. We seek to remember, and we try our best to understand why our world is the way it is now. We seek to reconcile that past with our present in an effort to find peace. When those ghosts of Gettysburg are caught on a tourist's camera (see *Gettyburg Ghosts* video) marching through the trees, we are seeing a living history played out before us, a glimpse into the experience of that time on camera. Seeing those ghosts is a personal, individual experience in which the viewer has somehow bridged a gap between the known and the unknown, the past and the present.

Obviously skeptics will seek to condemn such a video as a fraud or mistake on the part of the viewer, but it is nearly impossible to authenticate or debunk this experience. The viewer says it's real, others say it's not, but what *is* real is the desire to visit this holy ground, and the belief that there are spirits that walk the fields, woods, and inns. The belief of those who have encountered something they cannot explain is real; and the belief that they have witnessed something that is a direct remnant from the past is real, regardless of science. Not everybody comes to Gettysburg on an official ghost hunt, but everyone is, in some way, looking for ghosts.

Why do ghosts walk these old passageways and fields? It would seem a senseless act. Could it be they are there to remind us, to form a connection between the living and the dead, the past and the present? In gothic America, we are seeking out the dead so that we can better understand ourselves and the present. Author John Keel refers to this as "Our Haunted History," in that the world with all its cycles and patterns and incidents is far older than our comprehension. With that age comes history that we are just beginning to understand.

LIZZIE BORDEN TOOK AN AXE...

On August 4, 1892, the horrific murders of Andrew Borden and his wife Abby Borden were discovered. Both people had been hacked to death with a hatchet. Lizzie, their daughter, was the immediate suspect; as the case went to trial, it became a media sensation, sparking waves of controversy, debate, and folklore. It even spawned a nursery rhyme: *Lizzie Borden took and axe and gave her father forty whacks; after that, she wasn't done, she gave her mother forty-one.* Lizzie was eventually acquitted of the charges due to lack of hard evidence, though there was plenty of circumstantial evidence. However, she is still largely believed to be responsible for the murder of her parents. Today the Lizzie Borden House is not only a national historical landmark, but also a bed and breakfast that is reputedly very haunted and has been investigated by innumerable ghost hunting teams, including The Atlantic Paranormal Society (TAPS) of *Ghost Hunters* fame.

The Lizzie Borden trial has been compared to that of O. J. Simpson; one that captured the attention of the entire nation. In both cases, the defendant was found not guilty, and in both cases the public by and large believed the opposite. O. J.'s guilt, while not official in the courts, has been solidified in the national consciousness; comedians make references to it, scholars make excuses for it, and journalists make accusations against any and all parties involved. Regardless of the factual evidence of the case and that he was found innocent, the public consciousness has declared and accepted, not only his guilt, but also the idea that he got away with it. The Lizzie Borden case was similar; a gruesome double murder in an affluent part of town involving a family that was slightly out of the norm (O. J. and Nicole were a mixed-race marriage, while the Borden household was notoriously old-fashioned and resisted modern advances such as indoor plumbing), both murders involved bladed objects, and both involved circumstantial evidence that pointed to the defendant but couldn't prove the case. More important to this discussion is that each of the murders became part of the narrative of the American culture.

But why have these murders entered into the narrative of the United States, whereas others have not? One reason might be that these particular trials fit into the kind of narrative that the United States is writing for itself. Mark Edmundson, professor of English and author of the book *Nightmare on Main Street*, believes that the narrative of the United States may be a gothic tale, and these stories reinforce that tale. "Gothic shows the dark side, the world of cruelty, lust, perversion, and crime that, many of us at least half believe, is hidden beneath the established conventions . . . Gothic shows time and time again that life, even at its most ostensibly innocent, is possessed, that the present is in thrall to the past. All are guilty. All must, in time, pay up."[5] The Simpson and Borden cases, involving wealthy families, brutal murders, circumstantial evidence, and issues that are generally hidden behind closed doors, captured the public fascination because they fed into this gothic narrative of people being two-faced—inwardly violent while outwardly kind. And perhaps this American gothic narrative is what has kept the Lizzie Borden mythology alive, as people still seek out the ghosts of those who died to find a final answer to the question, who killed the Bordens?

And this is certainly not the only case that feeds into the gothic narrative. The Rosenberg trial fed the U.S. fascination with the double life, as well as the trial of the Menendez brothers in the murder of their parents. Both revealed inner realities far different from the exterior façade, and both became media sensations.

Perhaps one of the most evident and repeated of these story lines is that of the Salem witch trials. Salem, Massachusetts, in the 1690s was a puritanical society in which outward appearances of piousness and God-fearing morality were the standard by which a person was judged. However, the people were all too willing to accept a story about witches who hid beneath the veneer of godliness while convening with the devil in the woods by firelight and casting spells. The light was trying to reconcile with the darkness, the known with the unknown, and, unfortunately, the results were disastrous. In his work

"Young Goodman Brown," Nathaniel Hawthorne, a descendent of one of the witch trial judges, describes Goodman Brown's nighttime journey into the forest, where he stumbles upon all the good and decent townsfolk celebrating a witch's mass around a fire. He is unable to reconcile one image of reality with the other, and he is forever changed by his experience. One of the themes of "Young Goodman Brown," which has led to its inclusion in so many anthologies, is that the true nature of people is often hidden in the dark—in the woods. It wasn't just some odd coven of witches, but rather the *entire town* that was guilty. Those who died, died for the sins of all, not just their own.

Witch trials and witch-hunts have repeated through the ages in the American narrative. During World War II, Japanese Americans were rounded up and sent to internment camps for fear that they could be spies. In the 1950s McCarthyism tried to root hidden Communists from society, focusing mainly on rich Hollywood elites. During the 1980s the paranormal aspect of gothicism made a triumphant return with the satanic panic. Today, the witch-hunt is still on with the media frenzy that surrounds celebrities such as Paris Hilton, Britney Spears, and Lindsay Lohan. We follow their every move with moral criticism, as if none of us who watch the reports has ever had a few too many drinks in our early twenties. Also, fascination with the celebrity sex videos allows the moral public to shake a finger and say, "Shame on you," and ask, "What is happening to our young women?" More often than not, these issues end up in court with a vast amount of media coverage. They are our modern witches, guilty of not upholding imagined morals before a hypocritical public. Truly, those who forget the past are doomed to repeat it.

The literal witch-hunt may not be behind us, either. Feminism often asserts that the hunt for witches is actually nothing more than a hunt for strong, independent-minded women who do not conform to social norms. Wendy Kaminer, attorney and feminist author, wrote in 2000, "It has long been clear to feminists that crusades against witchcraft reflect a primal fear of feminine power and aim to punish women, most brutally, for transgressing gender roles."[6] She goes on to tell a story about a young aspiring writer who attended Columbine High School, the infamous site of the worst school shooting in U.S. history—an event, incidentally, that was surrounded by rumors of occult involvement on the part of the two perpetrators. The young girl, Brandi Blackbear, had apparently written a story about an incident at school, which prompted school officials to search her locker and confiscate her notebooks.

School officials found a story involving a shooting on a school bus and promptly suspended her. Ostracized and harassed by fellow students,

Blackbear returned to school in the fall of 1999 and began a private study of Wicca. Within a few months, a teacher was hospitalized for a still unknown ailment, and Blackbear says she was blamed: An aptly named assistant principal, Charles Bushyhead, accused her of practicing Wicca, casting spells, and causing the hospitalization of the mysteriously ill teacher. According to the lawsuit, Bushyhead called Blackbear an immediate threat to the school and suspended her for another 15 days.[7]

School officials being overly concerned about a girl writing a story about a shooting on a bus is understandable, particularly considering the context of what had just happened at Columbine. However, the charges of witchcraft due to an unforeseen illness illustrates how, in times of fear, misunderstanding, and chaos, people tend to revert back to the old gothic narratives which have persisted in the American culture.

During the 2010 Senate race in Delaware, Republican candidate Christine O'Donnell, favored by the newly formed and highly influential Tea Party, was targeted by the media, who cited O'Donnell's appearance on the Bill Maher show where she said that she had dabbled in witchcraft in high school. O'Donnell was already far behind in the polls but her presence in the race was highly polarizing, and the charges of witchcraft gained national media attention and was addressed by all sides of the political race.[8] While officially the statements were laughed off as the product of imaginative youth, the fact that this tactic was used in the first place and that it received so much attention attests to the fact that, as a nation, we are only a few nooses beyond Salem.

Christine O'Donnell is actually the perfect gothic figure when discussing the existing narrative in the United States; she's young, attractive, strong, independent, and Christian; but the idea that she is secretly involved in the demonic, the summoning of ancient, invisible powers, supercedes anything that she may be or profess to be. She is a metaphor for the modern American gothic, an attractive structure that hides deep, dark, supernatural secrets. Such is the fascination with the gothic narrative in the modern world.

Gothic castles are the classic haunted houses, and while there are very few castles remaining in the world, the ones that do remain are purportedly haunted. However, it's the American haunted house that now occupies the spotlight. They are places of old where, within their faded walls, great torture and pain and drama have unfolded which were often not realized by the public of that day and have only come to light through history's intervention. For children, the haunted house on the block is the old, run-down house with boarded windows and overgrown grass. Why? Because its look is that of abandonment, of secrecy behind its walls and the belief that something terrible must have happened to cause it to look this way. The haunted house is never believed to be the newly built raised ranch next door. But the gothic narrative, which repeats in the American culture, tells us that behind that new home there's something dark lurking in the depths of history. Edmundson paints a portrait with the Bates Motel from Alfred Hitchcock's *Psycho*:

> Alfred Hitchcock, in his most influential film, struck a blow against modern hubris. The way we signify our satisfaction with the highway motel we're compelled to stop at on our car trek cross-country is to say that it looks like no one has ever been there, it's so clean. In other words, it has no past. The ranch-style highway motel is a feat of architectural low modernism. But after Hitchcock it is difficult to say of a motel, especially while in the shower, that no one's ever been there. Hitchcock saw that the blank slate of modernist architecture could easily be invaded by the Gothic monster. After *Psycho*, motels are indissociable from loony Norman Bates and the glowering mansion next door (which Hitchcock thought of as one of the stars of the film).[9]

Edmundson was writing in the late 1990s as the nation was at the precipice of a new millennium and at the beginning of the paranormal revival in the United States. Perhaps, if we look at it from the *Psycho* standpoint, while the United States was realizing there was a gothic monster that stood behind its modern façade during the nineties, the new millennium has found the United States exploring that gothic construction, looking for the ghosts and demons that reside there. Programs like *Ghost Hunters* and *Paranormal State* are trying to find the ghosts that haunt the ancient castle that is the American landscape, and the public is fascinated. In this aspect, the United States is constantly in the midst of a narrative that involves ghosts, trying to reconcile the past with the present, the light with the dark, the known with the unknown, the mundane with the horror. For this reason our paranormal belief systems run the gamut from haunted histories to recollections of horror and pain. The stories that survive and get passed into mythology are the ones that best capture the gothic nature of the United States. The witch-hunts, the double lives, the murders, and the ghosts of houses where horror has unfolded are all part of the American landscape and the gothic narrative of our time.

BIGFOOT AND THE INNER WILD MAN

If the paranormal is a window to the unknown past, then what do we see when we view Bigfoot lumbering toward the dark reaches of the Pacific

Northwest wilderness through the lens of Patterson and Gimlin? Dr. Jeff Meldrum, with a PhD in anatomical sciences and an MS in zoology, may provide part of the answer.

Gigantopithecus blacki is theorized to have been a giant bipedal, ape-like creature that existed less than 1.6 million years ago on the Asian continent. It stood approximately nine feet tall and is estimated to have weighed around 700 pounds. The first remains of *Gigantopithecus* were found in the late 1950s in China, which, oddly enough, was when the Bigfoot phenomena began to manifest in the United States (though the abominable snowman was earlier, in the 1930s). Since that time, *Gigantopithecus* has been suspected as being both the abominable snowman of the Himalayas and the Bigfoot of the Pacific Northwest. Dr. Meldrum, in his immense work, *Sasquatch: Legend Meets Science*, theorizes that during the Ice Age *Gigantopithecus* migrated across the Bering land bridge and made its way into North America. "The compelling reason for this distinct possibility is that the land bridge between Asia and North America is known to have existed several times within the last million years, at various intervals during the Pleistocene or Ice Age. It appears that these hairy, human-like creatures, sometimes called sasquatch, could easily have migrated to North America at several times during the Ice Age."[10]

The world today is obviously not as it was during the Ice Age and the ages before. Whale fossils have been found in the deserts of Egypt and Peru, the Arctic Circle once averaged a balmy 74 degrees year round, and in July of 2010, scuba divers discovered the fossils of an extinct species of monkey in the ocean off the coast of the Dominican Republic. Probably most telling is the discovery of fossilized red panda remains in Tennessee, which was notably first reported by the Cryptomundo website, a site dedicated to the research and discovery of mysterious and unknown species. The scientific establishment often derides groups such as Cryptomundo because they search for Bigfoot and various other creatures of myth and legend. *The Huffington Post* reported on the discovery of the red panda remains: "It has the face of a giant panda bear and the body of a small raccoon. This unusual, cuddly-looking animal is the red panda, and until recently, was only believed to be native to the mountains of Nepal, Burma and China. Now, according to recent fossil findings, it appears the enigmatic red cousin to the black-and-white panda once roamed the long-ago forests of Tennessee."[11] The ancient world was a vastly different place. "It's here, at the Gray Fossil Site, where a startling number of mammal bones have been uncovered, including a saber-toothed cat, ground sloth, rhinoceros, alligator, camel, shovel-tusked elephant, Eurasian badger and a red panda, dating back more than 4 million years to the period known as the late Miocene era."[12] Many of these creatures, particularly the red panda, would have had to cross into North America via some land bridge, Bering or other.

The number and variety of species that have existed and disappeared greatly outnumber the number of current existing species. It is largely thought that humans, along with a number of other species, migrated from the Asian continent to the North American continent across the Bering land bridge when it was in existence. There is controversial evidence of early forms of man having existed on the North American continent before the officially recognized crossing approximately 12,000 years ago.

> Nearly as controversial as the sasquatch itself is the interpretation that a fragment of a fossilized human brow ridge found at Mexico's Lake Chapala may be from the skull of a relic *Homo erectus*...This Asian hominid is thought to have gone extinct within the last 100,000 years, possibly persisting until quite late, until less than 30,000 years ago on isolated Indonesian islands. That the notion of *Homo erectus* in North America is even entertained by serious researchers has implications for the potential range of *Gigantopithecus*. If red pandas, and perhaps *Homo erectus*, both sympatric contemporaries of *Gigantopithecus* in Asia, successfully migrated to North America, what would prevent a similar distribution of *Gigantopithecus*?[13]

Meldrum, of course, is not the first person to believe that the reports of Yetis and Sasquatch in Asia and North America were possibly sightings of an ancestral relative of man. During the 1930s Adolf Hitler dispatched a group of scientists to the Himalayas to search for the Yeti. Hitler believed that the Yeti might provide a link to the ancestry of the Aryan race. They came back empty-handed.

It is possible, though not probable, that a species such as *Gigantopithecus* could have survived undiscovered. New species are discovered every year, though they are usually quite small in size or minor variations of already known species. However, there have been a few exceptions. The megamouth shark, a 16-foot long, unusual-looking beast, was not discovered until 1976. The snub-nosed dolphin was discovered off Australia in 2005, and in 2008 a population of approximately 125,000 gorillas was discovered in the Congo; this discovery doubled the number of gorillas known to be alive worldwide. Obviously, these are rare cases, but there are still undiscovered areas of the world that occasionally reveal their secrets. Could a species like Sasquatch exist in the wilds of Canada and the Pacific Northwest? There are certainly plenty of people who claim to have seen them, and many more who believe that it is a distinct possibility.

So what do we see when we gaze upon the Patterson-Gimlin film of a Bigfoot hulking into the dark forest? What is it that confronts us when we see the footprints in the mud or sand? Is it an unknown past—a time in which the world was something alien and odd, when strange creatures wandered through areas that are now populated with suburbs, highways, and strip malls? The discovery, or even the possibility, of a creature like Sasquatch is a beacon to the modern world, a figure from an ancient time that serves to remind us of our short existence here and of the history and mysteries that the earth has hidden beneath our modern veneer. As we try to understand the history of our planet, Bigfoot is history staring right back at us. It exists as a window to the past, a reconciliation of the past and the present, the known and the unknown. It is no wonder that we seek him out or see him in the reaches of the forest and mountains. Even if Bigfoot isn't "real," even if visions of him walking in the forest and footprints in the sand are only anomalies or some kind of mass delusion, we still see him and create him in our minds for a reason. The symbol of Bigfoot and what he represents may be just as important as whether or not the creature is real.

There is a sociological aspect to Bigfoot as well. Bigfoot represents an ancient form of man: the Wildman, the Hairy Man that lurks beneath the modern man. The Sasquatch has entered into and remained a part of the American conscious for a reason; it represents a wildness that exists in the hearts of humans. While we may have civilized our lives over the course of history, there exists an animal element in our biological and psychological makeup, and Bigfoot feeds that element. Hence, throughout history there have been reports of "wildmen" who roam the forest, sometimes kidnapping women, sometimes savage, sometimes gentle, sometimes hairy and other times nearly completely human. Wildmen are part of the folklore and mythology of many different cultures and civilizations around the world, particularly the Pacific Northwest Native American lore.

Gayle Highpine is a Native American who has traveled extensively throughout the different tribes and studied Bigfoot in mythology. "Here in the Northwest, and west of the Rockies generally, Indian people regard Bigfoot with great respect. He is seen as a special kind of being, because of his obvious close relationship with humans. Some elders regard him as standing on the 'border' between animal-style consciousness and human-style consciousness, which gives him a special kind of power."[14] In many of the tales and traditions, Bigfoot is a supernatural being, a messenger that will warn the tribe that the Creator is angry with them.

Kathy Moskowitz Strain, the Heritage Resource and Tribal Relations Programs Manager for the Stanislaus National Forest in Sonora, California, is a frequent speaker at Bigfoot symposiums and has done extensive lecturing regarding Bigfoot in Native American folklore. One of her well-known contributions concerns Native American pictographs at Painted Rock, which depict a large, hairy, man-like creature (called Hairy Man) alongside several other known species. According to Moskowitz, the creature embodied several different narratives, from "protector of man" to "predator of man," and his legend is even associated with the beginning of the world.[15]

While the Native American legends have painted Bigfoot as a fairly benign being, referring to him as "elder brother" and "Hairy Man," Wildman depictions by European settlers, and the stories they inspired, painted a different picture. There were stories (usually second or third hand) of men being carried off in the middle of the night by large, hairy, man-like creatures. While these stories were quite rare, the media would often portray Bigfoot as a beast running off into the forest with a woman under his arm, and there were also scattered Native American stories about females being kidnapped or at least stalked by the beast. These images, and the idea of a "wild man" running off into the secrecy of the forest to have its way with a hostage woman, may have contributed to the association between Bigfoot, the Wildman, and the fascination that the 1950s and '60s culture had with the beast.

Joshua Blu Buhs has written perhaps the best analysis of the cultural significance of Bigfoot in his work, *Bigfoot: The Life and Times of a Legend*. "Throughout history stories of wildmen have provided a way of thinking about what it means to be human: the contradictions, the difficulties, limits, and the glorious wonder of it all."[16] Blu Buhs envisions Bigfoot as a confrontation between a vanishing culture of woodsman masculinity and the modern, consumer-driven culture of the fifties and sixties. The era that included women entering the workplace, the end of World War II, and protests of the Vietnam War was a time of great transition in the United States, especially among the working-class men. "White working-class men were frustrated and scared about the changing society, the changing economy, worried that they were failing. Many Bigfoot tales sought to ease these anxieties by affirming the culture of character, the importance of work, skill, and old-fashioned masculinity."[17] It was working-class men on a road construction job that first found the famous Bigfoot tracks. It was hunters and woodsmen that affirmed the tracks with further discoveries, sightings, and stories. They attained relevance through their interaction with the paranormal, spotting and documenting a mythical beast that was only known by them. The scientists were irrelevant and the women incapable or unwilling to make the deep long treks into the wilderness; so it was these blue-collar men, struggling to maintain their sense of self in a changing world, that ultimately sought out Bigfoot.

The Bigfoot craze allowed a generation of men whose world was changing to find some purpose to their existence, and in some ways that has not changed. Ghosts, UFOs, and Bigfoot remain symbols, regardless of their "reality." They are symbols of our desires, our fears, and our cultures. People still pursue and believe in Bigfoot with an almost religious-like faith. They spend time and money and sacrifice their reputations and relationships in pursuit of these things. The paranormal, the gothic, is a part of them.

Part of what fed the fascination with Bigfoot was the media portrayal of the creature. "[I]n the early 1970s Bigfoot began appearing at suburban drive-ins. These theaters, like rural areas, were largely ignored by Hollywood, so independent filmmakers supplied the theaters with so-called exploitation movies: cheaply made horror flicks and sexually charged films aimed at a mostly teenage audience."[18] Most of these films portrayed Bigfoot as a killer and a creature of horror. *The Legend of Boggy Creek*, in which a Bigfoot-type creature stalks the swamps of a rural area, frightening and attacking the townsfolk, actually became a huge commercial success. But it involved the sexualized, horrific aspect of the creature—the dark side of the Wildman; something that is still portrayed by the tabloids and movies to this day.[19] Every monster should have a movie, after all. These films are still produced today, though with a knowing, tongue-in-cheek homage to the seventies drive-ins. *The Wildman of Navidad* beautifully replicates the old drive-in creature features. These films both add a highly sexualized male component to the script. The camera captures a breed of man that has all but died off—the rugged, ugly, full-bearded ancient man in rural towns who hunts and fishes and is beyond the influence of the modern world. *Shriek of the Mutilated* brought the male sexuality to a new level and added a strong subterfuge of homosexuality between the men hunting the mythical and dangerous Yeti. These films concentrate on men, rather than on women; this male focus is very different from many other horror films. Why? Because they are the ones that are truly in danger of being killed off, not by the creature, but by society.

The Bigfoot legend and mythology has survived to a certain extent. Bigfoot has been transformed into a bit of a commercial on some level, as Blu Buhs points out, advertising beef jerky and even hosting his own television show for kids called *Bigfoot Presents*. However, the deeper mythology of Bigfoot has also survived, and the fascination remains, as evidenced by the new upsurge in interest from the public and by programs such as *MonsterQuest* and *Is It Real?* Ultimately, Bigfoot's survival is a part of the gothic narrative. "By imagining themselves into the body of Sasquatch, white working-class men could imagine themselves as black, as women, could come in contact with their own souls, their own repressed and forbidden desires."[20]

It is these "forbidden desires" that Blu Buhs mentions that may be the darker, gothic narrative for Bigfoot. Bigfoot's story is, in essence, one of history and repression; the history of an unknown and ancient past before man was a human, and the repression of the inner "wildman" in a culture that is more and more consumed with political correctness, consumerism, and modernity. There is an inherent antisocial darkness about the Wildman, a creature beyond the confines of civilization that kills its food and kidnaps its mate through violence. The media depictions of Bigfoot in both magazines and film have fed this idea of a dangerous creature that roams the forest and threatens the confines of civilization. But why does the idea of the Wildman fascinate us so? Why does the idea of this creature fit so well within our cultural story, our hopes, our dreams and fears?

The inner Wildman may be the inner horror that confronts the mundane of our lives. The idea of something deep within that is purely animalistic, powerful, and instinctual without the constraints of normal society is a dark and ultimately antisocial idea, and it is one that feeds the gothic narrative of Bigfoot. To confront Bigfoot in the woods is to confront a variety of things—the unknown, the dangerous, the wondrous, and the supernatural—and all are in direct confrontation with modern everyday life. Bigfoot is a reconciliation between these things; it represents a mysterious past and an unknown being with a possibly violent, repressed animal nature.

UFOs AND THE ANCIENTS

"As they were walking along and talking together, suddenly a chariot of fire and horses of fire appeared and separated the two of them, and Elijah went up to heaven in a whirlwind. Elisha saw this and cried out, 'My father! My father! My father! The chariots and horsemen of Israel!' And Elisha saw him no more. Then he took hold of his own clothes and tore them apart."[21]

While strange flying objects in the sky may seem like a more recent phenomenon, it is really not new. The Bible speaks of great pillars of fire by night and pillars of clouds by day that guided the Israelites through the wilderness; it tells of the chariot of fire that took Elijah up into heaven in a whirlwind, and great shining stars that signaled the birth of Christ. When talking of UFOs it is important to distinguish between unidentified flying objects and flying saucers. Anything can be an unidentified flying object until, of course, it is identified; but flying saucers are another matter. Not all UFOs are flying saucers, but all flying saucers are (thus far) UFOs; and flying saucers have been recorded throughout history, even farther back than the biblical records. Hieroglyphs on the Great Pyramid depict flying machines in the shape of discs and what appear to be modern-day astronauts descending from them. Images painted on cave walls during the Renaissance and Romantic periods show strange objects in the sky—sometimes threatening, sometimes enlightening, but always with an accompanying story.

Carl Jung examined the proclivity of the human mind to see circular objects in the sky in both dreams and artwork in his work, *Flying Saucers: A Modern Myth of Things Seen in the Skies*. The flying disc becomes a sign of epiphany from heaven. "In the present instance it seems to me sufficiently safe to conclude that in my examples a central archetype consistently appears, which I have called the archetype of the self. It takes the traditional form of an epiphany from heaven..."[22] The idea of flying saucers being heavenly psychic realizations is very interesting when looking at the biblical passage from 2 Kings quoted above. Elijah's apprentice, Elisha, asks that he be bequeathed a double helping of the spirit of Elijah. Elijah states that if God allows Elisha to view his ascent into heaven, then he would be granted his desire. Thus, the chariots of fire descend, and Elisha sees his teacher taken away and becomes endowed with a spirit greater than that of Elijah. "The company of prophets from Jericho, who were watching, said, 'the spirit of Elijah is resting on Elisha.' And they went to him and bowed to the ground before him."[23] Elisha goes on to perform miracles such as purifying the water in Jericho so the people can drink it. The vision of the chariots of fire imbued Elisha with mystical knowledge, an ability to perform miracles, and reverence from the people and prophets of Jericho. He was thus able to go to the land and help the people of Jericho.

Elisha is not the only person in history to claim a greater knowledge or power from their interaction with a UFO. People who claim to have been visited by alien creatures, or even abducted by them, often claim they have received a message regarding the fate of the world, or that they have been gifted with a vision of the star systems from which the aliens came. Barney and Betty Hill, the United States' first official abductees, recreated a star map from which the alien craft supposedly came. Whitley Strieber saw visions of doom and destruction during his time aboard the spacecraft. Some even claim to communicate with the aliens regularly and thus are able to relay messages from the aliens to mankind. Indeed, if one were to actually witness a flying saucer, and certainly, if one were to come in contact with the beings who are piloting the craft, he or she would be imbued with a knowledge and understanding that surpasses all currently accepted reality. To see this flying saucer, therefore, would be to gaze upon something that reflects both the known world (human technology) and the unknown world. It exists in our present world as an image of a reality that cannot be known. It is a gothic symbol from our subconscious.

So what does this have to do with the American gothic narrative? How would these visions in the sky fit into the overall gothic experience of a collision between past and present, known and unknown, mundane with horror? While we often associate flying saucers with images and ideas from science fiction, the phenomenon itself is as old as man's consciousness. Jung uses the flying saucer as an archetype for the interaction of the conscious and subconscious of man, something that is inherently part of the universal consciousness of human experience. But there are more concrete interactions.

On the moorlands of Britain stands a wonder of the world that has long been associated with the paranormal. Stonehenge, to this day, baffles scientists and anthropologists as to its origins and its meaning. It has been associated with witchcraft, mass burials, ancient calendars, and UFOs. The most obvious mystery is how this monument was constructed over 5,000 years ago by a society of hunters and gatherers. Some of the massive stones were transported to their present location from as far away as 200 miles. One can only speculate the purpose of this overwhelming task. It is a task that is very difficult to explain or comprehend and, thus, has become a thing of great paranormal speculation. Geoffrey Monmouth wrote of Stonehenge in his classic literary work, *History of the Kings of Britain*, "They are mystical stones and of medicinal virtue. The Giants of old stole them from the farthest coast of Africa and placed them in Ireland, where they inhabited at the time."[24] Merlin describes them as ". . . a structure of stones, which none of this age could raise without a profound knowledge of the mechanical arts."[25] They called these stones "Giant's Dance."

"Mechanical arts" could certainly be understood in today's technology, but 5,000 years ago, what constituted mechanical arts? Whatever methods were employed by ancient man to build Stonehenge have obviously been lost in time, as modern technology has erased our past knowledge of mechanical arts. And even if we were to definitively answer the question of "how," the question of "why" is of greater importance and even more mysterious.

In 1965, astronomer Gerald Hawkins put forth a theory as to the purpose of Stonehenge. As discussed in *Time* magazine, "In his analysis, he identified 165 separate points on the monument, and linked them to astrological phenomenon like the two solstices and equinoxes and lunar and solar eclipses. It's a difficult theory to disprove completely and some evidence is persuasive—at dawn on the summer solstice, for example, the center of the Stonehenge ring, two nearby stones (The Slaughter and Heel Stones) and the sun all seem to align."[26] But even these theories are met with skepticism from the scientific community, which states that there is no way ancient man had the precision or knowledge to construct such an intricate calendar. However, Hawkins's theories remain

one of the more legitimate and socially and scientifically acceptable of the reasons explaining "why." But this answers only part of the question.

> Four thousand years ago Great Britain was populated by a small group of
> people barely out of the Stone Age. They had a few primitive tools made
> of bones, and they probably eked out a living with only the greatest diffi-
> culty. Anthropologists estimate that there were probably about three hun-
> dred thousand of them. They were undoubtedly divided into warring
> clans and factions, since factionalism is a natural state of man. Yet some-
> how, thousands of these people managed to get together and spend many
> generations quarrying huge stones (some weighing thirty tons) in the
> Prescelly Mountains of Wales and hauling these enormous blocks
> 240 miles to Amesbury. There they systematically arranged these stones
> in a circle, following precise measurements—so precise that they were able
> to construct a mathematically correct astronomical calendar.[27]

Hawkins's argument of an astronomical calendar is impressive, but not as
impressive as the feat these ancient peoples undertook; in fact, by comparison, it
doesn't seem to make a bit of sense. Stonehenge literally took thousands of years
to construct. Even conservative estimates show this undertaking to be almost
unbelievable. As stated in Britannia History, "While we can't say with any degree
of certainty what it was for, we can say that it wasn't constructed for any casual
purpose. Only something very important to the ancients would have been worth
the effort and investment that it took to construct Stonehenge."[28]

This could almost be considered an unexplainable anomaly of human history, if Stonehenge stood alone in the world as a symbol of ancient man's
mysterious technology and endeavors; but it's not. It is one of many, many
mysterious and unexplainable structures that exist throughout the world.
They are structures that defy explanation and understanding and continually
defy our efforts to define them. Among these are the Great Pyramids and
the Sphinx, the faces of Easter Island, the temples of Tiahuanaco, the
Mayan calendar, and the Nazca Lines of Peru; all of these are ancient structures and creations that defy understanding and definition, and all of them
seem to contain an unknown knowledge of the ancient earth . . . and perhaps
something more. The intricacies of their mathematics, the mysteries of their
creations, the precision of their craftsmanship remain the center of much controversy. How did the Mayans create a calendar that is so precise that it even
accounts for the small wobble of the earth on its axis? Why are the Nazca
Lines only visible from a plane and seem to serve no practical purpose?

In 1968, German writer Erich von Däniken released his work *Chariots of
the Gods*; it became an instant best-seller. In it, Däniken hypothesizes that

the human race was more or less created by an alien race that visited earth millions of years ago and is ultimately responsible for humanity's ascension from primitive beast to a race of technological demigods through interbreeding with female earthlings and eliminating specimens that did not meet their requirements.

> Obviously the "man" of those times was no *homo sapiens* but something rather different. The spacemen artificially fertilized some female members of this species, put them into a deep sleep, so ancient legends say, and departed. Thousands of years later the space travelers returned and found scattered specimens of the genus *homo sapiens*. They repeated their breeding experiment several times until finally they produced a creature intelligent enough to have the rules of society imparted to it. The people of the age were still barbaric. Because there was a danger that they might retrogress and mate with animals again, the space travelers destroyed the unsuccessful specimens or took them with them to settle them on other continents.[29]

Sound insane? That's precisely what the critics thought. However, Däniken is not just randomly hypothesizing; he is focusing on the great similarity between ancient texts and legends from peoples around the world, which all seem to include gods descending from the heavens in "chariots" that generally consist of fire and thunderous sound, interbreeding with human women, imparting great knowledge to the ancient people, and then ascending back into heaven. The Sumerian *Epic of Gilgamesh*, the Bible, the Mahabharata, Egyptians, Tibetans, American Indians, Eskimos, and ancient Incas all have very similar stories concerning the origins of man and knowledge. Couple these legends and texts with massive stone structures created by "primitive" man, unusually precise measurements, and their understanding of the stars, calendars, mathematics, and metallurgy, and you suddenly have a very real and believable hypothesis that is antithetical to today's understanding of ancient history. "I am simply referring to passages in very ancient texts that have no place in the working hypothesis in use up to the present. I am drilling away at those admittedly awkward spots in which scribes, translators and copyists could have had no idea of the sciences and their products ... It is unworthy of a scientific investigator to deny something when it upsets his working hypothesis and accept it when it supports his theory."[30]

If Däniken was only offering an hypothesis, than Graham Hancock was offering proof of the theory in his massive and exhausting work, *Fingerprints of the Gods*, which incorporates much of Däniken's theories, though with much more evidence, research, field work, and history. Hancock does have his own take on the theory, postulating that there was a much more ancient and advanced human civilization that existed before recorded history, and who passed down their knowledge through construction of massive, enigmatic structures. Hancock concentrates largely on the legends of Viracocha—bearded, Caucasian, Christ-like god, whose idols the Incas worshipped and whose prophesied return they had long awaited.

> Indeed their legends and religious beliefs made them so certain of his physical type that they initially mistook the white and bearded Spaniards who arrived on their shores for the returning Viracocha and his demi-gods, an event long prophesied and which the Viracocha was said in all the legends to have promised. This happy coincidence gave Pizarro's conquistadores the decisive strategic and psychological edge that they needed to overcome the numerically superior Inca forces in the battles that followed.[31]

Hancock travels the world finding and cataloging not only the mysteries of ancient artifacts, but the similarities in the stories told from civilization to civilization. Modern-day fundamentalist Christian churchgoers would probably find it very interesting that the biblical stories they know have been recreated again and again in other cultures and religions; the great flood, heavenly beings taking human females as wives, and even the story of Christ. The Viracocha not only taught the Incas about mathematics and sciences, but also about love, benevolence, and morality, before he was carried out to sea on a raft made of snakes, promising to return one day. Both Däniken and Hancock postulate that humanity is much older than previously thought, and that the ancients were influenced and educated by beings far older and more advanced than we are even now.

Arthur C. Clarke and Stanley Kubrick collaborated to create *2001: A Space Odyssey*, the greatest science fiction story ever told thus far. The story is based around the idea of an alien race setting in motion the beginnings of mankind and then monitoring their progress of evolution from the development of tools in the opening scenes to man's ability to leave the confines of earth and reach for the stars. This ancient alien race was one that could be both benevolent and violent. The stark black monolith left by the alien race sounds like a beacon in the depths of space alerting the universe to our ever-growing presence. The idea is not without precedent. Some astronomers and scientists believe that the existence of water on earth could be due to an ancient collision with a comet comprised of ice, and that life on earth could have formed from bacteria and microorganisms that hitched a ride on a meteorite and eventually came to rest on this planet. Indeed, that is the explanation put forth by Charles Darwin as to how some land-based animals wound up on the Galápagos Islands.

In 2008 aerial photographs showed one of the last remaining tribes in the world that remain untouched by modern civilization in the Brazilian rainforest near the border of Peru. The flyover was conducted in order to prove their existence and thereby protect the land from deforestation and the tribe from extinction. The low-flying aircraft was met by tribesmen armed with bows and arrows and prepared to defend themselves from a machine that they feared and could not understand. "It is understood that when the plane first flew over the village, the people scattered into the forest. When it returned a few hours later they had painted themselves red and fired arrows into the sky. 'They must have suffered some sort of trauma in the past and must know that contact is not a good thing,' Fiona Watson, of Survival International, said."[32] Is it not possible to compare the fear and awe that this last surviving, isolated tribe felt when they sighted the airplane, with the fear and awe that has been passed down from generation to generation in the form of myths and legends about great gods that came from the heavens? Could our fascination with flying saucers be related to the deeply engrained myths of gods who possessed greater knowledge and power, and who descended from the skies to plant the seeds of our civilization? The gothic narrative of the flying saucer could be the ultimate reconciliation between the present and the ancient, ancient past, the heavens and the earth, the light and the dark. To see one of these alien craft or to have contact with alien beings is to commune with the gods. People who claim to have had these experiences come away forever changed; their old perceptions of reality have been altered and a new understanding has been imparted to them—just like Elisha after having viewed Elijah's ascent into heaven in a chariot of fire or the epiphany rendered by Jung's subconscious. Either way, the flying saucer embodies the idea of the past haunting the present, and the present reconciling itself to the past.

But what of the reconciliation between the mundane and the horror—the true cornerstone to the gothic ideal? There is a darker side to the flying saucer narrative, one that is more innately gothic and horrifying. In his collection of works, H. P. Lovecraft, the father of the modern horror story, talks about the "Old Ones"—ancient, malevolent beings that despise humanity and seek to harm and horrify humanity. Their evil is beyond the confines of human morality. "Never is it to be thought that man is either oldest or last of the Masters of Earth; nay, nor that the great'r part of life and substance walks alone. The Old Ones were, the Old Ones are, and the Old Ones shall be. Not in the spaces known to us, but between them...As a foulness shall They be known to the race of man."[33] Lovecraft's work involving the Old Ones became known as the Cthulhu Mythos. He wrote in the 1920s, and critics accused Däniken of being misled through Lovecraft's fiction.

John Keel, author of *The Mothman Prophecies* and *Our Haunted Planet*, also postulates that there are beings that are older than man who regularly interfere with the development and course of humanity, sometimes for good and sometimes for evil. Keel also draws on the ancient texts, the complexities of the great ruins, and the existence and persistence of world religions. He refers to these beings as "ultraterrestrials" rather than extraterrestrials because he is not certain that their origins are otherworldly, but are perhaps much more ancient beings who have left the confines of corporeal bodies. They manifest themselves in the mysterious visions that haunt our planet—UFOs, aliens, ghosts, spirits, and demons. "The startling truth, as carefully recorded by the ancient historians, is that the ultraterrestrials have always been in direct contact with millions of individuals and that they actually ruled directly over mankind for many years. In recent centuries their influence has become more subtle."[34] Keel's philosophies concerning UFOs, psychic encounters, and various other phenomena are all-encompassing and quite appealing, though they exist at the periphery of popular UFO and paranormal thought, belief, and influence.

Much more popular in our gothic culture is the idea of UFO abductions, cattle mutilation, and human experimentation. It has reached levels of both horror and comedy in popular culture, everything from *Fire in the Sky* to *The Simpsons*. People do claim that creatures from other planet have abducted them and that they have been subjected to probes and experimentation. Their lives are forever changed, and their experiences are often described as absolutely horrifying.[35] Whitley Strieber recorded his hypnotherapy sessions with psychiatrist Donald Klein and presented them in his book, *Communion*. "I saw something that looked like it had a hood on it, standing over by the wall near the corner in our bedroom [breaks into panic] and I don't want it to be there! I don't want it to be there! Please! God, it—What's it doing to me? Stop! Oh, oh, stop! What's it doing to me? [Screams, prolonged, twenty seconds.] I cannot recall experiencing at any time in my life such panic as was evoked at this point in hypnosis."[36] Certainly the idea of finding anyone, let alone an alien being, in your dark bedroom is a terrifying idea. But what often horrifies abductees even more is their inability to move, while at the same time sensing the overwhelming awareness of a presence in the room and seeing visions of figures leaning over them and floating outside through a window to a craft they have never before seen. This is the stuff of nightmares, the horror in contrast to the mundane.

While much fun has been poked at those who claim to have had these experiences, there is a very real human aspect of suffering involved that is often vented through psychotherapy and hypnotherapy. Professor of psychiatry at Harvard and Pulitzer Prize winner John Mack shocked the academic world when he began serious research on the UFO abduction phenomenon. He worked with such figures as Budd Hopkins, a famous proponent of and believer in the abduction theory, and Whitley Strieber.

Mack took the abductees' stories seriously; he listened to them and worked with them, much to the dismay of certain figures of the scientific and academic world. But Mack's compassion led him to work with a group of people who were isolated and unwilling to come forward for fear of mockery; individuals who had had very traumatic and horrifying experiences.

> The trauma has four aspects to it. The first element is the experience itself —to be paralyzed, to be taken against your will, to be subjected to these intrusive, terrifying procedures. The terror is enormous, and it is buried or repressed for the reasons that I mentioned. The second aspect is the isolation that these individuals feel. They are very reluctant to tell their parents. They get told they are too imaginative or that they are dreaming. As adults, if the guy who is abducted tells what happened, say, in a bar, he will be told he is crazy. So abductees have each learned, as one of them put it, to go "underground." They do not tell their experiences, so they feel very isolated. They know something of profound importance has happened in their lives, something that has great meaning; but they dare not talk about it. The third aspect, which is the one that has particular relevance to our discussion, is that it totally shatters their understanding of consensus reality, as of course it does for us.[37]

Mack admits that these stories do sound unbelievable, but the sheer numbers of unrelated individuals who claim similar, if not identical, experiences, and who have no history of psychiatric problems, lead him to conclude that there is something beyond the range of normal human experience that is occurring. "Keep in mind that I hear myself saying these words and I cannot believe I am saying them. You probably cannot either. Yet this is the consistent account of otherwise normal, healthy, sane people, who do not believe it either. They are only first confronting the truth of it with me or other investigators."[38]

As indicated before, part of the gothic nature of these experiences that has solidified them into the consciousness of the United States is the psychosexual nature of the experiences. "The most prominent aspect of the experience is the urological-gynecological probings. Instruments are inserted into the vagina. Often, mothers claim to have had fetuses removed. While there is not a physically documented case of fetus removal, the experience is that they have been pregnant and the fetus has been removed. Men have had sperm samples taken against their wills. It is highly distressing."[39] It is true horror, though Mack notes that the horror of the rape-like experience does not compare to the horror of having one's entire understanding of reality ultimately changed. It should also be noted that these reported abduction experiences coincided with Däniken's assertion that alien races bred with humans.

The horror of these incidents holds a dark fascination for the public. It would be different if the aliens all brought cookies and milk for the abductees and sat around chatting about *The Late Show*. Most people would not find it to be a very interesting story. The cultural fascination lies in the movie-like horror of the experience. In the same way that *Shriek of the Mutilated* and *The Legend of Boggy Creek* created staying power for Bigfoot by portraying him as a horrific, sexualized creature, so films such as *Fire in the Sky, Close Encounters of the Third Kind*, and more recently, *The Fourth Kind*, were able to take the abduction stories and turn them into entertainment, albeit scary entertainment. The abductions themselves, however, lay hidden behind the veneer of modern, scientifically fact-based life. It is the horror that lurks behind it all that man continually wants to explore. In essence, we want it to be true; we want the danger, we want the mystery, and we want the movies to be real. The stark reality for the abductees, however, is not a fun-filled movie adventure, but a true and horrifying experience. And the public fascination is one that is tied to the horror of these abductions, rather than to the transformative effects of these experiences.

What is truly interesting about the late John Mack's work is that ultimately the abductees saw these horrific experiences as a catalyst to personal transformation. As Carl Jung had indicated 30-plus years earlier, these visions of flying discs in the air and our psychic interaction with them is an epiphany, a new understanding of ourselves and the reality in which we exist. Sometimes those epiphanies and realizations can be painful and frightening, but the ultimate result is a new awareness and understanding.

> The second important dimension of the UFO abduction phenomenon, and one I want to underscore, is the element of transformation. What I and others who have worked with the trauma of this have discovered is that the abductees begin to feel that their experiences were for a purpose or had a positive meaning to them. That is, when the trauma has been fully experienced and processed intensely in the non-ordinary state of consciousness, after more than one, two, three, or four hypnosis sessions—something begins to happen in the abductees and in their perceptions of their experiences. They feel that the experience is expanding their consciousness, that they are connecting with themselves, that they are opening up to a whole new perspective on the universe.[40]

He notes that this only occurs through therapy; if left unresolved, the experience can actually have the opposite effect. But there it is in Mack's work: the spirit of Elijah imparted to Elisha the gift of understanding and prophesy—an image of the divine imparted to the ordinary. Confronted with the unexplainable, people experience horror and a breakdown of their vision of reality, but they emerge with a new understanding. The flying saucer narrative persists because of its uniquely American gothic qualities; the blurring of lines between past and present, known and unknown, the mundane and the horror. Only through the reconciliation of these things can a person find peace, understanding, and a new enlightenment.

Holy ground, the inner Wildman, and the vision of the flying disc in the sky all hold their witnesses in complete and utter awe. These visions, whether scientifically real or not, fundamentally alter the way an individual sees the world and the way he or she lives his or her life. No one can possibly step into the realm of the paranormal or the unknown and not be changed by it. The fascination with the paranormal persists, in part, because of the gothic nature of the phenomenon and the American culture. As Mark Edmundson put it, our modernism is like the Bates motel, quaint and new, but shadowed by a frightening, dark, and unknown Gothic castle. Now, in the twenty-first century, we are truly beginning to make our way into that castle of our own fears and dreams, absurdities and pathologies. We are fascinated by the dark, unknown reaches of life, and the paranormal provides that for us. Whether it is walking on the same ground where thousands upon thousands of soldiers died to birth a country, or finding a giant naked footprint in the sands of the wild, or seeing a disc that could not be anything man-made, these phenomena transcend our known reality and blur the lines between what we think we know and what we see; between what we read of the past and what was actually lived; between the mundane of our lives and the waiting horror that lurks beneath the quaint visage.

During times of trauma and great cultural change, people turn to the paranormal. Despite humanity's vast achievements in understanding the world, sciences and technology, it would appear that the paranormal and the gothic narrative belie all of it. Erich Fromm said that modern religion is merely a veneer painted over the ancient beliefs of totemism and animism. I would take it a step further, and say that our modern world of science, technology, and progress is merely a veneer over ancient, gothic belief systems. Witchcraft, wild giants in the forest, gods from heaven, and the darkest reaches of the human experience hover like a shadow over our brave new world—they walk where we walk, see what we see, live what we live.

They can also drive us to action the way that Christine O'Donnell's witch-craft comments drove the public debacle. And this can happen on a global scale. Throughout the centuries, dating back to pre-Roman times, the ritual-istic sacrifice of infants has been a recurring theme in the belief of witchcraft and evil, and one that was the major theme of the satanic panic. However, it was also cited as a reason to go to war with Iraq in 1990 following the Iraqi invasion of Kuwait. According to the *Guardian*:

> We recall the horrifying stories, incessantly repeated, of babies in Kuwaiti hospitals ripped out of their incubators and left to die while the Iraqis shipped the incubators back to Baghdad—312 babies, we were told. The story was brought to public attention by Nayirah, a 15-year-old 'nurse' who, it turned out later, was the daughter of the Kuwaiti ambassador to the US and a member of the Kuwaiti royal fam-ily. Nayirah had been tutored and rehearsed by the Hill & Knowlton PR agency (which in turn received $14 million from the American government for their work in promoting the war). Her story was entirely discredited within weeks but by then its purpose had been served: it had created an outraged and emotional mindset within America which overwhelmed rational discussion.[41]

We as a nation, incensed by this act of pure evil—one with its base in witchcraft and Satanism—cheered when the bombs began dropping.

The 2001 World Trade Center attack left the nation utterly speechless and terrified. It was an evil act on such a massive scale that the public had difficulty dealing with it emotionally and psychologically. However, a reason appeared in the smoke pouring from the North Tower: the demonic image of Satan.

> Ever since the commercial airline missiles destroyed New York City's World Trade Center on 9/11/01, images of violence and catastrophe have seared the collective mind. A popular image shot by freelance pho-tographer Mark Phillips seemed to capture the face of a demon in a large plume of smoke emanating from one of the twin towers. Soon after the Associated Press secured one-time printing rights to the so-called "smoke demon" image, it became available to Internet users who quickly disseminated it with foreboding commentary about the Christian apocalypse.[42]

The image appeared in newspapers across the country and George W. Bush's speeches took on an air of public exorcism, the spiritual confrontation between good and evil; "... just as some people found demons in the smoke of the World Trade Center's destruction in their attempts to organize and contain anxiety, so did Bush's speechwriters amplify the 'terrorist' attacks on U.S. soil as a violent, spiritual confrontation with hidden, malicious forces."[43]

Witchcraft, Satanism, infant sacrifice, and exorcism still form the stories told in our collective lives. Our brave new world is a veneer over an ancient one. While we may have progressed much in the fields of science and technology, can we really attest to having developed as much in the realm of the spiritual, emotional, and social? There are still witch-hunts, both symbolic and literal; there are still exorcisms; there are still legends of things in the woods and images of gods from the heavens before whom we tremble and shake. It is, however, during the times of greatest distress and social upheaval that we collectively and publicly turn to these long-held and hidden beliefs. They form the backbone of our social organization. It wasn't just happenstance that the Salem witch trials occurred on American soil; it was the culmination of ancient beliefs and fears in a new, strange land in a new and strange time. Whenever the land and time become strange to us, during those times of uncertainty and upheaval, we resort to those old beliefs and we find our witches and put them on trial again.

CHAPTER 14

The Ghost Hunter Age: Today's Paranormal Movement

So what of today's paranormal movement? It is a period of time marked by an explosion of television programs focused on the paranormal that have proved to be quite successful for a number of different channels, including National Geographic, the History Channel, A&E, the Syfy Channel, and Discovery. The recent spike in public interest in the paranormal comes after a lull during the 1990s as the nation attempted to regain its senses and forget about the satanic panic of the 1980s. It also comes on the heels of life-altering changes in technology, politics, and the devastating terrorist attacks of 9/11.

The period of time defining the ghost hunter age, like all the previous paranormal ages, is loosely defined and, as indicated before, does not mean that the beliefs disappear; it only means that public interest subsides during the intervals. Also, as demonstrated in chapter 6, each paranormal age is defined by the focus of paranormal interest as it relates to the recent social changes, largely spurred by changes in science and technology. The focus on witchcraft during the European witch craze was influenced by the Copernican revolution; the Spiritualist movement was tied to the Darwinian revolution; the flying saucer invasion was tied to the atomic age and Cold War fears; and the satanic panic was tied to the attempt to institutionalize folklore through therapeutic expertise. But these were not the only factors that contributed to the panics and movements; as in any social movement, there were a large number of factors. The repetition of the spike in paranormal belief, combined with the development of science and technology, recurs often enough to postulate a relationship between the two. Likewise, the current paranormal age can be tied to similar factors. The ghost hunter age has been spurred by three major changes to society: the sequencing of the human genome, the invention and adoption of the Internet, and the terrorist attacks on 9/11. These three factors have combined to create a spike in public interest in the paranormal, as evidenced by the numerous television programs dealing with the paranormal and recent polling data that indicates as many as 75 percent of Americans believe in some form of the paranormal.[1]

I am referring to this recent paranormal age as the ghost hunter age because of the success of the Syfy Channel's program *Ghost Hunters*, which features two men who are plumbers by day and ghost hunters at night. This program, with its "reality television" style and its reliance on technology as a means to find evidence of the paranormal, is the definitive manifestation of the current paranormal age. While there are several other programs and styles of program, *Ghost Hunters* has come to mark the pop-culture phenomenon of paranormal fascination.

Like all the ages before it, this one, too, must come to an end. In October of 2010 I attended a live presentation by the Ghost Hunters themselves, Jason and Grant. The theater was filled to capacity with an interested audience. Jason and Grant took the stage, not as paranormal plumbers, but as consummate showmen. With a large screen behind them, they dominated the stage. The show was animated and well performed, but mostly, it was funny and entertaining. The audience laughed with the two men over stories of crazed homeowners who believed their homes were haunted. There was merchandise for sale from The Atlantic Paranormal Society (TAPS). They showed grainy, night vision footage and pointed out the supposed ghost in each.

However, as funny and entertaining as the show was, the video evidence they presented was underwhelming. While Jason and Grant hinted at more revealing and terrifying encounters, they apologized that they were unable to show that footage due to privacy concerns for the people involved. But more revealing than the show itself was the audience reaction to the two men; the questions and comments focused on the relationships of present and former TAPS members, and numerous women fawned over the two men. It became apparent that the paranormal fascination had become an industry of fame, and that the audience was more fascinated with seeing two people who were on television than in any ghostly research. The audience came to see the living embodiment of the two spectral figures who haunt the television in their homes every Wednesday night. The paranormal had taken a back seat to a reality television fad; it had crossed the boundary between inquiry and entertainment—and entertainment can be as fickle and fleeting as the wind. The commercialization of the paranormal will ultimately be the end of the ghost hunter age. When it becomes too mainstream the paranormal will, inevitably, transform and move back to the periphery of society. I believe that day is coming soon.

However, it is important to examine the factors that have led to this recent age of paranormal fascination because, as surely as the ghost hunter age will end, another will begin. Considering the global impact that these ages have had on people's lives and on the course of history, studying the causes and outcomes of these social movements is important to the understanding of human history and human nature. Thus, we will begin our examination of the ghost hunter age with the advent of the Internet.

THE INTERNET

The Internet began as a military project in the 1960s that was designed to integrate the computer systems of different military bases and programs. The initial research and development was headed up by some of the finest and most prestigious institutions in the United States, including the Massachusetts Institute of Technology. It was developed over the next 30 years until it was finally introduced to the public in the mid-1990s. The commercialization of the Internet has resulted in possibly the most significant technological change to human life since the discovery of electricity. As of 2010, according to Internet World Stats, approximately two billion people worldwide are now connected to the Internet, the majority of those users coming from the wealthier Western nations in Europe and North America.[2] Usage across the world is expanding daily as the Internet begins to penetrate into the social and technological systems of third world Asian countries. The Internet has served to connect people in every country through one integrated medium and, unlike the television, has enabled them to actually participate in that medium and interact with each other. Today the Internet is used for business, advertising, communicating, building and/or maintaining relationships, news, research, entertainment, gambling, day trading, thievery and crime, opinions, and goofing off on the boss's dollar. People interact with each other under new names—aliases that separate them from their identity, making them simultaneously connected and anonymous; truly, ghosts in the machine. The average U.S. citizen has the ability to connect to the entire world in the matter of a few keystrokes and a few seconds; fortunes and fame are created online, changing the dynamic of Hollywood and the recording industry and making "stars" out of nearly anyone willing to put him- or herself on YouTube.

The result is a 24-hour, self-generating media blitz; cable news runs 24 hours a day, 7 days a week, and simultaneously generates news stories online. The average cable news anchor has a laptop in front of him and is plugged into the Internet that is streaming news from sources around the world. The Internet has resulted in a kind of limbo; the citizen of the United States or some other Westernized nation who is plugged into the 24-hour media cycle exists in a suspended state of information coming and going. As information is received, it is simultaneously old information at one end of the cycle and new information at the other, and the viewer exists trapped in the middle. Existing in the strange, nebulous world of the Internet results in the feeling of being groundless. Even the structural concept of the Internet closely resembles a star nebula that is suspended in dark, infinite outer space.

It is this groundless state of existence that now fuels and informs our ever-expanding and information-saturated world and has also fueled the ghost hunter age. The Internet has resulted in the dissolution of truth, the promulgation of apocalyptic fears, and the ability for people to find new and different belief systems, all while broadcasting their lives around the world. Ghosts exist in an ethereal world between the past and present; between the living and the dead; the existent and the nonexistent. Likewise, the new Internet world exists in a similar state of being and nonbeing. We communicate with the living through the nonliving computer; we form relationships with beings that we cannot see and know only by a name or a face that may or may not be their actual name or face; we simultaneously receive information and dispense information and are now members of a country numbering nearly three billion users as opposed to three hundred million. The Internet has made us at once smaller and bigger, powerful and powerless. The entire system exists in a state of contradiction. As discussed in the chapter "The Native Paranormal," the contradiction inherent in the founding of the United States fueled belief in the haunting presence of Native Americans; likewise the inherent contradictions of the Internet also fuel belief in the paranormal.

During my childhood, my father had a nightly tradition; every evening at 6:30 p.m. he would sit down and watch the nightly news with Dan Rather, and I watched with him. Every evening Rather's voice—authoritative, intense, and God-like—resounded in our cozy living room; it commanded attention and dispensed truth. For us and much of civilization at the time, information about the world and the current state of humanity was garnered through the evening news and the newspapers, and, for the most part, these institutions had a monopoly on the truth; they presented the world to us and shaped our perception of it through their manipulation of words, images, and ideas. We could rest well at night if Dan Rather confirmed that, for tonight, everything was okay.

The Internet has changed all that. Now instead of one voice ushering the truth into our homes, there are literally millions. News reports now stream

24 hours a day from competing news agencies allied with different political parties, who mold and shape the news to suit their interests; the blogosphere empowers ordinary citizens who do not work for any news organization to suddenly become reporters of the truth, and, in some cases, actually become relevant voices in the information cycle. Video via YouTube is streamed directly into the home through the Internet and cable news shows, from the cell phones and cameras of people around the world, sometimes in places that no journalist would have access to; and scientific information is acquired directly alongside contradictory scientific information. This is the democratization of information, but it is also the dissolution of truth, or, at the very least, the idea of truth. There are many reasons why this is a positive change for society; however, the loss of any notion of truth has created a void in our understanding of reality. Being groundless and left to float in the ether, we find ourselves communing with ghosts; searching for our own personal truth to questions for which there are no real answers outside personal perception.

To illustrate the effects of the democratization of information and the dissolution of truth, let us use the example of the global warming debate. "Debate" is the key word, because 25 years ago there would have been no debate. A group of scientists would have declared that empirical data showed that the earth was warming due to increased carbon in the atmosphere and that this was going to cause widespread environmental distress. A similar event actually did occur during the 1980s with the discovery of the hole in the ozone layer over Antarctica. Regulations were put into place that banned the substances and gases suspected of causing the hole, and, as *National Geographic* reported in May of 2010, "Today the ozone hole, which was first spotted 25 years ago, appears headed for a happy ending, thanks to unprecedented international action."[3] There was scientific consensus, which was reported by the media as being factual and "the truth"; and due to the subsequent action taken by the international community, it appears disaster has been avoided. Today, the ozone hole is a nonissue except that, as indicated in the same *National Geographic* article, the closing of the ozone hole may actually contribute to further global warming. The irony does not go unnoticed.

However, a very similar situation has occurred over the past decade with a remarkably dissimilar outcome; global warming, although pronounced as fact by compendiums and conferences of scientists, remains a debate rather than an accepted fact. Global warming has not been able to establish itself as a "truth"; "truth" has been rendered subjective largely because of the Internet and the availability of information, opinion, and technology. As a result, some people, politicians, and scientists accept global warming as fact while others do not, and some even claim that it is a hoax. What has changed in this period of time between the discovery of the ozone hole and the global warming alarm? It is the democratization of information through the 24-hour media cycle and unprecedented global access to information. It is also an irony that more information has led to less truth—to more questions than answers.

To a certain extent, truth has always been subjective, but that rested more with personal truths rather than public truths. Each individual may have had their own take on issues in the past, but with the advent of the Internet, those individual viewpoints have now become a part of the public discourse, and, in some cases, garnered much attention and public following. The Internet's unparalleled ability to connect people and ideas have allowed prominent scientists whose findings may be contrary to the popular opinion the ability to spread their findings and broadcast them to the world at large. A scientist such as Dr. Roy Spencer, who is openly critical of the belief that global warming is man-made, is able to offer his ideas, opinions, and research to the global community through his website. A very well-credentialed man, Spencer is a small voice in the scientific community regarding global warming, but his conclusions represent one of the inherent difficulties in the democratization of information—his ability to connect with billions of people.

This, of course, is not necessarily a bad thing, although global warming advocates bemoan the voices of those who disagree with their findings. If, in fact, global warming is not man-made or is actually yet another of mankind's mass panics, similar to *The Population Bomb* panic of the 1970s that asserted the earth could not continue to support its population growth and predicted mass starvation, then the work of these few objecting scientists is important to the lives of individuals and the interests of governments and business around the world. Similar to *The Population Bomb*'s dire warning of mass starvation, the United Nations warned of 50 million "environmental refugees" by 2010 due to global warming.[4] When these predictions failed to materialize by 2010, scientists reset the date for 2020 instead.[5] The fact that the cataclysmic and dire predictions regarding global warming have yet to be seen, combined with the availability of differing viewpoints and information, has resulted in a dramatic decrease in the number of people who consider it priority.

What has occurred is a virtual stalemate; no direct action has been taken by the international community as in the case of the ozone hole, and the protracted debate has left a public largely lackadaisical regarding global warming. Only time will tell if this is fortunate or disastrous.

Perhaps one of the biggest changes to science since the advent of the Internet is that science is no longer "science." For nearly every scientific study

and conclusion, one can go online and find a different set of studies and statistics that point to the opposite conclusion. Researchers and scientists flaunt
their credentials (sometimes impressive) and tout their conclusions, but what
would have been hard science is now being called into question by the average citizen. While the scientists among us may be able to draw their own conclusions, the new subjective nature of science leaves the average layperson
with no firm understanding of what is actually occurring in the world.
There is no truth. This same model can be applied to nearly every aspect of
life in which a person seeks stability upon which to build their notion of reality; politics, religion, history, current events, and science are now more fluid
than ever before, and the United States is awash in the ebb and flow of the
Internet's tide of information.

The democratization of information that began with the JFK assassination,
when average citizens decided not to accept the official story but investigate
for themselves, has reached its ultimate zenith—a world in which truth and
facts are subjective to the pre-conceived notions of the viewer. Some philosophers will argue that this has always been the case, and that may be, but never
has it been on such wild display and had such far-reaching implications as it
now does; the questions that once may have been only for the philosophers
have spilled over into the masses. Unfortunately, when we remove truth and
fact from the world, we are left with faith; and faith is the realm of the paranormal—a realm that holds no absolutes, no empirical evidence, no grounding upon which to set our feet. Our society has become simultaneously
faithless and yet full of faith in whatever institution we choose.

Is it any wonder that the paranormal has taken such a foothold in this society? With unprecedented access to people and to information that may
change or even contradict what has popularly been considered fact, the timeless saying that, "There is no such thing as ghosts," is rendered obsolete and
subjective. On a symbolic level, an individual's interaction with the Internet
in 2013 is very similar to an individual's interaction with the spirits through
a medium during the Spiritualist movement of the late 1800s. Nameless,
faceless, possibly false beings interact with us, making predictions and obser-
vations, telling of distant lands and new religions; they tell us of science and
the natural world and that we are all one being connected through the mysteries of life. Madame Blavatsky would be proud.

More specifically, the ghost hunter age combines faith with technology;
ghost hunters venture forth into haunted houses with infrared cameras, digital voice recorders, thermal night vision cameras, digital video recorders, and
a vast array of computer programs and hardware. They search for empirical
evidence of something that is notoriously devoid of anything that can be

conclusively proven; the rationale being that the improvement in technology will somehow be able to verify our faith and thus turn faith into reality. Oddly enough, it seems that the exact opposite has occurred; rather than eliminating the need for faith, the technology explosion, spurred by the advent of the Internet, has created more need for faith than ever before. The ghost hunters have faith that there exists a spirit world beyond our natural world; and as the grounding reality of the world we once knew falls away beneath our feet, we begin to wonder and become interested in the possibility of a spirit world. The pretenses of science in modern-day ghost hunting serve only to bolster the faithful with the notion of empirical evidence that does not really exist. As Shirley Jackson wrote in her work *The Haunting of Hill House*, "People . . . are always so anxious to get things out into the open where they can put a name to them, even a meaningless name, so long as it has something of a scientific ring."[6] But the paranormal is confined to the shadows and boundaries and darkness of the human experience; it is not so easily named.

In 2005 Dan Rather left *CBS Evening News* following a controversy regarding the truthfulness of a story that he had brought to light during the 2004 election. After 43 years, the voice of truth had been upset—dethroned, and dissolved in a bubbling cauldron of dissenting voices, competing stories, and multiple variations of truth. The major networks saw their ratings plummet as the whole idea of sitting down for the news at 7 p.m. faded in the wake of the Internet and the 24-hour news media cycle on cable news programs. Newspapers began to struggle for readership and had to quickly adapt to the Internet or be left behind. Today, we choose our truth; we choose our sources of information based on our personal idea of truth. If I choose to believe that aliens are secretly running the world, I can find validation— truth—on the Internet; I can converse with other people who believe the same, and together we can find evidences, narratives, and "scientific" proofs that uphold those beliefs. Twenty-five years ago I may have found myself relegated to the mental hospital.

The Raelians believe that, "Thousands of years ago, scientists from another planet came to Earth and created all forms of life, including human beings, whom they created in their own image . . . Once humanity reached a sufficient level of scientific understanding, the Elohim decided to make themselves more visible in UFO sightings and to conceive their final messages. Rael was given two missions: spreading that last message on Earth and preparing an embassy to welcome the return of our creators."[7] While earth and humanity have never had a shortage of people willing to follow strange cults and practice beliefs outside the mainstream of religion and science, as of this writing, the Raelian movement claims over 60,000 members worldwide and

4,866 people on Facebook who "like this." The Internet, through its unprecedented ability to link people together, has created a world in which our beliefs, no matter how outlandish they may seem to others, can find validation, evidence, and truth.

Our technology and science have betrayed us; we are now a nation based almost entirely on faith; faith in politics, faith in science, faith in religion, faith in our nation, and faith in our ideas. We have to have faith because the availability of contradictory information and opinion makes nearly any assertion debatable and subject to criticism, review, and, most of all, doubt. When we are constantly forced to ask ourselves, "Do I really know what I think I know?" we are forced to rely on faith instead of information and "facts" to support our reality. That faith reveals itself in the religious fervor by which people express their beliefs and in their willingness to sacrifice for them. While this has long been the case in religion, it has now spread itself to countless other areas of life, including science; because, in this new age, everything is in question. As Erich Fromm postulated, American beliefs are a veneer over the primitive totemism that was once merged with the American land. Once again, we find ourselves in a primitive frame of mind. We know nothing because everything is in question; therefore, we have only belief. The totem serves to turn belief into reality; it represents a spiritual connection between man and the physical world. Our totems are no longer plants and animals, but rather science, technology, religion, history, psychology, and politics. The land is the same, but the totems have changed.

Is it any wonder that the paranormal is thriving today? If you (rational being that you are) stood alone among 60,000 Raelians, you would be considered insane. Similarly, we sit alone in front of a computer screen, awash in a sea of nameless beings that offer to confirm or contradict our reality. Our allegiances and beliefs are subject to the click of a mouse, the choosing of a totem.

THE HUMAN GENOME PROJECT

In April of 2003, the Human Genome Project completed its five-year plan of mapping the human genome. The 20,000 genes in the human genome were identified, and some of them were even identified as to what role they played in development and disease. The fantastical double helix, the very puzzle of man's humanity, had been unraveled for the world. The building blocks of our very being had been disassembled and mapped out by a team of scientists. The mysterious double helix had been decoded, and as the world marveled at the accomplishment, there was a subtle, simultaneous gasp that the mystery of mankind was now less of a mystery. We had unraveled the foundation of our bodies and being and found . . . well, not much. While the mapping of the human genome is of great importance to the future of medicine and our ability to fight and prevent disease, it did surprisingly little for helping mankind understand his place in the world, aside from the rather humbling fact that the human genome contains only 20,000 genes—double that of the typical roundworm, and a far cry from the original estimate of 30,000.[8] There was no answer as to our origins; there was no key to the unlocking of life; there was no "God" gene, nor anything that pointed in the direction of man being anything other than an animal with opposable thumbs and a knack for math.

The influence of the successful mapping of the human genome on the world of the paranormal and the ghost hunter age is much more subtle than the influence of the Internet. It does not, necessarily, leave us awash in a sea of information; in fact, the sheer underwhelming nature of the discovery could be seen as a welcome bit of grounding for humankind. But, as with many other scientific discoveries that should have grounded mankind, the mapping of the human genome has helped spur a greater and more popular interest in spirits and life after death. There is a very human need being fulfilled with programs like *Ghost Hunters*—the need to feel that we are something more than animal and that our unique abilities, our self-awareness, is not just an accident of evolution or the result of a random sequence of amino acids. In essence, it is a search for purpose and a search for an answer to the question of "Why?" The double helix has been unwound, but the mystery still remains.

The Spiritualist movement, which began in the 1850s, was a uniquely American working-class movement, though it became very aristocratic in Europe. In a previous chapter we explored how that movement could have been affected by Darwin's *On the Origin of Species*. Darwin contended that man had evolved from lesser beings and, essentially, removed any notion of divine origins and an eternal soul. What should have been a grounding reality for humanity during that time was, instead, met with a large shift to Spiritualism, as mankind tried to confirm the existence of the soul after death; to affirm the belief that man is something more than animal and that death is not the end of our being. The Spiritualist movement was rife with fraud and trickery; however, even in the face of scandal, people kept returning to mediums, continuing to believe in spite of obvious fraud. There was a need that had to be fulfilled. It was faith that kept the Spiritualist movement alive in the face of contrary evidence: faith in God, faith in the soul, and faith in mankind. World War I largely ended that faith.

Likewise, the ghost hunter age has been a time of faith, as mankind seeks to establish the soul's continuance after death and to reaffirm that man is more than animal. While the mapping of the human genome is not as earth shattering as the *Origin* was, it is a rather disenchanting look at the basics of humanity. We have plumbed the depths of our bodies and found no soul, no spirit, no key that unlocks the mystery of our existence. The Human Genome Project reminded us that we are very closely related to all the other creatures that walk, crawl, or swim on this planet. It did not show us that we were extraordinary; rather, it showed the opposite. Thus, people during the ghost hunter age are seeking their own confirmation of the soul—the divine nature of man. During a time when everything is in doubt and everything is subject to faith, those who are looking for something more to believe in will find it in the paranormal world of the *Ghost Hunters*.

The ghost hunter age is actually nothing more than Spiritualism remade in the wake of technological achievements and reality television, and, similar to the Spiritualist movement, is a movement of the common man. Now, instead of sitting before a medium in a candlelit room of the medium's design, we venture forth at night into modern-day Gothic castles—old haunts and abandoned places where legends have grown from rumored whispers. We go with digital recorders and electromagnetic frequency detectors, infrared and night vision cameras, and we attempt to commune with the dead and find evidence that life continues after death. Mediums still play an active role in the hunt, but now their role is more passive, giving way to the real star of the show—technology, which will hopefully confirm our faith in the human soul. And these Spiritualist adventures are not limited to the few, but rather anyone can become a ghost hunter. Today, cities offer "ghost tours" that take tourists on a walk through the city's most famous haunted sites; legend-trippers are people who travel to places rumored to be haunted or possessed by the paranormal; courses in ghost hunting are available, and people with similar interests can form their own paranormal investigation group, set up a website, and interact with other ghost hunting groups in the area. All of this is an effort to preserve the mystery and confirm the deeply held belief that there is a purpose to our lives, a soul in our bodies, and a divinity in our existence. The Internet has made much of this possible through its democratization of information and the ability of people to communicate on an unprecedented scale. Thus, ghost hunting (Spiritualism) has become democratized as well; you don't need much—just the cover of night, a willingness to believe, and a place to explore. But it is not, necessarily, the haunted houses that we are exploring, but rather, ourselves; it is an attempt to find meaning in our lives. With the divinity of mankind cast into doubt through Darwin's work and then, once again, through the mapping of the human genome, the paranormal offers a way to sidestep that doubt and immerse ourselves in belief.

There is another side to the influence of the Human Genome Project. On December 27, 2002, a company called Clonaid announced to the world that it had successfully cloned a baby girl and named her Eve. This set off a firestorm of controversy surrounding the use of genetics for the cloning of human beings. Scientists had already been able to clone a variety of animals, most notably Dolly, the first cloned sheep, and there was much talk of cloning being used to help grow and replace failing organs in sick people. The notion of human cloning has obviously been visited in the past through films and books, but it was, and still remains, an ethical issue of the highest order. Clonaid is a company owned and operated by the Raelians, who believe that humanity was created by an alien race that made us in their own image through cloning. Therefore, the Raelians see cloning as a step toward immortality and achieving what the original "gods" had intended for humanity. They believe that when humanity has reached technological maturity, we will be reunited with our alien ancestors.

Clonaid was promptly brought to court with the child's welfare in question. However, Clonaid had relocated the family to Israel, which lacked any cloning legislation, and the judge was not able to issue any order for the return of the child. Clonaid has since claimed to have cloned many more children for clients around the world, though this has never been independently verified and has led to claims of a hoax. "Without the tests, the cloning claims cannot be validated. Some experts believe the whole thing is a hoax by the religious sect behind Clonaid, a group called the Raelians that believes life on Earth was started by space aliens."[9] However, there was a general unease about Clonaid's announcement, especially because they had the funds, facilities, and willing surrogates to complete such a project.

The news was unsettling for a variety of reasons, but one aspect that stands out is the incorporation of science and technology by the paranormal. The scientific community had been invaded, even usurped, by a group that believed humanity was fathered by an alien race that is communicating their message to man through the prophet Rael. The Raelians are one of many "UFO cults" that popped up during the UFO invasion. UFO cults claim that they are in direct contact with alien races that distribute knowledge of the origins of mankind and offer dire prophesies if we continue on our current path. The Raelians are certainly one of the most successful and lasting of those cults; most of them collapsed under the weight of their own prophesies, which never materialized into reality.

However, the Raelians, despite all logic to the contrary, continue on with the adoption of scientific technology for use in a belief system that is an affront to the very science it wields. The Raelians, naturally, are not the first group to claim that aliens spawned our existence. Erich von Däniken's book, *Chariots of the Gods*, became a popular best-seller when it used ancient texts and mythology to call into question the current understanding of earth and man's history, and it spawned numerous similar books and belief systems. However, mastery of the intricacies of human DNA has still not yielded an understanding or an answer to the great mystery of life: why are we here? While science may be able to provide the nuts and bolts of how it happened, the question of "why" remains a spiritual one. That is, once again, the realm of faith and the paranormal.

For every action there is an equal and opposite reaction; this is a basic law of physics. But it seems that this particular law may spread beyond the boundaries of the physical world into the social and spiritual realms. For every step taken toward the disenchantment of the modern world, there appears to be an equal and opposite step toward the belief in magic, spirits, aliens, and witches. We have not yet found, and may never find, the gene that seemingly hardwires our brains to seek out enchantment, magic, and mystery. Perhaps it is a defense mechanism against the lonely, stark reality of an existential universe, or perhaps it is the by-product of a highly complex brain, which rests in the only animal that is constantly aware of its own mortality.

Indeed, there are stories passed down through ancient texts that tell of the beginning of the world and our origins. The Bible, Sumerian texts, and the Hindu Vedas all offer explanation and history as to the origins of man, and all of them talk of gods that descended from the skies. Evolution opposes these myths, and the mapping of the human genome has reinforced that opposition. However, to exist in modern society is to exist in a place that is comprised of myths; total, absolute reality cannot be known by any single human mind, and in the ghost hunter age, it may be further away than ever before. Therefore, the mythology is reinforced, validated, evidenced, and shared. "The imagery of myth, therefore, can never be a direct presentation of the total secret of the human species, but only an attitude, the reflex of a stance, a life pose, a way of playing the game. And where the rules or forms of such play are abandoned, mythology dissolves—and, with mythology, life."[10]

Attempts to unravel secrets are met with resistance; people will clutch their mythologies as they would their very lives, because it is that mythology that enables them to live.

SEPTEMBER 11, 2001

On the morning of September 11, 2001, the world was forever changed. Nearly every American knows where they were and what they were doing when they first heard of an airliner crashing into the World Trade Center. With the crashing of the second airliner into the second tower and the crashing of a third into the Pentagon, it became obvious that this was a terrorist attack on the people of the United States. Fueled by pure, blind, murderous faith, 19 Arab hijackers successfully carried out the most devastating attack on American soil in the history of our nation. This act single-handedly shaped the course of the geopolitical world over the next decade and will continue to do so into the future.

It was, indeed, a massive shock to the American psyche. There was a new threat to people's lives and while part of that threat came from beyond our borders, the most dangerous and frightening part came from within. The hijackers had lived and worked, smiled and mingled, shopped and worshipped among us, blending with the very people they intended to slay. It was not necessarily the outside world that caused unease, but rather, the world within our borders; our house was haunted by malicious spirits that plotted against us and meant to unravel our very lives.

Naturally, this was not the first time the United States faced a threat, but the reaction with regard to the paranormal was different than would have otherwise been expected. The flying saucer invasion was spurred by a threat from Communist Russia. The threat of nuclear attack from the sky was an ever-present reality and thus people were looking to the skies and the notion of invaders from another planet, alien to our way of life, resonated with the public. But why would exploring haunted houses at night looking for signs of ghosts resonate with the public in the aftermath of 9/11?

Firstly, there was the gothic nature of the terrorists themselves; men who were leading double lives with dark intentions and plotting in their minds, an obsession with death and an addiction to blind faith that bordered on insanity. But there was also the nature of the attacks themselves. These devastating attacks were not from a foreign country. Military personnel did not pilot weapons of mass destruction with rising suns adorning their wings, as in the Pearl Harbor attack. The weapons were not missiles fired from thousands of miles away and altogether foreign-looking to the American public, nor were they bombers streaking overhead at 50,000 feet, as we feared during the Cold War. Rather, the weapons used were American Airline jets filled with unsuspecting, innocent civilians. On any given day, an American can look up into the sky and catch sight of the vapor trail left in the wake of a commercial airliner traveling from city to city across this nation, each one filled with our own people, representatives of our own way of life and our culture. It was those very things that were used against us. Our own citizenry, our friends and neighbors, were used as a weapon to kill more than three thousand people that morning who were participating in the daily grind of American life. The familiar sight of jetliners was suddenly rendered unfamiliar; they were not safe and stable transports anymore, but weapons turned against us. The fact that the terrorists were able to simultaneously hijack four different flights spurred fears that there could be more in the skies overhead. Jet fighters were scrambled by the air force with orders to shoot down any plane that would not comply with orders to identify themselves and land. The American skies were shut down for a week as the United States and the government tried to recover and determine what had occurred and who had perpetrated such an act. The effects were disorienting—familiar things were no longer familiar; the skies were patrolled by our own air force with orders to kill; more than three thousand families were suddenly torn apart, broken and mourning. Stephen King said that horror is the sense that things are in the unmaking—surely this was a time of horror across the United States.

Secondly, as the initial shock began to wane and the march to war began, there were factions of our society that questioned the role of the United States in the attacks, questioning whether or not American foreign policy and even our lifestyle and culture were to blame for fueling the attacks. Peter Bergen offered an organized overview of the many theorized causes of 9/11 in *Prospect* magazine, citing that some of the political rhetoric in the 9/11 aftermath placed blame on American culture that was flawed. Among them are the beliefs that the attacks were spurred by American occupation in Arab countries, by the CIA intervention in Afghanistan's battle against the Communist invaders, and—an idea propagated by George W. Bush in the time leading up to two wars—that "They hate us because of the freedom-loving people we are."[11] During the massive political battles that took shape over the next decade, both sides of the political aisle used these ideas, and each, in their own way, blamed the United States for the attacks. The liberal left cited American foreign policy and Arab poverty, while the conservative right cited a Middle Eastern culture that hated Western freedom. While Bergen points to flaws in each argument, the political weight of these arguments were enough to warrant their general acceptance among the public.

Thus, we were, at least according to the political rhetoric at the time, somewhat to blame for the horror of the 9/11 attacks. Either our freedom-loving lifestyle or American world dominance was the root cause of the most physically and psychologically damaging attack on the United States in history. Also, there was the undercurrent of the religious clash; the United States, a powerful country founded and dominated by Christianity, was suddenly in a clash with radicalized Islam. There exists a long history of violence between the two religions, and Christianity now had to defend its beliefs to reaffirm American values and traditions in the homeland, while the military avenged the attacks over seas. Part of that defense, however, involved demonizing other religious beliefs and peoples as "evil."

It is important to note that this was not a conscious decision or action on the part of the church or the American people; rather, it was an emotional reaction to a trauma. No one person or organization set forth to affirm national traditions and beliefs in the wake of 9/11, although there were surely cries from the pulpit that echoed such sentiment; there was simply a stirring in the subconscious of the collective American psyche that made the ghost hunter age not only possible but necessary in an effort to heal. It was in the years following 9/11 that we saw the spike in television programming about the paranormal. The most popular paranormal television series, the ones that have come to represent the ghost hunter age, were developed during this time. *Most Haunted* began in 2001, *Ghost Hunters* and *The UFO Files* in 2004, *A Haunting* in 2005, *Paranormal State* in 2006, and *MonsterQuest* in 2007. All of them follow a similar reality television format and are popular programs for their respective broadcast companies. While there was renewed interest in the paranormal in general, including cryptozoology and UFOs, the main point of interest was ghosts and other spirit phenomena. In these programs camera crews follow paranormal investigators during nighttime investigations and employ an array of technical devices in hopes of communicating with the spirits in the house or to offer some kind of evidence of the world beyond. Why the sudden and dramatic interest in the pursuit of ghosts?

Ghost hunting, as it is portrayed on these television programs, involves contact and communication with spiritual entities. It is Spiritualism updated for the modern era. There are no traditional séances with tables moving and candlelights flickering, but efforts are made to communicate with the dead; spiritual mediums are used regularly and the investigators ask questions in empty rooms hoping to record answers on digital voice recorders in a phenomenon known as EVP—electromagnetic voice phenomenon. Some investigators even employ Ouija boards to communicate with the spirits.

As the nation reeled in the wake of the 9/11 attacks, the United States was forced to look inward, rather than outward, and explore the thing that haunted its proverbial house. But this investigation into the world of ghosts and spirits may have been both a search for meaning and a reaffirmation of the nation's traditional belief system. Bill Ellis writes,

[B]oth activities [deliverance and Ouija] are alike in their goals—to allow participants to participate in the Christian myth directly. In most denominations believers are passive, with acts of power—prayer, healing, the consecration of the Eucharist—reserved for priests and other institutionally designated specialists. Bible reading and reflection on doctrinal issues may satisfy many believers, but others seek a more direct experience of the divine. Deliverance and Ouija are parallel paths to this close encounter with the world of angels and demons.[12]

Thus, as American traditions and values were being challenged, both from abroad and from within the country itself, many people sought out the paranormal as evidence to reaffirm their belief system in the wake of tragedy and chaos. Hence, the sudden popularity in programs which affirm life after death and the traditional Christian notions of spirituality; the image or idea of a ghost reaffirms the belief that a human being is a spiritual being and that life does not end after death—a comforting thought after watching the death of three thousand people on live television.

There is also something distinctly modern and similar between the reality television programs depicting ghost hunters and the military aftermath of 9/11. The U.S. government was now on a mission to hunt down both the terrorists living among us and those living abroad. Two wars, Iraq and Afghanistan, were waged in the aftermath of the 9/11 attacks, but they were not wars against nations; they were wars against individuals who secreted themselves among populations of innocents, who blended in and were nearly invisible—in effect, they were ghosts. The depiction of the war on television had a strangely similar effect as did the depiction of the ghost hunters on the various programs. U.S. citizens were able to watch the wars unfold as if they were part of a reality television series; the night vision cameras were right there filming the action as it happened—as the military personnel hunted down an adversary that was nearly invisible. Our technology was able to overcome, and our American spirit was not daunted; these military operations were patriotic reaffirmations of the national tradition, and the look was oddly similar to the look of *Ghost Hunters*.

In essence, the search for ghosts at home reflected the search for ghosts abroad, and both had similar goals—to reaffirm our American way of life and our belief tradition, and to bolster our mettle against those who challenged that belief system. The post-9/11 world was a world of mechanized warfare, but it was also a world of spiritual warfare, one belief system trying to destroy another, a clash of radicalized Islam and the Christian West. "In the many discussions of the 'root causes' of Islamist terrorism, Islam itself is rarely mentioned. But if you were to ask Bin Laden, he would say that his war is about defense of Islam. We need not believe him but we should nevertheless listen to what our enemy is saying. Bin Laden bases justification of his war on a corpus of Muslim beliefs and he finds ammunition in the Koran to give his war Islamic legitimacy."[13] Following 9/11 the popularity of paranormal-based television programs served to reaffirm American religious traditions and values, and reflected the idea that we had to look inward for the cause of this tragedy rather than outward. As we questioned our very way of life and our history, we looked to the paranormal to give us evidence of the unknown—a basis for our faith. The programs reflected the modern age of television and warfare, of spirituality and the American gothic tradition.

The ghost hunter age, like the paranormal ages before it, was spurred and defined by advances in technology and science that altered the way in which the world was experienced and questioned traditional values and belief systems. In the case of the ghost hunter age, the social tumult and upheaval caused by the 9/11 attacks also served to question traditional American belief systems. These times of paranormal focus and interest reflect changes in our society and, during these times of change, the gothic nature of the American culture becomes loudly evident; it is what we fall back on when our world is awash in chaos.

On May 1, 2011, President Obama announced that Osama Bin Laden, the mastermind of the 9/11 attacks, had been found and killed during a nighttime raid in Pakistan. The entire might of the United States armed forces in conjunction with the combined efforts of many other nations were not able to find Bin Laden for 10 years; it was thought by many that he may have died due to his failing health or that he was possibly buried under the rubble of a missile strike. Some people, including myself, had given up hope of ever finding him. He was, for all intents and purposes, a ghost. And then, suddenly and without warning, the ghost was found and killed. It had been made real again; it was flesh and bone and blood. As strange as it may sound, this could also be a signifier of the end of the ghost hunter age. A collective tension was relieved when that announcement was made, and a feeling of closure seemed to occupy conversations the following day. It was certainly not the end of the battle with terrorism, but it seemed that, at least temporarily, a sense of peace had come upon the collective American house. Our ghosts had been silenced and our demons had been exorcised . . . for now.

CHAPTER 15

Shirley Jackson's America

Shirley Jackson's 1959 novel, *The Haunting of Hill House*, has become the quintessential haunted house story and, oddly enough, has come to represent the gothic structure and haunting fear that defines the modern ghost hunter age. In the novel, Dr. Montague, an academic interested in the paranormal, invites 20 people to spend the summer with him at Hill House, a Gothic manor with a checkered past of suicide, insanity, family betrayal, and local rumor, in an effort to conduct a "scientific" study of psychic phenomena. He chooses people whom he thinks may, unknowingly, possess psychic gifts. Of the twenty that he invites, only two, Eleanor and Theodora, respond and agree to stay at the home and aid with the study. A fourth character, Luke, who stands to inherit the house from his aunt, is also invited as a representative of the family. Together, the four characters spend several days in Hill House and record the phenomena they witness. They are eventually joined by Montague's wife—a self-appointed medium blowhard and her assistant, an obnoxious private school teacher named Arthur. While the book begins with Dr. Montague, it is Eleanor who is the protagonist, and it is through her point of view that Hill House is explored.

At its most obvious and superficial, the story reflects the current structure of paranormal investigators in the ghost hunter age; a group of people enter a place with a dark history, which is the subject of local rumor and legend, in an effort to confirm once and for all the existence of the paranormal. Some of the group members, such as Eleanor and Theodora, are believed to have mediumistic gifts that make them more susceptible to spirit manifestations; Dr. Montague is there to prove the existence of the paranormal through scientific means; and Luke, playboy that he is, accompanies them for the fun of it. This is the basic structure of paranormal research groups: mediums to aid in communicating with the spirits, "scientists" to use technology to try to find evidence, and those who are merely along for the ride, to explore their world in all its mystery. Together, they enter the Gothic castles of the United States and they try to confer with the spirits and prove that life continues after death and that there exists a force outside the known limits of science. These are the ghost hunters. They are on television and on the Internet. They are small groups and large, sometimes famous and sometimes operating in the peripheries of our society; but either way, they exist and are living and working and striving to find something more than what is already known.

Dr. Montague represents our current reliance on technology and science. In an effort to find proof of the paranormal, investigators use modern technology and conduct what they believe to be scientific research and experiments on something that, by its very definition, defies those boundaries. But still they are searching. "Dr. John Montague was a doctor of philosophy; he had taken his degree in anthropology, feeling obscurely that in this field he might come closest to his true vocation, the analysis of supernatural manifestations. He was scrupulous about the use of his title because, his investigations being so utterly unscientific, he hoped to borrow an air of respectability, even scholarly authority, from his education."[1] Science and technology have come to define our reality. They are meant to represent the solid, unmovable, and unshakeable base of our existence. Thus, in an effort to give credence and legitimacy to their search for the paranormal, investigators turn to science and technology, believing that it may hold the key to defining the paranormal world once and for all. But, as Dr. Montague states somewhat contradictorily, "People . . . are always so anxious to get things out into the open where they can put a name to them, even a meaningless name, so long as it has something of a scientific ring."[2] The defining of the world through science and technology may simply be a veneer over a mysterious and undefined reality. As we scramble for an explanation, for a truth to believe in that will structure our world, we seek out science and technology to form that truth. However, in the modern ghost hunter age, that very science and technology that we seek has led us to more ambiguity and less definition. But still, as Dr. Montague points out, we try to give it a name with a scientific ring so that we can sleep comfortably at night, even if it really isn't science, but, rather, faith.

But the heart of Jackson's story isn't about science, just as the heart of the ghost hunter age is not about science and technology, but about something deeper and more psychological. While world-changing developments in the sciences and technology may have acted as a catalyst for the ghost hunter age, it is the search inward for an identity that truly defines the era. The search for identity is more than defining something by name or assigning it scientific significance, as we try to do during our various ghost hunts. The ghost hunt is a reflection of our search for the human identity—the human soul—that will truly define our mysterious existence.

Likewise, Eleanor, the main character of *The Haunting of Hill House*, has lived her entire life without definition, without identity. Isolated from her neighbors throughout her childhood due to her mother's paranoia, and then forced to devote her life to caring for her elderly mother as an adult, Eleanor has never had the opportunity to define herself. She has lived in perpetual isolation, physically and emotionally, and therefore does not have an identity outside the one provided by her mother. It is only upon her mother's death that Eleanor ventures out into the world, and her first trip toward identity is to Dr. Montague's haunted, Gothic castle set at the base of some dark brooding hills. Jackson's opening line of the novel establishes that "No live organism can continue for long to exist sanely under conditions of absolute reality; even larks and katydids are supposed, by some, to dream. Hill House, not sane, stood by itself against its hills, holding darkness within . . ."[3] Jackson establishes that Hill House has existed under conditions of absolute reality and is, therefore, not sane. It also establishes that Hill House is a living entity, which Eleanor is about to explore to define her life; but she is defining herself within something that has existed in absolute reality and is thus not sane. That insanity is a darkness, which the house holds within its walls.

Eleanor's situation is such that she has nothing about herself to tell to the others; she has no likes, no dislikes, no stories, and no experiences by which to define herself in relation to the others in the group and, tragically, in relation to the house. She creates a false life and false memories during her drive to Hill House, adopting images and characteristics of other people along the way. She imagines a life of definition and character; when she stops at a diner for lunch she admires a little girl who refuses to drink milk from anything other than her "cup of stars." "Don't do it, Eleanor told the little girl; insist on your cup of stars; once they have trapped you into being like everyone else you will never see your cup of stars again; don't do it; and the little girl glanced at her, and smiled a little subtle, dimpling, wholly comprehending smile and shook her head stubbornly at the glass. Brave girl, Eleanor thought; wise, brave girl."[4] She admires the character and definition that the little girl has established. Eleanor later passes the "cup of stars" story off as her own.

When she meets Theodora and they walk together down to the brook to talk and explore, Theodora tells Eleanor about her family, and Eleanor mimics and mirrors Theodora's stories and creates a nonexistent family and history for herself. She lies about having extended family members and memories of picnics in parks to such an extent that Theodora believes they must be long-lost cousins.

Does the United States lack such definition? Does humanity? We exist in a state of perpetual change on a small planet spinning alone in the vastness of space. Thus far, we cannot find any other species remotely like us, and it is our very aloneness in the universe that creates such a quandary for the understanding of humanity. Were we one of many other civilizations in our solar system, a scientific explanation of humanity would probably be more acceptable and comforting. However, as we are alone and, thus far, unique, we have no way to define ourselves. We feel more than animal but less than gods.

The United States is the melting pot of various cultures and peoples, some who have maintained their cultural identity and heritage and some who have not; there are some who have been relegated to the boundaries of our civilization, and some who are perhaps lost in the bubbling cauldron. Modern technology has added to the existential feeling of being alone and undefined. The Internet has expanded our world to vast proportions and has left us ill-defined in a world of competing "facts," opinions, and versions of reality. We interact with anonymous beings that, despite our best efforts, remain unknown and foreign because they exist in a computer—and we sit alone at a desk. In a particularly telling and prophetic scene in Jackson's work, the four newly acquainted participants make idle chatter in the parlor. During the conversation they humorously begin to make up false identities for themselves with elaborate and exotic backgrounds; Theodora claims to be the daughter of a lord, Luke claims to be a bullfighter, Dr. Montague claims to live in Bangkok where he habitually bothers women, and Eleanor claims to be an artist's model. As we try to establish our identity in this new world we are faced with people whose true identities remain unknown to us. We use false names and images to present ourselves to the outside world, all the while concealing the perhaps all-too-mundane truth about ourselves. The anonymity of the Internet allows us to become different people and act outside the standards that we would normally hold in front of seeing eyes and listening ears. We sit safe, protected, and alone before the computer screen, and when we no longer want to interact, we simply walk away or change our names and identities. Never before have we had the ability to function in such a manner. We are ghosts, and the ghost hunt is a search for ourselves; and, just as in Jackson's story, when confronted with a new world we turn to the Gothic castle as a place in which to define ourselves in this new world. The Gothic castle is our very own construction of reality, one that harbors secrets, darkness, and insanity. Thus, in those times of change and stress, the gothic nature of humanity reveals itself. We stalk the empty corridors, basements, and attics of the haunted houses that belie our modern, common, roadside motels. Perhaps that is why Hitchcock's *Psycho* resonated so deeply with audiences—we recognized the ancient, frightening house on the hill because there is one that looms over our own personal façade of reality.

The danger in this gothicism comes when we lose ourselves in that haunted place; when we can no longer separate ourselves from the Gothic castle, much like what happens to Eleanor in *Hill House* and which results in her death. This has happened before on massive social scales during such times as the European witch craze and the satanic panic. The public institutionalization of the gothic resulted in ruined lives and death. However, the same is true on an individual basis. The world of the paranormal can be dangerous territory for one's sanity. Whether real, imagined, or symbolic, demons, ghosts, and monsters do invade and haunt the psyche. If we lose ourselves in that haunted place or if we seek to define ourselves through that haunted place, we risk losing our sanity and even our lives. The history of the paranormal is littered with broken lives, ruined finances, insanity, and death.

Critic John G. Parks claimed that the new American gothic is narcissistic— a turning inward rather than outward. And Stephen King writes, "The new American gothic provides a closed loop of character, and in what might be termed a psychological pathetic fallacy, the physical surroundings often mimic the inward turning of the characters themselves..."[5] The terrorist attacks on 9/11 and the subsequent world upheaval caused us to look inward. The mapping of the human genome was the closest look at what constitutes humanity that man has ever endeavored. And the Internet is a virtual altar to narcissistic impulses as we broadcast ourselves out into the world, only so that we can gaze upon ourselves. In this Internet age, we digitally record ourselves doing any and everything and post it on the Internet as if we are stars, as if the world is hanging on our every word, our every foible, our every pseudo-intellectual, opinionated word rant. It is all so that we can gaze upon the glory of ourselves—become movie stars, as it were. Is there any doubt as to the narcissism of this ghost hunter age? But, according to the original myth, Narcissus dies—having wasted away at the edge of a reflective pool, gazing upon his own image. Eleanor also dies, unable to separate herself from Hill House. Likewise, perhaps we should beware the path that today's technology is taking. Without a strong identity and an understanding of ourselves, we can easily get lost and drown in a pool of ambiguity and emptiness.

The paranormal has always been with us and will continue to be with us. It is a uniquely human experience, and the mystery and wonder it breeds is a necessary part of existence. But as we explore the haunted house that is our world, it is important that we not try to define ourselves by it. The paranormal is the trickster's paradise, a place of ill-defined boundaries, shifting ideas, and ambiguous realities. To seek definition in such a place is to embrace such things, and this can be both fortuitous and dangerous. Just like the trickster, absolute reality is made up of ill-defined boundaries, shifting ideas, and ambiguous realities and, as Shirley Jackson said, no living thing can exist sanely under conditions of absolute reality. We seek to establish scientific fact everywhere we look, but the more we try the less we succeed. We assign scientific-sounding names so that we can identify some sort of solid ground on which to stand, but that ground shakes in the changing landscape of an information-saturated world. We try to define ourselves through science and logic and reason, but we continually fail.

In the past few chapters we have discussed the ways in which faith has taken on the veneer of different movements, from science to politics to the paranormal, and the way in which that faith has turned them into totems. But this is not true faith—it is totemism. Faith is the belief in that which cannot be proven and for which there is no evidence. Faith's greatest attribute is the one least often used: the recognition that one's belief cannot be proven as fact—that is precisely what makes it faith rather than science. As Dr. Montague so articulately said, we try to pull things that defy definition, coherence, rationality, and institutionalization out of the darkness and into the light by giving it some scientific credence or "facts" for which there exist antithetical "facts." Just as the ghost hunter tries to define the indefinable world of the paranormal through science and technology, the political activist seizes upon "facts" by which to march in the street, and the religious fanatic, driven by "facts," bombs a building. They have supplanted their faith with totems and rendered it a reality by which to act upon the world. Faith, however, acknowledges that while we may believe something to be true, it cannot be known for sure, and therefore, does not, or should not, compel us to act or declare something as fact. True faith is the recognition that we might be wrong.

But these totems cannot stand forever, and their shadows leave a long darkness on our civilization. It is the Gothic castle—that representation of the hidden and unknown—in which we search for ourselves. To search for identity is noble and time-worthy, but to try to create identity where one does not exist, as Eleanor did, will lead to a path of destruction, particularly when trapped within the haunted confines of our history. We parade our false identities online, but only to look upon ourselves and contemplate our image. It is not truth, and it is not character, and it is not faith. It is technology filling a void, creating something where there is nothing. The past

12 years have caused us to look inward, to confront questions and to seek answers. We try to form a firm ground on which to stand and by which we can understand ourselves and our world, but science and technology alone cannot create that understanding and cannot form that identity. That comes from something more—faith without the veneer of fact or truth or science.

As we search for meaning and identity at the dawn of this new century, we may begin to realize that the traditions shrugged off from years past that anchored our cultures in belief may be the only thing that can save us from drowning in ourselves. Awash in a sea of ever-changing truths, we may find that, perhaps, some things are better left to faith.

CHAPTER 16

Why Does the United States Need Ghosts, UFOs, and Bigfoot?

D espite centuries of scientific and social progress, we remain, at our most intimate level, believers. Religion, paranormal beliefs, politics, and sometimes even science have become beliefs that continue to be rationalized in lieu of our continuing history. Religion and paranormal beliefs must often change in the face of scientific developments and technologies; the believer, there-fore, must somehow account for these new developments in his or her belief system or risk abandoning those beliefs altogether and be sucked into a pit of cognitive dissonance. Likewise, true followers of a politician or political party must somehow forgive or account for the many errors, poor decisions, and indiscretions within their particular affiliation. And, alas, science occasionally has to deal with their predictions going awry, their numbers being rendered inaccurate, their theories and hypotheses not panning out in reality. Unfortunately, the true believer, bound by the need for order in the universe based on his or her belief system, will often undertake the Sisyphean task of maintaining and rationalizing that belief to fit the new world. The result is dogma, unquestioning faith, irrationalism, and occasionally violence; but this inherent need for belief surmounts all of that and renders any possible lessons learned in history without value and easily forgotten. So why is there so great a need to *believe* in something?

Matthew Alper is the author of *The God Part of the Brain* and postulates that mankind is genetically hardwired to believe in something more than the reality of the empirical world. He believes that it is a coping mechanism that the brain developed as a way of handling the knowledge of our own mor-tality. As he stated on the radio program *Coast to Coast AM*, "I believe that the anxiety was so overwhelming that it forced the selection of this cognitive modification which . . . compels us to believe that there is this other transcendental force . . . through which, even though we know the physical body will die, we now believe this spiritual component will live on forever."[1] He cites decreased blood flow to areas of the brain during prayer and meditation that may account for the feeling of spiritual serenity and also account for the sensations of religious experiences with the chemical interaction of the temporal lobe of the brain with the neurotransmitter glutamate. He also feels that the belief in UFOs and aliens is another way that people can escape the anxiety of death by believing that there is a deeper, supernatural and transcendent reality. That, of course, can be extrapolated to include ghosts, demons, and Bigfoot.

Why else would people devote their lives, careers, and reputations to pursuing these mysteries that have so eluded mankind for centuries? The mysterious—the paranormal—plays a necessary role in the development of society and in the personal lives of each and every individual. It satisfies a need for belief; whether genetically encoded, scientifically evidenced, personally experienced, or transcendent from God—humanity needs its mysteries.

Medieval maps used to depict beasts that inhabited the oceans and unknown lands, dragon-like serpents that warned of dangerous waters and places. They were places to encounter danger, but, more importantly, places to encounter the divine. Legends told of mermaids and various monsters that became folklore and legend, sometimes new and sometimes passed down through ancient texts.

Similar to Homer's *The Odyssey*, ancient mariners were warned of confronting the gods, of the sirens sent to tempt them, and the monsters, spirits, and unexplained phenomena that challenged them if they dared venture to the very limits of the known world. By pushing the limits of knowledge and human experience the adventurer would go forth into the frightening and dangerous world, well aware that he might face supernatural challenges; but if he overcame them, he would attain a new knowledge that could better the world. In many cases, the reward of the adventurer was the discovery of new lands. He would return to the old world and tell of the new, and the bounty that awaited those willing to make the dangerous trip. In effect, he came back enlightened; he had faced death, fear, and the unknown and had returned a hero. He had ventured to the limits—the very periphery of the earth, to encounter the unknown, the mysterious.

Today, the world is mapped. Our maps are filled with roads and cities. Nearly every piece of inhabitable land is occupied by mankind; our maps are no longer documents of the mysterious and unknown, but rather, the very details of the known world—every road rational, every highway another human vein on the body of earth. The modern map is a testament to the known world.

But there exists an unseen world not shown on maps; there are places in our world that occupy the realm of the mysterious. They form our legends and folklore, and they are celebrated in small towns and tourist areas throughout the country. They are not a part of the empirical world but, instead, have become part of the unknown recesses of our psyche. These places represent the dark unknown that has come to occupy a small but mysterious part of the human experience—places that have become epitomized by the paranormal.

Massachusetts, of course, boasts Salem, a monument to old belief systems and fears, but it also contains the Freetown State Forest, an area that has attained legendary status for its paranormal phenomena. The stories were collected and documented by Christopher Balzano, and he illustrates all the darkness that our candle of modern illumination cannot brighten.

> Most of what makes up this book comes from the people who experienced it, but much of it is also the child of legend and urban legend. Over three hundred and fifty years those lines get blurred, and looking at official documents can never tell the full story. Some of the stories come from news reports about true crime, but police reports only tell us the facts and leave out the emotion ... Any story of a town is never the full story.[2]

Hidden within our official modern histories are stories that have become legends, even myths, and the people who seek out these legends for the purpose of understanding the world or, perhaps, finding new questions.

In the town of Point Pleasant, West Virginia, there stands an eight-foot stainless steel sculpture known as the Mothman. It symbolizes a year in Point Pleasant's history when residents were reporting a giant, winged, human-like creature that was appearing on their roads and in their yards. It made local headlines, attracted author John Keel to the area, and spawned numerous theories concerning UFOs and otherworldly creatures. When the Silver Bridge collapsed in 1967, killing 46 people, the sightings of the Mothman abruptly ended; some concluded that the creature was somehow a warning to the town of the impending disaster. It became a book by John Keel and a subsequent film starring Richard Gere and Laura Linney. The sculpture stands as a symbol of that strange, tragic, and sometimes terrifying year in the town's history. The inscription on the sculpture reads,

On a chilly, fall night in November 1966, two young couples drove to
the TNT area north of Point Pleasant, West Virginia, when they realized they were not alone. What they saw that night has evolved into
one of the great mysteries of all time, hence, the Mothman legacy
began. It has grown into a phenomenon known all over the world by
millions of curious people asking questions. What really happened?
What did these people see? Has it been seen since? It still sparks the
world's curiosity—the mystery behind Point Pleasant, West Virginia's
Mothman.

The United States is dotted with these places of mystery and legend, which
do not comprise the rational and known world of our maps; rather, they
occupy the darker parts of our psyche and history. Some places are marked
with statues and sculptures as testament to the mystery; but there are many,
many more that are only known in local lore, but will occasionally make it
onto the Internet for a little more exposure or tourist dollars. Dudleytown
in Connecticut; the Pine Barrens in New Jersey; Flatwoods, West Virginia;
Roswell, New Mexico; Amityville, New York; Bray Road in Wisconsin; and
Willow Creek, California, are just a few of the many places that occupy a place
in the unknown history of the United States. Stop into any small town or
large city, and you can find a ghost story.

We designate these places through folklore and legend, and people seek out
these areas of mystery—whether nationally known, like Point Pleasant, or only
locally known, like the Green Lady Cemetery in Harwinton, Connecticut—in
an effort to encounter the mysterious. Bill Ellis describes legend-telling as "the
communal exploration of social boundaries. By offering examples of the extreme
of experience—unusual, bizarre, inexplicable, unexpected, or threatening incidents—members of the legend-telling circle attempt to reach some consensus
on the proper response to what is 'real.' "[3] He also describes "legend-
tripping," in which adventurous souls, traditionally adolescents, go to places
that are supposedly haunted—places associated with the supernatural—in order
to not only test the legend, but test themselves as well. It has traditionally been
an adolescent rite of passage, and these haunted areas afford teenagers the
secluded places where they can engage in forbidden activities with the added
thrill of a ghost story lingering in the darkness. Recently, seeking out legendary
creatures and haunts has become a more popular and serious matter. In essence,
it is no longer just adolescents exploring the boundaries of what is "real"; these
legends and legendary places represent the boundary where the known world
meets the unknown. We find these liminal places where the boundaries of the
known and unknown meet in nearly every town across the States. There is

invariably a haunted house, a haunted road, a story of a beast or lights in the sky; we designate these places in our collective consciousness as a way of assigning a totem for all that we do not understand or know, for those unexplained experiences in life for which science and modernity cannot account, and for which we ourselves cannot quite believe or disbelieve.

In essence, we *need* ghosts, UFOs, and Bigfoot.

A NEW AMERICAN MYTHOLOGY

The persistence of these legends—our need for them—is indicative of something deeper and more meaningful embedded in our paranormal culture. Every time we watch *Ghost Hunters*, every time we explore or stay overnight in a place that is haunted; every time we seek out a religious experience to be touched by God; every time we pay $10 to see a "true" story based on the paranormal; and every time we secretly hope that Bigfoot is out there stomping around in the mountains of the Pacific Northwest, we engage in something more than legend. The persistence of these beliefs and what they say about our society point to the emergence of a mythology—one that has become part of the American experience. The melting pot of American culture means that no one mythology brought over from the Old World, either from Europe, Africa, or Asia, can symbolize the American experience. Thus, a new mythology is born from the old, and a new and unique country requires a mythology that has been reworked in the modern world and fitted to the American experience. Thus, it is not God who descends in a fiery chariot, but extraterrestrials from scientifically advanced alien planets; it is not a dragon that is seen in Lake Champlain and Loch Ness, but a plesiosaur that has somehow survived the millennia in deep lakes around the world. Our new nation has adopted a new form of mythology by which to experience the world and touch the mysterious.

Bill Ellis writes, ". . . institutionalized myths, in the traditional sense of the word, are used to explain and validate contemporary social practices . . . beliefs are combined and linked in legends; legends are combined and linked in myths. Contemporary mythologies thus are scenarios made up of many beliefs and narratives which are accepted on faith and used then to link and give meaning to stressful events in terms of continuous penetration of this world by otherworldly forces."[4] And Joseph Campbell writes, "Mythology, we may conclude, therefore, is a verification and validation of the well-known—as monstrous. It is conceived, finally, not as a reference either to history or to the world-texture analyzed by science, but as an epiphany of the monstrosity and wonder of these; so that both they and therewith ourselves may be experienced in depth."[5]

Our various mythologies the world over are ancient explanations as to how the world came into being as it was understood in ancient times. Thus, there are gods and goddesses who frequently battle each other, commingle with mankind, and create magical and wondrous events that set into place things as average and mundane as the rising and setting of the sun. The Bible, *The Metamorphoses of Ovid*, the Mahabharata, and the Koran are all examples of this mythology—the mythology of us—recorded in ancient writings. These sacred texts are used to explain our existence and purpose, and thus, they guide our lives and our perceptions of reality. However, since the Copernican revolution and subsequent Enlightenment, advances in science, philosophy, and technology have rapidly broken down these mythologies.

However, this is not to blame science for ruining the party; much of the fault lies in the institutionalization of these mythologies and their adherents' religious desire to hold on to these mythologies as empirical truth. "Wherever the poetry of myth is interpreted as biography, history, or science, it is killed. The living images become only remote facts of a distant time or sky. Furthermore, it is never difficult to demonstrate that viewed as science and history, mythology is absurd. When a civilization begins to re-interpret its mythology in this way, the life goes out of it; temples become museums, and the link between the two perspectives is dissolved. Such a blight has certainly descended on the Bible and on a great part of the Christian cult."[6] In other words, the Garden of Eden story in the Bible, taken as literal fact and history, becomes absurd in light of scientific, anthropological, and historical developments. However, people still try to cling to that mythology as reality. This is not to say that there is no truth to the history of these texts; cities listed in the Old Testament have been uncovered by archeologists and have lent credence to the biblical stories. Moses composed the first five books of the Bible, and much of it involved him directly participating in the action. However, Moses could not record the beginning of the universe and man through direct experience because he did not yet exist. Furthermore, the stark similarities between the biblical story of creation and stories of creation in other mythologies as far away as the Orient indicate that the mythology of creation was spread across a vast number of cultures that substituted their own god or gods for the role of Yahweh. It is these mythologies that the ancients used to explain how life came into being; however, to regard these stories as actual histories eventually leads the believer into an unnecessary collision between mythology and science. Faced with impossible questions, believers feel that they must either abandon their faith or, conversely, follow their faith blindly as fact. Each tends to have dire consequences—either moral relativism or fanatical belief. Both have a long history of death and destruction.

Belief in the literal interpretation of these ancient texts substitutes faith for fact, spirituality for dogmatic religion, and gods for totems. The literal interpretation of these texts ignores the true importance and meaning behind them and their significance to our society. The mythologies of different cultures are, and should be, traditions meant to preserve those societies in their finest forms. They are codes of conduct meant to preserve a culture. However, literal interpretations of these myths, when confronted with emergent science, result in the exact opposite—a breakdown of that culture. When confronted with the Darwinian revolution, the atomic age, and the theory of relativity, the literal interpretation of a text such as the Old Testament does not hold up and results in the fracturing of a culture. As the United States became the epicenter for scientific development, technology, and modernity, its young culture became fractured, as literal and dogmatic religion collided with science. This inevitably led to two different conclusions: A. that there is no God; or B. that science is wrong and the Bible's story of creation is factual. While most people fall somewhere between the two extremes, the divide has resulted in a fractured society that has rather quickly given up any traditions that it may have formed in its brief history. The results have not been positive—fundamentalism clashing with moral relativism. It is dissolution of the American body.

The paranormal and religion are inseparable. Religion, throughout the history of the world, was the way in which man confronted the mysterious and experienced a revelation as to his place in the cosmos. However, the modern dissolution of religion has left a void in civilization. Man, due to his unparalleled intelligence, knowledge of his own mortality, and his communal nature has an innate need to confront the mysterious. Whether or not it is a genetically inherited trait, as Matthew Alper theorizes, is irrelevant. It could be argued that scientific development actually aids spirituality as science discovers our interconnectedness to the cosmos; we are, in fact, stardust. Likewise, science must confront its own mysteries and acknowledge that its understanding of even some of the most basic components of life is tenuous at best. Science and faith need not be mutually exclusive.

But where does this leave the world of the paranormal? The paranormal attempts to bridge the gap between science and faith—to form a new mythology and restore traditions that constitute a strong culture. Oftentimes, the true intent of the paranormal researcher is to be found between the lines, the place where the paranormal is most at home and most relevant. Take, for instance, the work of Erich von Däniken and his many, many imitators and collaborators. Däniken found a new interpretation for the ancient, mythological texts. He began to interpret them literally, as some religious fundamentalists have done; however, he interprets them through the belief that these were actual events caused by alien beings rather than gods. He uses the idea of a scientific and technologically superior race interceding in the creation and development of mankind, as a way to understand the ancient texts. Thus, he combines religion and mythology with technology and science. But, as Jason Colavito noted, as the belief in ancient alien creators progressed, it eventually became a moral, spiritual argument.

> Instead, the authors talk about the decline of Western civilization and accidentally reveal the true reasons for their work. Alternative archeology was nothing more and nothing less than a way to reconnect to the primal magic of better days. The promise of scientific progress had faded in the twentieth century, and the egalitarian ideals of Western democracy clashed with the elitist, specialist nature of industrial science ... Like creationism, it is a cultural revitalization movement of sorts. It is a replacement belief system, a faith in the greatness and goodness of the mysterious ancestors, be they human or alien, for a salvation through a return to the past, to childhood, to innocence.[7]

The paranormal has a long history of attempting to create a new mythology. The "alternative archeologists" who posit alien intervention in the creation of man and alien presence in our ancient texts are attempting to reinterpret the mythology that has formed the basis for our various cultures. These alternative archeologists find a way in which to encounter the divine through the study of ancient mysteries and texts. Prominent Spiritualists, such as Madame Blavatsky, would supposedly communicate with ancient spirits who talked of the lost civilizations of Atlantis and Mu. They would tell of technological wonders but also offer religious-like poetic proclamations about "the endless magnetic life of nature."[8] The Spiritualist movement, closely aligned with Christianity, was creating a mythology around mythical times and lands, but also incorporating Darwinian theory that life is all interconnected and sprang from one ancient source. It was the combination of Christianity and Darwinism, and communing with the dead was a way to assert the truth of Christianity told through a new mythos. UFO contactees during the 1950s and '60s issued similar ambiguous, spiritual messages, and, occasionally, dire warnings about the progress of humanity.

The paranormal is a way in which to experience the mythical, mystical, and mysterious. This was traditionally the domain of religion, but its dogmatism and literalism was its ultimate undoing; in light of scientific and technological advances, people began to seek a new way to touch the mysterious. It is an essential part of our being. There is so much that is not known, and probably cannot be known, about the universe and ourselves. Scientists, too, live with and study ghosts. Stars, long ago extinguished, still shine brightly in our night skies and are studied by astronomers seeking to understand the story of our creation. Just as ghosts are windows to the past, pyramids and UFOs inspire rethinking of archeology and history, and Bigfoot leads us to question the development of *Homo sapiens*, so the ghosts of faraway stars inspire new questions and theories about the origins and purpose of man. The difference is that the paranormal offers a fleeting glimpse, which inspires the individual to seek his or her own answers, while the starlight offers more permanence for scientific study. But they are both ghosts—glimpses into the past that inspire us to seek our origins, our future, and our purpose.

A BRAVE NEW WORLD

The opening stanza of *The Metamorphoses of Ovid* offers a prayer: "My soul would sing of metamorphoses. But since, o gods, you were the source of these bodies becoming other bodies, breathe your breath into my book of changes: may the song I sing be seamless as its way weaves from the beginning to our day."[9] It is a book of the ancient myths that helped shape the Western world, some eerily similar to biblical stories. But Ovid's prayer is that his book would help explain the changes that led to the world today. Mythology is ultimately about change; and the paranormal, if we are to understand it as a pursuit of modern American mythology, is also about change. As discussed earlier, times of great social change have often preceded times of great paranormal revival. Mythology forms the basis of culture. Therefore, the attempt to rebuild mythology in light of the modern world of science and technology is an attempt to rebuild the culture. But how are the paranormal investigators a part of this change—those believers who search for ghosts, demons, UFOs, and Bigfoot and offer up their lives and reputations, their money and beliefs in pursuit of something that has remained so elusive throughout the years? What does the mysterious offer that calls forth the pursuits of men and women toward the unknown?

The paranormal is ancient and influential. It is a reaction to modernism, but its pursuit is based in the mythological pursuits of ancient heroes—those who would change the world by touching the mysterious—thus it penetrates to the core of our culture and identity. It is a search for identity through a search for the mysterious. We ultimately remain mysterious to ourselves, alienated from our own understanding of purpose; and the search for our identity and meaning must touch the mysterious aspect of life. The paranormal offers answers—and questions—to investigators and believers. But, ultimately, it offers an identity and worldview that seeks to save those who believe. It is a new religion, much like many of the other new religions that have developed in light of the modern world. But this new religion is based on tradition, mythology, and spirituality rather than the atheistic base of scientism and modernism.

In his work *Hero with a Thousand Faces*, Joseph Campbell describes the journey of the archetypal hero of myth and postulates that this archetypal hero is the one who alters the course of human history. Jesus Christ, Mohammed, the Buddha, Viracocha, and any number of the Hindu gods—they are the creators of our civilization and culture, and their stories are strangely similar and follow similar tracks. Ultimately, the hero is one who has come into contact with the mysterious—or in the case, of Campbell's work, with the divine—and who then returns to society in an effort to change that society with the new knowledge he has attained. To paraphrase Campbell's summary of the hero's journey: the hero is called to adventure by either internal or external forces and encounters a shadow presence that the hero must battle and thereby transcend our reality into the "world of the unfamiliar yet strangely intimate forces"; he gains contact with and is illuminated by the divine and then returns to the known world; "the hero re-emerges from the kingdom of dread (return, resurrection). The boon that he brings restores the world (elixir)."[10] The story of the paranormal closely resembles this model of the archetypal hero. Those who dedicate their lives to investigating the paranormal are fulfilling the role of the hero. They are typically called forth into action by a paranormal encounter, such as seeing a ghost or some other phenomenon, and then plunge themselves into the unknown world of the paranormal—something hidden from the light of rational day. Eventually, their beliefs in a personal quest are verified through different strange encounters or paranormal manifestations (real or imagined). Following such encounters with the mysterious or divine, the individuals or investigators return to the world of the rational and attempt to tell their story. However, this is more difficult than it seems.

While the insight or enlightenment the individuals have gained has changed their perspectives and given them a glimpse at a side of the world that is normally hidden from view, their ability to properly translate their story and express their enlightenment to the world is often more difficult. "As dreams that were momentous by night may seem simply silly in the light of day, so the poet and the prophet can discover themselves playing the idiot before a jury of sober eyes."[11] In essence, the experience of the mysterious does not often translate well into the realm of the rational, thereby rendering it easy for the individual to be labeled gullible, a kook, a liar, or just plain insane by those who have not experienced such a transcendental moment. Like the prophets before them, those who have had contact with the mysterious and been changed by it will have believers and detractors—both those who seek mysterious encounters for themselves and those who believe that the realm of night is only for dreams. But the vast majority of people who have a paranormal experience use it to further their own personal understanding of their place and purpose in the world; they walk amongst us with their own knowledge of the mysterious intact, content to let everyone else do as they please. Their stories are occasionally roused in conversation but rarely revealed in the light of day. "The easy thing is to commit the whole community to the devil and retire again into the heavenly rock-dwelling, close the door, and make it fast."[12]

Then there are those who seek to bring the knowledge of the mysterious to others; those who attempt to bring the irrational night-world into the rational light of day. These are the individuals who try to tell the world—the ghost hunters featured on television, ufologists who argue with skeptics and challenge the establishment, monster hunters who seek to find that last remnant of the unknown world and bring it into the open. Theirs is a difficult journey. They are mocked, ridiculed, and criticized; they are torn between roles and rules they have established for themselves in the rational world, but they are proselytizing a world of the irrational in which rules and roles have no place. Thus, the modern prophets often find themselves not only at odds with the outside world but also at odds with themselves. These modern-day prophets attempt to bridge the divide between the known and the unknown, the rational and the irrational, the light and the dark. It is a monumental, if not impossible, task. Just as the twilight can play tricks on the eye, those who try to bridge that gap find it to be strange, tricky, inconsistent, and elusive. In biblical stories prophets were given visions and instructions from God, which they were to relay to the people. Prophets would warn of impending dangers if the people did not change their ways to act in accordance with God's will. They foretold the future and related stories of meetings with angels, burning bushes, chariots of fire, and demons. They warned that man must return to his traditional ways or face disaster. However, according to the Bible, a prophet would only be known as a true prophet of God if the prophesies he foretold came true; that, inherently, left any number of "prophets" making any number of predictions, and the people not knowing whom to believe until much later in the future.

A prophet of the paranormal is very similar to the biblical prophets, and the paranormal has, throughout history, been a catalyst for the prophet.

He or she experiences the mysterious and, if so inclined, returns to society to tell them, not only what happened, but what it means. In the Bible, God would appear to men like Saul, thus changing their lives and sending them out into the world to deliver his message; an encounter with the "Hairy Man" (Bigfoot) in Native American lore was said to be a warning that the tribe must return to their traditions or face destruction; spirits communicated with mediums during the Spiritualism movement to tell humanity that everything was connected and to cease its destructive ways, and, similarly, those who claimed to be contacted by alien beings also warned of impending, catastrophic doom if mankind were to continue on its present course. Encounters with the mysterious seemed to herald a message to humanity—repent and change your ways. These encounters were, in effect, both gateways to spiritual depth and warnings that society was collapsing, although many of those warnings have yet to come to pass.

Similarly, outside the realm of the mysterious, we encounter warnings from prophets. The public is bombarded with warnings from scientists about the dangers of man-made global warming and the possible destruction it will cause. The media uses nearly every natural disaster as further warning: repent and change your ways; the blight of oil must be stopped, and we must return to natural ways of producing energy. Terrorist attacks against the United States and its allies are seen by right-wing politicians as signs that the United States must change its progressive policies and revert to traditional, conservative policies. So, the rational world of light has its prophets as well, and which of those are true prophets has yet to be known.

Ray Kurzweil is, by nearly everyone's standards, a genius. Responsible for some of the greatest technological achievements in the modern world of computer technology, he is considered by many to be a prophet of technology. Kurzweil believes that by the year 2044, mankind will reach the "singularity"—a moment in time when technology enables information to be so quickly developed and expanded that the growth of information and technology will overtake humanity; we will, in essence, become fundamentally merged with computers. Some fellow scientists warn about the singularity as being tantamount to creating Armageddon, but Kurzweil sees it as a blissful, transcendent moment in time when man will finally evolve into something greater. We will have to wait and see. But the point is that prophets exist in both the irrational night-world of the paranormal, as well as in the rational light-world of science and technology. The prophet of the paranormal has his personal experience with the mysterious, which can never be shown to the public, while the scientist has charts, graphs, and computer models that are barely decipherable by the majority of the public or even by those who tout their findings, such as journalists. Oddly enough, it appears that both sides argue for putting the brakes on a society that seems to be tumbling toward the abyss.

When the paranormal is experienced on a personal, private level, it is a divine call to the individual to expand his understanding of the universe spiritually, mentally, and physically. However, the paranormal, when given public forum by a prophet, whether it is an investigator being interviewed by the media, or any of the paranormal programs being featured on television, is a warning to society to return to its traditional values or face a bleak future. Bigfoot is a warning to return to a more natural way of life that is in tune with nature; ghosts are a signal that there is a spiritual world and, aside from implying directly that God exists, they also tell us that our very souls are at stake in our worldly lives; and UFOs are warnings about our violent, warlike, and self-destructive nature. The essence of the paranormal is that there is more to the universe than we now know, and that our actions have long-term consequences for both our society and our souls. The high level of public interest signals openness and a yearning for that change. The paranormal heralds a brave new world—one that, oddly enough, calls for a return to traditional values, simplicity, and spirituality. As Jason Colavito said, it is "nothing less than a way to reconnect to the primal magic of better days . . . it is a cultural revitalization of sorts."[13]

The urge to return to a "primal magic" amounts to a need to find meaning in life. The magical belief system of the ancients and primitive man meant that everyday occurrences, which today go largely unnoticed, had real meaning. For instance, today the gathering of storm clouds on the horizon and the rumble of thunder may signal a low-pressure front colliding with a high-pressure system and thus producing rain and lightning, which is merely the exchange of electrons from the earth to the sky. It is cause to perhaps batten down the hatches, but also to sit on the front porch, have a drink, and watch the light show. However, in a magical belief system, the thunderstorm is an omen imbued with meaning; a signal from forces greater than our own. It is drama in its highest form acted out on the largest stage of all, and our lives and souls are at stake. In *The Metamorphoses of Ovid*, Byblis, in love with her own brother, calls a servant to deliver her love letter to him. As she hands him the letter, it slips and falls to the ground; "That omen troubled her, and yet she sent them on." Her brother's angered rejection leaves her broken, and she laments her decision to ignore the omen; "But I, in truth, had been forewarned: that omen—was it not clear that I must not pursue my love when those wax tablets slipped and fell as I was about to send them off? Did that not mean my hopes had fallen, too?" She spends the rest of her life, insane, wandering the countryside and weeping for her love.[14] Ignoring the omen had drastic consequences. In the magical belief system, there is no coincidence or random occurrence. Instead, life is imbued with meaning, and the world, therefore, becomes symbolic. This world of magical symbolism through paranormal beliefs is a way in which the individual can relate to the society and the universe as a whole; "The myths and rites constitute a mesocosm—a mediating, middle cosmos, through which the microcosm of the individual is brought into relation to the macrocosm of the all. And this mesocosm is the entire context of the body social, which is thus a kind of living poem, hymn, or icon of mud and reeds, and of flesh and blood, and of dreams . . ."[15]

This magical symbolism is not altogether something new; indeed, humans function with symbolism in the form of words, both written and oral. As far as we know, at this point, we are the only species to function on such a symbolic level that enables us to discuss philosophy, mathematics, science, and all the bigger questions in life. Therefore, a worldview that directly engages the world as symbolic of a greater or alternative reality has an innate appeal to us. It also allows for us to capture some of the lost curiosity, wonder, and magic of our childhood where we stood in wonder at the world; and the slightest details, easily overlooked in our adult years, took on the envious quality of opening worlds of understanding in our young minds. As adults, we may not marvel at a parade of ants marching in and out of an anthill (though maybe we should); instead, we walk over it having seen such things time and time again. However, the prospect of an unseen, magical world in which the banality and meaninglessness of life disappear, a world in which we become the hero imbued with new knowledge meant to save humanity, has overwhelming appeal. Even die-hard skeptics, like the late Carl Sagan, often state that they wish some of this were true. Some of them even began their careers engaged in searching for the mysterious only to reverse course after finding nothing to support their hopes. Indeed, finding proof of such an alternative reality would possibly be the greatest scientific achievement in history; to be the man or woman who discovers alien life, the spirit world, or Bigfoot would literally become a historical icon of science. However, since scientists have largely dismissed the paranormal, average citizens have taken up the cause. Spurred by encounters with strange phenomena, enabled through the democratization of science and technology, and encouraged by the faith and belief of millions, the seeker of the mysterious takes on the role of the mythological hero who encounters the divine and returns to society after fulfilling his or her mission.

This is not necessarily a bad thing. While many bemoan such paranormal beliefs as being archaic or ignorant or deluded and cringe as they watch person after person succumb to the appeal of pseudoscience, the actual over-all effect of the paranormal may be much more positive than that. Carl Jung believed that the vision of a flying saucer was akin to a great psychological awakening that ultimately became a catalyst for individual change. Similarly, paranormal experiences often change the worldview of those who have experienced them. People who are not necessarily religious suddenly have an experience that alters their worldview and imbues the world with meaning. The belief that there is something more than our daily waking reality gives our lives meaning and our actions long-reaching consequences. Religion has traditionally been a way to reach the mysterious divine; but, as religion is challenged throughout the world, people begin to seek the mysterious through alternative routes. There is a positive effect in this heroic quest; a world with meaning and purpose encourages individuals to think beyond their immediate circumstances—to ask the big questions and to live their lives according to a standard, recognizing that their actions carry meaning.

The easy argument against the symbolic world of meaning is that such "meaning" can take on dangerous forms. Suddenly, this profound meaning can include instructions from a supernatural being to kill all those who do not believe: for instance, nearly every war and crusade that has been fought has been fought on behalf of religion. This is the typical atheist argument against religion. However, a world without meaning—the Nietzschean existential world in which God is dead—is not necessarily more appealing: take a look at the Nazi and Communist movements. Clearly, both are extremes of each worldview, but it is often the extremes that form the best arguments against particular beliefs. However, the paranormal, in the form of ghosts, UFOs, and Bigfoot, has a fairly benign history. Aside from the occasional public panic, its history has not been littered with genocide and torture. The scientific community's incredulousness, the hoax, and the enigmatic nature of the paranormal keep the beliefs in check. The paranormal does not lend itself easily to dogma and fanatical proselytizing. Rather, most people quietly keep their beliefs to themselves, content with their own personal understanding of the mysterious, and not wanting to open themselves up to ridicule.

The paranormal imbues the world with a magical-symbolic meaning for individuals, but the larger public fascination with the paranormal, as evidenced by the surge of paranormal programs and their popularity, has larger societal implications. Its implications are similar to "Hairy Man" appearing before Native American tribes in the Pacific Northwest. As documented by Gayle Highpine, a Dakota Native American and son of a tribal spiritual leader said, ". . . The Big Man comes from God. He's our big brother, kind of looks out for us. Two years ago, we were really going downhill, really self-destructive.

We needed a sign to put us back on track, and that's why the Big Man appeared."[16] Similarly, these times of increased paranormal interest and fascination signal a need for change—a need to return to traditional values. This may explain why the paranormal sees such resurgence during times of social upheaval, when many people may feel that the world is spinning out of control and thus seek for a deeper meaning in the chaos. The paranormal is a warning that society has turned in the wrong direction and must return to traditional values in order to maintain its strength.

While the word "tradition" has become a dirty word in today's modernism, it is tradition that has enabled cultures to survive from ancient times. Orthodox Judaism is a good example of strict traditions ensuring cultural longevity; the strict rules of behavior and life, imbued with meaning, have ensured the survival of a culture through many centuries of hatred, difficulty, and homelessness. Their traditions were an anchor by which the culture was able to survive the devastating changes and challenges that have faced the Orthodox Jews throughout the centuries. If tradition is the physical enactment of myth, as Joseph Campbell contends, then a call for a return to traditional values is, essentially, a call for a return to the mythological sources of our culture. Thus, the archetypal hero of ancient mythology finds a new home and purpose in the exploration of the paranormal in modern society.

This modern world has left many people feeling lost in a sea of changing and competing information. The old institutions of government, religion, and science are collapsing, as information becomes so vast and readily available that nearly every institution is easily discredited, any theory easily debated, with just a few keystrokes. Our cultural ship is adrift and the renewed, fervent interest in the paranormal is an attempt to toss an anchor into this turbulent ocean. It is a call for a return to the myths and traditions that have previously rooted nations and cultures. Stephen King's definition of horror is the sense that things are in the unmaking, and during times of great social stress and change, such as this one we are currently living in, that horror manifests in the popular milieu of television and the Internet. The paranormal is a uniquely human experience—part of the human condition that touches upon the eternal mystery of life—and it is often the cause for change in one's personal beliefs and practices. However, those who publicly and privately work to discover, define, and prove the paranormal are engaged in a mythological hero's quest—an effort to experience the divine or mysterious, and then bring it back to society in an effort to change humanity. Indeed, the proving of any aspect of the paranormal would probably radically change humanity forever, more so than even the technological advances of the past few centuries. But that task is nearly impossible.

The heroism, then, may lie in the effort itself. What is the harm in trying to remake society for the better? To find meaning in what has essentially become a Nietzschean world? While attainable on a personal level, the path to this discovery finds much resistance and contempt in society at large. It seems that the elusiveness of the paranormal makes the effort to bring the mysterious to society a Sisyphean task. The believers continue to push the rock to the top of the hill only to have it roll back down for an infinite number of reasons. The pursuit of the paranormal is a pursuit of an unattainable social balance between the light and the dark, the earth and the sky, the past and the present, and the body with the spirit.

CHAPTER 17

Cry of the Banshee

While in graduate school and working for the writing lab at Western Connecticut State University, I encountered a woman from Ireland who was working her way toward becoming a teacher. I will call her Beth. She, like many others, had come to the writing lab for a review of her entrance essay to be admitted to the education program. During the course of our work together she informed me that once, as an adolescent living in Ireland, she actually heard the scream of a banshee. In Irish folklore a banshee is a feminine spirit who wails when someone is about to die; she has been portrayed both as frightful and comforting, occasionally attaching herself to particular families. However, on this particular night, as she was walking home at dusk, Beth heard the loud, audible scream of what she believed was a banshee. She was frightened and ran home to tell her family. Two days later her uncle died. She steadfastly believes in banshees—spirits who roam the Irish countryside warning of approaching death.

But death can also signal a change. Symbolically, death gives way to birth —the ushering in of a new life. Similarly, the cry of the banshee, while being a paranormal warning of approaching death, could also signal the beginning of something new. Certainly for Beth it signaled, not only the death of her uncle, but the beginning of belief in the paranormal and supernatural. Had she never heard the scream, or had her uncle not died and thus fulfilled the legend, she would never have come to believe in banshees and the paranormal as she so fervently does today. She knew in her heart that what she heard was real, and she could not believe otherwise, even when offered some possible alternative explanations. Her life had been forever changed at that moment.

One thing has been consistent in my experience over the past five years of researching and writing these books, and that is, whenever I tell an individual or a group of people what I'm working on, I almost always get a story from one of them detailing a paranormal experience they once had. This is across the spectrum of age, wealth, education, and religious affiliation. It is an experience they stand by, which causes them to believe for the rest of their lives that there is something paranormal, unexplainable, and mysterious at work in the world. These experiences are sometimes frightening and sometimes joyous, both curses and blessings, but the effects are the same—belief in spite of evidence or science or everyday experience.

In the course of my work, some stories have stood out more than others, and it is here at the conclusion that I would like to present those stories in an interview format—in their own words—so that perhaps it will shed light on the fact that the paranormal is not necessarily a supernatural experience, but rather, a uniquely *human* experience.

PAUL S.

(25, Single, Computer Technician)

MEF: Where did you grow up?

PS: I grew up in Hamden, Connecticut.

MEF: And why don't you start by telling us about your first experience that you couldn't explain or understand?

PS: I was in my early teens to mid-teens at my parents' house. They often worked late, so my brother would take care of us. We would just do our own thing—watch TV, play on the computer kind of deal. Typically, when my parents came home they would yell for us to come help with the groceries or whatnot, and all of sudden we heard our names being called; we were in different rooms and we all ran downstairs and no one was there. We were looking around and we turned on the lights outside to make sure whether someone was there or not. All of us ran down at the same time because we were trained to do that—to run down and help and then go back to doing our own thing. And when no one was there we all kinda looked at each other and freaked out, locked the doors, and ran back upstairs.

MEF: Where were your parents at the time?

PS: They were out with their friends . . .

MEF: So they were nowhere near the house . . .

PS: No. Typically the dogs would run downstairs to greet them.

MEF: Did the dogs run down that time?

PS: No, the dogs didn't, just us. Which is kind of strange, for it to happen, especially to all three of us. My—they're not joking around—and when you hear something similar to your mom's voice calling you, you run down to see what's going on. For all three of us to do it at the same time is kind of strange for that to happen. I mean you really can't shrug it off, there's two other people that heard what you heard . . . so you can't just shrug it off, go upstairs, and forget about the whole thing. That was the first initial thing that happened to me. You kinda . . . You think about it but then you try not to think about it because you don't want to seem crazy.

MEF: So you just put it out of mind?

PS: Yeah, I mean that's the best thing to do because you really can't investigate or try to figure out what it was without—I don't know—professionals or something. There's no way to prove that it happened, only to have witnesses or somebody that saw or heard the same thing . . . there is no other thing you can do after that happens, there's no set of guidelines when something like that happens.

MEF: Were there incidents after that?

PS: There were a couple incidents after that, you know . . . My brothers would be watching TV and I would get the old Super Nintendo to myself in my brother's room. I would be playing it and about an hour into it all of a sudden, things got really weird . . . I didn't lose consciousness, I didn't feel like I was dreaming, I totally saw what I was doing—playing a video game—but when I looked up I saw a six- to seven-foot shadow figure . . . I could see a black outline that said, "It's up there." That was all it said to me. It was a man's voice. I responded and said, "What's up there?" and then I, like, came to; it's like I got my sense back and realized that there was something going on here that was not right. I ran out the door to other people looking like I just saw a ghost . . .

MEF: 'Cause you kind of did . . .

PS: (laughing) Yeah. My parents were asking what was wrong, do you want to talk? But it was really weird . . . I didn't want to seem crazy by telling my parents that something just happened to me in my brother's room. I didn't want to tell my brothers about it, I just wanted to forget that it happened.

MEF: What do you think that meant, "It's up there"?

PS: I really thought about that for a long time. *It's up there.* Is it in the attic? There's nothing in the attic. It was a brand-new build of a house, we didn't have floors in the attic, it was just a narrow space with wires and beams and there is nothing up there, so ... I don't know. Is he talking about a heaven or hell type of deal? I just don't know.

MEF: Are you religious?

PS: My mom is ... I'm ... Not really. I don't go to church every week, I don't read the Bible. But ... things like that make you think, "What's going on?" At the same time, I'm more of a scientific guy; I'm into computers. There's a logical explanation behind everything, so I don't necessarily believe that God exists but when stuff like that happens, it's like, well, scientifically how do I explain this and when I can't ... What's left?

MEF: So you don't have any doubt as to what you saw and what you experienced?

PS: There's not a doubt at all. The strange thing is that it has been 10 years since this happened and I recall that perfectly, because that's what happened. I was younger but I know what happened. If I was dreaming ... How long do you remember a dream for? But to remember the same exact thing, the same exact phrase, the same exact voice after 10 years ... Something happened. I don't talk about it because I don't want to sound crazy but it's still something that happened.

MEF: Is this something that you tell other people?

PS: No. Clearly, I talk to my girlfriend but, to complete strangers or regular people, I don't like to talk about it, because you don't know how they're going to react or how they're going to judge you or they won't believe you. I'd rather not have that happen.

MEF: Both those incidents occurred in the same house. Was there something about the house that may have contributed to it?

PS: Well, my area, my town is really old ... like the 1700s. If you walk a half mile into the woods you'll see foundations of old houses, you'll see wells and property markings and stone walls for farmers. There's evidence that this place is really old. There's been a lot of people that have lived around there. When I was younger I'd walk around those areas with my brothers. Especially with a new build, who knows what happened to the land.

MEF: Have incidents happened since you left the house?

PS: The only thing that has really been happening, which is strange, is that I'll see shadows whiz by. I'll be looking down at, like, a piece of paper and I see something go by really fast. I'll look up and nothing is there. And I know I saw something go by, I know there's something going on but I try to tell myself that it was just the lighting or my eyes playing tricks on me. But when it happens consistently, it's like... there's something that is moving that is not human or physical being, it's something else. I don't know. A shadow figure, I guess. I've heard of other people and seen news or documentaries about shadow figures and I didn't really believe what I was seeing until I heard other people say, "Hey, I've seen shadow people." I was like, "Oh... that's what that was," because I had no other way to explain it. When other people say that they have seen the same thing, then you don't feel crazy anymore.

MEF: Do you like that any of this happens to you?

PS: You know... At first I was really scared, you want to get up and run away when you're younger and don't know what's going on. I don't mind it as long as it's not negative. If it's positive or it doesn't affect me, it's fine. Just knowing it is kind of unique, but I could certainly live without it. It's not something that I enjoy. It kind of freaks me out (laughing)—big time. I try to play it off like, "This is nothing, let's just watch some TV and turn the volume up," or whatever. It bugs me out. I try to keep cool, but when something like that happens it's kind of hard to ignore.

MEF: Has this changed your life at all?

PS: It's made me a little more paranoid than usual. I don't like being in older houses by myself. If I am by myself I like to have the TV on or the news where someone is talking. I don't like it to be dead silent. Besides that, nothing too negative. I just don't like being alone that much without some kind of physical media to distract me from being alone, because that is when it usually happens. That is the only thing that is negative. I try to kill the quietness with some kind of activity.

MEF: Has this made you think at all about what happens after we die or the bigger picture? Does that occur to you in light of this?

PS: Well, typically, you reach a particular age when you start to ask yourself that question of "What happens when I die?" Seeing that raises questions, but I don't know... I have no idea. There is something that happens—clearly—but I have no idea. I can't give you a straight answer.

MEF: Have you tried to pursue this at all or look into it?

PS: No. I hear my mom tell stories or my stepdad tell stories of things that have happened to them and it makes me feel better just knowing that it happens to other people. From there, if you don't feel comfortable with what happened to you, you don't pursue it.

Just let it go and pretend like it never happened. I don't know what these things are capable or doing or what's going on and I don't want to know. I just want to leave it alone because if you mess with it, bad things can happen. I think that is what most people do. They don't want to seem crazy so they just let it go.

VICKIE B.

(35, Married, Registered Nurse)

MEF: I understand that you had an experience when you were a teenager?

VB: It was in my parents' house—they still live there, actually—I was a freshman in high school, I believe—freshman or sophomore. One of my girlfriends was staying with me and we were—one of us was at the top of the stairs and one of us was at the bottom of the stairs and we were talking and a bright, white sphere came out through the bedroom door. It flew down the stairs then up to the ceiling then down to the floor and then flew out of sight.

MEF: Where were you standing?

VB: I was at the bottom of the stairs, she was at the top. It flew over her head and down right past me.

MEF: And you both saw it?

VB: Yes. 'Cause I looked at her and I said "Did you just see that?" And she described what I had just seen.

MEF: How did you react?

VB: Were just like "Holy shit!" (laughing)

MEF: Did you tell anybody about it?

VB: Um . . . You know there were these strange things that would happen at my parents' house. There were motion sensor lights that would go on at the same time every night. There were rocks from outside that would end up in the garbage disposal in the kitchen and I tried telling my father once that there was something in the house and they kind of laughed at me. So, after that . . .

MEF: Had you ever experienced anything before that? Besides those things?

VB: Not really. Occasionally afterwards, but only in my bedroom. The people before us had redone the room, it had been a master bedroom and one wall was entirely mirrored and you would be looking in the mirror and you would see it kind of go behind you . . .

MEF: The same kind of sphere?

VB: Yeah, it was more like a bright light, but a couple of times it was a black sphere and I could see it going by in the reflection. It was pretty neat. The room had originally been gray, I believe, and I painted it purple. It was after that that things started happening; the motion sensor going on and the visual spheres going around. After I moved out my parents painted it back to a neutral color and I never heard about anything happening again.

MEF: Do you have any theory as to why this happened or what caused it?

VB: Not really.

MEF: Had you been interested in these things before?

VB: Absolutely. (laughing) I was actually into witchcraft and stuff for a while, I had an altar room set up in my closet and would do little spells but nothing huge or anything.

MEF: Where did you learn the spells?

VB: Oh. Just from my friends, and you could pick up books at bookstores. It was nothing, just kind of a hobby. One of my friends was Wiccan, too.

MEF: Do you still do that?

VB: Oh God, no. I haven't in a long time. It was all little, innocent, white magic spells, you know? I don't know that any of it ever worked or anything . . . Though I remember one time I was meditating—I was doing a spell and meditating—and I had an out-of-body experience. I was all of sudden floating over myself, looking down and seeing everything. I was up in the corner of the room looking down.

MEF: Did that make you think any differently about things, especially after seeing the spheres?

VB: I don't think so . . . I was always pretty open to the possibilities of anything, whether it's ghosts or spirits or reincarnation or witchcraft . . . it's all in the realm of possibilities.

MEF: Did seeing the spheres confirm your intuition?

VB: Yeah, I would say that.

MEF: Are you religious at all?

VB: Not really. I grew up in a mixed religion household and wasn't really brought up to practice anything in particular.

MEF: Have you ever seen anything since that time?

VB: No, just at that house.

MEF: Was the experience scary for you at all?

VB: I don't know if scary is the right word, or creepy. Really just more unbelievable. I mean, "Oh my God (laughing) what the hell was that?"

MEF: If I was to tell you that it was a hallucination between you and your friend, what would you say?

VB: I wouldn't buy it. For both of us to share the same hallucination?

MEF: So you know what you saw and you're sure of that?

VB: Yes, I'm sure.

MEF: So you believe in the things that we cannot explain?

VB: Absolutely.

JESSICA D.

(32, Married)

MEF: Jessica, why don't you tell me what you saw?

JD: Well, I was getting ready to leave, my husband was driving me to work. We were leaving off of our back porch and as we looked over to the left, there was this large light in the sky. It lasted about five minutes and then disappeared . . . It was a large triangular beam of light coming down and all of Connecticut saw it. It was all over the news. There was a white aura around it and it was very bright.

MEF: About what time of night was this?

JD: It was about 10:30 at night.

MEF: What did it look like to you, what did you think it was?

JD: Well, I'm into all the UFO stuff so I was skeptical . . . I didn't know at first. My husband is a nonbeliever and he was like, "Wow," and was really caught at it. I'm really not sure. It wasn't something that you see every day. It was bright and it looked just like something in the sky that had a beam of light coming out of it, like a funnel.

MEF: Were you able to make out any structure to it or was it just a beam of light?

JD: It had structure. It was in the shape of a funnel upside down. An upside-down triangle . . . It was really, really weird and when I got to work I told everybody and it was all over the news.

MEF: A bunch of people saw it. What did the news say it was?

JD: They called it "a strange light in the sky over Connecticut." And, you know, by the morning, NASA said it was something else. They claimed it was some kind of rocket or satellite. But we definitely can't see a rocket from Florida.

MEF: They said it was a rocket from Florida?

JD: They didn't say, but the only place I know of that launches rocket is in Florida. And they tried to make up stories that it was a rocket and other stories said that it was a satellite, but it was clearly neither one because it just disappeared. The light faded but the aura was gone. It faded very fast.

MEF: What do you think it was?

JD: I believe that it could have been some type of aircraft.

MEF: You say that you have been a believer in the UFO phenomena?

JD: Oh, yeah. Anytime I see a strange light in the sky I stop and I'm like, "What's that?" (laughing) And my husband makes fun of me.

MEF: Well, what did he think when you saw this?

JD: When I noticed this, I was like, "Come here, come here! You have to look at this," and he was like, "Oh God . . ." And then he looked up and said, "Whoa, what is that?" And he was stuck there for a couple minutes looking at it.

MEF: Is he a believer now?

JD: No, he believes the same as I do: We believe that we were not created by God or Jesus. We believe that we were created by an alien. That's who placed us on this earth to provide, and that's what we believe. But as far as lights in the sky, my husband is not really one of those who really look. I am.

MEF: So he believes that human origin may have been extraterrestrial but he's not looking up in the sky thinking that everything he sees is a flying saucer?

JD: That's right. I like looking up at the sky, though.

MEF: Now, what inspired your views and beliefs?

JD: It started from somewhere . . . with our technology and our knowledge, there are some people who are smarter than others, there are people who can see into the future, there are people who are great builders or artists. I mean, it's hard to believe that some can be better than others. They have to be that way for a reason, for a purpose.

MEF: But where did you get the idea of extraterrestrial creation?

JD: That's just a conversation that my husband and I have had and it's something that we just decided and believe because nobody has ever seen this "God." Who made Adam and Eve? There's never an answer for that. And the universe is so big it's hard to believe that we're the only life forms.

MEF: So did seeing this thing in the sky change anything for you?

JD: No, because I've always been a believer.

MEF: And you don't believe what NASA said it was?

JD: No, I don't.

MEF: Are they just trying to cover something up?

JD: That's what I believe, yes.

MEF: Have you seen anything since then?

JD: Possibly . . . Could have . . . Well, yes, I actually have. About a year and a half ago, my children and I were coming back from the movies and it was about six or seven in the evening. We were coming over 72, the new expressway, and we saw a huge fireball coming across the sky, way in the distance. It was pretty far away. We tried to get it on video but the cell phone made it look like the size of a little peanut. But I saw it, my stepdaughter saw it, and my daughter saw it. We were hanging out of the car looking at it. To this day I don't know what it was. My mom said it probably could have been a meteor, but there was no coverage on it. The news didn't say that a meteor had passed over. There was nothing. This was definitely weird because it was bright orange and it was falling to earth, not traveling across the sky. My kids and I still talk about it to this day.

COLLEEN S.

(28, Married, Senior Relocation Accounting Analyst)

MEF: You say that you had an experience that you cannot explain when you were a child?

CS: Yes, I was about 9 years old.

MEF: And what happened?

CS: I was playing with a bunch of the neighborhood friends. We were playing what we called "War." Basically, the girls played against the little boys in the neighborhood. We each [team] had a "home base" and our home base ended up being at my house at the shed, which was off the side of the house. Our parents often didn't like it because there was a lawnmower and tools, but we did it anyway. And the guys in the neighborhood ended up invading my lawn and trying to capture one of the girls, so we were running away, laughing, giggling, and screaming. I ended up running around the house, toward the shed in the opposite direction and looking behind me every few feet to see if anyone was chasing me. Probably the last two or three yards I was looking behind me while running. It was a clear path ahead of me so I knew I could look behind me and I was looking to make sure no one was behind me. Right before I stopped to turn and go into the shed, I turned my head around and there was this huge ... and, the only way I can describe it was it looked like a moth but magnified times ten. It must have been about six feet tall and about the same across ... Just a moth, magnified with two tiny red, dead center red eyes. It was enough to stop me dead in my tracks and all I could do was scream. I screamed for my mom, I got so scared. I went from running to a dead stop; I was terrified. I turned around and ran away and when I looked back behind me it was gone. I ran inside and told my mother and she was like, "Oh, it's okay, don't worry about it," but I was petrified. Scared wouldn't describe it.

MEF: Do you have any idea what it could have been?

CS: No. Nothing. I'm not one to believe in these things. I don't believe in Bigfoot, I don't believe in the Loch Ness monster. I don't know ... any other way to say what it could have been besides other accounts of the Mothman and seeing pictures drawn and I look at them and say, "Oh my God, that's what I saw." I'm not trying to discredit myself or anything like that, but I'm not one to believe in superstitious things, but there is no other way ... I don't know how to explain it. I don't know.

MEF: Now you say that on the date this occurred that something else happened that you were not aware of.

CS: Yeah, I was not aware of it. It might not have been that day, but it was definitely that week.

MEF: And what happened?

CS: I don't want to go into too much detail because I don't know how this could ... I don't want to get in trouble for mentioning this because I don't know if it ever ... I don't even think it was mentioned in the paper. One of the girls that we played with was captured by one of the guys and ended up being ... we'll say ... molested, or pretty much raped by her brother's friends. They were part of the "guys." It was childhood guys against the girls, but they were slightly older.

MEF: And when did you find out about that?

CS: I didn't know. She had told me that something bad happened. The timeline is very blurred. Probably, if I had to guess, two weeks later when it was being investigated. The police officer came to my house to ask questions and that was when I started putting things together as to what happened. I'm probably being very obscure because I don't know to what extent . . .

MEF: I understand. You say that you don't believe in Bigfoot or the Loch Ness monster or anything like that, but did seeing this thing have any kind of effect on your beliefs?

CS: It definitely taught me to judge certain aspects; just because you don't see it doesn't mean it's not there. To a certain extent, I would say not really, I don't know, but I think there are definitely things that we cannot explain. I'm more likely to believe in ghosts and paranormal activity and UFOs. It would be naïve to think that we were the only living things in this universe. But as far as mythical creatures like Bigfoot, I'm . . . I know it's crazy to say, because the Mothman is along the same lines, but there's no logical explanation for it. There is not a single one. I don't remember a whole lot from my childhood but I remember that single event. I remember moving, which we did, from that neighborhood pretty soon after that happened, and I don't have any other way to explain it.

MEF: So seeing this thing was kind of a turning point; you moved out of the neighborhood and things changed for you.

CS: Yeah. A lot. After that all went down. It wasn't just bing-bang-boom but in the years following that incident we moved, I went to middle school and high school after that but with different friends. When I say we moved, we actually stayed in the same town but moved a couple miles away to a different area and different street. I would say it was kind of a precursor to . . .

MEF: Some people speculate that the Mothman is a warning of things that are about to happen.

CS: I do believe that, I do believe that. One thing that I can say that is different from the drawings I've seen is that it did not look like a man. It looked just like a moth but magnified. I was a 9year-old girl and it completely towered over me. It was like a black moth but with two beady red eyes and just huge, and I remember thinking, "Why don't I feel the air from the wings? Why don't I feel the push, it was so big?" To say that it could have been a bat that was magnified by sunlight when it flew out, I mean . . . it couldn't.

MEF: You said that you had no way to explain it or describe it until you heard about the Mothman . . .

CS: Yeah, when I was older I heard about that. I told my mom when it happened but she was just, "Oh, it's okay, it was just this or that."

MEF: Do you still feel scared when you think about it?

CS: Yeah. It gives me the creeps. It sends a chill down your spine. I mean, I wasn't in danger, I didn't fear for my life. I didn't think this thing would hurt me but, let's put it this way, I wouldn't walk around it nonchalantly and there was no way I was going to try to challenge it in anyway but it was just there. It wasn't trying to hurt me but . . . it was just there. It was one of those things that sat in the back of my mind until I saw that Richard Gere movie, *The Mothman Prophecies*, when they really started talking about it, and I was like, "Oh, my God." It was definitely a precursor of what came, and it is clear as day in my mind. I can see it.

Notes

CHAPTER 1

1. *Where Evil Lurks*, directed by David Haycox, performed by Anthony Call and Kelly Cherie Levander, New Dominion Studios, 2007, http://www.4shared.com/video/w83Jn5Pk/a_haunting_s04e06_-_where_evil.html.

2. David W. Moore, "Three in Four Americans Believe in Paranormal," Gallup Poll News Service, June 16, 2005, home.sandiego.edu/~baber/logic/gallup.html.

3. Zeeya Merali. "Splitting Time from Space—New Quantum Theory Topples Einstein's Spacetime," *Scientific American*, November 24, 2009, www.scientificamerican.com/article.cfm?id=splitting-time-from-space.

4. George P. Hansen, *The Trickster and the Paranormal* (Philadelphia, PA: Xlibris, 2001), 430.

5. "How Many North Americans Attend Religious Services (and How Many Lie about Going)?" ReligiousTolerance.org, www.religioustolerance.org/rel_rate.htm.

CHAPTER 2

1. Bill Ellis, *Aliens, Ghosts, and Cults: Legends We Live* (Jackson: University Press of Mississippi, 2001), 40.

2. Paul S. Boyer and Stephen Nissenbaum, *Salem Possessed: The Social Origins of Witchcraft* (Cambridge, MA: Harvard University Press, 2003), 2.

3. Boyer and Nissenbaum, *Salem Possessed*, 16.

4. Laura K. Leuter, "The Legend of the Jersey Devil," The Devil Hunters: The Official Researchers of The Jersey Devil, 2004, njdevil hunters.com/legend5.html.

5. Owen Davies, *The Haunted: A Social History of Ghosts* (New York: Palgrave Macmillan, 2007), 23.

6. Davies, *The Haunted*, 25.

7. Judith Richardson, *Possessions: The History and Uses of Haunting in the Hudson Valley* (Cambridge, MA: Harvard University Press, 2003), 78.

8. Richardson, *Possessions*, 79.

9. Lesley Pratt Bannatyne, *Halloween: An American Holiday, an American Tradition* (Gretna, LA: Pelican Publishing Company, 1990), 2.

10. John B. Kachuba, *Ghosthunters: On the Trail of Mediums, Dowsers, Spirit Seekers, and Other Investigators of America's Paranormal World* (Franklin Lakes, NJ: New Page Books, 2007), 199.

11. Hilary Evans and Robert E. Bartholomew, *Outbreak!: The Encyclopedia of Extraordinary Social Behavior* (San Antonio, TX: Anomalist Books, 2009).

12. Terence Hines, *Pseudoscience and the Paranormal* (Amherst, NY: Prometheus Books, 2003), 235.

13. Kendall R. Phillips, *Projected Fears: Horror Films and American Culture* (Westport, CT: Praeger Publishers, 2005), 58.

14. Hines, *Pseudoscience and the Paranormal*, 273.

15. Jeff Meldrum, *Sasquatch: Legend Meets Science* (New York: Forge, 2006), 64.

16. Patterson–Gimlin film, directed by Roger Patterson and Bob Gimlin, 1967, www.youtube.com/watch?v=Ol8ifMrFN9U.

17. Joshua Blu Buhs, *Bigfoot: The Life and Times of a Legend* (Chicago: University of Chicago Press, 2009), 126.

18. Donnie Sergent and Jeff Wamsley, *Mothman: The Facts behind the Legend* (Point Pleasant, WV: Mothman Lives Pub., 2002).

19. John Keel, *The Mothman Prophecies* (New York: Tor, 2002), 86.

20. Keel, *The Mothman Prophecies*, 7.

21. Phillips, *Projected Fears*, 104.

22. Jay Anson, *The Amityville Horror* (New York: Pocket Star Books, 1991), 291–92.

CHAPTER 3

1. *Fox News: Bigfoot Fake*, directed by Fox News, performed by Megyn Kelly, New York City, 2008, www.youtube.com/watch?v=1ubBss7tlAQ &feature=related.

2. Ker Than, "Bigfoot Hoax: 'Body' Is Rubber Suit," *National Geographic News*, August 20, 2008, news.nationalgeographic.com/news/2008/08/080820-bigfoot-body.html.

3. George P. Hansen, *The Trickster and the Paranormal* (Philadelphia, PA: Xlibris, 2001), 89.

4. "The Ghostly Drummer of Tedworth," Museum of Hoaxes, www.museumofhoaxes.com/hoax/archive/permalink/the_ghostly_drummer_of_tedworth.

5. "The Hoaxes of Benjamin Franklin," Museum of Hoaxes, www.museumofhoaxes.com/hoax/archive/permalink/benjamin_franklin.

6. "The Great Moon Hoax of 1835," Museum of Hoaxes, www.museumofhoaxes.com/hoax/archive/permalink/the_great_moon_hoax.

7. "The Great Moon Hoax of 1835," Museum of Hoaxes.

8. Owen Davies, *The Haunted: A Social History of Ghosts* (New York: Palgrave Macmillan, 2007), 201.

9. *Ghostwatch*, directed by Lessley Manning, performed by Michael Parkinson and Sarah Greene, BBC, 1992, video.google.com/videoplay?docid=6073447872198040913.

10. "Crop Circle Makers in Their Own Words: Doug Bower," www.ufologie.net, June 30, 2006, www.ufologie.net/htm/cropbower01.htm.

11. Robert L. Snow, *Deadly Cults: The Crimes of True Believers* (Westport, CT: Praeger, 2003), 154–55.

12. Carl Sagan, *The Demon-haunted World: Science as a Candle in the Dark* (New York: Random House, 1996), 227.

13. Sagan, *The Demon-haunted World*, 240.

14. Nina Bernstein, "On Welfare and Not Psychic? New York Provides Training." *The New York Times*, January 28, 2000.

15. Don Dahler and Glenn Silber, "Psychic Hoaxes," ABC News, July 21, 2006, abcnews.go.com/2020/story?id=2218064&page=1.

16. Dahler and Silber, "Psychic Hoaxes."

17. CNN, "Bigfoot Hoaxers Say It Was Just 'A Big Joke,'" CNN.com, August 21, 2008, edition.cnn.com/2008/US/08/21/bigfoot.hoax/.

18. David Brakke, "Monks, Priests, and Magicians: Demons of Monastic Self-Differentiation in Late Ancient Egypt," PDF, Indiana University.

19. Bob Young, "Loveable Trickster Created a Monster with Bigfoot Hoax," *The Seattle Times*, December 5, 2002, community.seattletimes.nwsource.com/archive/?date=20021205&slug=raywallaceobit05m.

20. Malcolm McGrath, *Demons of the Modern World* (Amherst, NY: Prometheus Books, 2002), 57.

21. McGrath, *Demons of the Modern World*, 57.

22. McGrath, *Demons of the Modern World*, 62.

23. Hansen, *The Trickster and the Paranormal*, 260.

24. M. Scott Peck, *Glimpses of the Devil: A Psychiatrist's Personal Accounts of Possession, Exorcism, and Redemption* (New York: Free Press, 2005), 38.

25. Peck, *Glimpses of the Devil*, 234.

26. John Briggs and F. David Peat, *Seven Life Lessons of Chaos: Timeless Wisdom from the Science of Change* (New York: HarperCollins Publishers, 1999), 9.

27. Hansen, *The Trickster and the Paranormal*, 31.

28. Hansen, *The Trickster and the Paranormal*, 270.

29. Tim O'Brien, *The Things They Carried: A Work of Fiction* (Boston: Houghton Mifflin, 1990).

CHAPTER 4

1. Yi-Fu Tuan, *Landscapes of Fear* (New York: Pantheon Books, 1979), 127.

2. Jay Anson, *The Amityville Horror* (New York: Pocket Star Books, 1991), 122.

3. Renée L. Bergland, *The National Uncanny: Indian Ghosts and American Subjects* (Hanover, NH: Dartmouth College, 2000), 53.

4. Bergland, *The National Uncanny*, 16.

5. Bergland, *The National Uncanny*, 3.

6. Malcolm McGrath, *Demons of the Modern World* (Amherst, NY: Prometheus Books, 2002), 57.

7. Tuan, *Landscapes of Fear*, 19.

8. Joseph Campbell, *The Masks of God: Primitive Mythology* (New York: Viking Press, 1969), 30–31.

9. Sigmund Freud, "The 'Uncanny' (1919)," PDF, University of Iowa.

10. Bergland, *The National Uncanny*, 11.

11. Stephen King, *Stephen King's Danse Macabre* (New York: Everest House, 1981).

12. Freud, "The 'Uncanny' (1919)."

13. Bergland, *The National Uncanny*, 50.

14. Claude Lévi-Strauss, *Totemism* (Boston: Beacon, 1962), 2–3.

15. Lance Michael Foster, "Old Indian Burial Grounds," Native American Paranormal Blog, February 1, 2008, nativeamericanparanormal .blogspot.com/.

16. Bergland, *The National Uncanny*, 26.

17. Erich Fromm, *Psychoanalysis and Religion* (New York: Bantam Books, 1967), 31–32.

18. Bergland, *The National Uncanny*, 7.

19. Lévi-Strauss, *Totemism*, 59–60.

20. Bergland, *The National Uncanny*, 161.

21. Foster, "Old Indian Burial Grounds."

22. Tuan, *Landscapes of Fear*, 127.

CHAPTER 5

1. Kathryn S. Olmsted, *Real Enemies: Conspiracy Theories and American Democracy, World War I to 9/11* (Oxford: Oxford University Press, 2009), 4.

2. Jeffrey Burton Russell, *Satan: The Early Christian Tradition* (Ithaca: Cornell University Press, 1981), 28.

3. Joseph McCarthy, "Speech at Wheeling, West Virginia," http://historymatters.gmu.edu/d/6456/.

4. Olmsted, *Real Enemies*, 134.

5. Olmsted, *Real Enemies*, 130.

6. Olmsted, *Real Enemies*, 146.

7. Stanton T. Friedman, *Flying Saucers and Science: A Scientist Investigates the Mysteries of UFOs: Interstellar Travel, Crashes, and Government Cover-ups* (Franklin Lakes, NJ: New Page, 2008), 53.

8. John G. Fuller, "Flying Saucer Fiasco," *Look*, May 14, 1968, www.project1947.com/shg/articles/fiasco.html.

9. Olmsted, *Real Enemies*, 136.

10. Philip J. Corso and William J. Birnes, *The Day after Roswell* (New York: Pocket, 1997), 4

11. Daniel Bates, "America's X Files: Top U.S. Airmen to Accuse Air Force of Cover-Up as They Claim UFOs Have Been Deactivating Nuclear Missiles since 1948," *Daily Mail Online*, September 28, 2010, www.dailymail.co.uk/sciencetech/article-1315479/Aliens-interfered-weapons-UFOs-deactivating-nuclear-missiles.html.

12. Fox News, "Aliens Are Monitoring Our Nukes, Worry Ex-Air Force Officers," FoxNews.com, September 23, 2010, www.foxnews.com/scitech/2010/09/23/aliens-monitoring-nukes-worry-ex-air-force-officers/.

13. Olmsted, *Real Enemies*, 185.

14. William J. Broad, " 'Urge to Investigate and Believe' Sparks New Interest in U.F.O.'s," *The New York Times*, June 16, 1987. www.nytimes.com/1987/06/16/science/urge-to-investigate-and-believe-sparks-new-interest-in-ufo-s.html?pagewanted=all&src=pm

15. George P. Hansen, *The Trickster and the Paranormal* (Philadelphia, PA: Xlibris, 2001), 245.

16. Lawrence Fawcett and Barry J. Greenwood, *Clear Intent: The Government Coverup of the UFO Experience* (Englewood Cliffs, NJ: Prentice-Hall, 1984), 50.

17. Fawcett and Greenwood, *Clear Intent*, 183–85.

18. Fawcett and Greenwood, *Clear Intent*.

19. *A Strange Harvest*, directed by Linda M. Howe, performed by Linda Moulton Howe, From Beyond, 1981, www.youtube.com/watch?v=i9B1rAy3a3E&list=PL943C82BB8F2ABD4D&index=1.

20. Friedman, *Flying Saucers and Science*, 103.

21. Travis Walton, *Fire in the Sky: The Walton Experience* (New York: Marlowe & Company, 1996), 277.

CHAPTER 6

1. Jeffrey Burton Russell, *Lucifer: The Devil in the Middle Ages* (Ithaca, NY: Cornell University Press, 1984).

2. Russell, *Lucifer*, 275.

3. Anne Llewellyn Barstow, *Witchcraze: A New History of the European Witch Hunts* (San Francisco: Pandora, 1994), 2.

4. Hilary Evans and Robert E. Bartholomew, *Outbreak!: The Encyclopedia of Extraordinary Social Behavior* (San Antonio, TX: Anomalist, 2009), 733.

5. Rosemary Sullivant, "An Unlikely Revolutionary: Nicolas Copernicus, Circumscribed by Orthodoxy and Steeped in Catholicism, Triggered a Scientific Transformation," *Astronomy* 52, 1999.

6. Russell, *Lucifer*, 303.

7. Barstow, *Witchcraze*, 60.

8. Sullivant, "An Unlikely Revolutionary."

9. Russell, *Lucifer*, 58.

10. Barstow, *Witchcraze*, 39.

11. Barstow, *Witchcraze*, 32–33.

12. Alan Charles Kors and Edward Peters, *Witchcraft in Europe 400–1700: A Documented History* (Philadelphia: University of Pennsylvania, 2001), 394.

13. Russell, *Lucifer*, 77.

14. Kors and Peters, *Witchcraft in Europe 400–1700*, 393.

15. Georgess McHargue, *Facts, Frauds, and Phantasms: A Survey of the Spiritualist Movement* (Garden City, NY: Doubleday, 1972), 1.

16. *Spirit Summonings* (Alexandria, VA: Time-Life, 1989), 23.

17. *Spirit Summonings*, 23.

18. McHargue, *Facts, Frauds, and Phantasms*, 39.

19. McHargue, *Facts, Frauds, and Phantasms*, 118–19.

20. *Spirit Summonings*, 62–63.

21. McHargue, *Facts, Frauds, and Phantasms*, 242.

22. McHargue, *Facts, Frauds, and Phantasms*, 171.

23. *Spirit Summonings*, 54.

24. McHargue, *Facts, Frauds, and Phantasms*, 217.

25. Stephen King, *Stephen King's Danse Macabre* (New York: Everest House, 1981), 4.

26. King, *Stephen King's Danse Macabre*, 5.

27. *The Day the Earth Stood Still*, directed by Robert Wise, performed by Michael Rennie and Patricia Neal, Twentieth Century Fox Film, 1951.

28. J. Allen Hynek, *The UFO Experience: A Scientific Inquiry* (Chicago: H. Regnery, 1972), 29.

29. Jerome Clark, "The Odyssey of Sister Thedra," in *Alien Worlds: Social and Religious Dimensions of Extraterrestrial Contact*, ed. Diana G. Tumminia (Syracuse, NY: Syracuse University Press, 2007), 25–42.

30. Bryan Sentes and Susan Palmer, "Presumed Immanent: The Raelians, UFO Religions, and the Postmodern Condition," in *Alien Worlds: Social and Religious Dimensions of Extraterrestrial Contact*, ed. Diana G. Tumminia (Syracuse, NY: Syracuse University Press, 2007).

31. Sentes and Palmer, "Presumed Immanent."

32. Desmond Leslie and George Adamski, *Flying Saucers Have Landed* (New York: British Book Centre, 1953).

33. *Earth vs. the Flying Saucers*, directed by Fred F. Sears, performed by Hugh Marlowe and Joan Taylor, Clover Productions, 1956.

34. Hynek, *The UFO Experience*, 138–39.

35. *Battle of L.A. UFO Attacked by U.S. Army: 1942*, December 17, 2006, www.youtube.com/watch?v=oQmbGMWlL7w.

36. David Seed, "Constructing America's Enemies: The Invasions of the USA," *Yearbook of English Studies* 37(2), 2007.

37. Seed, "Constructing America's Enemies."

38. Pia Andersson, "Ancient Alien Brother, Ancient Terrestrial Remains," in *Alien Worlds: Social and Religious Dimensions of Extraterrestrial Contact*, ed. Diana G. Tumminia (Syracuse, NY: Syracuse University Press, 2007), 264–91.

39. Malcolm McGrath, *Demons of the Modern World* (Amherst, NY: Prometheus, 2002), 97.

40. Associated Press, "Tells of Satan Kill," *The Odessa American*, October 18, 1973, NewspaperARCHIVE Elite.

41. Associated Press, "Tells of Satan Kill."

42. Jay Maeder, "Fearful Coed Flees 'Satanic Cult out to Kill Her,'" *Chronicle Telegram*, Elyria, OH, April 26, 1975, NewspaperARCHIVE Elite.

43. Jeffrey S. Victor, *Satanic Panic: The Creation of a Contemporary Legend* (Chicago: Open Court, 1993), 54.

44. Victor, *Satanic Panic*, 202.

45. Bill Ellis, *Raising the Devil: Satanism, New Religions, and the Media* (Lexington, KY: University of Kentucky, 2000), 79.

46. McGrath, *Demons of the Modern World*, 115.

47. Jon Trott and Mike Hertenstein, "Selling Satan: The Tragic History of Mike Warnke," *Cornerstone* 21(98), 1992.

48. Brian Siano, "Truth in Advertising for Satan Seller?" *The Humanist* 53(3), 1993.

49. Debbie Nathan and Michael R. Snedeker, *Satan's Silence: Ritual Abuse and the Making of a Modern American Witch Hunt* (New York: Basic, 1995).

50. Testimony by Dr. Bruce Woodling, director of medical examinations for Ventura County, law2.umkc.edu/faculty/projects/ftrials/mcmartin/woodlingtestimony.html.

51. Nathan and Snedeker, *Satan's Silence*, 189.

52. McGrath, *Demons of the Modern World*, 155.

53. McGrath, *Demons of the Modern World*, 93–94.

54. Ellis, *Raising the Devil*, 285.

CHAPTER 7

1. Joseph Campbell, *The Masks of God: Primitive Mythology* (New York: Viking, 1969), 30–31.

2. Lesley Pratt Bannatyne, *Halloween: An American Holiday, an American Tradition* (Gretna, LA: Pelican, 1990), 2–4.

3. Jennifer Rosenberg, "War of the Worlds Radio Broadcast Causes Panic," About.com, history1900s.about.com/od/1930s/a/warofworlds_2.htm.

4. Bill Ellis, *Aliens, Ghosts, and Cults: Legends We Live* (Jackson: University of Mississippi, 2001), 41.

5. Terence Hines, *Pseudoscience and the Paranormal* (Amherst, NY: Prometheus, 2003), 13.

6. Hines, *Pseudoscience and the Paranormal*, 34.

7. *Ghostwatch*, directed by Lessley Manning, performed by Michael Parkinson and Sarah Greene, BBC, 1992, video.google.com/videoplay?docid=6073447872198040913.

8. *MonsterQuest*, Season 1, Episode 2: "Sasquatch Attack," directed by Doug Hajicek, performed by Stan Bernard and Tod Disotell, Motive NYC, 2007, www.youtube.com/watch?v=8j0iFQIkNMo.

9. *X-Creatures*: "Shooting the Bigfoot," directed by Chris Packham, BBC, 1999, www.youtube.com/watch?v=jy4P2ZhQjmc.

10. The Devil Hunters, www.njdevilhunters.com.

11. *A Haunting*: "Where Evil Lurks," directed by David Haycox, performed by Anthony Call and Kelly Cherie Levander, New Dominion Studios, 2007, www.4shared.com/video/w83Jn5Pk/a_haunting_s04e06_-_where_evil.html.

12. "Fiendish Friday Interview: Larry Silverman of Discovery Channel's 'A Haunting,'" interview by iamlegend, The Haunted Report, October 5, 2007, www.hauntedreport.com/2007/10/fiendish-friday-interview-larr.html. Accessed 3/1/2010.

13. Fiendish Friday Interview.

14. Fiendish Friday Interview.

15. *Ghost Hunters*, Season 3, Episode 18: "Waverly Hills Live Results," performed by Jason Hawes and Grant Wilson, Alan David Management, 2007, http://www.youtube.com/watch?v=5qA9kNDbbfc.

16. Owen Davies, *The Haunted: A Social History of Ghosts* (New York: Palgrave Macmillan, 2007), 16.

17. Alvin Schwartz, *Scary Stories to Tell in the Dark* (New York: HarperCollins Publishers, 1981), 94.

18. Ellis, *Aliens, Ghosts, and Cults*, 188–89.

CHAPTER 8

1. Bill Ellis, *Aliens, Ghosts, and Cults: Legends We Live* (Jackson: University of Mississippi, 2001), 93–97.

2. Whitley Strieber, *Communion: A True Story* (New York: Harper, 2008), 253.

3. Strieber, *Communion*, 255.

4. Strieber, *Communion*, 88.

5. Mark 5:1–9 (New International Version).

6. George P. Hansen, *The Trickster and the Paranormal* (Philadelphia: Xlibris, 2001), 259.

7. Hansen, *The Trickster and the Paranormal*, 244.

CHAPTER 9

1. Jan Harold Brunvand, *The Vanishing Hitchhiker: American Urban Legends and Their Meanings* (New York: Norton, 1981).

2. Jay Anson, *The Amityville Horror* (New York: Pocket Star Books, 1991), 122.

3. Carl Sagan, *The Demon-Haunted World: Science as a Candle in the Dark* (New York: Random House, 1996), 180.

4. Stephen King, *The Shining* (Garden City, NY: Doubleday, 1977).

5. Christina Valhouli, "The Most Haunted Hotels," Forbes.com, accessed October 27, 2011, www.forbes.com/2002/10/31/cx_cv_1031feat.html.

6. Owen Davies, *The Haunted: A Social History of Ghosts* (New York: Palgrave Macmillan, 2007), 62.

7. King, *The Shining*, 328.

8. Bill Ellis, *Aliens, Ghosts, and Cults: Legends We Live* (Jackson: University Press of Mississippi, 2001), 197.

9. Dana Clark Felty, "More People May Believe in Ghosts Than You Might Think," SavannahNow.com, October 27, 2006, savannahnow.com/2006-10-27/more-people-may-believe-ghosts-you-might-think.

10. Stanton T. Friedman, *Flying Saucers and Science: A Scientist Investigates the Mysteries of UFOs: Interstellar Travel, Crashes, and Government Cover-ups* (Franklin Lakes, NJ: New Page Books, 2008), 23.

11. "Larry King Live on UFOs," directed by CNN, performed by Stanton Friedman and Jesse Marcel, 2007, www.youtube.com/watch?v=S2 eoCqwBCQI.

12. *Stanton Friedman Is Real*, directed by Paul Kimball, performed by Stanton Friedman, Red Star Films, 2002, www.youtube.com/watch? v=jFIUlcmRwgw.

13. Friedman, *Flying Saucers and Science*, 92.

14. Friedman, *Flying Saucers and Science*, 297–98.

15. Associated Press, "Relatives Convicted in 'Bizarre' Exorcism Death," June 13, 2009.

16. Edward Bulwer-Lytton, "The Haunted and the Haunters," in *The Mammoth Book of Haunted House Stories*, ed. Peter Haining (Philadelphia: Running Press, 2007), 21–22.

17. Sagan, *The Demon-Haunted World*.

18. Friedman, *Flying Saucers and Science*, 299.

19. Sagan, *The Demon-Haunted World*, 25.

CHAPTER 10

1. Peter Travers and Stephanie Reiff, *The Story behind The Exorcist* (New York: Crown Publishers, 1974), 158.

2. Roger Ebert, "The Exorcist," Rogerebert.com, December 26, 1973, rogerebert.suntimes.com/apps/pbcs.dll/article?AID=/19731226/REVIEWS/ 301010310/1023.

3. Travers and Reiff, *The Story behind The Exorcist*, 168.

4. Louise Sweeney, "Occult Interest Suggests Technology Faith Shattered," *The Christian Science Monitor*, April 20, 1974.

5. Thomas B. Allen, *Possessed: The True Story of an Exorcism* (Lincoln, NE: IUniverse.com, 2000), 232–33.

6. Travers and Reiff, *The Story behind The Exorcist*, 16–17.

7. Rev. Carl Vogl, *Be Gone Satan* (Rockford, IL: Tan Books & Publishers, 1973), 9.

8. Vogl, *Be Gone Satan*, 14.

9. Travers and Reiff, *The Story behind The Exorcist*, 83.

10. Matt Baglio, *The Rite: The Making of a Modern Exorcist* (New York: Doubleday, 2009), 67.

11. Rosemary Ellen Guiley, *The Encyclopedia of Demons & Demonology* (New York: Checkmark Books, 2009), 197.

12. Sweeney, "Occult Interest Suggests Technology Faith Shattered."

13. Richie Rathsack, "Foolishness or Ghoulishness? Film Puts Spotlight on Meridan Ave. House," *MyRecordJournal.com*, March 14, 2009.

14. Ray Garton, Ed Warren, Lorraine Warren, Al Snedeker, and Carmen Snedeker, *In a Dark Place: The Story of a True Haunting* (New York: Dell, 1994), 189.

15. Guiley, *The Encyclopedia of Demons & Demonology*, ix.

16. Rathsack, "Foolishness or Ghoulishness? Film Puts Spotlight on Meridan Ave. House."

17. Joe Nickell, "Demons in Connecticut," *The Skeptical Inquirer* 33(3), May/June 2009.

18. Nickell, "Demons in Connecticut."

19. "Damned Interview: Ray Garton," interview by Ray Bendici, Damned Connecticut, www.damnedct.com/damned-interview-ray-garton/.

20. "Carmen Reed CNN Interview," interview by Melissa Long, CNN, April 22, 2009.

21. Carmen Reed, "About Carmen Reed," www.carmenreed.com/about.htm. Accessed 1/23/2010.

22. Garton et al., *In a Dark Place*, 100.

23. Garton et al., *In a Dark Place*, 122.

24. Associated Press, " 'Struck by Light Ray,' Missing Man Found by Brother," *Press Telegram* (Long Beach, CA), November 11, 1975.

25. Travis Walton, *Fire in the Sky: The Walton Experience* (New York: Marlowe & Company, 1996), 83.

26. Walton, *Fire in the Sky*, 91.

27. Walton, *Fire in the Sky*, 86.

28. Walton, *Fire in the Sky*, 222.

29. Walton, *Fire in the Sky*, 6.

30. Walton, *Fire in the Sky*, 93.

31. Walton, *Fire in the Sky*, 92.

32. Budd Hopkins, *Missing Time: A Documented Study of UFO Abductions* (New York: R. Marek Publishers, 1981), 63.

33. Stephen King, *Stephen King's Danse Macabre* (New York: Everest House, 1981), 22.

34. King, *Stephen King's Danse Macabre*, 131.

CHAPER 11

1. Frank Newport, "More Than 9 in 10 Americans Continue to Believe in God," Gallup; June 3, 2011, www.gallup.com/poll/147887/americans-continue-believe-god.aspx

2. "How Many North Americans Attend Religious Services (and How Many Lie about Going)?" ReligiousTolerance.org, www.religioustolerance.org/rel_rate.htm.

3. Paul Kurtz, *The Transcendental Temptation: A Critique of Religion and the Paranormal* (Amherst, NY: Prometheus, 1991), 454.

4. Max Weber, *The Sociology of Religion* (Boston: Beacon, 1993), 1.

5. Weber, *The Sociology of Religion*, 25.

6. George P. Hansen, *The Trickster and the Paranormal* (Philadelphia: Xlibris, 2001), 87.

7. Weber, *The Sociology of Religion*, 7.

8. Hansen, *The Trickster and the Paranormal*, 105.

9. Erich Fromm, *Psychoanalysis and Religion* (New York: Bantam, 1967), 2.

10. Fromm, *Psychoanalysis and Religion*, 22.

11. Kurtz, *The Transcendental Temptation*, 457.

12. John Briggs and F. David Peat, *Seven Life Lessons of Chaos: Spiritual Wisdom from the Science of Change* (New York: HarperCollins Publishers, 1999), 2.

13. Fromm, *Psychoanalysis and Religion*, 112.

14. Robert L. Snow, *Deadly Cults: The Crimes of True Believers* (Westport, CT: Praeger, 2003), 135.

15. "Haitians React to Televangelist Pat Robertson's 'Devil Pact' Remarks," performed by Pat Robertson, *The Miami Herald*, January 14, 2010, www.youtube.com/watch?v=DN_goSKPCaM&feature=related.

16. Jeffrey Burton Russell, *The Devil: Perceptions of Evil from Antiquity to Primitive Christianity* (Ithaca, NY: Cornell University Press, 1977), 33.

17. Russell, *The Devil*, 17.

18. Russell, *The Devil*, 27.

19. Matt Baglia, *The Rite: The Making of a Modern Exorcist* (New York: Doubleday, 2009), 84.

20. Baglia, *The Rite*, 111.

21. Francisco Radecki and Dominic Radecki, *Tumultuous Times: The Twenty General Councils of the Catholic Church and Vatican II and Its Aftermath* (Wayne, MI: St. Joseph's Media, 2004).

22. Radecki and Radecki, *Tumultuous Times*, 282.

23. Paul Burnell, "Exorcisms on the Rise," *National Catholic Register*, June 4, 2000.

24. Tracy Wilkinson, "Vatican Backs Exorcism Course: Church Lacks Priests to Practice Ritual," *Los Angeles Times*, February 18, 2005.

25. Richard E. Gallagher, "'Among the Many Counterfeits: A Case of Demonic Possession," *New Oxford Review* (2008).

26. Gallagher, "Among the Many Counterfeits: A Case of Demonic Possession."

27. Russell, *The Devil*, 21.

28. Russell, *The Devil*, 19.

29. Wilkinson, "Vatican Backs Exorcism Course."

30. Stephano Maria Paci, "Vatican Exorcist Amorth Speaks on Satan's Smoke," *Spero News*, March 16, 2006.

31. Wilkinson, "Vatican Backs Exorcism Course."

32. Paci, "Vatican Exorcist Amorth Speaks on Satan's Smoke."

33. Wilkinson, "Vatican Backs Exorcism Course."

34. Fromm, *Psychoanalysis and Religion*, 33.

35. "How Many Wiccans Are There? Estimates for the United States and Canada," ReligiousTolerance.org, December 28, 2009, www.religious tolerance.org/wic_nbr3.htm.

36. Baglia, *The Rite*.

CHAPTER 12

1. Michelle Green and Civia Tamarkin, "A Boy's Love of Satan Ends in Murder, a Death Sentence—and Grisly Memories," *People Weekly* 26, no. 154 (December 1, 1986).

2. "Members of Satanic Cult Who Confessed to Ritual Slayings Await Sentencing," *America's Intelligence Wire*, February 22, 2005.

3. Andrew Osborn, "Satanic Cult Teens 'Sacrificed' Victims Then Ate Them," *The Telegraph*, May 24, 2010.

4. Jeffrey S. Victor, *Satanic Panic: The Creation of a Contemporary Legend* (Chicago: Open Court, 1993), 142.

5. Anton Szandor LaVey, *The Satanic Bible* (New York: Avon Books, 2005).

6. Rosemary Ellen Guiley, *The Encyclopedia of Demons & Demonology* (New York: Checkmark Books, 2009), 217.

7. Jeffrey Burton Russell, *Mephistopheles: The Devil in the Modern World* (Ithaca: Cornell University Press, 1986), 219.

8. Russell, *Mephistopheles*, 221.

9. J. K. Huysmans and Robert Irwin, *Là-Bas (Lower Depths)* (London: Dedalus, 1986), 248–49.

10. *Häxan: Witchcraft Through the Ages*, directed by Benjamin Christensen, performed by Benjamin Christensen and Elisabeth Christensen, Aljosha Production Company, 1929, www.youtube.com/watch?v=ltDAAu7uEjw.

11. Guiley, *The Encyclopedia of Demons & Demonology*, 31.

12. LaVey, *The Satanic Bible*.

13. LaVey, *The Satanic Bible*.

14. LaVey, *The Satanic Bible*.

15. *Satanis: The Devil's Mass*, directed by Ray Laurent, performed by Anton LaVey, Sherpix, 1970, www.youtube.com/watch?v=0QHgZY 75TxE.

16. Blanche Barton, "Church of Satan—A Brief History: Lucifer Rising," Church of Satan, 2003, www.churchofsatan.com/home.html.

17. Barton, "Church of Satan."

18. LaVey, *The Satanic Bible*.

19. Ande Yakstis, "6000 in U.S. Worship Devil," *Alton Evening Telegraph*, January 20, 1968.

20. Owen Davies, *Grimoires: A History of Magic Books* (Oxford: Oxford University Press, 2009), 275.

21. Davies, *Grimoires*, 177.

22. Dave Smith, "Founder of First Church of Satan Believes in Showmanship," *The Los Angeles Times*, May 26, 1970.

23. Smith, "Founder of First Church of Satan Believes in Showmanship."

24. Peter Dizikes, "The Meaning of the Butterfly," *The Boston Globe*, June 8, 2008.

25. Blanche Barton, "Church of Satan—A Brief History: Diabolical Endeavors," Church of Satan, 2003, www.churchofsatan.com/home.html.

26. LaVey, *The Satanic Bible*.

27. Joseph Campbell and Bill D. Moyers, *The Power of Myth* (New York: Doubleday, 1988).

28. LaVey, *The Satanic Bible*.

29. LaVey, *The Satanic Bible*.

30. LaVey, *The Satanic Bible*.

31. LaVey, *The Satanic Bible*.

32. LaVey, *The Satanic Bible*.

33. Diane Vera, "Who and What Is the Christian 'God,'?" Theistic Satanism.com, theisticsatanism.com/CoAz/belief/theology.html#Xian.

34. Diane Vera, "First Serious Attempt at Building a Local In-Person Group, Beginning April 2009," TheisticSatanism.com, theisticsatanism.com/CoAz/history.html#local.

35. Diane Vera, "Background up to 2004," TheisticSatanism.com, theisticsatanism.com/CoAz/history.html#early.

36. Campbell and Moyers, *The Power of Myth*.

CHAPTER 13

1. *Gettysburg Ghosts*, directed by Tom Underwood, History.com, November 30, 2009, www.history.com/shows/monsterquest/videos/gettysburg-ghosts#gettysburg-ghosts.

2. Bill Ellis, *Aliens, Ghosts, and Cults: Legends We Live* (Jackson: University of Mississippi, 2001), 94.

3. Kendall R. Phillips, *Projected Fears: Horror Films and American Culture* (Westport, CT: Praeger, 2005), 188.

4. Phillips, *Projected Fears*, 190.

5. Mark Edmundson, *Nightmare on Main Street: Angels, Sadomasochism, and the Culture of Gothic* (Cambridge, MA: Harvard University Press, 1997), 5.

6. Wendy Kaminer, "American Gothic," *The American Prospect* 11(26), 2000.

7. Kaminer, "American Gothic."

8. *Christine O'Donnell: I'm You*, performed by Christine O'Donnell, Christine4Senate, October 4, 2010, www.youtube.com/watch?v=tGGAgljengs.

9. Edmundson, *Nightmare on Main Street*, 119.

10. Jeff Meldrum, *Sasquatch: Legend Meets Science* (New York: Forge, 2006), 95.

11. Lee Spiegel, "Seeing Red: Discovery of Red Panda Fossils in Tennessee," *The Huffington Post*, August 9, 2010, www.aolnews.com/2010/08/09/exclusive-a-red-panda-in-tennessee-fossils-confirm-n-american/.

12. Spiegel, "Seeing Red."

13. Meldrum, *Sasquatch*, 96.

14. Gayle Highpine, "Attitudes Toward Bigfoot in Many North American Cultures," *The Track Record*, 1992, www.bigfootencounters.com/legends/highpine.htm.

15. Kathy Moskowitz, "*Mayak Datat*: An Archaeological Viewpoint of the Hairy Man Pictographs," Proceedings of International Bigfoot Symposium, www.bigfootproject.org.

16. Joshua Blu Buhs, *Bigfoot: The Life and Times of a Legend* (Chicago: University of Chicago, 2009), 3.

17. Buhs, *Bigfoot*, 160.

18. Buhs, *Bigfoot*, 157.

19. *The Legend of Boggy Creek*, directed by Charles B. Pierce, performed by Willie P. Smith and John P. Hixon, P&L, 1972.

20. Buhs, *Bigfoot*, 164.

21. 2 Kings 2:11–12 (New International Version).

22. Carl G. Jung, *Flying Saucers: A Modern Myth of Things Seen in the Sky* (Princeton University Press, 1991), 101.

23. 2 Kings 2:15 (New International Version).

24. Geoffrey of Monmouth, *The History of the Kings of Britain*, trans. Aaron Thompson (Cambridge, Ontario: In Parantheses Publications, 1999).

25. Geoffrey, *The History of the Kings of Britain*.

26. Dan Fletcher, "Stonehenge Theories," *Time* magazine, 2009.

27. John A. Keel, *Our Haunted Planet* (Lakeville, MN: Galde, 2002), 41.

28. "Stonehenge," Britannia History, www.britannia.com/history/h7.html.

29. Erich von Däniken, *Chariots of the Gods: Unsolved Mysteries of the Past* (New York: Berkley, 1999), 64–65.

30. Däniken, *Chariots of the Gods*, 82–83.

31. Graham Hancock, *Fingerprints of the Gods* (New York: Three Rivers, 1995), 45.

32. James Sturcke, "Aerial Images Prove Existence of Remote Amazon Tribe," *The Guardian* [London], May 30, 2008.

33. Howard Phillips Lovecraft and S. T. Joshi, *The Call of Cthulhu and Other Weird Stories* (London: Penguin, 2002), 109–10.

34. Keel, *Our Haunted Planet*, 129.

35. *The Fourth Kind: Alien Abduction Stories*, performed by George Knapp and Budd Hopkins, Abovetopsecret.com, October 1, 2009, www.youtube.com/watch?v=tFBdimN2G6o.

36. Whitley Strieber, *Communion: A True Story* (New York: Harper, 2008), 54.

37. John E. Mack, "The UFO Abduction Phenomenon: What Does It Mean for the Transformation of Human Consciousness?" *Primal Renaissance: The Journal of Primal Psychology* 1(1), 1995, www.johnemackinstitute.org.

38. Mack, "The UFO Abduction Phenomenon."

39. Mack, "The UFO Abduction Phenomenon."

40. Mack, "The UFO Abduction Phenomenon."

41. Brian Eno, "Lessons in How to Lie about Iraq," *The Guardian*, August 16, 2003, www.guardian.co.uk/politics/2003/aug/17/media.davidkelly.

42. Joshua Gunn, "The Rhetoric of Exorcism: George W. Bush and the Return of Political Demonology," *Western Journal of Communication* 68(1), 2004.

43. Gunn, "The Rhetoric of Exorcism."

CHAPTER 14

1. David W. Moore, "Three in Four Americans Believe in Paranormal," Gallup Poll News Service, June 16, 2005, www.gallup.com/poll/16915/three-four-americans-believe-paranormal.aspx.

2. "United States of America Internet Usage and Broadband Usage Report," Internet World Stats: Usage and Population Statistics, www.internetworldstats.com/am/us.htm.

3. Brian Handwerk, "Whatever Happened to the Ozone Hole?" *National Geographic*, May 5, 2010, news.nationalgeographic.com/news/2010/05/100505-science-environment-ozone-hole-25-years/.

4. David Adam, "50M Environmental Refugees by End of Decade, UN Warns," *The Guardian*, October 11, 2005, www.guardian.co.uk/environment/2005/oct/12/naturaldisasters.climatechange1.

5. Joanna Zelman, "50 Million Environmental Refugees by 2020, Experts Predict," *The Huffington Post*, February 22, 2011, www.huffingtonpost.com/2011/02/22/environmental-refugees-50_n_826488.html.

6. Shirley Jackson, *The Haunting of Hill House* (New York: Penguin, 1984), 71.

7. "Message from the Designers," International Raelian Movement, 2012, www.rael.org/message.

8. "The Human Genetic Code—The Human Genome Project and Beyond," Centre for Genetics Education, www.genetics.edu.au.

9. Associated Press, "Clonaid Chief: Baby Eve Alive in Israel," Fox News, January 30, 2003, www.foxnews.com/story/0,2933,77024,00.html.

10. Joseph Campbell, *The Masks of God: Primitive Mythology* (New York: Viking, 1969), 131.

11. Peter Bergen, "What Were the Causes of 9/11?" *Prospect*, September 24, 2006, www.prospectmagazine.co.uk/2006/09/whatwere thecausesof911/.

12. Bill Ellis, *Raising the Devil: Satanism, New Religions, and the Media* (Lexington, KY: University of Kentucky, 2000), 79.

13. Bergen, "What Were the Causes of 9/11?"

CHAPTER 15

1. Shirley Jackson, *The Haunting of Hill House* (New York: Penguin, 1984), 4.

2. Jackson, *The Haunting of Hill House*, 71.

3. Jackson, *The Haunting of Hill House*, 1.

4. Jackson, *The Haunting of Hill House*, 12.

5. Stephen King, *Stephen King's Danse Macabre* (New York: Everest House, 1981), 168.

CHAPTER 16

1. George Noory, "The Brain & Spiritual Beliefs: Matthew Alper," *Coast to Coast AM*, July 8, 2011, www.coasttocoastam.com/show/2011/08/07.

2. Christopher Balzano, *Dark Woods: Cults, Crime, and the Paranormal in the Freetown State Forest* (UK: Schiffer, 2007), 12–13.

3. Bill Ellis, *Aliens, Ghosts, and Cults: Legends We Live* (Jackson: University Press of Mississippi, 2001), 11.

4. Bill Ellis, *Raising the Devil: Satanism, New Religions, and the Media* (Lexington, KY: University Press of Kentucky, 2000), 5.

5. Joseph Campbell, *The Masks of God: Primitive Mythology* (New York: Viking Press, 1969), 181.

6. Joseph Campbell, *The Hero with a Thousand Faces* (Novato, CA: New World Library, 2008), 249.

7. Jason Colavito, *The Cult of Alien Gods: H. P. Lovecraft and Extraterrestrial Pop Culture* (Amherst, NY: Prometheus Books, 2005), 253.

8. Georgess McHargue, *Facts, Frauds, and Phantasms: A Survey of the Spiritualist Movement* (Garden City, NY: Doubleday, 1972), 54.

9. Allen Mandelbaum, trans., *The Metamorphoses of Ovid* (New York: Harcourt Brace & Company, 1993).

10. Campbell, *The Hero with a Thousand Faces*, 245–46.

11. Campbell, *The Hero with a Thousand Faces*, 218.

12. Campbell, *The Hero with a Thousand Faces*, 218.

13. Colavito, *The Cult of Alien Gods*, 253.

14. Mandelbaum, *The Metamorphoses of Ovid*, 307–16.

15. Campbell, *The Masks of God*, 150.

16. Gayle Highpine, "Attitudes Toward Bigfoot in Many North American Cultures," *The Track Record*, July 18, 1992, www.bigfooten counters.com/legends/highpine.htm.

Index

About the Author

MARC E. FITCH is a graduate of the Western Connecticut State University Master of Fine Arts Program. He is the author of the novel *Old Boone Blood* and has numerous short fiction and nonfiction publications. He works in the field of mental health and lives in Harwinton, Connecticut, with his wife and three children. He spends his free time watching horror movies and reading noir fiction. More information and links to his published works can be found at www.marcfitch.com.